The Oath Is Dead and Gone

Jim Maher

LONDUBH BOOKS

In memory of my grandfather, Michael McSweeney, and my father and mother,
and for my wife, Mary, and my sons, Michael and Tom

First published in 2011 by

Londubh Books

18 Casimir Avenue, Harold's Cross, Dublin 6w, Ireland

www.londubh.ie

1 3 5 4 2

Cover by siné design

Origination by Londubh Books

Printed by ScandBook AB, Sweden

ISBN: 978-1-907535-19-2

Contents

Acknowledgements

A book such as this is completed only after much research and study and as a result I owe a debt of gratitude to many people.

During my long years of research I spent a great deal of time in the Franciscan Library, Killiney, County Dublin, where the curator, Father Ignatius, looked after me well and the late Breandán Mac Giolla Choille gave me personal insights into troubled years of Irish history.

I also owe a debt of gratitude to those who contributed personal recollections and placed documents and literature at my disposal. In this regard I particularly acknowledge Éamonn Gaynor for making available relevant parts of Father Pat Gaynor's papers and An t-Athair Ua hUallacháin for giving me access to his father's memoirs, Gearóid Ua hUallacháin's *Mo Scéal Féin*.

While I was writing this book I met the late Brian Lenihan TD after he had been the guest speaker at an annual dinner of the 1916-21 Club. We discussed my proposed book and he said that he would get permission for me to consult the minutes of the Fianna Fáil organisation in the UCD Archives. He did as he promised and because of this and the added recommendation of Seán Fleming TD, a past pupil who is still a close friend of mine, I was able to acquire important information. Unfortunately, Brian did not live long enough to read this book. *Ar dheis Dé go raibh a anam dílis.*

I greatly appreciate the assistance and courtesy of Séamus Hefferty in the UCD Archives. Séamus provided all the historical documents that I requested and guided me to others that were important. He facilitated me particularly by providing five of the photographs reproduced in this book. Amongst other members of the staff who assisted me in the UCD Archives were Orna, Kate, Jennifer and Dónal.

I cannot forget the many visits I made to the Gilbert Library, Pearse Street,

Dublin, where I was always made to feel at home. The staff there provided me with many relevant books, hard copy of daily newspapers, copies of Republican publications and issues of the early Fianna Fáil paper, the *Nation*. If I were to name everyone who assisted me in the Gilbert Library I would have a very long list but I feel I should mention Maura Kennedy, Divisional Librarian, Special Collections, with whom I have had a long association, and Dublin City Archivist Mary Clarke. Others among the staff of Dublin City Library and Archive who facilitated me in every respect were Andrew O'Brien, Pádraig O'Brien, Anne Keane, Clodagh Kingston, Leo Magee, Donna Behan, Fergus Byrne, Michael O'Dwyer and Brian Monahan.

I spent many years doing research in the National Library of Ireland and always got great help from all the staff. Among those who assisted me in obtaining six of the photos reproduced in this book were Elizabeth Kirwan, Keith Murphy, John O'Sullivan, Glenn Dunne and Bernie Metcalfe.

Many a pleasant day I spent in the National Archives, Bishop Street, Dublin, reading the minutes of Sinn Féin and Provisional Government meetings. I thank Christy Allen, John Delaney (retired) and Paddy Sarsfield for their help.

I wish to thank Jo O'Donoghue, publisher and editor of Londubh Books, for her great interest and expertise in editing and publishing this book. She has given meticulous attention to every detail of the production. I am also grateful to Jo for the index. Her son, David Parfrey, used his computer skills to lay out the photographic section.

I also wish to thank my wife, Mary, for her help, patience and forbearance while I was writing this book. She deserves a holiday far away from the din of a working printer and a document-shredder.

To anyone else who helped me in any way I offer thanks.

Preface

A veteran of the War of Independence once told me that he came from a part of County Cork 'where neither the king's nor the queen's rule ever ran' and that in the 1920s and early 1930s he was many times tempted to leave Ireland for the USA because he never felt comfortable living in an Ireland where the elected TDs and many senior public officials were obliged to swear allegiance to a reigning British monarch.

Many other young men and women like him, who took an active part in the national struggle between 1916 and 1921, were unable to accept Article 4 of the Articles of Agreement signed by the British and Irish delegates on 6 December 1921, which stated:

> The oath to be taken by Members of the Parliament of the Irish Free State shall be in the following form:
>
> I _____ do solemnly swear true faith and allegiance to the Constitution of the Irish Free State as by law established and that I will be faithful to HM King George V, his heirs and successors by law, in virtue of the common citizenship of Ireland with Great Britain and her adherence to and membership of the group of nations forming the British Commonwealth of Nations.

This book traces the many steps that had to be taken after the establishment of the Free State government finally to rid the Constitution of any reference to this controversial Oath of Allegiance. It is the only book devoted wholly to this subject and traces the Oath from its first introduction into the Westminster parliament in the reign of Henry VIII to its unilateral removal by Éamon de Valera in the Constitution (Removal of the Oath) Bill 1933 and the consent of the British government to its absence from the new Constitution of 1937. Since then Dáil Éireann has been open to all Irish citizens duly elected in a valid constituency in the twenty-six counties.

1

THE OATH RAISES ITS DIVISIVE HEAD

At the turn of the twentieth century, Irish Party MPs sat in Westminster; Irishmen and women debated in Ireland, sang Gaelic songs, learned the Irish language and played Gaelic games. There was little talk of Irish freedom. Then Arthur Griffith founded a newspaper, the *United Irishman*. He propounded within its pages a new policy to win freedom for Ireland – abstentionism – a policy whereby Irish parliamentary representatives would absent themselves from the House of Commons.

The strongest political party in Ireland at this time was the Irish Parliamentary Party. Its members attended the House of Commons in Westminster. It had been responsible for many reforms in land law and local affairs and it was still high in popular esteem.

Griffith launched Sinn Féin in the Rotunda, Dublin, on Tuesday, 28 November 1905. That evening, after the official launch, the Round Room of the Rotunda was thronged for a meeting to announce the Sinn Féin programme to the general public. Griffith had declined to accept the presidency of the new organisation. Instead Edward Martyn, a wealthy County Galway landowner, was made president. He addressed the gathering:

> This meeting has been assembled to endorse the Sinn Féin policy, which may be defined as the awakening of a sense of justice in our rulers by the force of passive resistance.[1]

John Redmond was leader of the Irish Parliamentary Party, which was determined to continue its attendance at Westminster and through its alliance with the Liberal Party to get a majority in the British parliament to vote for

Home Rule for Ireland. Even after Home Rule was won, the party envisaged that it would still have Irish members sitting at Westminster to assist in legislation concerning the collective interests of Great Britain and Ireland.

Neither Sinn Féin nor the Irish Party was concerned by the fact that elected Irish representatives were obliged to take an Oath of Allegiance to the ruling British monarch before they were allowed to take their seats in the House of Commons. At this point, Sinn Féin had little intention of sending any representative to the House of Commons so the question of the Oath did not arise. However, members of John Redmond's Irish Party formally took this Oath of Allegiance and did not express any conscientious objection to taking it.

How did this Oath of Allegiance to a British monarch come about? The first parliament summoned by an English king was called in 1295 by Edward 1 but no member of either of the two houses of parliament was obliged to take an Oath of Allegiance to the British monarch. It was not until 1532 that the Tudor King Henry VIII, who had declared himself Supreme Head of the Church, introduced an Oath of Supremacy, which had to be taken by all officers of the state, both ecclesiastical and temporal. They had to testify and declare that 'in my conscience the bishop of Rome ought not to have jurisdiction, power or authority within the realm'. The same oath contained a further promise: 'that I shall bear faith, truth and true allegiance to the King's Majesty and to his heirs and successors'. This was an Oath of Allegiance to the British monarch.

Henry's daughter, Mary, a Catholic, repealed the Oath of Supremacy when she came to the throne in 1553. She restored the official position of the Catholic Church within her dominions and abolished the title of Supreme Head of the Church that Henry VIII had claimed for himself. But when she died in 1558 her half-sister, Elizabeth, who succeeded her, was as great a champion of the Reformation as Mary had been of Catholicism. Her aim was ecclesiastical uniformity throughout her dominions and the establishment of a well-ordered state church of which she herself should be the head. To this end and in order to ensure that parliament would carry out her wishes in all decrees that applied to her reign,[2] she created a new, more concise Oath of Supremacy and Allegiance to be taken by all ecclesiastical officers and ministers and all temporal officers of the crown. They had to declare that the queen was the only supreme governor of the realm in all spiritual and temporal matters and affirmed that they bore faith and true allegiance to the queen, her heirs and lawful successors. A few years later, the obligation to take this oath was extended to include all MPs.

During the reign of James I, who succeeded Elizabeth in 1603, Guy Fawkes and his Catholic conspirators plotted to blow up the Houses of Parliament in what became known as the Gunpowder Plot. This produced a new wave of indignation and anti-Catholic panic in England. The king enacted a more severe Oath of Allegiance and Supremacy to discover and repress Roman Catholics who refused to attend Protestant services. Members of the House of Commons were required to take the oath 'before he or they shall enter the House.'[3]

In 1672, during the reign of Charles II, a declaration against transubstantiation was added to the Oaths of Allegiance and Supremacy by means of a new penal statute entitled 'An Act for preventing dangers which may happen from popish recusants.'[4]

On 5 July 1828, Daniel O'Connell was elected MP for County Clare, defeating William Vesey-Fitzgerald. The Oath of Supremacy made it impossible for believing Roman Catholics like O'Connell to enter the House of Commons because it contained a passage denying the spiritual jurisdiction of the Pope and a declaration against transubstantiation. On 13 April 1829, a new Bill – the Emancipation Bill – received the Royal Assent, permitting Catholics to enter Parliament by taking a new Oath. On 15 May 1829, Daniel O'Connell presented himself at the House of Commons to claim his seat but MPs voted 190 to 116 against his entry on the grounds that the Emancipation Bill authorising the new Oath was not retrospective and did not become effective until after his election. A new election, to be held on 30 July 1829, was declared for County Clare and this time O'Connell was returned unopposed.

On 4 February 1830, O'Connell took his seat in the House of Commons. He was the first Catholic in modern history to do so.[5] From then on Catholic

MPs took the new Oath before taking their seats: 'I _____ do sincerely promise and swear that I will be faithful and bear true allegiance to his Majesty George IV.'[6] Protestant MPs continued to take the old form of the combined Oaths of Allegiance and Supremacy before taking their seats.

In 1868 a different form of Oath for both Protestants and Catholics was adopted. This new Oath required MPs to promise:'I _____ do swear to be faithful and bear true allegiance to her Majesty Queen Victoria, her heirs and successors according to law.'[7] Standing at a table in front of the speaker, MPs read from a paper the words of the Oath, which they then signed. In 1884 Lord Randolph Churchill declared with reference to the Oath:

> It had been the proudest boast of the Commons of England that, however their political differences might be, they were at any rate united in one sentiment in that of loyalty to the Crown: and they gladly testified to that fact when they took the Oath of Allegiance at the table.[8]

It may have been the proudest boast of Englishmen to swear allegiance to the British monarch of the time but elected members of the Irish Party who attended the House of Commons took the Oath because there was no alternative if they wanted to occupy their seats there.

Sinn Féin was the first nationalist organisation to develop a systematic philosophy of abstention from the British parliament. It advocated that Irish MPs should abandon Westminster and form their own national assembly in Dublin. As early as 1908 Sinn Féin began to go into decline, becoming almost moribund. Interest now centred more and more upon parliamentary affairs and the fortunes of the Irish Parliamentary Party in its endeavours to win Home Rule. In this atmosphere the abstentionist policy of Sinn Féin was not likely to prosper.

In tandem with the constitutional campaign of the Parliamentary Party, the physical force tradition was represented during the second part of the 19th century and the start of the 20th by the Irish Republican Brotherhood (IRB), a secret, oath-bound underground organisation that believed that

Irish independence could be won by armed revolution. At Easter 1916 prominent IRB members, among whom were Pádraig Pearse, Tom Clarke, Thomas MacDonagh, Joseph Mary Plunkett, Éamonn Ceannt and Seán Mac Diarmada, in conjunction with the Irish Citizen Army under the leadership of James Connolly and in the hope of receiving help from Germany, led their followers into insurrection against British forces in the heart of Dublin. They managed to hold Dublin for five days with a small force of about twelve hundred volunteers. British troops used artillery to suppress the Rising and the British administration had the leaders executed by firing squad. Many others who participated were interned.

After the execution of the 1916 leaders there was a huge change in public opinion in Ireland about those who had fought against Britain in the rebellion. Many of the internees were released at Christmas but the sentenced prisoners were held in British prisons until June 1917.

The Sinn Féin organisation revived itself and the new Sinn Féin was launched at its 1917 *ard-fheis*. Although the name remained the same there were very few similarities between the new and the older organisation. The new movement was far more Republican in outlook. The old Sinn Féin with its one hundred and fifty delegates at the *ard-fheis* of 1914 gave way to this new organisation that was able to muster 1700 delegates for the *ard-fheis* of 1917.[9] A new Constitution was approved. Éamon de Valera was unanimously elected president of Sinn Féin.

The question of abstention was finally decided: all factions were in agreement that the MPs elected for the party should not attend Westminster but should set up an administration at home.

The First World War ended on 11 November 1918 and the British Prime Minister, David Lloyd George, thinking the moment opportune, decided to go to the polls. Sinn Féin operated under great handicaps. A hundred of its most prominent leaders were in jail and political novices had taken their places. Sinn Féin itself had been banned and all Republican papers had been suppressed.[10]

Polling day was 14 December. It was the mildest December for many years and this helped Sinn Féin in their last canvassing push. There was a relatively good turnout of 69 per cent of the electorate, especially considering that there was an epidemic of the deadly 'great flu' at the time.

Sinn Féin won seventy-three seats out of a total of a hundred and five. The Irish Party won six seats. Unionists won twenty-six seats – twenty-five of them in Ulster and one in the Dublin (Rathmines) constituency where Sir Maurice Dockrell polled more than the combined Sinn Féin and Irish Party votes.

Many British policies had played into the hands of Sinn Féin: draconian measures after the Easter Rising; the so-called 'German Plot' in April 1918 that led to the wholesale arrest of many of the prominent Sinn Féin leaders on the false charge of entering into 'treasonable communication with the German enemy'; the threat of partition; the threat of conscription; and the death in Mountjoy Jail of the hunger striker, Thomas Ashe, while being forcibly fed, on 25 September 1917.[11]

Sinn Féin had won the general election of 1918 on its abstentionist policy from the House of Commons and its denial of the right of the British government to legislate for Ireland. It had no alternative now but to set about establishing a separate Irish parliament and to render powerless any system of English government in Ireland.

Twenty-six of the elected Sinn Féin representatives met and decided to invite all MPs (Unionist, Irish Party, Nationalist and Sinn Féin) to the opening session of Dáil Éireann.

At 3.30 on the afternoon of 21 January 1919, the very first Dáil Éireann met. The proceedings, which were mostly in Irish, took less than two hours. The Unionist members and the six survivors of the old Parliamentary Party had declined the invitation to attend and the new Dáil comprised only Sinn Féiners. Of the seventy-three Republicans elected just twenty-seven were in attendance: almost all the remainder were 'faoi ghlas ag Gallaibh' (imprisoned by the foreigners). Count Plunkett proposed Cathal Brugha as presiding officer for the day. The assembly passed the Provisional Constitution of the Dáil. Everyone stood as Ireland's Declaration of Independence was read and all the deputies replied in unison when they repeated the Pledge of Allegiance contained in the declaration.

Now, therefore, we, the elected representatives of the ancient Irish people in National Parliament assembled, do, in the name of the Irish nation, ratify the establishment of the Irish Republic and pledge ourselves and our people to make this declaration effective by every means at our command.[12]

At a meeting of Dáil Éireann on 20 August 1919, which forty-two Republican deputies attended, Cathal Brugha proposed an Oath of Allegiance to the Irish Republic. Traolach Mac Suibhne (Terence MacSwiney) seconded the motion. Every elected Republican deputy, officer and clerk of the Dáil and every member of the Irish Volunteers (later the Irish Republican Army) was obliged to take this Oath to the Irish Republic and to the Dáil. It was adapted from the Oath of Allegiance taken in the USA by all congressmen and senators and read:

I _____ do solemnly swear (or affirm) that I do not and shall not yield a voluntary support to any pretended government or authority or power within Ireland hostile and inimical thereto, and I do further swear (or affirm) that to the best of my knowledge and ability, I will support and defend the Irish Republic and the government of the Irish Republic, which is Dáil Éireann, against all enemies, foreign and domestic and I will bear true faith and allegiance to the same, and that I take this obligation freely without any mental reservation or purpose of evasion, so help me God.[13]

The Dáil, on a division, carried this motion and adopted this form of the Oath.

Meanwhile the Irish Volunteers, using guerrilla tactics, were fighting a military campaign against British forces in Ireland. Competent leaders such as Michael Collins, Richard Mulcahy, Tom Barry, Seán Treacy, Dan Breen, Liam Lynch, Seán Mac Eoin and Ernie O'Malley directed the war. The IRA got the upper hand over British troops in many rural areas.

In mid-May 1921 moves were afoot in London and in Dublin to find a solution to the whole Irish problem. Lloyd George admitted that the British had failed 'to restore order' and that they wouldn't succeed in doing so for some months but claimed they would get there in the end.[14] Winston Churchill said, in the same debate, that it was of great public importance to get a respite in Ireland. The British were getting a bad reputation and the problems in Ireland were poisoning their relations with the United States. They could continue as before but they should do everything to get a settlement.[15] In an interview with the *New York Herald*, de Valera expressed a willingness to open conversations with Lloyd George.

Lloyd George wrote to de Valera, inviting him to a conference in London. After an exchange of letters between the two leaders, a truce was arranged for noon on 11 July 1921. The purpose of the truce was to allow negotiations to take place between representatives of the British government and Sinn Féin.

After months of negotiation, the Irish plenipotentiaries, Arthur Griffith, Michael Collins, Éamonn Duggan, George Gavan Duffy, Robert Barton and the secretary, Erskine Childers, reported to the Dáil cabinet on Saturday, 3 December 1921. They met Éamon de Valera, Cathal Brugha, Austin Stack, William T. Cosgrave and Kevin O'Higgins to give them a report on how their negotiations were progressing with Lloyd George and his team of negotiators. There was still a crux over the Oath of Allegiance to the British king that Lloyd George considered essential in any Treaty settlement. The form of the Oath proposed by the British was:

I _____ solemnly swear to bear true faith and allegiance to the Constitution of the Irish State and the community of nations known as the British Empire; and to the King as head of the State and of the Empire.[16]

Griffith spoke strongly in favour of accepting the Oath. He believed that if the cabinet rejected this form of the Oath 'the country would not fight on the question of allegiance and there would be a split'.

Éamonn Duggan agreed with him. 'This was England's last word,' he said.

Robert Barton disagreed: 'Britain will not declare war on the question of allegiance and England's last word has not been heard.'

Michael Collins was prepared to accept the Treaty as a whole but had reservations about the Oath: 'The Oath of Allegiance will not come into force for twelve months. Would it be worth while taking that twelve months and seeing how it would work?' But he would recommend non-acceptance of the Oath as it stood.[17] Éamon de Valera stated emphatically that he could not subscribe to the Oath of Allegiance as outlined in that form.[18]

Cathal Brugha objected to any type of Oath. 'Of course,' he said, 'if the British wanted an Oath from us to respect whatever Treaty was made, we might give it provided they swear to us in return.'[19]

De Valera then suggested: 'If we get all else we want, what harm would there be if we had an Oath something like this:

I _____ do solemnly swear true faith and allegiance to the Constitution of the Irish Free State, to the Treaty of Association, and to recognise the King of Great Britain as Head of the Association.'[20]

There was no direct swearing to the King in this form of the Oath and de Valera thought it would unify the cabinet and prevent a split in their ranks. Austin Stack accepted de Valera's suggested Oath and tried to convince Cathal Brugha to do likewise. 'Nothing doing,' retorted Brugha. 'There is going to be no unanimity on such an Oath as that.'[21]

There were only minutes left before the plenipotentiaries had to leave to catch the boat to London that night so the cabinet made a quick final decision. Colm Ó Murchadha recorded it in his minutes of the meeting:

Delegation to return and say that cabinet won't accept Oath of Allegiance, if not amended, and to face the consequences assuming that England will declare war.[22]

The plenipotentiaries and secretaries returned to London and tried to persuade the British delegation to amend the proposed treaty. Griffith raised the question of the Oath. Lord Birkenhead intervened and said that Michael Collins had handed him a copy of an Oath on which he (Collins) had been working. Birkenhead made some small alterations to the text suggested by Collins and at that moment produced his version.[23] This Oath became Article 4 of the official 'Articles of Agreement for a Treaty between Great Britain and Ireland signed by both British and Irish delegations in London at 2.15am on Tuesday, 6 December 1921. It read:

> I _____ do solemnly swear true faith and allegiance to the Constitution of the Irish State as by law established and that I will be faithful to HM King George V, his heirs and successors by law, in virtue of the common citizenship of Ireland with Great Britain and her adherence to and membership of the group of nations forming the British Commonwealth of Nations.

This form of the Oath of Allegiance aimed to keep Ireland on a basis of common citizenship with England and countries within the same Commonwealth. It pledged, by Oath, direct faithfulness to the King and allegiance to the Constitution of the Free State of which the King was part.[24]

Later that morning Michael Collins found himself looking out on the cold damp streets of London. He should have been happy with himself after signing the Articles of Agreement for a Treaty between Great Britain and Ireland. But his mind was uneasy: although he was satisfied with the settlement he had got for Ireland, he knew that many would not be happy with it. He wrote to a friend:

> Think – what I have got for Ireland? Something which she has wanted these past seven hundred years. Will anyone be satisfied at the bargain? Will anyone? I tell you this – early this morning I signed my death warrant…These signatures are the first real step for Ireland. If people will only remember that – the first real step.[25]

Notes

1. The *United Irishman*, Dublin, 9 December 1905.
2. Diarmuid Ó Cruadhlaoich, *The Oath of Allegiance*, pp. 2, 3.
3. *Ibid.*, pp. 8, 9.
4. Pollock on *The Oath of Allegiance in English History, Online Library of Liberty.*
5. Michael MacDonagh, *The Life of Daniel O'Connell*, pp. 188, 189, 190.
6. Ó Cruadhlaoich, *op. cit.*, p. 71.
7. *Ibid.*, p. 24.
8. *Ibid.*, p. 98.
9. *Sinn* Féin, 17 January 1925.
10. Dorothy Macardle, *The Irish Republic*, p. 262.
11. P.S. O'Hegarty, *The Victory of Sinn* Féin, p. 29.
12. *Sinn* Féin, 20 December 1924 and *Dáil Éireann Debates*, 1919-21, 21 January 1919, p. 16, Col. 1.
13. *Ibid.* and *Dáil Éireann Debates 1919-21*, 20 August 1919, Private Session, p. 151, Col. 2.
14. Thomas Jones, *Whitehall Diary*, Volume III, (cabinet meeting, 12 May 1921), p. 68.
15. *Ibid.*, p. 69.
16. *Dáil Éireann Debates*, Private Sessions, 1921-22, Volume 4, 16 December 1921 (George Gavan Duffy), p. 183.
17. NAI, Notes of Colm Ó Murchadha of meeting of the cabinet and plenipotentiaries, 3 December 1921.
18. Frank Pakenham, *Peace by Ordeal*, p. 209.
19. *Ibid.*, p. 210.
20. *Dáil Éireann Debates*, Private Sessions, 1921-2, 16 December 1921, Robert Barton p. 190; Erskine Childers, p. 91; Pakenham, *op. cit.*, pp. 210, 211.
21. *Ibid.*, 16 December 1921, Cathal Brugha, p. 187.
22. NAI, Notes of Colm Ó Murchadha of meeting of the cabinet and plenipotentiaries, 3 December 1921.
23. Pakenham, *op. cit.*, pp. 232, 233.
24. *Ibid.*, p. 233.
25. Rex Taylor, *Michael Collins*, p. 152.

2

DEPUTIES OPPOSE THE TREATY

When the details of the Articles of Agreement of the Treaty and particularly of the Oath of Allegiance reached Dublin, Éamon de Valera and other ministers of the cabinet of Dáil Éireann – Cathal Brugha and Austin Stack – received the news with much dissatisfaction and disappointment. The Oath of Allegiance that they had seen at the cabinet meeting the previous Saturday had been amended but not sufficiently for their approval. Their biggest objection was that it contained a direct pledge of faithfulness to King George V. The elected representatives of the Irish Free State would be obliged to take this Oath before entering the Irish parliament.

There was a long discussion in Dáil Éireann on Arthur Griffith's motion: 'that Dáil Éireann approves of the treaty between Great Britain and Ireland'. Many of the Sinn Féin TDs who made up the Dáil found it extremely difficult to vote for a settlement that included the Oath of Allegiance. These Dáil deputies found themselves in a moral and conscientious quandary over the Oath and during this long debate they expressed their genuine and serious misgivings about the matter. Sinn Féin deputy, Austin Stack, a staunch Republican who represented the constituency of Kerry-Limerick West explained why he could not contemplate taking this Oath. 'You are British subjects without a doubt and I challenge anyone here to stand and prove otherwise than that according to this document.'[1]

Count Plunkett, father of the executed 1916 leader, Joseph Mary Plunkett, whose victory in the North Roscommon by-election started the Republican revival in January 1917, was not prepared to sacrifice his personal honour by taking this Oath:

You are told…that by swearing an Oath of Allegiance to the English king, that this is the means by which you will achieve your liberty…I am faithful to my Dáil Oath. I am faithful to my own boys, one of whom died for Ireland with his back to the wall and the other two who were sentenced to death…Under no circumstances will I sacrifice my personal honour in such a manner.[2]

The Limerick City-Limerick East TD, Katherine O'Callaghan, wife of the former Mayor of Limerick, Michael O'Callaghan, who was murdered in his own home by armed police in March 1921, stated that she would never take this Oath of Allegiance: 'I still fail to see how in swearing an Oath of Allegiance to the Free State I avoid King George. He is in the Constitution. Why am I a widow? Was it that I should take an Oath to be a faithful citizen of the British Empire?'[3]

Kathleen Clarke, widow of Tom Clarke, the executed 1916 leader, who represented Dublin-Mid, declared that no power on earth would force her to take this Oath of Allegiance:

I heard big strong, military men say here they would vote for this Treaty, which necessarily means taking an Oath of Allegiance, and I tell these men there is not power enough to force me, nor eloquence enough to influence me in the whole British Empire into taking that Oath, though I am only a frail scrap of humanity. I took an Oath to the Irish Republic, solemnly, reverently, meaning every word. I shall never go back from that.[4]

The already famous Sinn Féin TD for Dublin South, Countess Markievicz, who was Minister for Labour in that second Dáil, also rejected this Oath of Allegiance. 'Now personally,' she said, 'I, being an honourable woman, would sooner die than give a declaration of fidelity to King George or the British Empire.'[5] Brian O'Higgins, one of de Valera's running mates in Clare, vehemently denounced this Oath of Allegiance:

> My conscience tells me the Oath embodied in the Treaty in
> London is an Oath of loyalty to the English king: an admission
> that the King of England is King also of Ireland, that I am a
> British subject, that my children are British subjects: such an
> admission I never intend to make so long as I have control of my
> will and reason, no matter what material advantage it may be
> supposed to gain for Ireland.[6]

Almost every anti-Treaty speaker who spoke in this long Treaty debate referred directly or indirectly to the Oath of Allegiance and castigated it in the strongest of terms.[7]

Other members of Dáil Éireann and Sinn Féin were able to accept the Oath of Allegiance and had no scruples of conscience about it. Arthur Griffith, one of the plenipotentiaries who negotiated the Treaty in London, said:

> It is an Oath of Allegiance to the Constitution of the Free State
> of Ireland and of faithfulness to King George V, in his capacity
> as head and in virtue of the common citizenship of Ireland
> with Great Britain and the other nations comprising the British
> Commonwealth. That is an Oath, I say, that any Irishman could
> take with honour.[8]

Kevin O'Higgins TD (Leix-Offaly), Assistant Minister for Local government, denied that it was an Oath of Allegiance at all:

> It is not an Oath of Allegiance. There is a difference between
> faith and allegiance. Your first allegiance is to the Constitution
> of the Irish Free State and you swear faith to the King of
> England. Now faith is a thing that can exist between equals.[9]

Many of the other pro-Treaty deputies in Dáil Éireann held similar views and affirmed that the only allegiance promised in the Oath was to the

Constitution of the Irish Free State.[10]

The acrimonious debate ended on 7 January 1922. The result of the vote taken was sixty-four in favour of the Treaty that included the Oath of Allegiance, fifty-seven against.

Little was said about Ulster or partition during the long debate on the Treaty. The Government of Ireland Act 1920 had partitioned the island into two regions, separating the six counties of Northern Ireland from the other twenty-six counties. Northern Ireland had already established a government in Stormont. There was provision in the Treaty for a Boundary Commission that could adjust the border which had been decided in 1920. Most leaders in the south, both pro-Treaty and anti-Treaty, assumed that this commission would transfer predominantly nationalist areas such as County Fermanagh, County Tyrone, south Derry, south Armagh, south Down and the city of Derry to the Free State. They expected that what remained of Northern Ireland would not be economically viable and that the statelet would eventually opt for union with the Free State. Most of the deputies in this Second Dáil believed that there was no better solution to partition.

On 9 January, Dáil Éireann defeated by sixty votes to fifty-eight a motion by Kathleen Clarke to re-elect Éamon de Valera as President of the Irish Republic.

Michael Collins then proposed that Arthur Griffith be appointed president of Dáil Éireann. The time was approaching for a division when de Valera rose and announced that he, at any rate, was not going to be a party to the election of someone who was bound by the Treaty conditions to undermine the Irish Republic. He left the room, followed by all the anti-Treaty TDs. As they left there was a sharp exchange of taunts between Collins and those who were leaving. When the roll to vote was called there were only sixty-one deputies left in the chamber and they unanimously supported Michael Collins's motion. The ship of state had a new captain, Arthur Griffith.

This incident was not the start of a de Valera-led anti-Treaty policy of abstention from Dáil Éireann. In fact de Valera and his fifty-six anti-Treaty deputies absented themselves from the Dáil for less than three hours, which included the lunchtime break. They were back in their seats by five o'clock to resume the debate on the future of Ireland in a political and constitutional manner. The anti-Treaty deputies continued to attend Dáil Éireann up to the break at the end of May to prepare for the Pact election of 16 June 1922.[11]

The Treaty negotiations had shown that British representatives were not prepared to yield on the symbol of the king in Irish political affairs. The crux was that there were many in Ireland who would not surrender the symbolism of the Republic. 'Many, as Sceilg [J.J. O'Kelly] has told us,' said Justice Kingsmill Moore in his summary of the Sinn Féin funds case, 'felt themselves bound in conscience by their Oath to the Republic which they regarded as sacrosanct in all changes of circumstances.'[12]

Éamon de Valera met anti-Treaty members of the Dáil at the Mansion House on 8 January 1922, the day after the ratification of the Treaty, to discuss what action they should now take as they were a minority in Dáil Éireann, strongly opposed to putting the Treaty into operation. They formed a new political party called Cumann na Poblachta (Republican Party).

Once the Treaty was ratified the next step, according to its provisions, was the setting up of the provisional government. One of the conditions of the agreement was that a meeting of members elected to the southern parliament in the general election of 1921 must be summoned to constitute a provisional government. The British government would transfer to that government the powers and machinery necessary to establish the Irish Free State – but they would deal only with the provisional government and not with Dáil Éireann. A Westminster committee under Winston Churchill pushed for the setting up of this government, wanting its representatives to come to London as soon as possible to discuss the removal of British troops, an amnesty for prisoners and the submission of the Articles of Agreement of the Treaty to the House of Commons for ratification.[13]

Arthur Griffith moved quickly. As chairman of the Irish delegation of plenipotentiaries, he issued a summons in January 1922 to all the elected representatives for the twenty-six counties to attend a meeting to give formal approval for the setting up of a provisional government. The southern parliament he called together included only candidates elected in the twenty-six counties in the 1921 general election, so it effectively recognised partition for the first time. Seán O'Mahoney, Sinn Féin deputy for Fermanagh-Tyrone, was not invited to attend because he represented one of the excluded Northern Ireland constituencies, although one where nationalists were in a majority.[14] If he had presented himself at Arthur Griffith's gathering he would have been ejected. The four Unionist members for Trinity College were invited and attended.

Éamon de Valera's answer to the summons was: 'We [he and the other anti-Treaty deputies] don't recognise any such parliament.' The anti-Treaty deputies refused to attend because the function of this provisional government was to put into operation the terms of a treaty which they, as republicans, despised, principally because of the Oath of Allegiance and partition. A correspondent from *The Irish Times* said that De Valera by his absence 'has committed public suicide'.[15]

Griffith's meeting first ratified the 'Treaty between Great Britain and Ireland – Articles of Agreement'. Then it approved of a provisional government of eight pro-Treaty ministers who were virtual rulers of Ireland until the Irish Free State came into existence. The southern parliament never met again and left the transitional work to the eight ministers. Michael Collins was elected Chairman of the Provisional Government at its first cabinet meeting on 16 January 1922.[16]

The refusal of anti-Treaty deputies to recognise the Provisional Government was the first act of abstention and non-recognition by any group of a native Irish assembly. As a result of the absence of anti-Treaty elected representatives, the eight pro-Treaty ministers of the Provisional Government got all the credit for the transfer of British installations and barracks into the hands of the Irish people. The Provisional Government was also in a position to sanction and distribute payments to local authorities for various relief schemes. For example, the minutes of its meeting of 10 May 1922 reported that it had sanctioned the payment of £8000 to Tipperary North Riding, £11,000 to Dublin County Borough, £15,000 to Limerick County Council, and £14,000 to Clare for the relief of unemployment.[17] This distribution of huge sums of money helped to relieve distress in many areas and resulted in the members of the Provisional Government winning significant local support for their policies, a support that would help them when the next general election came around.

In mid-January Sinn Féin issued a report stating: 'in the political situation of the moment and considering the aims of the organisation as set forth in its Constitution, there were sharp differences of opinion as to what should be the future policy of the organisation'. The mainstream Sinn Féin movement was split right down the middle by the Treaty. Each *comhairle ceanntair* (district council) met to elect representatives to an extraordinary *ard-fheis* to be held on 7 February 1922 to consider the situation. De Valera was still president of the organisation and there were thousands of Sinn Féin *cumainn* (local clubs) throughout the country.

At the end of January 1922 Father Pat Gaynor, North Tipperary, attended a meeting of the *Ard-Chomhairle* (Supreme Executive Council) of Sinn Féin, convened to arrange the holding of the February *ard-fheis*. He was uncommitted on the Treaty question at this stage. He observed that for the first time since its foundation, there were two Sinn Féins – the Sinn Féin of Michael Collins who had set up the Provisional Government and the abstentionist Sinn Féin Party under de Valera that had refused to recognise or become members of that assembly. Father Gaynor wrote a vivid account of this meeting:

> Cathal Brugha was there, grimly silent: so were Mrs Sheehy Skeffington, cold and implacable, and Mrs Wyse Power, a lifelong friend of Arthur Griffith, who seemed nervous and worried (she was a very refined and gentle lady). There was an atmosphere of politeness and courtesy such as you might expect between combatants and their seconds at the venue of a duel. De Valera and Michael Collins discussed the matters on the agenda calmly and – to all appearances – in mutual goodwill and friendship. They held the stage. Arthur Griffith and a few other members may have spoken briefly now and then but that was all. For once in my life, I sat in frozen silence.[18]

It became obvious to Father Gaynor: 'that the intention of de Valera was simply to launch a new party in constitutional opposition to the Treaty'. Dev hoped that the founding of such a party, with intent to proclaim a republic in due time by the will of the Irish people, would satisfy opponents of the Treaty and induce the irreconcilable minority to have patience. 'Cathal Brugha and Austin Stack would have stood by de Valera in that policy,' wrote Father Gaynor.[19] The priest was enraged by the idea that Sinn Féin must divide and as a gesture of protest, rather than with any real hope, Father Gaynor exercised his right as a member of the Supreme Council to place a resolution on the agenda of the *ard-fheis*: 'that we declare a truce on the Treaty issue for two years and devote our energies to organising the country'.[20]

After detailed preparation, more than three thousand delegates from all parts of Ireland met in the Mansion House for the *ard-fheis*.[21] *Comhairlí ceanntair* (district councils) and *cumainn* had chosen their delegates to represent either the pro-Treaty or anti-Treaty viewpoint – whichever predominated in their respective areas. Éamon de Valera proposed a resolution that advocated adherence to the spirit and letter of the Sinn Féin Constitution, declaring that the aim of the organisation should continue to be international recognition of Ireland as an independent republic. Part of his resolution read:

> That in accordance with their programme, the organisation… shall support at the coming parliamentary elections, only such candidates as publicly subscribe to it and pledge themselves not to take the Oath of fidelity to or owe allegiance to the British king.[22]

Arthur Griffith appealed to opponents not to obstruct those who saw a chance of salvation for the nation in the Treaty. Michael Collins urged unity.[23] Father Gaynor observed that at a moderate estimate, three-fifths, if not two-thirds of the delegates were on de Valera's side.[24] He was of the opinion that if a vote were taken, Dev's motion to keep to the spirit and letter of the Sinn Féin Constitution and not to take the Oath of Allegiance would prevail.

When Father Gaynor spoke the attitude of the delegates changed. He suggested that de Valera and Griffith and their friends should try to come to an agreement to carry on and cooperate without an election and in an assembly in which they could all sit without offending any of their principles. He then proposed his own resolution: 'that they declare a truce on the treaty issue for two years'. Dick Mulcahy suggested an adjournment to let the leaders confer. Éamon de Valera and Austin Stack on behalf of the anti-Treatyites met Arthur Griffith and Michael Collins, who represented the pro-Treaty side. They decided to adjourn the *ard-fheis* for three months. The new Constitution of the Irish Free State would then be ready and could be published and debated before parliamentary elections were held.[25]

At this time the Sinn Féin *cumainn* throughout the country were beginning to fall to pieces. Feelings were too high for adherents of opposing views to meet in goodwill within the confined ambit of a *cumann*. It was mostly those in favour of the Treaty who tended to stay away.[26]

The announcement of the Collins-de Valera Pact on 20 May 1922 re-injected some life into the Sinn Féin organisation and for a time both parties tried to implement this agreement but the former unity of the movement was never restored.[27]

The Constitution that was drafted and agreed to by the British government under Lloyd George and Churchill did contain the controversial Oath of Allegiance. There was no ambiguity about the compulsory nature of this Oath: 'Such Oath shall be taken and subscribed by every member of the Parliament/Oireachtas before taking his seat therein before the representative of the crown, or some person authorised by him.' The named representative of the crown was the governor-general.[28] The daily newspapers printed the terms of the Constitution on the morning of 16 June, the day of the 1922 Pact general election. Many of the electorate did not have time to study the long and involved document before casting their votes and this was to the advantage of the pro-Treaty candidates. Frank Aiken noted: 'the Constitution was published on the morning of the election. Daily paper readers were small in number then.'[29]

Only twenty constituencies were contested in this 1922 Pact general election. Pro-Treaty and anti-Treaty candidates were returned unopposed in the remaining eight constituencies. Proportional representation was the method used for electing deputies.

The pro-Treaty party did well in the election and Michael Collins obtained the highest vote in the country. The anti-Treaty party gained only nineteen seats in the contested constituencies. The Labour Party had a remarkable success. They nominated eighteen candidates and seventeen were elected. The Farmers' Party put forward twelve candidates and seven were elected.

The final result of the 1922 general election, taking into account the contested and uncontested constituencies, was: fifty-eight pro-Treaty Sinn Féin; thirty-six anti-Treaty Sinn Féin; seventeen Labour Party; seven Farmers' Party; six Independents and four Unionists representing Trinity College.

The thirty deputies elected on the tickets of the Labour Party, Farmers' Party, Independents and Unionists were in favour of attending the third Dáil and taking the Oath of Allegiance – all except one Labour deputy, Patrick Gaffney, elected for Carlow-Kilkenny.

One hundred and forty-one thousand Irish people had cast their votes for representatives who would not take the Oath of Allegiance. Harry Boland considered that these Republicans were 'disfranchised under the Constitution and representation is denied them in parliament by the Oath of Allegiance.'[30] Éamon de Valera's opinion of the new Constitution was that 'as it stands it will exclude from the public service and practically disfranchise ever honest Republican (because of the Oath of Allegiance).'[31]

It did not take long after the general election for war to ferment. Shortly after 4am on 28 June 1922 the Free State army opened fire on a force of diehard Republicans who had occupied the Four Courts in Dublin ten weeks earlier. From that on the Free State Army and anti-Treaty forces were embroiled in a tragic civil war.

After a month of conflict it became apparent that the Free State forces enormously outnumbered the anti-Treatyites and were far better equipped with guns and artillery. One by one the cities and towns that the anti-Treaty forces had held along the borders of Munster and in Cork and Kerry were taken. Liam Lynch evacuated Fermoy on 11 August as Free State troops advanced in numbers towards it, burning the barracks before he retreated. The last town held by the Republicans had fallen and their prospects were poor. The community's support for them was dwindling because the Irish people were war-weary. All that faced them was a prolonged winter campaign of guerrilla warfare.

July and August 1922 were black months for the Irish nation because the country lost some of its greatest sons. Early in July Cathal Brugha TD, the cabinet member who had stated that he would not accept any type of Oath of Allegiance, died outside the Hammam Hotel in O'Connell Street in Dublin as a result of wounds inflicted by Free State forces. Big-hearted Harry Boland TD, who had declared his total opposition to the Oath of Allegiance, went peacefully to his maker on the evening of 1 August when he died of wounds received when Free State forces surrounded him in the Grand Hotel in Skerries, County Dublin. On 12 August Arthur Griffith TD, the founder and father of Sinn Féin, now President of Dáil Éireann, died unexpectedly of a cerebral haemorrhage. Overwork and the strain of Civil War had affected his health. On 22 August Michael Collins TD, Commander-in-Chief of the Free State army, who had tried hard but in vain to persuade the British government to accept an Irish Free State Constitution without the Oath of Allegiance, fell mortally wounded in Béal na mBláth in County Cork in an ambush carried out on his convoy by Republican forces.

After a long delay following the Pact election of 16 June the Provisional Government summoned Dáil Éireann to meet in Leinster House on 9 September 1922. Some Republican deputies held the view that the Second Dáil had never been formally dissolved and that therefore no other assembly was legal. Éamon de Valera pointed out that, for this reason, the assembly summoned to meet was the provisional parliament and not Dáil Éireann. He recommended non-attendance but agreed that Laurence Ginnell, the Republican TD for Longford-Westmeath who had been elected in the 1922 Pact general election, should attend.

Laurence Ginnell was an elderly, dedicated Sinn Féin deputy, once a member of Redmond's Irish Party, who had not been militarily active in the Civil War. For fear of being arrested, very few, if any, of the other Republican

TDs could take the risk of attending the Dáil, even had they been willing to do so. The four Trinity College Unionist deputies were present at this meeting. Mr Ginnell took a seat at the corner of a front bench near a gangway to the left of the chair. The Clerk of the Dáil, Colm Ó Murchadha, read the several proclamations postponing parliament on five separate occasions since the June 1922 general election. He then called on the members to come forward and sign the roll. The first to do so was W.T. Cosgrave TD, followed immediately by the most senior members of his party and then by other Dáil deputies. By signing the roll the deputies signified that they accepted the terms of the Anglo-Irish Treaty of 1921. The process took half an hour. Laurence Ginnell made no effort to sign the roll and took no interest in the proceedings. W.T. Cosgrave asked the Dáil to elect a Ceann Comhairle (Speaker) for the House and called upon the clerk of the House to accept that motion. Mr Ginnell then interjected, 'May I ask at this stage whether all the deputies are supposed to sign the roll?' Cosgrave confirmed that this was the case.

Professor Michael Hayes TD (National University of Ireland constituency) was elected Ceann Comhairle.

There followed an acrimonious debate between Mr Ginnell and the Ceann Comhairle.

An Ceann Comhairle: Deputies who have not signed the roll have not the right to speak.

Mr Ginnell TD: I have been elected to Dáil Éireann. Are my constituents to be disfranchised by you, Sir?

A deputy: By yourself.

W.T. Cosgrave moved a motion that Mr Ginnell be excluded from the House as only members who had signed the roll had the right to appear there. The motion was passed.

An Ceann Comhairle: The motion has been carried that the person interrupting be removed.

Mr Ginnell was then requested to leave by one of the officials.

Mr Ginnell TD: You have to begin your proceedings by expelling a member. I am a member of Dáil Éireann. Take care about expelling me.[32]

After Laurence Ginnell had again been requested to leave by an official, an officer of the House in civilian dress approached him. Mr Ginnell was then ushered out of the House by three attendants using some force but careful not to cause the elderly man of small frame any physical injury.[33] As he was ushered out he continued to protest. The prompt ejection of Laurence Ginnell from Dáil Éireann was proof enough that Leinster House was no place for any TD who did not subscribe to the Treaty.

General Richard Mulcahy proposed the election of W.T. Cosgrave as President of Dáil Éireann. Professor Eoin MacNeill seconded the motion and W.T. Cosgrave was duly elected. The President then nominated the cabinet and all the ministers were approved by the elected deputies present.

On 18 September the new government introduced the Constitution Bill. It was on 3 October that Kevin O'Higgins, the Minister for Home Affairs, moved Article 17 of the Constitution Bill which read:

> *The Oath to be taken by Members of Parliament/Oireachtas*
> Such Oath to be taken and subscribed by every member of the Parliament/Oireachtas before taking his seat therein before the Representative of the Crown or some person authorised by him.[34]

O'Higgins defended the Oath:

> We have an Oath which gives the first allegiance of the Irish citizens to the Constitution of their own State, and which subsequently promises faithfulness to King George V, his heirs and successors…We do not think that in the mind of any signatory, British or Irish, there was the idea that this Oath… would be anything else but an Oath to be taken by all Members of Parliament, and to be taken as a condition precedent to their taking their seats and acting and voting in Parliament. This Treaty has been accepted by the late Dáil: it is unquestionably accepted by the people.[35]

George Gavan Duffy, a Dublin County TD and barrister-at-law and one of the plenipotentiaries who had signed the Treaty, urged that every member of the Dáil should not be compelled to take the Oath. This was a contract and should not be inserted in the Constitution as a command:

> I believe that something like 90 per cent of the opposition to the Treaty would disappear or cease to be active, if this Dáil recognised that it had the right of granting exemption. I do not want to see anti-Treaty men who object to the Oath or members of the Labour Party who will not take it, driven into direct action by a misconstruction of the Article of the Treaty.[36] Article 4 does not say 'the Oath to be taken by every Member of Parliament.' It does not even say, 'the Oath to be taken by the Members of Parliament' just 'to be taken by Members.'[37] I think the English knew well they were leaving this possibility of exemption.[38]

Kevin O'Higgins interjected:

> I can put it here to this Dáil that is the custodian of the honour and dignity of this nation; that if it takes the lines requested by Deputy Gavan Duffy, on this particular article, the nation will not be cutting either a very honourable or a very dignified figure.[39]

Labour Party leader Thomas Johnson said that the clause which they were asked to insert would have:

> …the effect of depriving this country of the services of quite a number of very estimable and very capable men and women and for that reason alone I think it very undesirable that this clause should be retained in the Constitution…An Oath of this kind is a survival of the feudal age, when men were supposed to give their personal allegiance to an individual King or Prince.

This Oath placed His Majesty, King George V in a position of superiority over all other mortals in the community.[40]

Another Labour member, Patrick Gaffney, who represented Carlow-Kilkenny, opposed the Oath.[41] Gaffney, a staunch Republican, born in Killeshin, County Carlow, had caused a major surprise in his constituency by heading the poll in the June Pact election, outpolling W.T. Cosgrave, now President of the Irish Free State, by more than 3500 votes. He was forthright in his comments in the debate: 'I rise to oppose the Oath and I do so…because it rather puts me in the category, not of association but of subjection. I refuse to take such an Oath.'[42] And he never did take it. Because of his stance on the Oath he could not register his opposition in the subsequent vote on the motion. This was his last appearance in the Dáil.

(The motion 'that the Article 17 be added to the Bill' was put and agreed to. Fifty deputies were for the inclusion of the Oath in the Constitution and seven against. The seven who voted against were all Labour TDs: Robert Day (Cork Borough); Thomas Nagle (Cork Mid, North, South, South-East and West); Thomas Johnson (Dublin County); William O'Brien (Dublin South); Hugh Colohan(Kildare-Wicklow); John Lyons (Longford-Westmeath); Cathal O'Shannon (Louth-Meath). The Oath of Allegiance was passed by Dáil Éireann and became part of the Constitution.

A hundred-and-twenty-eight TDs had been elected in the June 1922 Pact election. Four of these elected TDs had died since the outbreak of the Civil War. Only fifty of the remaining deputies had voted to make the Oath of Allegiance part of Constitution of the Irish Free State: the motion had been passed by the votes of a minority of the members of Dáil Éireann.

The Standing Committee of Sinn Féin met on 6 October 1922 at the request of Éamon de Valera. He could not attend as he was on the run but he appointed P.J. Little as his substitute. Kathleen Lynn, a vice-president of the organisation and a well-known Dublin doctor, chaired the meeting. There was an attendance of thirteen but some were proxy representatives for elected members who were unable to be there because of the Civil War. A resolution was put and carried that 'in order that the routine business of the Sinn Féin organisation may continue, it is agreed that the Standing Committee carry on the work of the organisation until the meeting of the *Ard-Chomhairle*'.[43] De Valera considered that the officer board of Sinn Féin was still the executive authority and that the Sinn Féin offices should be kept open with a representative of the organisation in attendance. He also contended that the Sinn Féin organisation could not be brought to an end except by a regular resolution of an *ard-fheis*.[44]

This Standing Committee of Sinn Féin was again convened on 6 November. Dr Kathleen Lynn again presided. Kathleen Clarke represented Austin Stack and P.J. Little represented Éamon de Valera. This time Jennie Wyse Power and Éamonn Duggan, past treasurers but now on the pro-Treaty side of Sinn Féin, attended to make their position clear. They declared that they had no objection to calling an *Ard-Chomhairle* meeting but it was the function of the Standing Committee to call it and this was impossible at that time owing to the chaotic state of the country and the non-availability of many of its members. They refused to recognise the authority of the officer board who had summoned that particular meeting. Having thus clearly stated their position, the two ex-treasurers left and the members who remained passed a resolution reopening the Sinn Féin offices and appointing Miss McDonnell as acting secretary.[45]

These meetings – of the Standing Committee in October 1922 and the officer board in November 1922 – were the last meetings of any executive or governing body of the national Sinn Féin party dating from the 1917-21 period.[46]

Republicans now found themselves barred from all channels of parliamentary action and with no policies other than a military one that was failing. De Valera and other anti-Treaty leaders saw that they were losing out to Free State forces. The anti-Treaty army and the Republican party searched for some way to keep alive the thirty-county Dáil Éireann established on 21 January 1919. The anti-Treaty army executive declared itself willing to give allegiance to a Republican government under the presidency of Éamon de Valera but reserved to itself power in the matter of peace and war.[47] As a result of this decision, Republican deputies, members of the Second Dáil, who were now a minority, because the Second Dáil had gone against their wishes in approving the Treaty by sixty-four votes to fifty-seven, held an assembly in Dublin. They came to the view that their assembly represented deputies who remained faithful to the Republican Oath and that they still constituted the Second Dáil because that assembly had never been formally brought to an end. They called upon Éamon de Valera 'in the name of all the loyal citizens of the Republic' to resume his presidency of Dáil Éireann. Republicans in general refused to call the new Free State government 'Dáil Éireann' but many of them called it 'the Dáil'.

De Valera was appointed 'President of the Republic'. He nominated twelve members of the Second Dáil to act as 'a council of state and executive ministers'.[48] This meant that Éamon de Valera was proclaiming a rival Dáil to that set up by the pro-Treaty side of the divide. This Second Dáil was to function until 'such time as the parliament of the republic is allowed freely to assemble, or the people are allowed by a free election to decide how they shall be governed'.[49] The Second Dáil, as the anti-Treaty side named it, was recognised by a sizeable portion of the public, although a minority. It was not able to function properly but it did place on record its protests at many of the draconian acts carried out both by the Provisional and the Free State government during the Civil War.

On 6 December 1922, exactly a year after the signing of the Articles of Agreement, the Irish Free State officially came into existence and the Provisional Government went out of existence. It had by this time adopted its own Constitution. That historical day began at Glenaulin, near Chapelizod, County Dublin, the residence of the Governor-General, Tim Healy. He was the first to take the Oath of Allegiance in the presence of the Lord Chief Justice Molony and other civil functionaries.

> I _____ do solemnly swear that I will be faithful and bear true allegiance to his Majesty, King George the Fifth, His Heirs and Successors according to law. So help me God.

The Governor-General immediately afterwards administered the Oath of

Allegiance prescribed by Article 17 of the Constitution of the Irish Free State to Professor Michael Hayes TD, the Speaker of Dáil Éireann. It was the same Oath of Allegiance that was part of the Treaty of December 1921.

When Hayes had taken the Oath, Healy authorised him to administer the same Oath to each member of Dáil Éireann.[50]

At 5.15 that evening, the members of the Free State parliament met and took the Oath of Allegiance to the British monarch. This was done in a very formal and official manner. The Ceann Comhairle rose and said: 'I have been authorised by the Governor-General of the Irish Free State to administer the Oath to the Deputies of Dáil Éireann'. Then President Cosgrave and his ministerial colleagues came forward to the table in succession and repeated the Oath. They then signed the roll and returned to their seats.[51] After that the back-bench TDs came forward and were sworn in rapid succession, the Ceann Comhairle all the time standing at the table. The occupants of the Labour benches did not come forward to take the Oath until all the TDs supporting the government had been sworn. Then Thomas Johnson, Labour Party leader, rose and read a statement:

> We recognise the act of taking 'an Oath of Allegiance' as a formality – a condition of membership of the legislature, implying no obligation, other than the ordinary obligation of every person who accepts the privileges of citizenship... We make our Declaration of Allegiance intending to fulfil our pledge with the proviso that, if at any time, it shall be deemed wise and expedient by the people of Ireland in the exercise of their sovereign right to denounce the Treaty or alter or amend the Constitution in any respect whatever, nothing in our Declaration of Allegiance shall be a barrier to our freedom of action.[52]

Johnson said that all the members of the Labour Party had signed his statement. However, an absentee from the Labour Party's ranks was Patrick Gaffney, TD for Carlow-Kilkenny[53], who, even before his election, had made no secret of the fact that he would not take the Oath because of his Republican principles.

Thus the Irish Free State came into existence. It was not a totally satisfactory outcome after the struggles of the previous six years. No anti-Treaty TD attended this first meeting of the Free State parliament, leaving thirty-four seats unoccupied by anti-Treaty TDs who had been elected by the votes of the people. By not signing the roll they forfeited their right to a TD's salary, as did Patrick Gaffney of the Labour Party. The protocol of the whole occasion was in itself sufficient to deter sincere Republicans from participation. It would have been anathema for some of the traditional Republican TDs to have submitted themselves to such a ceremony, given that in some of their families the king's writ had never been recognised. Nor should it be forgotten that a bitter civil war was raging in the country at this time. It would have been impossible then for Éamon de Valera to lead his party into the Free State parliament as the Labour Party had done, even if he had wished to do so.

When the Seanad met on 11 December 1922, the Oath of Allegiance was administered to each member by Éamonn J. Duggan, Minister without Portfolio, acting on the authorisation of the Governor-General.[54]

Éamon de Valera made a firm decision to keep Sinn Féin alive. On 1 January 1923, in a letter to all Sinn Féin clubs and all Sinn Féin members, he announced that he was resuming his office as President of Sinn Féin and that he would reorganise the party. Austin Stack was the surviving secretary and he also signed the notice that stated: 'The object for which Sinn Féin was reconstituted five years ago has not been achieved. Its aims and Constitution are as appropriate and as necessary for the national purpose today as they were in October 1917.'[55]

In 1948, Justice Kingsmill Moore commented on de Valera's letter to Sinn Féin members:

> I am not satisfied that this letter reached these members of Sinn Féin who had adopted the Free State side. I am satisfied that, one way or another, it probably reached those who had actively or

even passively adopted the Republican side and that a few clubs whose attendance was composed of Republicans may have tried to affiliate as a result of the communication. De Valera seems to have been alone in his belief that Sinn Féin was still alive.[56]

On 18 January the Adjutant-General of the IRA, Pádraig Ruitléis, issued a letter to O/Cs of all divisions and independent brigades stating that it was 'the duty of the IRA officers and men to do their utmost to assist in getting all former Sinn Féin clubs to work actively as quickly as possible and to encourage membership of Sinn Féin'. The letter continued: 'It is being arranged that organisers will visit all areas in the near future and they should receive all assistance possible from the army.'[57] Even though civil war still stalked the land in all its ferocity, it was clear that a move was on foot by Republicans to get involved once again in constitutional politics.

During the early months of 1923 the anti-Treaty forces suffered severe losses. The Republican army was in decline. Free State forces killed many of the best guerrilla fighters. Prisons and internment camps were packed with captured Republicans, many of whom were under sentence of death.

In April the Free State government sent thousands of troops in giant swoops through the mountains of Tipperary and Waterford in an attempt to flush out anti-Treaty leaders sheltering in valleys and woods where there was cover. On 10 April, Liam Lynch, Chief-of-Staff of the anti-Treaty forces, was mortally wounded near Croach, about three miles south-west of Newcastle in County Waterford, as he made his way over a rise in the Knockmealdown Mountains while trying to elude encircling pro-Treaty troops.

After Liam Lynch's death an adjourned meeting of the Republican army executive was held in Poulacapple, Mullinahone, County Tipperary. Frank Aiken was elected chief-of-staff to replace Liam Lynch. He urged an end to hostilities. The meeting of the anti-Treaty officers, with the aid of Éamon de Valera, set out principles on which they were prepared to negotiate. One proviso demanded that 'no individual or class of individuals who subscribe to the principles of national right, order and good citizenship can be justly excluded by any political Oath, test, or other device from their proper share and influence in determining national policy or from the councils and parliament of the nation'.[58] Éamon de Valera for the Republican government and Frank Aiken, on behalf of the anti-Treaty forces, signed proclamations ordering the suspension of all aggressive action by Republican forces from noon on Monday 30 April 1923.

Senators James Douglas and Andrew Jameson conveyed the Free State government's terms to Éamon de Valera: that the government would not undertake to negotiate with the British government with regard to the Oath, then included in the Free State Constitution. Éamon de Valera replied that he felt it his duty to make it clear that the full and satisfactory cooperation of all citizens for the good of Ireland could not be assured if elected representatives were prevented from taking part in any future parliament because of the Oath to which they could not honourably subscribe.[59]

In the Dáil debate on 10 May 1923 Labour party leader, Thomas Johnson, said he absolutely subscribed to de Valera's objection to the Oath. He added: 'A combination of those outside, who refuse to come in because of the Oath, with those who are willing to come in and still call it unjust [mainly the Labour Party] would, most certainly, in my view, bring about the removal of this injustice.'[60]

George Gavan Duffy said that there was one thing more certain politically than any other and that was that the Oath had to go, for two reasons: 'The first of which is that this country cannot afford to have driven into the wilderness of unconstitutional opposition those who are entitled to and ought to be encouraged to constitutional opposition'. The second reason was startling in Gavan Duffy's case, as he was one of the signatories of the Treaty: 'because the clause, as it stands, went a good deal beyond what we pledged ourselves to in the Treaty.'[61]

A surprise interjection came from Alderman Liam de Róiste, Cork City, a pro-Treaty deputy, who said, 'I am one of those who entirely disagree with having any test for entrance into the Assembly. I think there should be no such test.'[62]

Slightly taken aback by that comment by a TD of his own party, William T. Cosgrave rose to reply and ruled out any possibility that the Oath would be repealed in the near future: 'Is it peace or is it political careers these people want who have been waging destruction and creating disaster right through the country for the last ten months?'[63]

On 13 and 14 May the Republican cabinet and army council met again. They decided to order a 'cease fire' and 'dump arms'. Frank Aiken issued this order on 24 May 1923. The Civil War was over.

Notes

1. Official Report, Debate on the Treaty between Great Britain and Ireland, Stationery Office, Dublin, p. 28, Col. 1.
2. *Ibid.*, p.29, Cols. 1, 2.
3. *Ibid.*, p. 60, Col. 1.
4. *Ibid.*, p. 141, Col. 2.
5. *Ibid.*, p. 188, Col. 2.
6. *Ibid.*, p. 191, Cols. 1, 2.
7. See *Official Report*, Debate on the Treaty: Seán Etchingham (Wexford) p. 55, Col. 2: Seán T. O'Kelly (Dublin Mid) p. 65, Cols. 1, 2: Dáithí Ceannt (Cork East and North-East) p. 94, Col. 1, p. 95, Cols. 2, 3: Seán Ó Ceallaigh, (Louth-Meath) p. 134, Col. 2: Mary MacSwiney (Cork Borough) p. 126, Col. 1: Art O'Connor (Kildare-Wicklow) p. 175, Col. 1: Margaret Pearse (Dublin County) p. 122, Col. 2: John O'Mahoney (Fermanagh and Tyrone) p. 244, Col. 1: Dr Ada English (National University of Ireland) p. 247, Col. 2: Dr Bryan Cusack (Galway) p. 252, Col. 2: Dr Francis Ferran (Sligo-Mayo East) p. 286, Cols. 1, 2: Séamus Robinson (Waterford-Tipperary East) p. 289, Col. 1: Éamonn Aylward (Carlow-Kilkenny) p. 298, Cols. 1, 2: Harry Boland (Mayo South-Roscommon South) p. 302, Col. 2: Count Patrick O'Byrne (Tipperary Mid, North and South) p. 308, Col. 2: Cathal Brugha (Waterford -Tipperary East) p. 325, Col. 2, p. 329, Col. 1.
8. *Dáil Éireann Debates*, Treaty Debate, Nollaig 1921-Eanáir 1922, Arthur Griffith, p. 22, Col. 2.
9. *Ibid.*, Kevin O'Higgins, p. 46, Col. 2.
10. *Ibid.*, W.T. Cosgrave, p. 108, Col. 1; Eoin MacNeill, p. 149, Col. 1; Dan McCarthy, p. 246, Col. 1.
11. Jim Maher, *Harry Boland,* p. 178.
12. NAI, Judgement Hon. Kingsmill Moore, Sinn Féin Funds case, 26 October 1948, pp. 18, 19.
13. Maher, *op. cit.*, p. 180: *The Irish Times*, 10 January 1922.
14. Papers of Father Pat Gaynor, member of Sinn Féin executive 1922.
15. *The Irish Times*, 13 January 1922.
16. NAI, Minutes of meeting of Provisional Government, 16 January 1922, G 1/1 16 January-24 March 1922.
17. Ibid, 10 May 1922, DT – G1/2/63-76, NAI.
18. Papers of Father Pat Gaynor, 1922.
19. *Ibid.*
20. *Ibid.*
21. Jim Maher, *op. cit.*, p. 185: *The Irish Times*, 22 February 1922.
22. NAI, Judgement Hon. Kingsmill Moore, Sinn Féin Funds case, 26 October 1948, p. 25.
23. The *Nationalist*, Clonmel, 22 February 1922.
24. Papers of Father Pat Gaynor, 1922.
25. *Ibid.*
26. NAI, Judgement Hon. Kingsmill Moore, Sinn Féin Funds case, 26 October 1948, p. 30.
27. *Ibid.*
28. D. H. Akenson and J.F. Fallin, 'The Irish Civil War and the Drafting of the Irish Constitution', *Éire-Ireland*, 1970.
29. UCD Archives, O'Malley Papers, File P/7b/90, Frank Aiken.
30. Harry Boland to a friend, 21 June 1922, de Valera Papers, Franciscan Library, Killiney, File 253/3.
31. The *Free Press*, Wexford, 24 June 1922.

32. *Dáil Éireann Debates*, Volume 1, 9 September 1922, pp. 8-13.
33. The *Irish Independent*, 11 September 1922.
34. *Dáil Éireann Debates*, Volume 1, 3 October 1922, Constitution of Irish Free State Bill (Committee) Article 17, p. 1039.
35. *Ibid.*, p. 1040.
36. *Ibid.*, p. 1042.
37. *Ibid.*, p. 1043.
38. *Ibid.*, p. 1046.
39. *Ibid.*, p. 1047.
40. *Ibid.*, pp. 1046-1049.
41. Alec Burns, 'Pádraig Mac Gamhna'.
42. *Dáil Éireann Debates*, Volume 1, 3 October 1922, p. 1063.
43. NAI, Judgement Hon. Kingsmill Moore, Sinn Féin Funds Case, 26 October 1948, p. 34.
44. *Ibid.*, pp. 34, 35.
45. *Ibid.*, p. 36.
46. *Ibid.*, p. 37.
47. Dorothy Macardle, *The Irish Republic*, p. 807.
48. The twelve members of the Second Dáil whom Éamon de Valera nominated to act 'as a Council of State and Executive Ministers' were Austin Stack, Robert Barton, Count Plunkett, J.J. O'Kelly, Laurence Ginnell, Seán T. O'Kelly, Katherine O'Callaghan, Mary MacSwiney, P.J. Ruttledge, Seán Moylan, Michael P. Colivet and Seán O'Mahoney.
49. *The Irish Times*, 27 October 1922: 'A Rival Dáil Proclaimed'.
50. Brendan Sexton, *Ireland and the Crown*, pp. 88, 89.
51. *The Irish Times*, 7 December 1922.
52. *Dáil Éireann Debates*, Volume 2, 6 December 1922, p. 3.
53. *The Irish Times*, 7 December 1922.
54. Sexton, *op. cit.* p. 90.
55. Macardle, *op. cit.*, p. 829.
56. NAI, Judgement Hon. Kingsmill Moore, Sinn Féin Funds case, 26 October 1948, p. 39.
57. NAI, S1297, Pádraig Ó Ruithléis, Adjutant-General IRA to O/Cs all Divisions, 18 January 1923.
58. *The Irish Times*, 28 April 1923.
59. *Ibid.*, 10 May 1923.
60. *Dáil Éireann Debates*, Volume 3, 10 May 1923, pp. 789, 790.
61. *Ibid.*, p. 799.
62. *Ibid.*, p. 815.
63. *Ibid.*, p. 818.

3

THE GAP NARROWS

The efforts of the Republicans to keep their thirty-two-county Irish Republic in existence had been crushed by Free State forces. However, Éamon de Valera and P.J. Ruttledge, Adjutant-General IRA, were in close touch and debating how to involve the members of the defeated Republican army in the reorganisation of Sinn Féin. De Valera believed that the time for fighting had passed and that it was now a time for political thinking. It had been Dev's philosophy for some time now that once an Irish government and state machine had been set up, it was a sheer impossibility to dislodge it except by constitutional politics. Though many in Sinn Féin disagreed strongly with the civil war policy of the Republican militants, they remained anti-Treaty in outlook and opposed to the Oath of Allegiance. On the other hand W.T. Cosgrave and Kevin O'Higgins claimed in Dáil Éireann that the Irish Free State government was obliged to uphold the Oath of Allegiance clause in the Treaty, as the Oath was embodied in the Free State Constitution, 'that had been approved by a majority vote of the Irish people.'[1]

Dev's prompting had the desired effect because on the 28 May 1923, four days after the end of the Civil War, P.J. Ruttledge dispatched a communiqué to the O/Cs of the divisions and brigades of the IRA, pointing out 'that Sinn Féin must be reorganised throughout the country as it was organised after Easter Week'. The same letter declared that it was: 'the duty of every volunteer therefore to immediately join and organise Sinn Féin clubs and work earnestly and energetically to make the organisation an effective weapon for the attainment of our ideals.'[2]

Frank Aiken, Chief-of-Staff IRA, sent a memo to all IRA officers on the same day: 'We must join the Sinn Féin organisation and make sure the nation is represented by men who have our ideal and objective.'[3]

On 31 May Éamon de Valera, who was still on the run and unable to appear publicly for fear of arrest, advised that 'when circumstances permit, an *ard-fheis* of Sinn Féin should be called by either the personnel of the *ard-fheis* of a year ago or an *ard-fheis* comprised of [sic] the newly-affiliated *cumainn*.'[4]

Dr Kathleen Lynn chaired a public meeting in the Mansion House on 11 June to test Republican feeling on the matter. Between a hundred and a hundred and fifty people attended, representing sixteen Sinn Féin *cumainn*. This compared very unfavourably with the beginning of 1922, when 1485 *cumainn* (clubs) were regularly affiliated. The members present passed a resolution: 'That in their opinion the reorganisation of Sinn Féin as a national organisation is a national necessity and that the meeting should nominate a committee to undertake that task'.[5] In her report of the meeting Kathleen Lynn remarked: 'All present seemed to be glad that the time had arrived when they can [sic] come out and work as formerly.'[6]

De Valera sent a notice to his Republican followers to the effect that: 'All public meetings organised by our side should be held henceforth under the auspices of Sinn Féin.'[7] But the old officer board and the old Standing Committee were ignored and a new ad-hoc committee, which subsequently called itself the 'official Standing Committee' was set up. In his summary of the Sinn Féin funds case Justice Kingsmill Moore concluded that this new committee recreated rather than continued the old Sinn Féin organisation.[8] Joseph Connolly, chairman of the reorganisation committee, admitted that no attempt was made to get in touch with members of the old Standing Committee or to procure the old minute book and records. Owen O'Keeffe, secretary to the reorganised committee, stated that 'neither then nor afterwards was there any real attempt made to approach persons who were pro-Treaty.'[9]

At a meeting of the Standing Committee of reorganised Sinn Féin on 26 June 1923 the following resolution was carried unanimously, 'that Sinn Féin be organised as a constitutional movement'.[10] The organisation issued a draft of its proposed programme on 11 July 1923. With regard to the aims of the organisation:

We maintain that no elected representative of the people may take an Oath of Allegiance to any foreign power. We propose to achieve our programme by securing the election to all national and local government bodies of representatives who will faithfully carry out the Sinn Féin programme.[11]

The new Sinn Féin programme was ratified at a meeting in the Mansion House on 17 July 1923.[12] National Sinn Féin was at an end. Sinn Féin was now made up of members strictly Republican in outlook. The third phase of Sinn Féin – Republican Sinn Féin – was well and truly launched at this meeting.

The announcement that he was instigating a revival of Sinn Féin was a wise move by de Valera. Everything looked bad for Republicans at this time but de Valera was keeping a tight grip on Sinn Féin. W.T. Cosgrave and his ministers completely overlooked Sinn Féin, the biggest Irish mass movement in the 20th century. The only political development on the government side in 1923 was the foundation of its new political party, Cumann na nGaedheal, but, in the words of Gerry Boland, 'it was a party without a tradition and lacking the fire of the revolutionary Sinn Féin.'[13]

W.T. Cosgrave, President of the Executive Council of the Irish Free State, announced a general election for 27 August 1923. There were still eleven thousand Republicans in custody, two-hundred-and-fifty of whom were women. These anti-Treaty prisoners would be out of circulation for the duration of the election.

In the course of an interview with W.H. Brayden of the Associated Press of America in mid-1923, Éamon de Valera rejected any claim that Republicans intended a renewal of hostilities. 'It is not the intention of the Republican government or army executive to renew the war in the autumn or after the elections. The war, so far as we are concerned, is finished.'[14]

The government contested the 1923 general election under the umbrella of its newly-formed Cumann na nGaedheal party. Advertisements described the party as the national organisation formed to carry out the policy adopted by Arthur Griffith and Michael Collins and continued by the government of President Cosgrave.[15] This Cosgrave party had been in government for almost a year and as an advertisement in the *Cork Examiner* pointed out 'the Free State had paid unemployment benefit to a weekly average of 30,000 [people] since the previous October and that furthermore 12,000 workers had been placed in employment.'[16]

Though de Valera had reorganised Sinn Féin, he fought this election under the banner of the Republican Party – fully committed, if elected, to govern the country along the lines of 1919 Sinn Féin.[17] Because of its poor performance in the 1922 general election, the party felt insecure and fearful for its future. Any further slippage of support would cause such a loss of morale that the future of their Republican movement and, in fact, Republicanism itself would be bleak indeed. But newly revived Sinn Féin had dedicated party workers who were determined to drive themselves to exhaustion in an effort to avenge their military defeat in the Civil War and the death of many of their comrades.

This general election to the Fourth Dáil was held by means of proportional representation. The only constituency in the country where no contest took place was Trinity College where three candidates, all Unionists, had been nominated for the available three seats.

Before the election de Valera and Michael Colivet, Minister for Economic Affairs in the Republican government, prepared a draft social-democratic programme designed to improve the lot of the workers in the towns and the countryside.[18] But the abolition of the Oath of Allegiance still remained one of the most urgent Republican objectives.[19] The immediate release of the political prisoners was another demand. De Valera found himself much more at home in political work than in military activities.

The Catholic bishops continued to support the pro-Treatyites. But the anti-Treatyites had one friend in the hierarchy, Most Reverend Doctor Mannix, although he was domiciled far away from home as Archbishop of Melbourne. He claimed 'that there were thousands in Ireland, who in the circumstances, would never accept the terms of the London Treaty or swear with their lips an Oath of Allegiance which they could not ratify in their hearts.'[20]

The daily papers of 14 August announced that de Valera would speak in Ennis the following day. Up to then local men did almost all the work of addressing meetings on the Republican side. The anti-Treaty leaders were careful not to appear on public platforms in their constituencies for fear of arrest but it was widely known locally that Dev would address a meeting in the Square in O'Connell Street in Ennis on the afternoon of 15 August.

Large numbers of people assembled from midday on that day. At 2 pm a motor car turned into the square carrying de Valera, Reverend Brother Barrett (brother of Frank Barrett, a Sinn Féin candidate in Clare), and Ruairí de Valera, Dev's fifteen-year-old son.[21] At 2.30 Éamon de Valera rose to speak. The cheering rose in volume as he came to the front of the platform. He rapped out a dozen sentences in Irish. Then he spoke a few sentences in English. There was another outburst of cheering.

Just as silence settled on the crowd again, a woman shouted from the edge of the throng, 'The soldiers are coming. Here are the soldiers.' Two files of soldiers came around the corner of O'Connell Street on foot, followed by an armoured car. They made their way through the crowd, which gave way at their approach. Then de Valera could be heard shouting, 'They are coming for me, boys.' The soldiers surrounded the platform and de Valera raised his hand and shouted to the crowd, 'I am glad it is in Clare that I am being taken.' At that moment a number of shots rang out from the position that the soldiers had taken and immediately the crowd scattered in disarray.

Éamon de Valera was taken into custody and marched down O'Connell Street to the barracks, guarded on each side by military officers. He was moved to Limerick soon afterwards under heavy escort.

The Republican publicity department issued a statement informing the Irish public that Pádraig Ó Ruithléis, (Patrick Ruttledge), Minister for Home Affairs, had been appointed 'Deputy and Acting President of the Republic' by Éamon de Valera, hours before he left to address the meeting in Ennis.

Pádraig Ó Ruithléis immediately issued a statement as 'Acting President of the Republican government' that W.T. Cosgrave had said in Tralee, 'We claim that the people's representatives have a right to be heard.'[22]

In reply, a Free State publicity statement said:

De Valera now tries to shelter himself behind the political campaign but he must take his place with his associates and dupes until such time as he and the others can be released without injury to public safety.[23]

President Cosgrave announced at Drogheda that Cumann na nGaedheal had asked a Free State minister, Major General Joseph McGrath, to contest North Mayo against Ruttledge, 'to drive him out of public life so that he can no longer say he represents people in this country'.[24]

Arguments about the Oath of Allegiance continued on all sides in the lead-up to the election. Alderman William O'Brien, Labour candidate for Dublin City South, asserted 'that the Labour Party would do its best to have the Oath deleted from the Constitution'.[25] Major Bryan Cooper, an Independent candidate with a Unionist background, said in Skerries, 'that if he were returned he would resist any attempt from any quarter whatever to interfere with a settlement (the Anglo-Irish Treaty) which had been accepted and ratified by the representatives of the Irish people'.[26] In Clonmel, W.T. Cosgrave said 'that the most important thing in this election was the return of people who would take their seats in parliament and would sit, act and vote there'.[27] Mary MacSwiney said in Monaghan on the eve of the poll: 'I am going to obey no law made by any man giving allegiance to the King of England'.[28] In Dublin, R.J. Connolly, son of the dead patriot James Connolly, asked, 'Why not let the Republican majority or the Labour cum Republican majority after the election, walk into the Dáil and – remembering that oaths were neither sacrosanct nor immutable – pass as a first act an amendment to the Free State Constitution which would delete the Oath of Allegiance to the king'.[29]

Polling took place on 27 August 1923. The results showed that Free State ministers dominated the election as vote-catchers. Cumann na nGaedheal was way ahead of the Republican Party in the National University of Ireland, Dublin County, Dublin South, Dublin North, Cork City, Monaghan, Meath, and Carlow-Kilkenny. In the boroughs of Dublin and Cork the pro-Treatyites had an overwhelming victory over Republicans: in these two centres the anti-Treatyites recorded their lowest percentages of the vote. On the other hand,

Cumann na nGaedheal got no seats in Cork North or Waterford. The poor showing of Dr Vincent White (Cumann na nGaedheal) in Waterford can be attributed to the election there of Captain William Redmond, standing as an Independent and attracting the old Waterford Redmondite vote. In Dublin University (Trinity College) three Unionist candidates were returned unopposed.

Republicans got more votes and won more seats than Cumann na nGaedheal candidates in six constituencies out of twenty-nine – Clare, Cork North, Kerry, Longford-Westmeath, Wexford and Waterford. They got more votes but an equal number of seats in Leix-Offaly. The anti-Treatyites also polled strongly in Galway and Tipperary. Republicans performed worst – and gained no seats – in Kildare, Meath, Wicklow and the National University of Ireland.

It was a surprise that Éamon de Valera, in Clare, got the highest percentage poll in the whole country – 45 per cent (17,762 votes). The media, which were totally unsympathetic to the Republican cause, correctly continued to refer to General Richard Mulcahy's 22,205 votes (40 per cent of the poll) in Dublin North as the highest number of votes in the land, but never admitted that de Valera had obtained the highest percentage vote nationally. De Valera's vote emphasised the fact that the Free State government had made a cardinal error in arresting him in Ennis on 15 August. As most people regarded his arrest as a restriction on free speech, it put many extra votes on the ballot sheets of Republicans, not only in Clare but throughout the whole country.

Major General Joseph McGrath did not succeed in ousting Paddy Ruttledge, Acting President of the Republican government, in North Mayo as President Cosgrave had predicted. Ruttledge headed the poll there with 8997 votes to Major McGrath's 8011 and both were elected on the first count.

The state of the parties following the general election was: Cumann na nGaedheal sixty-three seats, Republicans forty-four, Independents seventeen, Farmers fifteen, and Labour fourteen. There were now a hundred-and-fifty-three seats in the House compared to a hundred-and-twenty-eight in the dissolved Dáil. The government had gained five seats, the anti-Treatyites eight, the Farmers eight and independents seven, while the Labour party had lost three seats. Overall Cumann na nGaedheal received 39.1 per cent of the total poll while Republicans obtained 27.4 per cent.

A slightly disappointed W.T. Cosgrave was interviewed at Holyhead on his way to Geneva:

> We, as ministers, regard the results as the complete endorsement of the policy of the government…It may be a complaint that we adopted a too conservative policy but the people have declared themselves to be very well satisfied…[30]

The *Freeman's Journal*, a pro-Treaty paper, commented on the election:

> The PR system enabled the anti-Treatyites to do much better than most people expected, and they remain a compact force which must be reckoned with as a political factor.[31]

Nearly 300.000 people, in voting for Republicans, protested against the imposition of the Oath of Allegiance. Nevertheless more than twice that number were not concerned that it was part of the Irish Constitution and voted for pro-Treaty candidates. The verdict of the majority of the people represented the view that it was better to accept the Treaty than to vote for Republicans who could upset the whole apple-cart again by rejecting parts of the Treaty, principally the Oath of Allegiance, thus, it was feared, sparking another round of guerrilla warfare with Britain.

With all results in, the government was certain of more than a working majority, even if the Republicans entered the Dáil and took the Oath and their seats. Even if the Labour Party combined with the anti-Treatyites in the event of the latter group taking their seats, the Cumann na nGaedheal Party would outnumber the combination by five seats.

In addition W.T. Cosgrave was almost certain of the support of practically all the independents and farmers. Three members of the defunct Irish Party had been elected as independents – Captain William Redmond (Waterford), Alderman Alfred Byrne (Dublin North) and James Cosgrave (Galway). How these deputies would vote in a tight situation was a matter of conjecture.

What use would the anti-Treatyites make of their improved strength? Rumours circulated that they, or at least some of them, were considering the question of entering the new Dáil. The *Freeman's Journal* commented that 'the more resolutely the anti-Treatyites hold aloof from the political conduct of affairs the more certain is their cause to perish of sheer futility.'[32]

In the absence of Éamon de Valera, who was in prison, the acting leader of the anti-Treatyites, Patrick Ruttledge, a solicitor and TD for North Mayo, issued a statement alluding to the gravity of the decisions that had to be taken and demanding the release of the prisoners and the removal of the Oath. 'No member of the party will take the Oath under any consideration and enter the Free State Dáil,' he said. 'While the Oath of Allegiance to England and all it implies is [sic] imposed on Ireland there can be no lasting peace or unity.'[33]

Ruttledge summoned all Republican deputies to a meeting on 14 September 1923 to consider the way forward. Included in the invitations were Republican TDs of the Second Dáil elected in May 1921 and those returned in the Pact election in June 1922 as well as the TDs returned in the most recent general election of August 1923. The majority of them were still in prison or on the run. Only eleven deputies, all of whom had been returned in the election of August 1923, including the chairman, Count Plunkett, were able to make their way to the meeting.[34] Acting President Ruttledge did not attend for fear of arrest by Free State forces.

The meeting of these eleven deputies constituted the first assembly of *Comhairle na dTeachtaí*, which was intended to be a consultative council of all Republican deputies, who would meet, advise and make recommendations on questions of policy to the twelve members of the Second Dáil, under the presidency of Éamon de Valera – the group that had been nominated 'as a council of state and executive ministers' on 25 October 1922. After the meeting the eleven elected deputies issued a statement:

> Forty-four (Republican) deputies have been elected by the people – in spite of English guns, bayonets and armoured cars, and the detention of 13,000 of our best and most prominent

workers…Because of their determined opposition to that foreign authority, exercised through the imposition of an Oath of Allegiance and all that Oath entails, twenty-seven of the elected deputies are in jail, including our president, and six of our colleagues are evading arrest. Only eleven – exactly one-fourth of those elected – are at present free.[35]

Mary MacSwiney, who had attended the *Comhairle* na dTeachtaí meeting, wrote to Patrick Ruttledge to give him an account of what transpired and noted: 'Louis O'Dea, Dr Conor O'Byrne and Frank Fahy were particularly insistent that our constituents expected us to go into the Irish Free State Dáil or try to do something. No one, I am glad to say, looked at the possibility of taking the Oath.'[36]

The Governor-General of the Free State, Tim Healy, issued a proclamation in mid-September 1923:

In the name of His Majesty the King and with the advice of the Executive Council of the Irish Free State I do hereby summon and call together the Oireachtas of the Irish Free State and each house of the said Oireachtas to meet in the city of Dublin on 19 September 1923 for the dispatch of such business as shall be submitted to the respective Houses.[37]

All the deputies returned in the August election, including the forty-four Republicans, had also received a notice to attend at the office of Colm Ó Murchadha, the clerk of the Dáil, before the date of the meeting of Dáil Éireann, for the purpose of taking the Oath of Allegiance. At first the eleven available elected Republican TDs, members of *Comhairle na dTeachtaí*, intended to make some appearance at this first meeting of the Fourth Dáil. Patrick Ruttledge, Acting President of the Republic, issued a statement:

This meeting called for 19 September 1923 is not to be regarded as a lawful government, to which citizens should give obedience and recognition. The object of attending this is (a) to give our opponents the opportunity of recording their willingness to cooperate in this work by their non-insistence on the taking of the political Oath which is the most immediate obstacle to peace and unity. (b) If admitted, Republican representatives will only remain long enough to ensure that the Oath is not insisted on and then withdraw until imprisoned representatives are released as the next step towards peace and unity.[38]

Shortly after this the eleven available Republican TDs changed their minds about making an appearance on the opening day of the Fourth Dáil. Acting President Ruttledge wrote to Countess Markievicz on 17 September 1923: 'The position has somewhat altered owing to our opponents having taken certain steps that indicate their insistence on the Oath of Allegiance to Britain and prevent our people from attending the meeting of the 19th. In view of this I am having action previously decided upon reconsidered by the cabinet and hope you and other deputies will hear further from me tomorrow.'[39] The cabinet of the Republican Second Dáil that had been chosen by de Valera on 25 October 1922 decided that for the eleven Republican TDs to attend the opening of the Dáil session on 19 September would serve no useful purpose as the Free State authorities had adopted new tactics for administering the Oath.[40]

These tactics comprised a new procedure by which elected deputies were obliged to attend at the office of the Clerk of the Dáil, Colm Ó Murchadha, prior to the meeting of the Dáil, for the purpose of taking the Oath. The Oath had to be taken and subscribed to in front of the representative of the crown or some person authorised by him – in this instance the clerk of the Dáil.[41] This change in procedure was a wise move by the Cumann na nGaedheal government as it prevented what would probably have been a noisy protest by the anti-Treaty deputies in the Dáil chamber itself.

Over a three-day period from Monday 16 September, pro-Treaty deputies called by invitation to Leinster House and took the Oath. A special room was prepared and there the Clerk of the Dáil was ready with the assistance of some of the staff to administer the Oath. All the elected deputies took the Oath with the exception of the forty-four anti-Treaty deputies who did not turn up. Instead the eleven available Republican TDs, on behalf of the other Republican deputies who were either prisoners or fugitives on the run, issued a statement explaining in no uncertain terms why they could not attend the opening session of the Fourth Dáil.

> We would consider it a duty to take part in the deliberations of the newly-elected assembly…on the following two conditions. The first is the abolition of the Oath of Allegiance to the King of England as a condition of taking our seats and the other is the immediate release of those of our colleagues in prison whom their constituencies have commissioned to represent them.[42]

The Fourth Dáil held its first meeting on Wednesday, 19 September 1923. The meeting got under way when Colm Ó Murchadha read out the entire list of deputies who had subscribed to the Oath of Allegiance prescribed in the Constitution and were therefore eligible to sit and act in the house. W.T. Cosgrave was again elected President of the Free State Parliament. The President then nominated his ministers for the Executive Council and they continued the business of ruling the country.

The Republican *Comhairle na dTeachtaí* held a meeting in Suffolk Street, Dublin, on the same day as the Dáil came together. This time ten Republican TDs attended under the chairmanship of Dr Kathleen Lynn TD. During the course of the meeting there was a discussion on the Civil War that had come to an end earlier that year. Mary MacSwiney, who acted as Secretary at this meeting, noted that 'Frank Fahy said (and I think Louis O'Dea agreed with him) that in no circumstances would he agree to a renewal of the Civil War with half of Ireland and all England against us.'[43]

For a while *Comhairle na dTeachtaí* was not certain which course it should pursue. However the acting president, Patrick Ruttledge, gave the group strong and enlightened leadership. He wrote in a letter to Dáithí Ceannt, Republican TD for Cork East: 'We must concentrate all our efforts on the

Oath of Allegiance and the release of the prisoners. The immediate work before us is to organise solidly and effectively the entire country through Sinn Féin.'[44]

In correspondence with the *Irish Independent* Countess Markievicz referred to the Oath of Allegiance:

> The will of the people who voted Republican is that we should be true to our Oath of Allegiance to the Republic. For me to take the Free State Oath would involve the breaking of the second commandment twice as I would be taking a false Oath and breaking a lawful one. First I should break my solemn Oath of Allegiance made without reserve to the Irish Republic, and under no duress. Secondly I should take a false one if I took an Oath of Allegiance to a foreign king not intending to keep it.[45]

An opposing view from 'A Real Republican' appeared in the letters' column of the same paper strongly criticising the abstentionist policy of the anti-Treatyites. 'Refusing to sit in the Dáil is useless as a political weapon, for it only strengthens instead of weakens their political opponents.'

More than a thousand delegates, representing six-hundred-and-eighty *cumainn*, attended the newly organised Sinn Féin *ard-fheis* which opened in the Mansion House on 16 October 1923. Two notable absentees, still on the run, were Patrick J. Ruttledge TD and Frank Aiken TD. In the absence of Patrick Ruttledge, Dr Kathleen Lynn temporarily took the chair. Her proposal that Mary MacSwiney preside was received with acclamation. Women were now playing very active roles in Sinn Féin to compensate for the enforced absence of many of the menfolk.

Éamon de Valera, although still in prison, was unanimously re-elected president. Elected as vice-presidents were Dr Kathleen Lynn TD, Father Michael O'Flanagan, P.J. Ruttledge TD and Mary MacSwiney TD.[46] Secretaries elected were Austin Stack TD, then in prison, and George Daly. Mrs Caitlín Brugha TD (wife of the late Cathal Brugha, Minister for Defence in the War of Independence) and Stephen O'Mara, former mayor of Limerick, were elected treasurers.

On the motion of Dr Kathleen Lynn, seconded by Patrick Cahill, TD for Kerry, a resolution was passed protesting at the taking of any Oath derogatory to or constituting a denial of the sovereignty and integrity of the Irish nation.[47] There is no doubt that this proposal referred to the Oath of Allegiance and it meant that no Republican TD should take this Oath under any circumstances whatever.

In his judgement on the Sinn Féin Funds issue Justice Kingsmill Moore had this to say about this first *ard-fheis* of the newly reorganised Republican Sinn Féin:

> On 10 October the affiliation fees of almost seven hundred *cumainn* were accepted. The *ard-fheis* was held on 16 October. By the existing rules, *cumainn* were not entitled to be represented at an *ard-fheis* unless they had been affiliated for three months previous to the date of holding the *ard-fheis*. Accordingly a mere fraction of the delegates who appeared and debated and voted on 16 October had any right to be present... The *ard-fheis* was not properly constituted according to the rules and its actions and resolutions can have no validity in preserving the continuity of the organisation.[48]

A by-election occurred in Dublin South in October 1923. This constituency was a Cumann na nGaedheal stronghold. Addressing an election meeting at Inchicore, Michael O'Mullane, the Republican candidate, said 'that priests and nuns in the North of Ireland were made take an Oath of Allegiance to the king before they were allowed to teach. How could the Free Staters protest when Sir James Craig could retort: "You won't let anyone enter your parliament unless he takes an Oath of Allegiance to the king."'

The Cumann na nGaedheal candidate, Hugh Kennedy, the former attorney-general, was elected with a big majority but the Republican vote in Dublin South rose from 21 per cent in the general election of August 1923 to 33 per cent in this October by-election. The Republicans had expected a greater increase in their vote but in this part of Dublin, where many people clamoured for employment and better housing, their abstentionist policy was a hindrance at the polls.

There was a further by-election at the beginning of November – this time in the National University, the constituency that had given the highest percentage vote in the country to Cumann na nGaedheal in the 1923 general election. Patrick McGilligan of the same party was elected with as large a majority as in the earlier election. The National University remained a pro-Treaty bastion.

Patrick Baxter, Farmers' Party TD and Cavan poll-topper, referred to the absence of the elected Republican TDs in Dáil Éireann in a Dáil debate:

> Twenty-five per cent of the deputies who were elected to represent the people of the Saorstát are not here. But I think that despite the fact that they are not present here, they do represent the twenty-five per cent of the Irish people who selected and elected them, and their point of view and their position in the Ireland of today and the Ireland of tomorrow must be taken into account by everybody who looks to any future for this country at all.[49]

Thousands of political prisoners, both male and female, were released from Free State prisons and internment camps in December 1923, seven months after the conclusion of the civil war, but not all the internees were freed. Among those still in custody were Éamon de Valera and Austin Stack. By this time good progress had been made on the formalising of the Republican Second Dáil. Printed notepaper had been procured and the office occupied by P.J. Ruttledge, Acting Republican President, had been named *Oifig an Uachtaráin.*

The young men released from Free State prisons found it extremely difficult to get employment. The President, W.T. Cosgrave, made an appeal in the public press on 1 January 1924 that demobilised officers and men of the Free State Army be given preference in the matter of jobs. Government agencies, local authority bodies and employers did as he asked. There were no jobs for the IRA volunteers who had fought the British in the Black and Tan War but had taken the side of the defeated anti-Treatyites in the Civil War. Many of them emigrated to the US, particularly to New York, to procure employment. The Secretary of Sinn Féin reported to the *Ard-Chomhairle*: 'We cannot stand by and watch our people starve. Every *cumann* in Ireland must…find employment for the unemployed.'[50]

Divisions began to appear among Republican TDs with regard to the validity of the claim of the Second Dáil to function as a government. These doubts came to the surface during a meeting of *Comhairle na dTeachtaí* held at 23 Suffolk Street, Dublin in mid-January 1924 that was attended by seventeen of the members of the group. Seán T. O'Kelly TD remarked that since his release from jail he had noted 'the swing round of the people to the position of 1918.' He asked for opinions as to how the Second Dáil could function as a government. Countess Markievicz TD (Dublin South) was the first to speak. She said, 'It is nonsense to call ourselves a government when the people have turned us down. We have the majority against us and until we have the majority with us again, we are not a government.'[51] Count Plunkett TD (Roscommon) sprang to his feet to refute this suggestion of the Countess. 'The present Free State government was set up by England,' he claimed. 'The men of 1916 had declared the Republic and established a provisional government.'[52] Louis O'Dea TD (Galway) asked: 'Are we entitled to form a government in present circumstances?' Mary MacSwiney TD (Cork Borough) supported the view of Count Plunkett: 'I deny that the right of the majority extends to the surrender of the independence of the nation.' Dr Kathleen Lynn TD concurred: 'No generation can surrender the independence of the country.' Frank Fahy said that the Second Dáil government must be there as a symbol: 'However it would be unjust to the majority of the people of the country if it tried to function.' Dan Breen TD (Tipperary) spoke with his defiant Republican spirit. 'The government is not ours to give away.' Finally Louis O'Dea proposed a resolution: 'That this meeting of Republican *Teachtaí Dála* heartily approves of the Republican cabinet appointed by President de Valera, which cabinet is to continue as the government of the republic.' Count Plunkett seconded the motion and it was passed unanimously. Before the session concluded, Madame Markievicz amended her opening statement by saying that she agreed that the government should exist (as a symbol) but that it had no right to legislate.[53]

The sudden death of Cumann na nGaedheal TD Philip Cosgrave, brother of W.T. Cosgrave, caused a by-election in Dublin South in March 1924. The candidates were James O'Mara (Cumann na nGaedheal); Seán Lemass (Republican); and John O'Neill (Independent). O'Mara, a businessman, had won South Kilkenny for Sinn Féin in 1918 and was now a staunch supporter of the Treaty. Seán Lemass had been second in command in the Four Courts when Free State forces attacked the building and was elected to the Standing Committee of Sinn Féin at the 1923 *ard-fheis*. At this stage he had no objection to the Sinn Féin abstentionist policy. He had been chosen as a candidate without his knowledge, a sign that there was no rush by Republicans to enter politics at this time.[54] The third candidate was John O'Neill, a well-known cycle manufacturer, who advocated a strong protectionist policy for Irish industry. 'I am not,' he said laughingly, 'an anti-Treatyite but we want to revive the country and we want protection for our industries.'[55]

During the campaign Lemass did not overstate the Sinn Féin abstentionist policy but emphasised in his speeches that he had a socialist as well as a Republican slant. At one meeting he pointed out 'that the Free State had a social system repugnant to the ideas of the Irish people.'[56]

The poll in Dublin South took place on 12 March and only 40 per cent of the total electorate cast their votes. O'Mara (Cumann na nGaedheal) polled 15,884 votes, Lemass (Republican) got 13,639 and O'Neill (Independent) obtained 2928 votes. It was a surprise that Lemass got within 2245 of his Cumann na nGaedheal rival. The election went into a second count but when O'Neill was eliminated the transfer of his second preference votes gave four times as many votes to O'Mara as to Lemass and O'Mara was elected.

The percentage Republican vote in Dublin South in the general election of August 1923 had been 21 per cent. In this March 1924 by-election, Seán Lemass brought it up to 42 per cent, a remarkable increase considering that Sinn Féin was still wedded to a policy of abstention from Dáil Éireann.

The accidental death of Michael Derham TD, also of Cumann na nGaedheal, meant the holding of another by-election in the constituency of Dublin County. Dublin County had given the anti-Treatyites a very low percentage vote in the 1923 general election. Batt O'Connor was selected as the Cumann na nGaedheal standard-bearer. Batt had been an intimate associate of Michael Collins right through the Black and Tan War. Seán MacEntee was the anti-Treaty candidate. He had been a Sinn Féin TD for Monaghan South in the first Dáil but stood unsuccessfully for Dublin County in the 1923 general election. The Labour Party selected Archibald Heron. A surprise last-minute candidate was Matthew Good, a solicitor, who was nominated by the Business Party.

The poll took place on 19 March 1924. Batt O'Connor (Cumann na nGaedheal) polled 16,456 votes. Seán MacEntee got a much-improved Republican vote of 10,263. Matthew Good received a creditable 9158 but Archibald Heron came in fourth position with 6287. Batt O'Connor was declared elected after a third count.

In this by-election, held less than a year after the general election, the Republican vote had risen from 14 per cent to 24 per cent, while the Cumann na nGaedheal vote had fallen from 48 per cent to 39 per cent.

The gap between Cumann na nGaedheal and abstentionist Sinn Féin was narrowing but no Republican candidate had yet been elected in any by-election. Republicans were, however, hugely determined to overturn the military defeat of the Civil War by constitutional success at the polls and they were making slow but steady progress towards that end.

Notes
1. *Dáil Éireann Debates*, Volume 1, 3 October 1922, p. 1040.
2. NAI, File S1297, P. Ó Ruithléis, Adj.-General IRA to O/Cs Divisions, 28 May 1923.
3. NAI, Frank Aiken, Chief of Staff to all IRA officers, 28 May 1923.
4. NAI, Éamon de Valera to reorganised Sinn Féin, 31 May 1923.
5. NAI, File S1297, Mansion House Meeting.
6. *Ibid.*
7. *Ibid.*
8. NAI, Judgement Hon. Kingsmill Moore, Sinn Féin Funds case, 26 October 1948, p. 46.
9. *Ibid.*, 26 October 1948, pp. 46, 47.
10. *Ibid.* and minutes of Standing Committee meeting, 26 June 1923.
11. NAI, Aims of Sinn Féin, 11 July 1923, File S1297.
12. NAI, Judgement Hon. Kingsmill Moore, Sinn Féin Funds case, 26 October 1948, p. 48.
13. Gerry Boland's story as told to Michael McInerney, Irish Times, 10 October 1968.

14. *The Irish Times*, 23 July 1923.
15. The *Irish Independent*, 3 August 1923.
16. Micheál Martin, *Freedom to Choose*, The Collins Press, Cork, 2009, p. 94, and the *Cork Examiner*, 21 August 1923.
17. The *Irish Independent*, 23 July 1923.
18. Gerry Boland story as told to Michael McInerney, *The Irish Times*, 10 October 1968.
19. Seán Lemass: An interview with Michael Mills, *Irish Press*, 23 January 1969.
20. The *Irish Independent*, 13 August 1923.
21. *Ibid.*, 16 August 1923.
22. *Ibid.*
23. *Ibid.*
24. *Ibid.*, 18 August 1923.
25. *Ibid.*, 23 August 1923.
26. *Ibid.*, 24 August 1923.
27. *Ibid.*, 23 August 1923.
28. *Ibid.*, 27 August 1923.
29. *Ibid.*, 24 August 1923.
30. *Ibid.*, 31 August 1923.
31. The *Freeman's Journal*, 3 September 1923.
32. *Ibid.*
33. The *Irish Independent*, 4 September 1923.
34. The eleven deputies who attended were: Caitlín Bean Brugha (Waterford); Constance Countess Markievicz (Dublin South); Dr Caitlín Ní Linn (County Dublin); Máire Ní Shuibhne (Cork); Conchubhair Ó Broin (Longford-Westmeath); Séamus Ó Cillín (Longford-Westmeath); Seán Ó Cruadhlaoich (Mayo North); Lughaidh Ó Deagha (Galway); Proinsias Ó Fathaigh (Galway); Micheál Ó Seallaigh (Carlow-Kilkenny); George Nobel Count Plunkett (Roscommon).
35. UCD Archives, de Valera Papers, File P/150/1944: Minutes of the meeting of available TDs, 14 September 1923.
36. UCD Archives, de Valera Papers, File P/150/1944: Letter from Mary MacSwiney to the Acting President.
37. *Dáil Éireann Debates*, Volume 5, 19 September 1923, p. 1.
38. UCD Archives, de Valera Papers, File P/150/1944.
39. UCD Archives, de Valera Papers, File P/150/1944: Letter from P.J. Ruttledge TD to Countess Markievicz, 17 September 1923.
40. UCD Archives, de Valera Papers, File P/150/1944: P.J. Ruttledge to Count Plunkett, Chairman *Comhairle na dTeachtaí*, 18 September 1923.
41. The *Freeman's Journal*, 14 September 1923.
42. UCD Archives, de Valera Papers, File P/150/1944.
43. UCD Archives, de Valera Papers, File P/150/1944: Minutes of the meeting of *Comhairle na dTeachtaí*, 19 September 1923.
44. UCD Archives, de Valera Papers, File P/150/1944: P. J. Ruttledge to Dáithí Ceannt TD, 19 September 1923.
45. The *Irish Independent*, 28 September 1923 and 2 October 1923.
46. *Ibid.* 17 October 1923.
47. *Ibid.*, 18 October 1923.
48. NAI, Judgement of Hon. Kingsmill Moore, Sinn Féin Funds Case, 26 October 1948, pp. 48, 49.
49. *Dáil Éireann Debates*, Volume 5, 16 November 1923, p. 973.
50. NAI, Sinn Féin Minutes, Report of Honorary Secretary, 27 Samhain 1923, File 2B/82/116/117, p. 77.
51. UCD Archives, de Valera Papers, File P/150/1945: Minutes of the meeting of *Comhairle na dTeachtaí*, 15 January 1924.
52. *Ibid.*
53. *Ibid.*
54. Horgan, John, *Sean Lemass: The Enigmatic Patriot*, pp. 30, 31.
55. The *Freeman's Journal*, 14 February 1924.
56. *Ibid.*, 25 February 1924.

4

DE VALERA FREE AGAIN

The Free State government experienced a serious setback when an army mutiny began on 6 March 1924. Two Free State officers, Liam Tobin and Charles Dalton, presented an ultimatum to the Cosgrave government. The mutineers declared that Michael Collins and the Irish people had accepted the Treaty only as a stepping-stone to a republic. They felt that the Free State rulers had become complacent with the constitutional position of the country. They also demanded the immediate suspension of demobilisation from the army as, they claimed, old IRA volunteers were being dismissed while ex-British-army officers were being retained.

About a hundred army officers throughout the country supported the ultimatum. The mutineers received assistance from Joseph McGrath TD (Mayo North), Minister for Industry and Commerce, who acted as a mediator between them and the government.

The crisis ended in serious controversy on 18 March when the Minister for Defence, General Richard Mulcahy, without government approval, authorised military action against the mutineers, who were holding a meeting at Devlin's public house in Parnell Street. As a result of this incident, General Mulcahy was obliged to resign as minister. Joseph McGrath, who sympathised with the mutinous officers, resigned as Minister for Industry and Commerce. In a compromise agreement, the mutineers won a concession that 'all men with active service records in the War of Independence would be retained in the army'.

The resignation of McGrath and Mulcahy from the Executive Council was a severe blow to the government. Kevin O'Higgins emerged as the strongest man in the cabinet and declared that in future the government would expect and demand 'absolute discipline, absolute loyalty, absolute obedience from every man in military uniform.'[1]

Joe McGrath announced that other Cumann na nGaedheal deputies supported the mutineers' claim that Michael Collins and the Irish people had accepted the Treaty only as a stepping-stone to a republic. Reliable sources estimated that there could be up to eight Cumann na nGaedheal TDs on his side. But these dissidents held many diverse views about the road forward. Joe McGrath declared: 'We will take up an independent line of action in Dáil Éireann, always guided by what we consider to be in the best interests of the country.'[2] In a subsequent statement he stated that he was an independent Republican. Professor Alfred O'Rahilly, Cumann na nGaedheal TD for Cork borough, who supported McGrath, hoped for the gradual emergence of a constitutional Republican party, the members of which would take their seats in Dáil Éireann.[3] In the short term, the strategy followed by this new group was to keep a vigilant eye on government policy and vouch criticism where it seemed needed.

Because de Valera and Austin Stack were in prison, TDs P.J. Ruttledge and Mary MacSwiney were guiding Republican policy in the *Comhairle na dTeachtaí* assembly. In the course of a speech she made in London, Mary MacSwiney said that 'Republicans did not recognise the Constitution of the Free State just as they did not recognise the British Constitution in Ireland before the Treaty.'[4]

P.J. Ruttledge was anxious that Sinn Féin TDs should take measures to ensure that their supporters avoided making 'war speeches' in their areas. In a letter to Seán T. O'Kelly he advised:

> Our strength is now such that we believe it may be possible to win recognition of Ireland's independence without further recourse to internal war or war with Great Britain. Our people are war-weary and any statements stressing the possibility of further war will entail loss of support.[5]

Speaking to an *Irish Independent* representative, Joe McGrath TD, leader of the group that had broken with Cumann na nGaedheal over the army mutiny, and Dan McCarthy TD, (Dublin South) a well-known GAA figure and member of the break-away band, said that their new group in the Dáil would in future be known as the National Group. The objectives of their party were complete independence, restoration of territorial unity and economic progress. They made their position clear: unlike Sinn Féin, they agreed with the Treaty enacted between Great Britain and Ireland and individually had no objection to the Oath of Allegiance:

> We are satisfied that we have sufficient powers under the present Irish Constitution to obtain our objectives. One big reason that we go into opposition is the apparent disinclination of the present government to make the most of the position gained by the Treaty or rather to have a tendency to lose sight of that position.[6]

Due to the resignation from the Dáil of the deputy for Limerick, Dr Richard Hayes (Cumann na nGaedheal), a crucial by-election occurred in that county in May 1924. The Republican vote had improved consistently and considerably in the Dublin area over the previous nine months. Would this trend be repeated in a rural constituency like County Limerick, where resistance to British forces in the War of Independence had been as strong as in any part of Ireland?

Cumann na nGaedheal chose Richard O'Connell as their candidate while the Republicans selected Tadhg Crowley at a Republican convention chaired by Dáithí Kent TD. A sign that the anti-Treaty side was taking a serious view of this election was the fact that they decided to send two paid organisers to the constituency.[7]

There was a surprise development when members of the National Group, led by Seán Milroy, promised to support the Cumann na nGaedheal candidate, Richard O'Connell, and pledged their services to help his election.[8] This emphasised the fact that the break-away McGrath group did not want any working relationship with anti-Treaty Sinn Féin.

The President, W.T. Cosgrave, visited County Limerick and addressed many meetings. In Newcastle West, scene of some of the toughest fighting in the Civil War, he surprised many when he said that he looked forward to the day 'when our opponents will realise their responsibilities and come into the parliament of the nation and accept their responsibilities there.'[9]

The anti-Treaty side realised that they could win the by-election. Sinn Féin workers from Killarney to Ennis invaded Limerick to whip up every possible vote for Tadhg Crowley. Their hopes were dashed when the Cumann na nGaedheal candidate, Richard O'Connell, was elected with an overall majority of 4505 votes. In this two-party by-election contest, the Dublin trend had continued with the gap narrowing between the Cumann na nGaedheal and the anti-Treaty vote.

In a statement on the election result P.J. Ruttledge said:

> I am satisfied with the result which I hold, taken with the recent Dublin results, reveals a magnificent national advance and proves conclusively that accession of support to the Republic is universal, steady, continuous and irresistible.[10]

Republicans displayed a spirit of euphoria after the result. At a public meeting in O'Connell Street, Dublin, Dr Kathleen Lynn claimed that the Republican vote in Limerick had risen by 80 per cent. 'Before long,' she added, 'Republicans would have the whole country.'[11]

Limerick City executive of Cumann na nGaedheal said in reply to these claims:

> There are many whose pensions and salaries were cut, workers who cannot secure employment, certain farmers who think agriculture has been neglected and many other strong Treatyites who think by giving the government a jolt they will get their particular grievances attended to.[12]

The anti-Treatyites had now fought five by-elections since the general election of August 1923 but although their vote was consistently on the increase, they had failed to win even one by-election. Was their abstentionist policy preventing them from winning seats in contests where the margin between victory and defeat was narrowing? The results of the by-elections indicated that they would win extra seats in a general election.

Seán Ó Dálaigh, Sinn Féin secretary, made an optimistic report to the *Ard-Chomhairle* in which he claimed that the organisation was continuing to expand. He said that 876 *cumainn* of Sinn Féin were fully affiliated and on their books. This showed a vast improvement for the third Sinn Féin – Republican Sinn Féin – that had started from sixteen branches. The organisation was strong in all parts of Ireland except the six counties, where only eleven branches existed. Munster had more *cumainn* than any other province – three hundred and twenty.[13]

Some of the Republican TDs were finding it hard to make ends meet as they received no remuneration because they did not take their seats in Dáil Éireann. A number of rural TDs found that they could not afford the high cost of travelling to Dublin to attend monthly meetings of *Comhairle na dTeachtaí*. Dr James Ryan TD (Wexford) proposed a motion at a meeting of *Comhairle na dTeachtaí* in May 1924 that the cabinet of the Second Dáil be asked to refund the travelling and out-of-pocket expenses of TDs going to these meetings. Dr Patrick McCarvill TD (Monaghan) seconded the proposal and it was passed unanimously.[14]

Sinn Féin got a big boost from a totally unexpected source. At the consecration of a new bishop, Dr Dignan, as Bishop of Clonfert in Loughrea, County Galway, on 1 June 1924, Sinn Féin delivered an address to him and the new bishop responded:

> I stand as I did in 1918. I believe as strongly as I did then in the right of Ireland to complete independence...But as a democrat, I feel bound to obey the rule of the majority as much as I may regret that the majority did not vote in 1923 as I did in 1918. This does not prevent you from using moral and peaceful means

to persuade the people to go back to that position. I predict that the Republican Party is certain to be returned to power in a short time.[15]

The new bishop was the first member of the Irish hierarchy to express any measure of public support for the anti-Treatyites since the signing of the Treaty in 1921. Most of the support for the government of W.T. Cosgrave was coming from the well-off sections of the community – the Church, business interests, big farmers, old Irish Parliamentary Party members, and former unionists who lived mainly in the cities of Dublin and Cork. Support for the anti-Treatyites came mainly from working-class people and small farmers.

A discussion took place in Dáil Éireann in late June 1924 about the release of prisoners. Joe McGrath, leader of the National Group, said that the most dangerous men had been released or allowed to be at large while 'politicals' of the type of Austin Stack and Éamon de Valera were detained. 'I am quite satisfied,' he said, 'that if the list of persons interned is produced to me and to other deputies in the House that we could point to seventy or eighty per cent of those who are well known to the deputies and to the people of Ireland not as criminals but as purely political class.'[16]

A Labour government under Ramsay MacDonald had replaced the Conservative government in Westminster. Some optimistic people in both Ireland and England thought that if the Free State government made a fresh demand for an Irish Republic it might be granted by the new administration. But J.H. Thomas, the new colonial secretary, made the policy of the Labour government clear in the House of Commons:

> Once and for all let it be understood that any such demand would receive from His Majesty's present advisers the same reply and none other than it would, I believe, have received from either of the two previous governments which had been in office since the Treaty was signed.[17]

Sixteen Republican TDs attended a meeting of *Comhairle na dTeachtaí* on 10 July 1924. The group was in a poor financial state. Mrs Katherine O'Callaghan, elected a TD in the Pact general election of June 1922, said that they were in debt in Limerick to the tune of £1000 – a huge sum of money in those days – as a result of the high cost of the by-election campaign the previous May. Countess Markievicz said that Limerick was simply flooded with Sinn Féiners from outside the constituency. Formerly people went down to take part in a by-election and paid all their own expenses. 'Now the people simply had not got the money,' she added. 'Many of those who came to help from outside had not got a penny,' said Mrs Katherine O'Callaghan. 'Their hotel expenses had to be paid.'[18] Louis O'Dea TD (Galway) pointed out that the motion sent to the cabinet of the Second Dáil proposing the payment of travelling expenses to rural TDs attending Comhairle na dTeachtaí monthly meetings had been turned down. The chairman, Seán T. O'Kelly, said that the Republican government would be willing to pay travelling expenses to quarterly meetings of Comhairle na dTeachtaí where necessary.[19]

It was decided at a cabinet meeting of the Free State parliament on 5 July 1924 that all the remaining non-criminal prisoners should be released in batches of twenty or so a day.[20] The government had bowed to the pressure of popular opinion to free the non-sentenced prisoners who were still in custody after the Civil War.

Éamon de Valera and Austin Stack were released unconditionally from Arbour Hill Barracks on 16 July 1924. Both were looking well. They were met by Seán T. O'Kelly and taken in a taxi to Sinn Féin Headquarters in Suffolk Street. There they met Seán MacEntee, Art O'Connor, Peter Murney, George Daly, Secretary of Sinn Féin, and Director of Elections, Éamon Donnelly. Dev and Stack chatted with their colleagues for a quarter of an hour. Éamon de Valera then went by car to his home but found on his arrival that his wife, Sinéad, and children had left the city a week earlier, unaware that his release was imminent.[21]

In the Dáil lobby, President Cosgrave said to Patrick Baxter, the Farmers' TD from County Cavan who had long championed the release of the prisoners: 'We have released your friends this evening. I signed the order for their release yesterday.'[22]

Notes

1. *Dáil Éireann Debates*, Volume 6, 19 March 1924, p. 2217.
2. The *Irish Independent*, 28 March 1924.
3. *Ibid.*, 3 April 1924.
4. *Ibid.*, 7 April 1924.
5. UCD Archives, de Valera Papers: letter from P.J. Ruttledge TD to Seán T. O'Kelly TD, 10 April 1924,
6. The *Irish Independent*, 10 May 1924.
7. NAI, Sinn Féin Standing Committee minutes, 3 March 1924.
8. The *Irish Independent*, 23 May 1924.
9. *Ibid.*, 26 May 1924.
10. *Ibid.*, 31 May 1924.
11. *Ibid.*, 2 June 1924.
12. *Ibid.*, 3 June 1924.
13. NAI, File 2B/82/116/17: Sinn Féin secretary's report and organisation report to *Ard-Chomhairle* Sinn Féin, 2 June 1924.
14. UCD Archives, de Valera Papers, File P/150/1945, Minutes of meeting of *Comhairle na dTeachtaí*, 13 May 1924.
15. The *Irish Independent*, 2 June 1924.
16. *Dáil Éireann Debates*, Volume 8, 27 June 1924, Release of Prisoners, p. 78.
17. The *Irish Independent*, 27 June 1924.
18. UCD Archives, de Valera Papers, File P/150/1945, Minutes of the meeting of *Comhairle na dTeachtaí*, 10 July 1924.
19. *Ibid.*
20. NAI, File C.2/114: Minutes of meetings of the Executive Council, 5 July 1924.
21. The *Irish Independent*, 17 July 1924.
22. *Ibid.*

5

First Post-Civil-War Win by Sinn Féin

When Éamon de Valera resumed his leadership of the Republican movement on his release from prison, Sinn Féin members believed that he would have a big influence on whether Republicans would go into or stay out of the Free State Dáil.

Among the prisoners released at this time was Gerry Boland, brother of Harry, who had been fatally wounded by Free State forces at the beginning of the Civil War. Some years later Gerry Boland said, 'The time of fighting was over and we were not that good at it. The time had come for Sinn Féin to put Cosgrave out.'[1]

Mary MacSwiney and Éamon de Valera were on friendly terms when he was released from prison. Though Dev knew that Mary MacSwiney's view was more extreme than his own in regard to abstentionism, this did not harm the good relationship between the two – at least not at this time. But Miss MacSwiney wanted her will to prevail in the anti-Treaty party.

Éamon de Valera attended a meeting of his supporters in a packed Mansion House in Dublin four days after his release. He was accompanied by a number of Republican TDs, including George Count Plunkett, Countess Markievicz, Mary MacSwiney, Seán T. O'Kelly, Austin Stack and Dan Breen. For the first time, a mixed choir sang a rousing new anti-Treaty anthem entitled 'Legion of the Rearguard', the only nationally-known ballad composed to commemorate Republican forces in the Civil War. During the course of his speech de Valera said:

> There has been a military defeat but the end has been achieved. The political victory that you have achieved is that you have

left this nation free by your protest. No power can make us take an Oath of Allegiance to a foreign power. We want to build a great nation and we want to let every shade of the political thought into it. Why do the Free State ministers accept…such a degrading Oath.[2]

Austin Stack resumed his work as secretary of Sinn Féin. Éamon de Valera came out firmly on the side of not entering the Free State Dáil. He went further and stressed that if any of the Republican TDs persisted in their intentions of doing so, they would have to sever their connection with the party.

By his presence De Valera had brought back unity of purpose among Republicans but there appeared to be no hope of the Oath being removed by the Free State government in the foreseeable future. All other paths towards Republican progress seemed blocked so de Valera now pinned his hopes on winning an electoral majority.

In August 1924, in a continuing effort to concentrate all Republican authority in one body, Dev recommended that *Comhairle na dTeachtaí* be continued and reconvened. P.J. Ruttledge, who had been Acting President of the Second Dáil while de Valera was in prison, Seán T. O'Kelly, who had chaired the meetings of *Comhairle na dTeachtaí* when Ruttledge was on the run from the Free State authorities, and Mary MacSwiney, the secretary, called a meeting of *Comhairle na dTeachtaí* for 7 August 1924, the first that Éamon de Valera had attended. For this special occasion the cabinet of the Second Dáil paid the railway expenses of all the authorised deputies in order to encourage a full attendance. Fifty-five past and present Republican TDs were present – the biggest attendance at any *Comhairle* meeting so far.[3]

Éamon de Valera took the chair. He declared:

The cabinet are of the opinion that it would be wiser to still regard the Second Dáil as the '*de jure* government and legislature', but the whole body of Republican TDs should act as the council of state (*Comhairle na dTeachtaí*) and be the actual government of the country. This government would then be ready to take full control as soon as the people turned down the present junta.[4]

The President called special attention to the position of Seán O'Mahoney, the Sinn Féin member elected for Fermanagh-Tyrone in the May 1921 general election for the parliament of Northern Ireland, and he emphasised that his presence at the meetings of *Comhairle na dTeachtaí* 'would act as the symbol of the unity of the country.'[5] De Valera claimed that the Second Dáil, that had voted in favour of the Treaty in January 1922, was not yet dissolved, nor the Third Dáil legally summoned.[6]

Countess Markievicz TD, who was constantly doubting the legality of the claim that the Second Dáil was the *de jure* government of the twenty-six counties, questioned the powers of this 'emergency government' on the ground that it was not a majority government of the people. Seán MacEntee supported her argument. After some debate the meeting agreed that power over life and death and the property of citizens should for a time be in abeyance.[7]

The Second Dáil then came formally into session and Seán T. Ó Ceallaigh TD was appointed Ceann Comhairle. Mary MacSwiney TD proposed: 'that the emergency (Second Dáil) government be continued.' Count Plunkett TD seconded the proposition and it was passed unanimously. The Republican TDs re-elected Éamon de Valera as president of the Second Dáil. De Valera then nominated the following ministers for his cabinet:

President and Minister for Foreign Affairs: Éamon de Valera
Minister for Home Affairs and Minister for Finance: Austin Stack
Minister for Economic Affairs and Local Government: Art O'Connor
Minister for Defence: Frank Aiken
Ministers without Portfolio: P.J. Ruttledge; Robert Barton

The Ceann Comhairle, Seán T. O'Kelly, asked de Valera for a clearer definition of the relationship between the Second Dáil and *Comhairle na dTeachtaí*. After some discussion and explanation President de Valera defined the position as he saw it:

> The executive formed as an emergency government in October 1922, by the faithful surviving members of the Second Dáil…is responsible to *Comhairle na dTeachtaí* that consists of…: (a) The surviving members of the Second Dáil who remained faithful to the republic; (b) Republican deputies elected in the Pact election in June 1922; (c) Republican deputies elected in the August 1923 general election; (d) Any other Republican deputies who may be hereafter elected (in by-elections or elections) during the existence of the emergency government.[8]

Before this session of the Second Dáil came to an end, all present took the Oath of Allegiance to the Irish Republic declared by Pearse and his comrades at the start of the 1916 Rising and ratified by Dáil Éireann on 21 January 1919. De Valera and other Republican TDs envisaged a day when Sinn Féin TDs, after receiving a majority in a general election, would meet outside Leinster House and use the structure of the Second Dáil to re-establish the republic.[9] Desmond Fitzgerald, a veteran of 1916 and the first Minister for External Affairs in the Cumann na nGaedheal government, also thought that, if they ever achieved a majority, the anti-Treatyites would reconstitute the Second Dáil and approach their problems with England on an entirely new basis.[10]

Mary MacSwiney continued to express extreme ideas on abstentionism. She would not recognise the Free State government under any circumstances. She explained her position at a meeting of *Comhairle na dTeachtaí*, 'We will only go into Dáil Éireann – we will go into no parliament called by them (Free Staters).'[11] For Mary MacSwiney and many other Republicans, participation in what they called 'the Free State legislature' would involve the recognition of an institution completely British in origin. Abstention was for them an absolute principle.

Éamon de Valera thought it would be a good political stroke to address a meeting in Ennis on 15 August 1924 because it was on that date and in that place one year previously that Free State forces had arrested him. He travelled to County Clare by train and got a tremendous reception all the way down.

Men and women walked and cycled long distances to Ennis on that day and the narrow streets were packed with Republicans. De Valera began his speech from a raised platform in the middle of the square by quipping, 'Well as I was saying to you when we were interrupted.' Cheers and again cheers. Later he said:

> There are basic principles on which we stand. Things may be forced on us, we may have temporarily to submit to certain things but our consent they can never have…We are never going to drink of the pool they have brought us to. Don't forget for a moment there is a vast difference between patiently submitting when you have to for a time and putting your signature to a consent or assent to these conditions.[12]

A reunion of the friends and associates of Michael Collins was held in Dáil Éireann under the auspices of Joe McGrath's National Group. Seán Milroy, one of the deputies who had resigned from Cumann na nGaedheal with Joe McGrath, said:

> Those who adhere to the traditional line of working towards the old national objective were opposed on the one hand by an element lacking in reason (Republicans) and on the other hand by an element lacking in national vision (Free Staters). We stand in opposition to the former element and in an attitude of acute criticism to the latter. The alternatives to our line of thought are in the case of Republicanism anarchy and destruction or in the second case (present Free State government) the re-establishment of the old regime.[13]

Dáil deputies were startled at the end of October when Joe McGrath, leader of the National Group, announced his resignation from Dáil Éireann.

He explained: 'we (the National Group) have come to the conclusion that there is no room in this small country for three parties all claiming to be national.'[14] Seven other members of his group followed his example the following day, when the Ceann Comhairle announced their resignations to a packed Dáil.[15] Some of them had hoped that the National Group would remain in the Dáil as a political party with stronger nationalist views than the ruling Cumann na nGaedheal Party. The Free State government viewed their resignations with alarm as each seat vacated necessitated a by-election and they wondered if these ex-National Group TDs had plans to stand in the various constituencies against candidates nominated by Cumann na nGaedheal.

There was no softening of the Free State government's stance on the Oath of Allegiance. Kevin O'Higgins addressed the Irish Society at Oxford on 31 October: 'The new tyranny had to be met and smashed and the right of the people to found a state on the basis of the Treaty had to be vindicated.'[16] The Free State government was claiming the support of the will of the people for their rigid stance on keeping the controversial Oath of Allegiance in operation.

The 1924 Sinn Féin *ard-fheis* was held on 4-5 November. Thirteen hundred delegates represented seven hundred and seven affiliated *cumainn*. Éamon de Valera was again elected president of the party.[17]

There was no discussion in public on the Oath of Allegiance or abstentionism but a motion came from the Fitzwilliam (Dublin) *cumann* of Sinn Féin 'that all candidates nominated by the Sinn Féin organisation be pledged to give allegiance to no foreign King.'[18] This proposal was considered in private and the Republican stance in regard to the Oath of Allegiance was once again ratified.

Five by-elections were due to be held on 18 November, in the constituencies of South Dublin, Cork City, East Cork, Donegal and North Mayo.[19] W.T. Cosgrave described the forthcoming by-elections as 'a mini-general election'.

Sinn Féin determined to pick the very best candidates available. The organisation gave guidelines for the qualities desirable in candidates: they should have sincerity, trustworthiness, be likely to advance the cause of Republicanism by devotion to duty and have a good national record.[20]

A circular from Sinn Féin appealed to their *cumainn* in Britain for financial aid to fight the elections, on the grounds: 'that the harvest prospects and economic conditions generally are poor in Ireland at present and so our people at home are not in a position to give as much as was always given by them in the past.'[21]

At a Cumann na nGaedheal public meeting in Dublin South, Senator McLoughlin said that 'his anti-Treaty opponents were always promising things to happen – tomorrow.'[22] In Cork, Kevin O'Higgins asked: 'How, if he abstained from the Dáil, could French, the Sinn Féin candidate and his associates, fulfil their promises about housing, pensions and the devil knows what?'[23] At a meeting in College Green, Dublin, a large crowd heard the Sinn Féin candidate, Seán Lemass, proclaim that they [Sinn Féin] were the party of the working class, and that when his party got control of the machinery of government 'they would see that it moved in the interests of the whole Irish people and not in the interests of a small and privileged class.'[24]

In Glenties, County Donegal, as J. McDevitt was addressing a Sinn Féin meeting on behalf of Thomas Daly, the Republican candidate, a motor car containing Fionán Lynch, the Free State Minister for Fisheries, drove up flying the Tricolour. 'There they come, boys,' declared McDevitt, 'carrying the flag of Pearse. These men will appeal to you to vote for a man who will take the Oath of Allegiance to King George.'[25] But Richard Mulcahy explained at a well-attended public meeting of Cumann na nGaedheal 'that when Griffith and Collins signed the Treaty and put into it the British Crown, they did it as the price of an undivided Ireland.'[26] Free State politicians believed that the Boundary Commission would resolve the partition issue, that the recognition of the Crown was necessary to entice Unionists into a united Ireland and that Northern nationalists, especially those living in areas of nationalist majority, had full confidence in the Boundary Agreement.

There was a rumour in Cork that Lord Mayor, Seán French, the Sinn Féin candidate, would break with the principle of abstentionism, if elected, and attend Dáil Éireann, but at a meeting in Dillon's Cross on the eve of the poll,

French told his audience: 'I will not attend in the Dáil, if elected…I am myself an honest man.'[27]

Polling took place in the constituencies of Dublin South, Mayo North and Cork East on 18 November. The people of Cork City went to the polls on 19 November and Donegal voted last on 20 November.

Loud cheers echoed through the streets in Dublin South on 19 November when Michael O'Mullane rushed from the count centre shortly after midday to announce that Seán Lemass had won the seat by about a thousand votes. Seán Lemass was the first Sinn Féiner to be elected in any by-election since the Treaty. The *Sinn Féin* newspaper commented: 'We frankly did not expect this tremendous victory in a former stronghold of British imperialism.'[28] Seán MacEntee, a prominent Sinn Féiner at this time, referred to the election of Seán Lemass years later: 'The victory was so utterly unexpected that it startled even extreme Republicans. It was the end of one epoch – that of physical force – and the beginning of a new, the era of parliamentary politics.'[29]

Hardly had Republican cheers died away in Dublin South than Sinn Féin flags began to wave in another constituency. Dr Madden, the Republican candidate, was declared elected in North Mayo with a majority of 870 votes. A jubilant crowd chaired him from the counting centre.

Cumann na nGaedheal candidates were successful in the constituencies of Cork East, Cork Borough and Donegal but with reduced majorities.[30] In the five contested constituencies there was still a combined majority of 22,000 in favour of Cumann na nGaedheal but the most significant factor about this 'mini-general election' was that the overall Republican vote showed an emphatic increase of 28,500 votes. The *Sinn Féin* newspaper declared:

> Four of the five contested areas were overwhelmingly Free State at the last general election…The tremendous Free State majorities have come tumbling down while the vote for Sinn Féin has almost doubled. A new era opens for Sinn Féin. But the Sinn Féin organisation needs money.[31]

Tom Maguire, sitting Sinn Féin TD for South Mayo, commented later on:

'Our hope was to achieve a majority: in other words, after another twenty seats or so we would reconvene the Second Dáil and proceed away from the Treaty position. This was agreed by de Valera and everybody else within the organisation.'[32] A Sinn Féin activist who had taken part in the Donegal by-election gave his version of the election contest:

> The Unionist Party are said to be 20,000 strong on the register and I am satisfied that they polled half their registered strength…That they voted Free State they made no secret of… The chief Republican strength was in the western mountains. With the exception of one district in the west, nearly all the Irish speakers in Tír Chonaill were Republican.[33]

The fact that the Free State government had reduced old-age pensions in September 1924 had annoyed many voters, particularly in North Mayo. Some of the increase in the Sinn Féin vote could be attributed to the desire of voters to register a protest against Cumann na nGaedheal on this issue.

Because of the loss of two seats to Sinn Féin and the defection of the National Group, Cumann na nGaedheal's strength was now reduced to fifty-three seats in Leinster House. Sinn Féin held forty-six seats, just seven seats behind the government party, and there were seven by-elections to elect nine new Dáil deputies pending in early 1925. It was not beyond the realm of possibility that in the near future Sinn Féin in abstention could have more seats than Cumann na nGaedheal in government.

Cumann na nGaedheal reacted with urgency to the results of these five by-elections. A meeting of the *Coiste Gnótha* of the party summoned all Cumann na nGaedheal deputies to take stock of the position 'and to decide on common action and on agreed lines with a view to retaining or improving their hold on public opinion.'[34] Arising from this meeting a special committee on organisation was set up to take charge of arrangements for the pending by-elections.[35] J.J. Walsh TD, Cork City, was appointed Cumann na nGaedheal general organiser for the seven by-elections, which were scheduled for March 1925.

There were sharp differences in opinion within Cumann na nGaedheal at the close of 1924. A group of deputies headed by Pádraig Ó Máille, Deputy Ceann Comhairle and C.M. Byrne, TD for Wicklow, urged a fresh effort to reunite with the resigned deputies of the National Group. Cumann na nGaedheal leaders were not in favour of this and viewed the idea as indicative of a definite move on the part of another group within the party that could cause further disunity.[36] Party leaders realised they had a stiff political battle on their hands with anti-Treaty activists. They had come to recognise that the Sinn Féiners were more skilled in political matters than the anti-Treatyites had been in military affairs.

Notes

1. Franciscan Library Killiney, de Valera Papers, File 1301, Gerry Boland to Michael McInerney, *The Irish Times*, 8 October 1968.
2. *The Irish Times*, 22 July 1924, and *Éire*, 2 August 1924.
3. UCD Archives, de Valera Papers, File P/150/1945, Minutes of the meeting of *Comhairle na dTeachtaí*, 7 August 1924.
4. *Ibid.*
5. *Ibid.*
6. *Ibid.*
7. *Ibid.*
8. *Ibid.*
9. J. *Bowyer* Bell, *The Secret Army: The IRA*, p. 49.
10. UCDA, Papers of Desmond Fitzgerald, P/80/847/32.
11. UCDA, Papers of Mary MacSwiney, P/48a/290/56.
12. *Sinn Féin*, 23 August 1924.
13. The *Irish Independent*, 25 August 1924. Those present at that meeting were Dan McCarthy TD (Dublin South); O.G. Esmonde TD (Wexford); Seán McGarry TD (Dublin North); Henry J. Finlay TD (Roscommon); Frank Cahill TD (Dublin North); Seán Gibbons TD (Carlow-Kilkenny); Alexander McCabe TD (Leitrim-Sligo) and Seán Milroy TD (Cavan).
14. The *Irish Independent*, 30 October 1924.
15. The following members of the National Group resigned from Dáil Éireann: Dan McCarthy (Dublin South); Seán Milroy (Cavan); Seán McGarry (Dublin North); Alasdair McCabe (Sligo-Leitrim); Thomas Carter (Leitrim-Sligo); Henry J. Finlay (Roscommon); Seán Gibbons (Carlow-Kilkenny).
16. The *Irish Independent*, 1 November 1924.
17. Elected vice-presidents of Sinn Féin were P.J. Ruttledge TD, Mary MacSwiney TD, Father Michael O'Flanagan and Dr Kathleen Lynn TD. Chosen as joint secretaries were Austin Stack TD and Scoirse Daly. Elected joint treasurers were Caitlín Brugha and Mollie Childers. (The *Irish Independent*, 6 November 1924).
18. UCDA, Papers of Mary MacSwiney, File P/48a/78a.
19. Dublin South became vacant on the appointment of Hugh Kennedy TD (Cumann na nGaedheal) as Chief Justice. Alfred O'Rahilly, Cumann na nGaedheal TD for Cork Borough, although sympathetic to Joe McGrath's National Group, remained independent and resigned of his own volition, claiming that Cumann na nGaedheal had no strong nationalist policy of its own. The Cork East contest followed the death of Cumann na nGaedheal deputy, Thomas O'Mahony. The vacancy in Donegal was caused by the resignation of sitting Cumann na nGaedheal TD Peter J. Ward for no clear reason. Harry Coyle, Cumann na nGaedheal deputy for Mayo North, forfeited his seat on technical grounds.
20. NAI, File 2B/82/116/7, Minutes of Standing Committee of Sinn Féin p. 185.

21. *Ibid.*, File 2B/82/116/18, 10 November 1924, p. 11.
22. *Sinn Féin*, 15 November 1924.
23. *Ibid.*
24. The *Irish Independent*, 10 November 1924.
25. *Ibid.*, 13 November 1924.
26. *Ibid.*, 10 November 1924.
27. *Ibid.*, 17 November 1924.
28. *Sinn Féin*, 22 November 1924.
29. *The Irish Times*, 'From Sinn Féin to Fianna Fáil – Seán MacEntee – 2': Franciscan Library, Killiney, de Valera Papers.
30. Michael K. *Noonan* won for Cumann na nGaedheal in Cork East with a majority of 5300 votes, Michael Egan held Cork City for Cumann na nGaedheal with a majority of 12, 300 and Denis McCullough won for Cumann na nGaedheal in Donegal with a majority of 6500 votes.
31. *Sinn Féin*, 29 November 1924.
32. Uinseann Mac Eoin, *Survivors*, p. 300.
33. *Sinn Féin*, 27 December 1924.
34. UCDA, Mulcahy Papers, File P 7b/60 (143).
35. UCDA, Mulcahy Papers, File P7b/59 (17), 28 November 1924: this special committee on organisation consisted of fourteen members including ministers and prominent Cumann na nGaedheal members. Ernest Blythe, Kevin O'Higgins, Patrick McGilligan, Fionán Lynch, Paddy Hogan, J.J. Walsh, Eoin MacNeill, Jennie Wyse Power, Michael Tierney, Richard Mulcahy, T. Montgomery, Senator McLoughlin, Michael Egan (recently elected in Cork City) and M. O'Hanlon (solicitor) were the members of the special committee.
36. The *Irish Independent*, 22 December 1924 and UCDA, Mulcahy Papers, File P 7/C/99/87, 6 December 1924.

6

HARD TIMES FOR REPUBLICANS

Thomas Johnson, the Labour Party leader, wrote an open letter to de Valera in mid-January 1925 in which he criticised the Republican policy of abstention. He told the Sinn Féin leader that his present policy of not recognising the Constitution 'would destroy all hope of social change in this generation.'[1]

On 4 February 1925 Dr Douglas Hyde, President of the Gaelic League and later President of Ireland, was co-opted to fill a vacancy in the Seanad caused by the death of Colonel Sir Hutchinson Poe. Dr Douglas Hyde 'took and subscribed to the Oath of Allegiance forthwith by coming to the table of the House.'[2]

Many of the best Sinn Féin organisers were forced to emigrate to the US, especially New York, as they could not find employment in Ireland. Some felt they could not make the declaration of allegiance to the Free State and its Constitution that was required for many government and local-authority posts. Many private employers, conservative by nature, feared Republicanism and were reluctant to give employment to applicants known to have or to have had Republican leanings. The secretaries of Sinn Féin (Stack and O'Daly) stated in *Sinn Féin*, the Republican newspaper, that 'we are hampered by the fact that our people suffer from the present economic depression to a far larger degree than our opponents.'[3] Seán Gibbons, elected as a Cumann na nGaedheal TD for Carlow-Kilkenny in the 1923 general election but who had resigned from the National Group and Dáil Éireann, asked at a meeting in Kilkenny: 'How can we expect peace while the men who risked their all and gave their all for Ireland are outlawed?'[4]

Séamus Dolan, Cumann na nGaedheal TD for Leitrim-Sligo, moved the writ for the seven by-elections to elect nine new members to Dáil Éireann on 18 February 1925. The Free State government had a distinct advantage going into the by-elections as it was in charge of the nation's purse strings and could dole out grant reliefs in the constituencies where by-elections were pending. An *Irish Independent* correspondent reported from Sligo-Leitrim, a constituency that had two Dáil seats up for grabs: 'The government has given a grant of many thousand pounds for relief of unemployment and distress in County Sligo. The money will be utilised for road repairs and drainage.'[5]

Seán Milroy, formerly of the National Group, who was among the eight deputies who had resigned from Dáil Éireann, used the occasion of a meeting in Dún Laoghaire to explain why his party had taken this action. Milroy said that he had read in a Dublin newspaper that a prominent Free State minister had stated: 'What the country wanted was one shilling off income tax, better prices for cattle and pigs and not drivel about men who fought and died.' Milroy rejected this sentiment: 'It was because we believed that that was what the government was standing for,' he continued, 'that we took the drastic action we did to raise the country to an understanding that the position gained by the Treaty was being captured by those who wanted to rehabilitate West-British ascendancy.' When asked to explain what he meant by 'West-British ascendancy', he replied: 'The men who fought the British and died did not do so in order when the battle was won that the old gang would come back to power.'[6]

Sinn Féin wanted to reaffirm that all their candidates in the coming by-elections agreed with the principle of abstentionism. At a meeting of the Standing Committee in January 1925 a resolution was passed 'that Sinn Féin candidates be pledged against Allegiance to a foreign king'.[7]

In early 1925, 'Politicus', political correspondent for the *Sunday Independent,* wrote an article in that paper in which he claimed that there was 'undoubtedly a section within the Anti-Treaty party which is opposed to the present policy of abstention and in the provincial centres there are local differences which make political progress difficult.' He added that the splits in the Treaty party had done more than anything else to preserve the appearance of unity in the anti-Treaty ranks. He concluded that in his opinion 'a very faint gesture on the part of the supporters of the Treaty would secure the attendance in Dáil Éireann of practically all the anti-Treaty TDs.'[8]

The pro-Treaty Party knew that they had a strong argument against anti-Treaty candidates in all elections because Republican candidates would not take the Oath of Allegiance or enter Dáil Éireann, if elected, to work for their constituents. Canon Butler, Administrator, Sligo, presiding at a Cumann na nGaedheal public meeting, referred to abstentionists as: 'men who called themselves Republicans, who asked the people to fight for them and yet refused to move hand or foot to improve the country.'[9] At the Roscommon County Convention of Cumann na nGaedheal in Strokestown, Kevin O'Higgins declared that 'he saw no prospects for the country in the repudiation of the Treaty except the permanent loss of six counties and the permanent and definite crippling of the twenty-six counties.' But he added that he thought it possible to build, on the basis of the Treaty, a strong worthy state that 'would in time assimilate the elements standing out in the north-east.'[10]

As the election campaign got into full swing, President W.T. Cosgrave returned from a holiday abroad that he had been advised to take: he was suffering from fatigue as a result of his arduous labours over the previous two years.

The Labour Party decided to contest the vacant Dublin seats in these by-elections and at this stage, rightly or wrongly, they reached the conclusion that Irish voters were becoming more interested in 'bread and butter' issues than national issues. Denis Cullen, the Labour candidate in North Dublin, said: 'Whether they had a Republic, a Free State, or a Dominion was all the same to the average man or woman – the breadwinner in each family had to face "bread and butter problems every day".'[11]

Professor O'Rahilly, the former Cork Cumann na nGaedheal TD, made a suggestion that the anti-Treatyites should enter the Dáil because he believed the 'Oath of Allegiance was theologically not an Oath at all'. This comment angered Éamon de Valera, who referred to it at an anti-Treaty meeting in Thomas Street, Dublin. 'If this Oath was not an Oath,' he said, 'it ought to be a very easy matter for the Free State to remove it.'[12] In his speech, de Valera explained his attitude further – not realising that this might be a problem for him a couple of years later. 'I regard as the worst form of blasphemy to take an Oath, not meaning to keep it.' He objected to the Oath from a democratic as well as from a moral point of view: 'I believe that when oaths are to be taken they should be taken to the people of the nation and not to any king.' Thirdly he objected to the Oath as an Irishman: 'because it would be doing what the nation had refused to do for 750 years – to give willing allegiance to a foreign monarch.'[13]

Moss Twomey, then Adjutant-General and later Chief-of-Staff of the IRA, drew attention to the fact that the number of Sinn Féin supporters who were emigrating was increasing all this time. He wrote: 'Republican prisoners who had been released were unable to secure work.' He reminded the people of Ireland that the families of Republican activists had suffered great poverty while their breadwinners had been on the run or in jail during the War of Independence and Civil War. According to Moss Twomey, these same families were under even greater economic and financial pressure at that time because many of their menfolk were without work. He declared that many of these Republicans, 'faced with starvation were compelled to emigrate to America and Australia'[14], and observed that this fact could detrimentally affect the Republican vote.

In fact there was a huge increase in emigration in 1925: 16,000 people emigrated to the US in 1923, a figure that increased to 17,000 in 1924 and peaked at 27,000 in 1925.[15] Mick McCarthy, a lifelong Republican activist, was interviewed by Uinseann Mac Eoin for his book, *The IRA in the Twilight Years 1923-1948*. He said, 'I am old enough to remember the hardships imposed upon the losers after the Civil War…I remember the denial of work to them that followed. They were marked men; they were avoided. So many of them – certainly many in this county – simply had to get out – to leave for America.'[16] It was a pity that so many of these young Irishmen and women, who had played prominent roles in gaining independence for most of Ireland, now had to take the emigrant ship to America and other distant lands. Many of them never returned to live in Ireland.

Other intelligent young men, who had fought with the IRA in the War of Independence but who had been on the defeated Republican side in the

Civil War, remained in Ireland – often frustrated, disillusioned, idle and with no prospects. Some suffered from shattered nerves as a result of close armed combat in the ambushes that were part of guerrilla warfare and found it hard to adapt to normal lifestyles when the conflict was over, particularly when their jobs were gone and they had no work to do. De Valera began to think seriously about the question and saw that it was his duty to do something worthwhile to rehabilitate these young Irishmen. He began to ask himself if abstentionism from Dáil Éireann was the best way to go about solving this problem.

The Free State government also realised that economic conditions were deteriorating in the twenty-six counties at this time. They feared that acute poverty in parts of Mayo and Leitrim might lead to a famine if the crops failed. Before the end of 1924 they had allocated £500,000 to be used in underprivileged areas to distribute free coal and seed potatoes to those in need. The government planned to use more money for the relief of unemployment and to supply free school meals to poor children in these areas.[17]

Séamus Burke, Minister for Local Government and Public Health, made a fact-finding visit to a very distressed district in north Mayo – the area stretching from Tallaghan Bay along the barren rock-bound coast to Drumaddacon Bay, taking in Geesala, Pullathomas, Bangor, Erris and Belmullet. He saw 'emaciated, famished, half-clad children in their rain-drenched cabins'. He was deeply moved 'by the spectacle indicating conditions of acute privation'. At a meeting held later in Geesala, he outlined the relief schemes that the government was processing.[18] These relief works were introduced during the election campaign but were withdrawn immediately after polling day.[19]

The stage was now set for the seven by-elections to elect nine new members to Dáil Éireann, to be held in the constituencies of Mayo North; Cavan; Leitrim-Sligo; Dublin North; Roscommon; Dublin South and Carlow-Kilkenny.

In Mayo North, Professor Michael Tierney of University College, Dublin, who had been pipped at the post by Dr John Madden (anti-Treaty) in the

November 1924 by-election, was again nominated to stand for Cumann na nGaedheal. Thomas Derrig, a War of Independence volunteer who had lost an eye in the Civil War while on active service with the anti-Treaty side, was the Sinn Féin nominee. In this constituency the contestants spared no punches. Addressing a big meeting at Swinford, Professor Tierney declared that 'de Valera said they (the anti-Treatyites) were too proud to take the Oath,' but, continued Tierney, 'they had not been too proud to take the money out of the banks and to use it to their own advantage.'[20] Thomas Derrig, the anti-Treaty candidate, declared in Kilkelly, County Mayo, that 'the people of Mayo would never sell their independence for coal or seed potatoes.'[21] Professor Michael Tierney converted a defeat of 870 votes in the previous by-election into a majority of 4927 when he won the vacant seat, defeating the anti-Treaty candidate, Thomas Derrig.

In Cavan there was a three-cornered fight for the vacant seat. Dr J.J. O'Reilly was a popular Cumann na nGaedheal candidate, J.F. O'Hanlon was nominated by the Farmers' Party and Philip Baxter was the anti-Treaty nominee. Patrick McKenna, Farmers' TD for Longford, who spoke in favour of his party's candidate, said jocosely that if they elected the Republican, Philip Baxter, in that constituency, 'he would sit at home in Ballinagh and talk of Brian Boru and Myles the Slasher but what was wanted were men who would slash out in the Dáil for the interests of the people.'[22] In Cootehill Ernest Blythe, Free State Minister for Finance, surprised some people when he stated: 'We have no desire to change the present Free State into a Republic. Our political object is the unity of Ireland.'[23] In this by-election Dr O'Reilly (Cumann na nGaedheal) headed the poll and was elected after the second count. Surprisingly J.F. O'Hanlon of the Farmers' Party was close behind him and Philip Baxter (anti-Treaty) came in third with 9774 votes, just five hundred votes behind O'Hanlon.

Four candidates contested two vacant seats in Sligo-Leitrim: Martin Roddy (Cumann na nGaedheal), Andrew Mooney (Cumann na nGaedheal), Frank Beirne, farmer (anti-Treaty), and Samuel Holt, former local authority clerk (anti-Treaty). Shortly before this, Holt had been removed from his job by 'sealed order' of the (Free State) Local Government Board because of his

Republican sympathies. This election contest was also bitter and contentious. At a Cumann na nGaedheal meeting in Ballymote, County Sligo, Very Reverend Canon Quinn PP, who presided, declared: 'From what we have experienced in the past from our opponents, it would be well if they put another supplication in the Litany, "From the Republic, O Lord, deliver us."'[24] Samuel Holt, the stronger of the two anti-Treaty candidates, won one of the two vacant seats. Martin Roddy (Cumann na nGaedheal) won the other seat.

In Dublin North, there were five nominees for two vacant Dáil seats. Cumann na nGaedheal hoped to win the two seats and nominated Donald O'Connor and Patrick Leonard. The Labour Party chose Denis Cullen as its candidate. Oscar Traynor, a 1916 veteran from Fairview, was nominated by the anti-Treaty party. De Valera said about him, 'In the days when they were fighting the British, Oscar Traynor held the flag of the Republic as Commanding Officer of the Dublin Brigade.'[25] Seán Milroy (formerly National Group) caused a surprise when he stood as an Independent Nationalist after his own party decided not to field any candidates to defend the seats they had resigned. Oscar Traynor polled well and won one of the Dublin North two vacant seats. Patrick Leonard of Cumann na nGaedheal captured the other seat. Denis Cullen, the Labour candidate, got the third-highest number of first preferences but was far below the quota when he was eliminated. Seán Milroy, then an Independent Nationalist, polled a small number of first-preference votes and was eliminated early in the count.

In County Roscommon there was a straight fight between Martin Conlon, Cumann na nGaedheal, a rate collector with Dublin Corporation but a native of the county, and J.J. O'Kelly (anti-Treaty) – otherwise known as 'Sceilg' – an Irish-language enthusiast and writer. Sinn Féin recalled Father Michael O'Flanagan from the USA to help the Republicans fight the by-elections as he was one of their finest orators and he played a prominent part in the Roscommon by-election campaign in support of 'Sceilg'. He was unpopular with the local clergy, a large majority of whom backed Cumann na nGaedheal. During his speeches Father O'Flanagan was cheered at times but at other times severely heckled. 'I was accused of being everything from Luther to Antichrist,' he claimed.[26] In St Mary's Hall, Ballaghaderreen, County

Roscommon, General Richard Mulcahy, speaking on behalf of Cumann na nGaedheal, said he would like to tell Father Michael O'Flanagan and de Valera, 'that the problem of 1925 was very different from that of 1919. The problem of 1925 was an economic one – that of feeding the hungry, increasing our trade, reducing taxation, and laying the foundation to solve the housing problem.'[27]

Father O'Flanagan harked back too often to the Civil War and bitterly criticised Michael Collins and Arthur Griffith for signing the Treaty: even some of his own supporters thought he should not be so critical of these dead patriots. The election in Roscommon finished in a very bitter and insulting exchange of views between Martin Conlon and J.J. O'Kelly, the anti-Treaty candidate. Conlon had a majority of 7708 votes over O'Kelly, who declared after the result was announced that he would not let the election close without replying to the slanders levelled at him and his family by priests in the constituency. 'I didn't come to Roscommon to be catechised by Father Brennan,' O'Kelly said. Father Brennan interjected, 'You got your answer now.' Minutes later Martin Conlon, the successful Cumann an nGaedheal candidate, addressed a large crowd of supporters on the steps of the courthouse. Referring to Father O'Flanagan, he said, 'His speeches have brought the blush of shame to the face of every decent Irish Catholic. The names of Michael Collins and Arthur Griffith were endeared in the hearts of every true Irishman, yet this man does not hesitate to outrage the feelings of the people.'[28]

There was one vacant seat in Dublin South. Dr Thomas Hennessy was considered to be a strong Cumann na nGaedheal contender. The anti-Treaty candidate was Professor Michael O'Mullane, who had stood unsuccessfully in the constituency before Seán Lemass captured a seat for the anti-Treatyites in the November 1924 by-election. Alderman Thomas Lawlor, standing for Labour, had only an outside chance of election. Dr Hennessy won the seat. Michael O'Mullane's anti-Treaty vote showed a decrease of 3397 on Lemass's vote of the previous November while the Cumann na nGaedheal vote showed an increase of 6000. Alderman Lawlor polled badly for Labour. O'Mullane caused dismay in his own party when, after the election, he commented on speeches made in Roscommon by Father Michael O'Flanagan in support of 'Sceilg', the anti-Treaty candidate: 'I did not agree with the statement made about the leaders of the Free State party, neither did I agree with the platform of a party being used for an attack on the bishops and clergy.'[29] O'Mullane claimed that his vote in South Dublin had suffered as a result.[30]

In Carlow-Kilkenny there were only two candidates for one vacant seat. Thomas Bolger, a member of Carlow County Council, was selected by Cumann na nGaedheal. Kevin O'Higgins, campaigning for Bolger, referred to the refusal of the anti-Treaty party to take the Oath of Allegiance: 'Idealism is the salt of the earth but you cannot live on it – a certain amount of bread and butter and meat go well with it.' Michael Barry, from Rathvilly, County Carlow, was the anti-Treaty candidate. He was a brother of Kevin Barry who had been executed by the British during the War of Independence, and he had stood unsuccessfully as a Republican candidate in this constituency in the 1923 general election. At a well-attended anti-Treaty meeting in Kilkenny, Éamon de Valera emphasised that the anti-Treaty party declined to declare allegiance to the 'Constitution of the Irish Free State as by law established' because it was a Constitution:

> dictated by England and forced upon Ireland – a Constitution which recognises the British king as king in Ireland and which subordinates the representative institutions of the Irish people to British government control…The king of England has no right to faithfulness or allegiance from the Irish people.[31]

The Cumann na nGaedheal candidate, Thomas Bolger, defeated the anti-Treaty Michael Barry by 7312 votes. This was not surprising as this constituency had given poor support to abstentionist Republican candidates since the Treaty. However Carlow-Kilkenny Republicans were satisfied with the performance of Michael Barry, who polled almost 17,000 votes, an increase of 7000 on the 1923 general election. After the result, Mr O'Duffy, the anti-Treaty director of elections in Carlow-Kilkenny, said, 'We were up against great forces which I might style the three Ps – the press, pulpit and police.'[32]

In the 1925 by-elections, Cumann na nGaedheal won seven seats and Sinn Féin had two new TDs – Traynor in North Dublin and Holt in Sligo-Leitrim. According to the *Irish Independent*: 'the Cumann na nGaedheal party has not only maintained its position but has recovered the ground it lost in the last by-elections.' Referring to the electoral performance of Seán Milroy in North Dublin the same newspaper declared: 'The insignificant poll recorded for Milroy is clear proof that the people are not prepared to countenance revolts in the government ranks.'[33]

The Free State government celebrated its sweeping electoral victory with a big demonstration in College Green, Dublin. President W.T. Cosgrave said: 'I say we will have peace in spite of them [anti-Treatyites].'[34]

Although obviously disappointed, de Valera put the best face he could on the results: 'Some Republicans have been unreasonably optimistic…We have not secured a majority vote yet, but with steadfast perseverance and devotedness on our side, it will come.'[35]

When the Republican Party, the name under which all anti-Treaty candidates appeared on the ballot paper prior to 1927, completed its analysis of the final results, President de Valera issued a second statement claiming that the Republican vote had increased by 28,316 in the seven areas contested. The Republican percentage of the total poll had increased from 26.7 per cent in the 1923 general election to 36.3 per cent in these by-elections.[36]

In a letter to the *Irish Independent* Seán Lemass, TD for Dublin South, made it clear that he endorsed everything that Father O'Flanagan had said during the Roscommon by-election campaign 'about the use of altars of the Catholic Church as political rostrums'. Lemass declared: 'I believe, I can, in this matter, speak for the vast majority of the Irish Republicans. The question of the political influence of the Catholic clergy has to be faced sooner or later.'[37] He continued: 'Dublin people, I believe, can have no conception of the manner in which God's altar was degraded in certain western constituencies in order to secure victory for the Free State party.' He further claimed: 'If we succeed in destroying the Catholic Church influence, we will have done good work for Ireland and I believe for the Catholic religion in Ireland.'[38] In a report to Cumann na nGaedheal minister Desmond Fitzgerald at this time, Colonel

Michael J. Costello, Director of Intelligence, wrote: 'Seán Lemass's letter about the Catholic Church may be taken as the opinion of the Irregular cabinet.'[39] At the Sinn Féin Standing Committee meeting on 4 May 1925, Michael O'Mullane, the anti-Treaty candidate in Dublin South, was expelled from Sinn Féin because of his outspoken negative comments about Father Michael O'Flanagan.[40]

In a final comment on the results of the by-elections President W.T. Cosgrave said: 'The results showed that the people are solid behind the Treaty, and are standing firmly for the programme and policy that we advocate.'[41] He summed up: 'The by-elections had been a complete test and there is no necessity for a general election.'[42]

Prominent leaders of the anti-Treaty party, including Éamon de Valera, recognised that its abstentionist policy made it difficult for Republicans to make any significant progress at the polls.

Notes

1. NLI, Johnson Papers, Ms 17, 230, Open letter to de Valera from Thomas Johnson, 15 January 1925.
2. *Seanad Éireann Debates*, Volume 4, 4 February 1925, Election of Senator.
3. *Sinn Féin*, 7 February 1925.
4. The *Kilkenny People*, 17 January 1925.
5. The *Irish Independent*, 6 January 1925.
6. *Ibid.*, 12 January, 1925.
7. NAI, File 2B/82/117/23: Minutes of Standing Committee of Sinn Féin, 15 January 1925.
8. The *Sunday Independent*, 18 January 1925.
9. The *Irish Independent*, 19 January 1925.
10. *Ibid.*
11. *Ibid.*
12. *Ibid.*, 29 January 1925.
13. *Ibid.*, and *Sinn Féin*, 7 February 1925.
14. UCDA, Moss Twomey Papers, P69/62 (10), 'General Outline of the Present Movement'.
15. Figures supplied by the late Tom Halpin, Kilkenny. Source of Data: Historical Statistics of the USA, US Bureau of Census, Washington DC.
16. Uinseann Mac Eoin, *The IRA in the Twilight Years*, p. 653.
17. The *Irish Independent*, 9 February 1925.
18. *Ibid.*
19. John M. Regan, *The Irish Counter-Revolution*, p. 242.
20. The *Irish Independent*, 2 February 1925.
21. *Ibid.*, 9 February 1925.
22. *Ibid.*, 6 February 1925.
23. *Ibid.*, 2 February 1925.
24. *Ibid.*, 9 March 1925.
25. *Sinn Féin*, 10 January 1925.
26. Denis Carroll, *They Have Fooled You Again: Michael O'Flanagan (1876-1942)*, p. 150.
27. The *Irish Independent*, 9 February 1925.
28. *Ibid.*, 14 March 1925.
29. *Ibid.*, 13 March 1925.

30. Carroll, *op. cit.*, p. 151.
31. *Sinn Féin*, 14 February 1925.
32. The *Irish Independent*, 13 March 1925.
33. *Ibid.*
34. *Ibid.*, 14 March 1925.
35. *Ibid.*, 14 March, 1925 and *Sinn Féin*, 21 March 1925.
36. *Ibid.*, 16 March 1925.
37. *Ibid.*, 14 March 1925.
38. *Ibid.*, 14 March 1925.
39. UCDA, Papers of Desmond Fitzgerald, P80/847 (80), 29 March 1925.
40. NAI, File 2B/82/117: Minutes of Sinn Féin Standing Committee, 4 May 1925.
41. The *Irish Independent*, 16 March 1925.

7

THE TURNING POINT

There were continuing sharp differences in point of view within Cumann na nGaedheal. A group of deputies headed by Pádraig Ó Máille, TD for Galway and Deputy Ceann Comhairle, and C.M. Byrne TD, Wicklow, was urging a fresh effort at reunion with the resigned deputies of the National Group. But Cumann na nGaedheal leaders were not in favour of this and viewed the idea as indicative of a definite move on the part of another faction within the party.[1] Early in 1925 Pádraig Ó Máille and Christopher Byrne were expelled from Cumann na nGaedheal.[2]

In April 1925 Ó Máille presided at a private conference in Mills Hall, Dublin, at which a new national political party was established, although not named. The gathering brought together representatives from all over the twenty-six counties, including prominent ex-Free-State officers who had resigned from the National Army at the time of the Army Mutiny and several ex-Cumann na nGaedheal TDs who had resigned from the party at the same time. This new party aimed to work by constitutional means, through the machinery of the Treaty, to establish beyond question the independence of Ireland, the complete supremacy of the nation in its economic life and the early restoration of Ireland's territorial unity. In his address Ó Máille said: 'They believed that the anti-Treaty Party would best serve Ireland if they took their seats in Dáil Éireann.'[3]

It seemed possible that Republicans could be permanently locked out of national politics when the North Dublin constituency committee of Cumann na nGaedheal proposed a motion at the party's national convention:

> That we urge the government to introduce legislation whereby
> a duly elected candidate, who fails to take his or her seat in An
> Dáil within three months from the date of election, shall be
> declared disqualified and the seat allocated to the unsuccessful
> candidate who, at the same election, obtained the next highest
> number of votes.[4]

But for the fact that President W.T. Cosgrave put up a spirited opposition
to this motion, it might well have been passed by the convention. Cosgrave
argued that 'political fever had been running at a higher temperature in the
country than was likely for another generation or two…and it was more
than possible that within the next two years, by the time that the next general
election was due, very few people in this country would stand for non-
representation in the national assembly.'[5] President Cosgrave's intervention
was timely in resisting the attempts of some of the most vehement enemies of
Republicanism in his party to prevent the future election of any anti-Treatyites.

From the time that the results of the seven by-elections of March 1925
were announced, the whole future policy of the Republican organisation was
discussed at length behind closed doors. Although de Valera did not reveal
his true feelings to his colleagues or to the Irish public he was shattered that
Republicans had won only two of the nine contested seats. He was aware that
some Republican TDs were prepared to take the Oath of Allegiance and enter
the Free State Dáil. As a result his mind began to focus on whether continued
Republican abstentionism was practicable.

However, he and forty-four of his TDs issued a statement: 'We, the
undersigned, do not recognise the legitimacy of either the "Free State" or
"Northern" parliaments.' The anti-Treaty TDs also denied 'that we or any of
us or at any time contemplated entering the Free State parliament and taking
the Oath of Allegiance to the British king.'[6] This denial was a stratagem to
keep extreme Republicans from becoming apprehensive about future policy
until the anti-abstentionist lobby at the top got the opportunity to formulate
a pragmatic new policy that could put an end to all-out, rigid abstentionism.

The signatures of three elected Republican deputies were missing from this statement, which denied that Republicans were in any way interested in entering either the Free State or the Northern Ireland parliament: those of Seán T. Ó Ceallaigh, Ernie O'Malley and Mary MacSwiney, who were all out of the country at the time. Mary MacSwiney, one of the staunchest supporters of abstentionism, was domiciled in the US on Republican business. However Joe Begley, who was working in the New York offices of the Republican paper, *An Phoblacht*, wrote to her informing her of the changing atmosphere in Ireland:

> Have a letter from mother in which she says that everybody is demanding to know why don't we devise some means of entering the Dáil and putting out the other fellows...When arguing for abstention in the case of Westminster parliament, you could always say that our handful of Irish members could do nothing effective except in the very odd occasion of securing the balance of power. In the present case, that is no longer effective. People say, 'You have forty-eight members – almost as many as the government party – Labour and some Farmers and Independents will vote for you – why the hell don't you go in and beat them and then start something – abolish the Oath, set up the Republic and so on.' I am only speaking the voice of the ordinary man – that much maligned 'man in the street'.[7]

Mary MacSwiney had no intention of wavering. In a curt answer to Begley a month later she wrote: 'The trouble is that we can give no answer except the one – we cannot take the Oath. It is quite clear that a big effort is being made to split our ranks on that very issue.'[8]

A correspondent using the pen-name 'Randall' wrote a letter entitled 'Why not enter the Free State' to the editor of *Sinn Féin*:

> Several well-meaning people who are not Republicans have said to me, 'Why not enter the Free State parliament?' I replied that every member of the Free State parliament must take an Oath of

Allegiance. The member swears solemnly: (a) To be faithful and give allegiance to the Free State Constitution, twelve clauses of which emphasise the over-lordship of the British king in Ireland; (b) to be faithful to the British king, his heirs and successors, in virtue of the common citizenship of Ireland with Great Britain.

The case of the Free State apologists is that Ireland is as free as France or Germany but no member of the French Chamber of Deputies or the German *Reichstag* is asked to take this Oath... If Ireland is as free as they say, they can prove it by removing the Oath.[9]

An editorial in *Sinn Féin* on the same day commented: 'The Belfast parliament imposes an Oath upon its public servants; then the Free State imitates it. In the end the whole population will be forced to take oaths to the king and his parliaments or become outlaws.'[10] The editorial affirmed: 'the very bedrock of Republicanism is the refusal to give allegiance to a foreign king.'[11]

However, the discussion of Republican abstentionism continued among anti-Treatyites. The second official debate occurred at the Sinn Féin Standing Committee meeting on 7 May 1925. This time a motion was proposed by stalwart Republican, Art Ó Conchubhair (Art O'Connor) and seconded by Gearóid Ó Beoláin Gerry Boland) that 'the President may act on the assumption that the question of Republicans entering the Free State "parliament", if the Oath were removed, is an open question, to be decided on its merits when the question arises on a practical issue.'[12] Mary MacSwiney was absent from this meeting as she was still in the USA, as was Father Michael O'Flanagan, who would, in all probability, have opposed the motion. Around this time Bishop Bernard Coyne of Elphin had suspended him from his priestly ministry because of the pronouncements he had made against the Catholic Church during the Roscommon by-election of March 1925.[13] The motion passed, signalling for a first time a definite review of the Sinn Féin policy of abstentionism.

Seán Lemass became more prominent in Sinn Féin as chairman of the reorganisation committee of the party for Dublin city and county. He gradually became known for his flexible and pragmatic political outlook and it became clear that he had shifted from his former militant stance. He was convinced that the party was likely to decline in terms of finances, total membership and vote-catching power if it persisted with its abstentionist policy.[14] In the course of a report about his work reorganising Sinn Féin in Dublin city and county he declared that Sinn Féin should be: 'doing ourselves what should be done and not merely criticising others for their neglect.'[15]

During a meeting of the finance committee of the Dáil on 28 May 1925, the estimates for public services were discussed. The Minister for Finance, Ernest Blythe, moved that a sum of £76,700 be granted to complete the amount necessary to defray the salaries and expenses of Oireachtas members (TDs and Senators) during the year ending 31 March 1926. Blythe explained that for the coming year the government had thought it right to provide for the full complement of deputies although he did not think it likely that all the members who had been elected would take their seats. Republican deputies would not receive the salaries or expenses payable to TDs unless they entered the Dáil and participated in the workings of the national assembly.

'Does the minister want them?' Conor Hogan, the Farmers' Party TD for County Clare, asked.

'We thought we ought not to neglect to make provision for their doing what they ought to do,' Blythe replied.

D.J. Gorey, Farmers' Party TD for Carlow-Kilkenny, took up the matter as soon as he was allowed to enter the debate:

> What [sic] is a member of this House? First they have to be elected, then they have to come here and subscribe to the Constitution and sign the roll. There is a good deal of doubt as to the position of those who have not come into the Dáil. It is questionable whether some of the seats have not been automatically vacated.

The President, W.T. Cosgrave, replied to D.J. Gorey in a very fair and balanced manner:

> No act has been passed declaring that a deputy must comply with the terms of the Constitution within a given period. It would be open to anyone on the last or any of the final days of the sitting of the Dáil to enter the House and become a member....My personal view is that it is better to let those matters rest.[16]

W.T. Cosgrave was keeping the door of the Dáil open for Republican TDs and, in insisting on this, he was treating the viewpoint of Republicans with respect. But he insisted that Sinn Féin TDs take the Oath of Allegiance before participating in the workings of Dáil Éireann, which Republican TDs stoutly continued to refuse.

A fresh opinion on the question of the abstentionism appeared in the persons of three Irish ecclesiastics. First there was Monsignor John Hagan, Rector of the Irish College in Rome, who had supported de Valera throughout the War of Independence and Civil War. Secondly, there was Archbishop Daniel Mannix, based in Melbourne, who had stood by Éamon de Valera both in dark and pleasant days. Finally there was Father Peter Magennis, who had been appointed Superior-General of the Carmelites and had taken up residence in Rome in 1919.[17] Before he was elevated to his order's highest office he had spent some time ministering in New York and had befriended Éamon de Valera and Harry Boland when they arrived in the US in 1919 to promote Ireland's claim to independence.

Monsignor Hagan believed that the policy of abstentionism was going nowhere. He drew up a paper for de Valera, in which he suggested that Republicans would have to change their policies if they hoped to take over the reins of government from Cumann na nGaedheal. Monsignor Hagan declared that, to start this process, 'Republicans must first take an Oath of Allegiance to the English crown.'[18] In May 1925 Monsignor Hagan became aware that Archbishop Mannix was to travel to Rome as leader of an Australian pilgrimage. He went out of his way to meet Mannix in Rome to discuss with him what they could do to influence de Valera to enter Dáil Éireann. Hagan got the impression that Mannix would be willing to approach de Valera on the subject provided that he was not the cause of a split in the Republican movement in Ireland. After this meeting with Mannix, Hagan relayed to de Valera the paper he had prepared proposing a new Republican policy that included taking the hated Oath. He also sent to de Valera a theological justification for entering the Dáil without losing too much face.[19] Monsignor Hagan then got in touch with the Carmelite Father Peter Magennis to enlist his support. Father Magennis stated that while he would not pressurise de Valera to swallow the Oath of Allegiance, he would not oppose the move, provided it was an unanimous decision of Republicans.[20]

As a result of this correspondence Éamon de Valera, accompanied by Seán MacBride, made a secret visit to Rome in early June 1925 to confer with Dr Mannix, Monsignor Hagan and Father Magennis on whether or not Republicans should recognise the Free State Parliament and enter the Dáil. De Valera had private meetings with the three churchmen in the Irish College. Seán MacBride attended most of the discussions and later described the consultations:

> It was very hush hush. He (de Valera) had a great many talks with Mannix; very long sessions. They went on for three or four days. Mannix, I knew, was pressing him to recognise the Free State Dáil. I felt this was a turning point.[21]

The politicians and the clerics discussed the creation of a policy for entering the Dáil and solving the vexed question of the Oath of Allegiance but took no formal decision to go ahead with any proposal. Seán MacBride said later: 'Father Peter Magennis was not so enthusiastic and was somewhat apprehensive and so was I.'[22] Tom Maguire, at this time anti-Treaty Sinn Féin TD for Mayo South, said of de Valera's meeting with Dr Mannix: 'de Valera never reported on this meeting to the Sinn Féin *Ard-Chomhairle* or to the second Dáil.'[23] MacBride and de Valera returned to Ireland on 9 June. The three churchmen and de Valera followed up on these talks in the months that followed.

Éamon Donnelly, MP for Armagh and Director of Organisation for Sinn Féin, signalled in a letter to Annie MacSwiney, sister of Mary MacSwiney, a subject of possible dissension within Republican ranks. He asked: 'Is it true… that efforts are being made to form some kind of new party whose object is the promulgation of some policy other than that of HQ?'[24]

Éamon Donnelly, although somewhat wide of the mark, was right that there was an atmosphere of change in the Republican movement. *Comhairle na dTeachtaí* held a meeting on 22 June 1925 that thirty-three anti-Treaty TDs attended and of which J.J. O'Kelly acted as chairman. The meeting developed into a debate on whether Sinn Féin deputies should enter Dáil Éireann or not if the Oath of Allegiance were not a precondition. Kathleen Clarke saw no reason for not going in any more than for not acting on county councils but Dublin-based Professor William Stockley said that he was against going in. Séamus Fitzgerald (Cork East) thought that the Free State government would insist on some kind of Oath or faithfulness to the Constitution that would debar Republicans from taking their seats. Both Seán Buckley TD (Cork West) and Art O'Connor (Kildare) spoke against going in.

Seán Lemass TD (Dublin South) expressed some reservations about the policy of abstention. He mentioned some alternative policies and said he believed that 'as a minority we could go in there, attack the legality of the parliament but recognise only that it is the parliamentary machinery of the government of the country.'[25] But he also remarked: 'I am not certain that this would be the best policy.'[26]

After Seán O'Mahoney (Fermanagh and Tyrone) had cautioned that the discussion was too serious to be brought to a conclusion by the small number of deputies present, Frank Aiken TD (Louth) proposed that the matter be adjourned to a weekend meeting that would be easier for more of the rural deputies to attend. The meeting agreed to this proposal. It is noteworthy that the most confirmed abstentionist of them all, Mary MacSwiney TD (Cork Borough) did not get the chance to contribute to the debate because she was still abroad in the USA on Second Dáil business.

When this adjourned meeting of *Comhairle na dTeachtaí* was reconvened on 28 June 1925, Éamon de Valera raised the matter of abstentionism. Mary MacSwiney TD was still absent in the USA. De Valera said that a few days beforehand Count Plunkett had written to him expressing his opposition to entering the Dáil.[27] Dev then attempted to summarise the feelings of *Comhairle na dTeachtaí* members about entering the Dáil:

> The most important business of *Comhairle* meetings is to discuss and advise on general policy. Everyone realises that the Republican movement has not the 'drive' in it that there should be for success and every member doubtless has his views as to the cause of the apathy...Some time ago there were rumours that certain Republicans regarded the present position as hopeless. They advocated as a way out entry into the Free State parliament, Oath and all. It was hinted that there were some Republican *teachtaí* [TDs] who were ready to take that course. A document signed by every *teachta* [TD] denying such an intention has been published. I take it that the signed declaration equally precludes any verbal declaration or any formal acceptance of the Treaty or the Free State parliament.[28]

De Valera raised the hypothetical question of what Republicans should do if the Oath of Allegiance were abolished by the British and Irish authorities; he suggested that in this case a brand-new scenario would exist:

> Suppose there was no Oath or declaration or formal acceptance of the Treaty policy or its consequences demanded from Republican representatives. Would they still be debarred by Republican principles from entry?...The present position, when an Oath of Allegiance to King George has to be taken; when Republican representatives are obliged to make formal acceptance of the so-called Treaty and the Constitution it imposes, that is, when Republicans are obliged to renounce their own policy and accept that of their political opponents – this is a

different position altogether.[29]

Finally he asked the members of *Comhairle na dTeachtaí* to express their own opinions as to what they thought the proper course of action should be:

> Is it a matter of principle or is it not?…That is a question for the *Comhairle* itself to decide. The *Comhairle* must say whether it is an open question for Republicans or not. The President's own judgement is that it is an open question, one that may and should be discussed if the members of *An Chomhairle* are to act up to their responsibilities and not exclude any means that is not dishonourable – which may lead to securing the ultimate objective – the independence of the country and its recognition as a sovereign republic.[30]

Seán MacEntee asked Éamon de Valera what power *Comhairle na dTeachtaí* had to decide on such matters and de Valera said that *Comhairle na dTeachtaí* had been given 'certain powers by the Second Dáil as it was constituted as a body to which the cabinet (of the Second Dáil) would report.'[31] De Valera elaborated on his views by referring to the possible outlook of a new generation:

> I could see a new generation, if we do not do it, regarding this as an open question and rousing and organising the Irish people against the Free State Oath and smashing it, and with the Oath the whole Treaty position, at once, bit by bit. I hold that we have no right to put up any barriers against taking such a course either for ourselves or others.[32]

De Valera concluded with the warning that in any decision reached, 'it will be understood that there is no question of considering that the present *teachtaí* can enter Dáil Éireann in any circumstances, unless they are released from their present obligations at a general election.'[33] He was reminding his deputies that they had been elected as abstentionist TDs. In his opinion Republican TDs would have to be returned by the electorate on a non-abstentionist ticket before they could contemplate entering the Dáil.

Notes

1. The *Irish Independent*, 22 December 1924 and UCDA, Mulcahy Papers, File P 7/C/99/87, 6 December 1924.
2. John M. Regan, *The Irish Counter-Revolution*, p. 251.
3. The *Irish Independent*, 16 April 1925.
4. UCDA, Papers of Ernest Blythe, Cumann na nGaedheal Convention, mid-May 1925: motion to disqualify elected Dáil candidates if they failed to take their seats.
5. The *Irish Independent*, 15 May 1925.
6. *Sinn Féin*, 25 April 1925, p. 5.
7. UCDA, Papers of Mary MacSwiney, File P48a/120/(18)/3: Joe Begley to M. MacSwiney, 23 April 1925.
8. *Ibid.*, File P48a/120 (22): Máire Nic Shuibhne to Joe Begley from Chicago, 25 May 1925.
9. *Sinn Féin*, 4 April 1925, 'Why not enter the Free State parliament?'
10. *Ibid.*, editorial.
11. *Ibid.*
12. NAI, File 2B/82/117/24, 7 May 1925: minutes of Standing Committee of Sinn Féin.
13. Denis Carroll, *They Have Fooled You Again: Michael O'Flanagan (1876-1942)*, p. 158.
14. Brian Farrell, *Seán Lemass*, pp. 12-13: J. Bowyer Bell, *The Secret Army: The IRA*, pp. 50, 51, 52 and Peter Pyne, 'The Third Sinn Féin Party, 1923-26', p. 40.
15. Farrell, *op cit.*, p. 13.
16. *Dáil Éireann Debates*, Volume 11, 28 May 1925, pp. 2455, 2457.
17. Dermot Keogh, *The Vatican, The Bishops and Irish Politics, 1919-39*, p. 19.
18. Patrick Murray, *Oracles of God*, p. 208.
19. Keogh, *op cit.* p. 131.
20. *Ibid.*
21. Uinseann Mac Eoin, *Survivors*, p. 121.
22. Review by Seán MacBride of *The Vatican, The Bishops and Irish Politics, 1919-39*, *Irish Press*, 12 April 1986.
23. Mac Eoin, *op cit.*, p. 298.
24. UCDA, Papers of Mary MacSwiney, File P48a/41 (2): Éamon Donnelly, D/Organisation, Sinn Féin to Miss A. MacSwiney, 16 June 1925.
25. UCD Archives, de Valera Papers, File P150/1945: Minutes of the meeting of *Comhairle na dTeachtaí*, 22 June 1925.
26. *Ibid.*
27. Thomas P. O'Neill, 'In Search of a Political Path: Irish Republicanism, 1922 to 1927', and UCD Archives, de Valera Papers, Count Plunkett to É. de Valera, 25 June 1925.
28. UCD Archives, de Valera Papers, File P150/1945: Minutes of the meeting of *Comhairle na dTeachtaí*, 28 June 1925.
29. *Ibid.*
30. *Ibid.*
31. *Ibid.*
32. *Ibid.*
33. *Ibid.*

8

A Second Path

Late in June 1925, to the surprise of many, Archbishop Mannix arrived in Ireland with a group of Australian pilgrims.[1] De Valera and Count Plunkett met him at Dún Laoghaire.[2] This was the sequel to de Valera's visit to Rome where he had consulted with Archbishop Mannix, Monsignor Hagan and Father Magennis on the whole vexed question of the Oath of Allegiance. De Valera had arranged a provisional schedule for the archbishop's visit that included public appearances in some of Ireland's biggest cities.[3]

Members of the Free State government soon noted his presence in Ireland. At a Cumann na nGaedheal meeting in Mullingar, where large crowds gathered to welcome President W.T. Cosgrave, Senator McLoughlin, still one of Cumann na nGaedheal's most vehement opponents of Sinn Féin, launched into an outright attack on Éamon de Valera and referred to the visit of Dr Mannix. He claimed that de Valera was using the visit to solve his own political problem of entering the Dáil. 'Notwithstanding official denials from the Republican headquarters,' Senator McLoughlin declared, 'one of their prominent leaders was going around plucking the soutanes of high ecclesiastics to enlist their help to make the fall easy.'[4] 'But,' he warned, 'if they [Republicans] want to enter the Dáil, there will be no special terms for them. They will have to comply with the same formalities and take the same Oath that better Republicans and better Irishmen than they took.'[5]

In a jubilant tour of Ireland Archbishop Mannix received numerous enthusiastic receptions in villages and towns.[6] The freedom of many cities was conferred on him by the new municipal corporations that now had Republican representatives among their members – representatives who had been elected in the 1925 local government elections, the first since the

Treaty. However, during his visit to Ireland, neither Church nor state officially acknowledged Mannix. The Catholic hierarchy ignored him and he was not invited to visit Maynooth, an institution of which he had been president.[7]

After Limerick Corporation had conferred the freedom of that city on him, Archbishop Mannix referred to the Oath of Allegiance in the Free State Constitution and said: 'If I had been in Ireland when the Treaty was signed, I would have endeavoured to keep the Oath out of the Constitution and thereby make it easier for those who, at the moment, were in a minority.'[8]

He was given the freedom of Waterford a week later and he acknowledged the honour by strongly advocating peace among Irishmen: 'I am just as much opposed to the Oath as ever I was – an Oath to a foreign monarch – and I am also opposed to fratricidal strife between Irishmen which could lead to nothing at the moment but untold misery for many people in Ireland.'[9]

When Archbishop Mannix was presented with the Freedom of the Borough of Wexford he commented: 'We still have the Oath of Allegiance and young men were still emigrating in great numbers.'[10]

At the end of October Archbishop Mannix spoke in the Pillar Room of the Rotunda in Dublin, which was unable to accommodate the huge number of people who came to hear him. He spoke to the crowd outside: 'Those who ask us to act constitutionally should remember that the way out for them is – let them agree upon an Irish Constitution. The Irish people would never give allegiance to a foreign king: they would be loyal to the nation.'[11]

Monsignor Hagan came from Rome and had discussions with Archbishop Mannix about how they could persuade a majority of anti-Treaty TDs and Sinn Féin supporters to change the party's policy of abstention from the Dáil. De Valera was under pressure from some of his closest associates, who included Gerry Boland TD, Seán Lemass TD and Seán T. O'Kelly TD to declare openly a new policy on abstentionism.[12]

As the visit of Dr Mannix to Ireland came to an end it was apparent that the series of meetings he had addressed had served to infuse a certain amount of new life into the Republican party. Many Republicans who had fought on the anti-Treaty side in the Civil War had reorganised themselves to prepare peaceful receptions for the one leading Irish-born prelate who had defended their anti-Treaty stance during that tragic period of fratricidal strife.

When Archbishop Mannix was on his way back to Australia after his four-months' visit to Ireland, the Irish in London made a presentation to him of an illuminated address in Irish. In response, Dr Mannix made a lengthy statement that summarised his observations during the course of his Irish visit:

> Under the Treaty, Ireland's elected representatives were forced to take an Oath of Allegiance to the king of England and even the ordinary civil servants were forced to take that Oath which they would not be asked to take in England or Scotland. When in Ireland I was asked if it would not be possible to get the Republican deputies into the Dáil. I was asked the question by supporters of the Free State. I replied that it was impossible for Republicans to take the Oath of Allegiance.[13]

Not all Irish people were pleased with the unofficial stopover of Archbishop Mannix in Ireland. D.P. Moran, editor of the *Leader,* a publication that remained detached from Free Staters and Republicans alike, declared that Mannix 'had quite crudely played to the anti-Treaty gallery and had not added to his dignity by allowing his visit to be worked by Republicans for all it was worth to them.'[14]

In the autumn of 1925 Seán Lemass wrote a series of articles that was published in *An Phoblacht.* In one he wrote that 'the optimistic hopes held at the time of the last *ard-fheis* have all been disappointed. In places where the Republican spirit is strong we have merely held our own: in other places we have lost ground...Judged by results the older men have failed, so let us give the younger men their chance now.'[15] Patrick O'Shea, the secretary of the Seán Mac Diarmada Sinn Féin *cumann,* replied to Lemass saying that this new hopeful [Lemass] considered that old members were a menace when elected to positions on Sinn Féin officer boards but 'let us (older members) say we are decidedly opposed to members, temporarily in a position on the governing committees of the Sinn Féin movement, expressing discordant opinions like "acceptance of the Oath conditionally".[16] Lemass continued to suggest new operational methods for Sinn Féin through the columns of *An Phoblacht*, although he did so in language that was opaque. He was aware that the 1925 Sinn Féin *ard-fheis* was fast approaching and he knew that an effort would be made at this congress to change the abstentionist Sinn Féin policy. 'There is something in the air,' he wrote, 'that tells us we have reached a parting of the ways. One way leads to victory and the other to defeat. The representatives of Republican Ireland, when they assemble next month, must choose which path the movement is to take. We must be very certain that we are right before we attempt to commit the movement to our views.'[17]

Mary MacSwiney TD, who consistently refused to give an inch on Sinn Féin's abstentionist policy, was still posted to the US but she was concerned about stories she had heard from Ireland that there could possibly be a change in Republican policy towards entering Dáil Éireann. In a letter to President de Valera and members of *Comhairle na dTeachtaí* she stated:

> The continuous crop of rumours of division in Republican ranks…render imperative some form of statement more than a mere denial of such divisions or a declaration of our determination to carry on.
>
> At present the businessmen have no faith in the ability of our party. Labour is afraid we are too reactionary. Capital fears we are Bolshevist. The young men and women who are Republican, but who are unable to see the vital importance of preserving the continuity of the government established in 1919, are more than half-inclined to look upon the elected (Republican) TDs pretty much as we looked upon the Irish Party in 1912-13.[18]

Two surprising occurrences at the end of October 1925 caused two by-elections. Darrell Figgis, an old Sinn Féin activist but then an Independent deputy for Dublin County who supported the Treaty, was found dead in a room in London filled with gas from a jet which had been turned on.[19] Seán McGuinness, Republican TD for Leix-Offaly, was disqualified from holding public office when he was sentenced to eighteen months imprisonment with hard labour for assaults on members of the Civic Guards in two different licensed premises in his own constituency.[20] Republicans stood a chance of retaining the McGuinness seat in Leix-Offaly but had no chance whatever of winning the Figgis seat in Dublin County.

Pádraig Ó Máille, former Cumann na nGaedheal TD from Galway, and other ex-Free-State-government deputies held a notable and unusual meeting with some Sinn Féin TDs and other prominent Republicans in the first week of November 1925. This group of unattached TDs tried to prevail on the anti-Treatyites to enter the Dáil. Dan Breen, Republican TD for Tipperary, who had built up a rapport with Ó Máille, was present at this meeting. Breen told the meeting that the Republican TDs were split on the issue.

On 13 November 1925 the *Ard-Chruinniú* (*ard-fheis*) of Cumann na mBan, the Republican Women's Association, took place in Dublin. The sixth resolution to be discussed on the agenda asked 'whether Republican TDs should enter Dáil Éireann.' From the moment the discussion began, it was obvious that the question would provoke considerable controversy. The strong Republican from Kerry, Gobnait Ní Bhruadair, was entirely against the idea of Republican TDs going into the Dáil but the chairperson and president of Cumann na mBan, Countess Markievicz, did not concur. She put it to the conference: 'Should they, in the case of securing a majority in an election, not go into the Dáil to have the Oath removed, then get rid of the king and the Constitution in which there is a king.?' She added: 'She would not think it any more disloyal to go into the Dáil to have the Oath removed than to go into an urban or county council.' After a long debate the *Ard-Chruinniú* of Cumann na mBan passed the resolution, that in order 'to prevent the spiritual annihilation of the existing Republic, we demand that the government [the Second Dáil] declares a working policy and reorganises the Republican organisation and we demand that under no circumstances should Republican *teachtaí* enter the Free State parliament.'

Though there was a majority in favour of the motion, Countess Markievicz dissented.[21] She made a surprise announcement later that evening:

In view of the resolution which has been passed regarding policy, after very careful consideration and with the greatest reluctance, I have decided that the only honourable course open to me is to resign my position as President of Cumann na mBan. I feel I could not have my hands tied in the event of certain circumstances arising.[22]

Mary MacSwiney, who had by this time returned from the US, refused a nomination from Gobnait Ní Bhruadair for the vacant presidency of Cumann na mBan on the grounds that she was about to change residence to Cork. Eithne Ní Chumhail was elected president after defeating Maighréad Ní Scineadóra by twenty-three votes to ten.[23]

Meanwhile, a crisis was looming in the IRA. The army executive met and agreed to call an army convention in November. Many IRA volunteers were not willing to accept the Free State Dáil under any circumstances or to turn to politics. These volunteers believed that after the end of the Civil War and the 'dump arms' order, all their efforts should have been directed towards a second conflict with the Irish Free State. IRA officers such as Seán Russell, Jim Killeen, Dave Fitzpatrick, Mick Price, Moss Twomey, Seán MacBride, Tom Barry, Andy Cooney and George Plunkett (son of Count Plunkett) thought that political activity did nothing at all to advance the Republican ideal.[24]

Like Éamon de Valera, Frank Aiken, then Chief-of-Staff of the IRA and Seán Lemass, Minister for Defence in the Second Dáil, had gradually come to the conclusion that a second armed conflict with Free State forces was out of the question. These three believed that one civil war in a generation was definitely enough.[25]

On the evening of 14 November 1925, the IRA general army convention opened in Dalkey. The most controversial resolution came at the end of the evening. This resolution, framed by Peadar O'Donnell and sponsored by the Tír Chonaill battalion of the IRA, proposed:

That in view of the fact that the government [the Second Republican Dáil] has developed into a mere political party and has apparently lost sight of the fact that all our energies should be devoted to the all-important work of making the army efficient so that the renegades who, through a *coup d'état*, assumed governmental powers in this country, be dealt with at the earliest possible opportunity, the army of the Republic sever its connection with the Dáil [Second Dáil], and act under an independent executive.[26]

George Plunkett asked Frank Aiken to state whether there was a 'new departure' within Sinn Féin to enter the Free State parliament. Aiken replied that there was formal discussion within Sinn Féin at that time about entering the Dáil. Moss Twomey expressed the view that 'it was bad for a revolutionary organisation like the IRA to be under the control of a semi-constitutional political party.'[27]

An emotional debate followed in which many delegates demanded that the IRA be saved from the humiliation of surrendering to the politicians of Leinster House. They alleged that Frank Aiken, their chief-of-staff, was selling them out; Frank Aiken resented this charge. The Tír Chonaill motion was passed. When the voting for a new executive took place those who were known to support the 'new departure' of entering Leinster House failed to get elected. The new army council elected Andy Cooney as chief-of-staff instead of Frank Aiken.

Seán Lemass, Minister for Defence in the Second Republican Dáil, was informed that the IRA had 'withdrawn allegiance from the Republican Dáil and had set up the army council as the supreme governing body.'[28] This meant that Lemass had no further authority over the army of the republic and his position as Minister for Defence was no longer recognised by the Republican army.

De Valera was not unduly upset by this split with the IRA. He had feared that a series of events similar to those prior to the outbreak of Civil War in 1922 could occur and that he might once again be held responsible for an outbreak of hostilities.

Matters looked complicated as the 1925 Sinn Féin *ard-fheis* approached.

To make matters worse Caherciveen (County Kerry) Sinn Féin *cumann* had put forward a controversial motion asking the *ard-fheis* to adhere to the Sinn Féin abstention policy of not entering the Dáil under any circumstances:

> Owing to the insidious rumours that Republicans will enter the 'Free State Parliament', if the Oath be removed, we call on Sinn Féin to get a definite statement from the government (*Comhairle na dTeachtaí*/the Republican Second Dáil) that they will adhere to the policy of Cathal Brugha, Erskine Childers and their fellow-martyrs, and enter only an Irish Republican parliament for all-Ireland.[29]

Not surprisingly, Éamon de Valera did not agree with this motion. This proposal directly opposed the new thinking about the abolition of the Oath that de Valera was formulating around this time. He now realised that, in order for him to survive as leader of Sinn Féin, he would have to come out in public and fight for the new policy he had in mind.

At the meeting of *Comhairle na dTeachtaí* held on 15 November, two days before the *ard-fheis*, de Valera decided to take a firm stand on his projected future policy to get rid of the Oath of Allegiance. There was an excellent attendance of around fifty Republican TDs and ex-TDs. De Valera was the first to speak. He affirmed that the time had come for Sinn Féin to abandon its present policy on abstention and begin a new chapter:

> We ought to go out definitely to the country and try to organise the people who don't want that Oath but do want stability – to organise them to smash the Oath…The position up to the present is that you have tried to maintain the *de jure* position of a government [Second Dáil] that was not able to function. Bit by bit your supporters are going away from you.'[30]

J.J. O'Kelly, TD for Meath, who was chairing the meeting, refused to stay in the chair if his function was to preside over any body of Republican TDs 'whose first business will be to discuss the question of going into the Free Sate parliament – that partitioned parliament.'[31] He requested that de Valera propose somebody else to take over as chairman of the meeting. De Valera ignored the request and went on with the debate. As the deliberations went on Dev became angry and said that he had one resort left to him: as the only nominee for President of Sinn Féin: 'I want everybody who would elect me to the office to know where I stand. I will not allow myself to be re-elected unless I have the opportunity of telling the *ard-fheis* what my views are and what we must do.'[32]

To get themselves out of the tight corner into which they were drifting the meeting agreed to resolve itself into a meeting of Cumann na Poblachta instead of the convened *Comhairle na dTeachtaí* conference that they were attending. Cumann na Poblachta was a Republican political party that de Valera and the anti-Treaty TDs had set up in early January 1922 after the passing of the Treaty.

At the Cumann na Poblachta meeting the following day, de Valera launched his plan of campaign to get rid of the Oath of Allegiance. 'If we were able to get the country on the Oath question – if that Oath were removed,' he said, '…under such circumstances I would be prepared myself to advise entry.'[33] He then asked if there was an alternative method. 'A few here in Dublin and a few around the country regard themselves as particularly pure Republicans. They will try to carry on for a time but then they will blow up. We have got very near that stage already – blowing up and eternal friction.'[34] Furthermore, he said: 'I would encourage the people to mass against the weakest point of the enemy's flank, finish that Oath – not by negotiations and going over to Churchill but get the Oath removed by massing the Irish people on the basis of realising that they can…sweep (away) that Oath and not risk war.'[35]

Frank Fahy, TD for Galway, was the first deputy to speak. He agreed with de Valera. 'There is no use disguising the facts,' he said. 'We can see the economic ruin that is coming upon the country. The IRA will soon be in America [because of emigration] and not in Ireland. At the next election we may get twenty [seats], and at the next ten. I think it is necessary to get an answer to this Oath question.'[36]

Professor William Stockley (NUI) took the opposite line. He addressed Éamon de Valera: 'The younger men feel you have given it up and that you are standing for what the people stood for whom you condemned a short time ago. They will feel that this going into the Free State parliament is an admission that you are accepting what is a giving up of your principle.'[37]

The issue divided the attendance almost equally. Gerry Boland TD (Roscommon) took de Valera's side: 'I would be inclined, if the Oath were removed, to go to that assembly (the Free State Dáil). I am out to win and to establish a Republic that will work. There might be a steeping stone.' He added: 'I am as much entitled to speak for the dead as anybody. The dead are dead and let them rest.'[38]

Staunch Republican TD Brian O'Higgins, from Éamon de Valera's own constituency of Clare, was having none of this. He retorted, 'I feel that even with the Oath removed, I could never go into what I consider the Dublin branch of the British parliament.'[39]

Seán O'Mahoney, who represented Fermanagh and Tyrone in the Second Dáil, regretted that he could not support the policy of President de Valera that night as 'even though the Oath were removed, was not every act in the Constitution vested in the King of England?'[40]

At this stage Éamon de Valera was unsure whether or not he had the support of the majority of his fellow-Republican deputies at the meeting. He was somewhat disappointed that he was not getting more support from the floor. 'My usefulness ends here if the policy which I put forward is not accepted,' he said. 'I feel rather sore about it that the word traitor should be flung around.'[41]

Donegal Republican TD, Joe O'Doherty, took de Valera's side. He believed that 'through the President we should tell the *ard-fheis* to consider it as the best policy [to go into Dáil Éireann if the Oath of Allegiance were removed] – risk the split in the hope that it would be a friendly split and that we could arrange with whatever divisions there would be – arrange some way of working in cooperation to bring about the fruition of all our hopes in this generation.'[42]

Mary MacSwiney, Cork Borough TD, rose to speak and there was no doubt in the mind of anyone present that she would refuse to go into the Free State parliament in any shape or form. 'I could not sit in parliament with men who had murdered my comrades,' she declared.

The stage arrived when thirty-two members of *Comhairle na dTeachtaí* had given their views on whether elected Sinn Féin TDs should or should not enter Dáil Éireann once the Oath of Allegiance was abolished. Eighteen Republican deputies had definitely stated that they would not enter Dáil Éireann even if the Oath were removed.[43] Twelve had affirmed that they would support Éamon de Valera's proposal to enter Dáil Éireann once they were not required to take the Oath of Allegiance to do so.[44] Two members of *Comhairle na dTeachtaí*, Oscar Traynor, TD, Dublin North and Éamon Donnelly, MP for Armagh, signified that they would require more time to make up their minds.

Mary MacSwiney came up with a suggestion. She believed: 'The only ground on which we can have unity would be when the thing comes up at the *ard-fheis* to discuss it fully and reasonably and then adjourn the *ard-fheis* for three months without a decision – tell them to go back to the *cumainn* (branches) and discuss the matter there – the more discussion you have the better.'[45]

President de Valera thought a decision should be reached at the *ard-fheis*: 'If the majority goes against me, we will do our utmost to give whatever help we can to the Republican movement.'[46]

At this stage of the debate Seán MacSwiney proposed an adjournment until 11 o'clock the following morning. When the conference reassembled, President de Valera pointed out: 'If the majority at the *ard-fheis* declares that they cannot enter the Free State Dáil, even if the Oath is abolished, and that it is a matter of Republican dogma or Republican principle not to do so – then I cannot conscientiously hold on. I would be misrepresenting the majority.'[47] He proposed an alternative motion:

> That this is not a question of Republican principle but of policy
> merely; that Republicans and members of Sinn Féin are at

liberty to hold and to advocate their individual views on the subject.[48]

Mary MacSwiney concurred. She said that she thought a split that day would be deplorable and that it was up to them all to prevent it. 'I think this properly-worded resolution will cover the President's position fully.'[49] The meeting of *Comhairle na dTeachtaí* accepted this resolution.

In the interval of two days between this meeting and the Sinn Féin *ard-fheis*, Éamon de Valera put together a short note defining in a more detailed manner the line of policy he proposed to take in the future:

> I am convinced that if we publicly declare this an open question and concentrate on the abolition of the Free State Oath, we shall bring to our side a number of people who are strongly national...The majority of the people of the country are prepared, in my opinion, to go to any length they can which does not appear to mean a renewal of the warfare with England...If we bring them to our side on any issue, and that we bring it to a successful conclusion, they will be prepared to accompany us in the fight for further and greater issues...If we do not attract them now – if we repel them by what they regard as an impossible attempt on our part, we shall miss the tide.[50]

At the Sinn Féin *ard-fheis* in the Town Hall, Rathmines, on 17 November 1925, the Caherciveen motion that Sinn Féin should adhere to the old policy and 'enter only an Irish Republican parliament for All-Ireland' was put to a packed hall of delegates from all parts of the country. The discussion that followed lasted for the best part of two days. Éamon de Valera argued that Republican deputies should enter Dáil Éireann once they were not obliged to take the Oath of Allegiance. As the debate progressed, it became clear that some of de Valera's longest-standing and oldest supporters were now entrenched on the other side of the divide. Count Plunkett TD, Father Michael O'Flanagan TD, Mary MacSwiney TD, Dr Kathleen Lynn TD, and J.J.

O'Kelly would not be prepared to sit in the Free State Dáil even if the Oath of Allegiance were removed.

There was stalemate until two women TDs, Mary MacSwiney and Countess Markievicz, proposed a compromise motion that was passed by the assembled Sinn Féin *ard-fheis* delegates:

> That no change be made in the policy of the Sinn Féin organisation at the *ard-fheis* but it is agreed that no subject of discussion is barred from the whole organisation or part of it, with the exception of the question of acceptance of allegiance to a foreign king and the partition of Ireland. And, if at any time a change of policy is proposed, an *ard-fheis* must be summoned to deal with the proposal.[51]

Seán Lemass supported the resolution. De Valera, Lemass and other supporters of this *modus operandi* had gained ground once the *ard-fheis* compromise motion had deferred any definite decision on the matter.

An editorial of the Republican newspaper, *An Phoblacht*, gave an account of the two different viewpoints in the *ard-fheis* debate:

> One point in the official report is of extreme interest to the public. From time to time those outside the organisation, seeing the state to which the country is reduced, have pleaded with Republicans, 'Would you not go into the assembly, take the Oath under protest and drive those scoundrels who are running the country out of public life.' Once more and very definitely the answer has been given by the *ard-fheis* to all such specious pleading. The acceptance of allegiance to England or the partition of Ireland is incompatible with membership of Sinn Féin.[52]

Éamon de Valera was again elected President of Sinn Féin and to cover the cracks of dissension, Father Michael O'Flanagan and Mary MacSwiney were elected vice-presidents. Austin Stack was chosen as one of the two joint secretaries.[53]

At the invitation of two Sinn Féin *cumainn* in Cork City, Cumann Tomás Ághas and Cumann Tomás MacCurtain, Mary MacSwiney attended their general meetings and explained why she had not striven to get the Caherciveen motion through the *ard-fheis*:

> It was evident that a division on the Caherciveen resolution would precipitate a division in the Sinn Féin organisation all over the country and in the opinion of some of us it was absurd to have a split on a mere hypothesis which might never arise.[54]

After the decision of the *ard-fheis* to allow the question of Sinn Féin entering the Free State Parliament as an open topic for discussion – 'with the exception of the question of acceptance of allegiance to a foreign king and the partition of Ireland' – *Comhairle na dTeachtaí* issued a document that contained suggestions for a basis of debate on future political policy. This statement contained fresh insight into where Sinn Féin might be going:

> It will be well for all of us to face the obvious truth, viz; that the Free State government is functioning, that its decrees are, in the main, being observed and administrated in its own area and that it is moulding, guiding and directing, however badly or otherwise, the fate of the citizens of the twenty-six counties. As time goes on, however, the difficulties of defeating the present government may increase for it may as well be admitted that... the administration of the Free State has been 'comparatively' successful. However, Republicans feel that the evils of imperialism are ever-present...Republicans are right in their judgement on the imperial connection but, in times of peace and comparative normalcy, it is not easy to drive home the truth of these menacing elements.[55]

The *ard-fheis* delegates, by not endorsing the Caherciveen motion, left the way open for de Valera to pursue further his aim of altering Sinn Féin's abstentionist policy. De Valera became ever more convinced that by going into the Dáil – if the Oath of Allegiance were abolished – his Republican party might eventually be able to dismantle any repugnant measures that were part of the Treaty of 1921.

Notes

1. Patrick Murray, *Oracles of God*, p. 213.
2. Dermot Keogh, *The Vatican, the Bishops and Irish Politics 1919-39*, p. 131.
3. Murray, *op. cit.* pp. 213, 214.
4. The *Irish Independent*, 27 July 1925.
5. *Ibid.*
6. Archbishop Mannix passed through Callan, County Kilkenny, on Monday, 12 August 1925. He received an enthusiastic reception from a large crowd. A procession formed and was led by the Kells Pipers' Band and the Kilmoganny Fife and Drum Band. It proceeded to the Square where Michael Shelley TD read an address of welcome from the Callan Town Commissioners. (The *Kilkenny People*, 15 August 1925).
7. Patrick Murray, *op. cit.* p. 217.
8. The *Irish Independent*, 6 August 1925.
9. *Ibid.*, 13 August 1925.
10. *Ibid.*, 3 September 1925.
11. Franciscan Library, Killiney, de Valera Papers, File 1452, 'Speeches of the Most Reverend Dr Mannix, Archbishop of Melbourne, in the Rotunda, Dublin', 22 and 29 October 1925.
12. Keogh, *op. cit.*, p. 131 and Seán T. O'Kelly to Monsignor Hagan, 30 November 1925.
13. The *Irish Independent*, 9 November 1925.
14. The *Leader*, 15 August 1925 and Patrick Murray, *op. cit.*, p. 217.
15. *An Phoblacht*, 9 October 1925.
16. *Ibid.*, 16 October, 1925.
17. *Ibid.*, 23 October 1925.
18. UCDA, de Valera Papers, File P/150/1946: Letter from Mary MacSwiney in the USA to President de Valera and members of *Comhairle na dTeachtaí*, 19 October 1925.
19. The *Irish Independent*, 28 October 1925.
20. *Ibid.*, 30 October 1925.
21. UCDA, Papers of Mary MacSwiney, File 48a/15, 13 November 1925: Minutes of *Ard-Chruinniú* Cumann na mBan.
22. *Ibid.*
23. *Ibid.*
24. J. Bowyer Bell, *The Secret Army: The IRA*, p. 52.
25. Brian Farrell, *Seán Lemass*, p. 12.
26. Bell, *op. cit.*, p. 53.
27. UCDA, Moss Twomey Papers, P69/62/ (10).
28. Brian P. Murphy, *Patrick Pearse and the Lost Republican Ideal*, p. 151.
29. The *Irish Independent*, 19 November 1925.
30. UCDA, de Valera Papers, File P/150/1946: minutes of the meeting of
31. *Comhairle na dTeachtaí*, 15 November 1925.
32. *Ibid.*
33. *Ibid.*
34. *Ibid.*
35. *Ibid.*
36. *Ibid.*

37. *Ibid.*
38. *Ibid.*
39. *Ibid.*
40. *Ibid.*
41. *Ibid.*
42. *Ibid.*
43. *Ibid.*
44. The eighteen *Comhairle na dTeachtaí* deputies who had stated that they would not enter Dáil Éireann even if the Oath of Allegiance were abolished were: Ceann Comhairle J.J. O'Kelly (Louth-Meath, 1922); Seán O'Mahoney (Fermanagh-Tyrone, 1921); Brian O'Higgins TD (Clare); Dáithí Kent TD (Cork East); Seán MacSwiney (Cork Mid, North, South, South-East and West, 1921); Austin Stack TD (Kerry); Seán Buckley TD (Cork West); Laurence Brady TD (Leix-Offaly); Seán Farrell TD (Leitrim-Sligo); Professor William Stockley (National University of Ireland, 1922); Mary MacSwiney TD(Cork Borough); Séamus Fitzgerald (Cork East and North-East, 1921); Mrs Caitlín Brugha TD (Waterford); Art O'Connor (Kildare-Wicklow, 1921); Mrs Katherine O'Callaghan (Limerick City-Limerick East, 1922); Thomas Maguire TD (Mayo South); Dr John Madden TD (Mayo North) ; Dr John Crowley TD (Mayo North): as per UCDA, de Valera Papers, File P150/1946, Minutes of *Comhairle na dTeachtaí*, 15 November 1925.
45. The twelve deputies who stated that they would agree to enter Dáil Éireann once the Oath of Allegiance was abolished were: President Éamon de Valera TD (Clare); Frank Fahy TD (Galway); Gerry Boland TD (Roscommon); Peadar O'Donnell TD (Donegal); Séamus Robinson (Waterford-Tipperary East, 1921); Kathleen Clarke (Dublin Mid, 1921); Seán MacEntee (Monaghan, 1921); Joe O'Doherty TD (Donegal); Louis O'Dea TD (Galway); Countess Markievicz TD (Dublin South); P.J. Ruttledge TD (Mayo North); Seán Moylan (Cork Mid, North, South, South-East and West, 1922).
46. UCDA, de Valera Papers, File P/150/1946: minutes of the meeting of
47. *Comhairle na dTeachtaí*, 15 November 1925.
48. *Ibid.*
49. *Ibid.*
50. *Ibid.*
51. *Ibid.*
52. *Ibid.*
53. The *Irish Independent*, 19 November 1925.
54. *An Phoblacht*, 27 November 1925.
55. *Ibid.*, 20 November 1925.
56. UCDA, Papers of Mary MacSwiney, File P48a/73/1: Statement of Mary MacSwiney to Cumainn Tomás Ághas and Tomás MacCurtain (Cork), after the 1925 Sinn Féin *ard-fheis*.
57. UCDA, de Valera Papers, File P/150/1946 (3).

9

The Boundary Agreement

The Free State government suffered a setback on 21 November 1925 when
Dr Eoin MacNeill announced that he was resigning from the Boundary
Commission before that body had issued its long-awaited report. At Emyvale,
County Monaghan, on 22 November 1925, W.T. Cosgrave explained the
reason that forced MacNeill to take this step:

> The Irish nominee on the tribunal (Dr Eoin MacNeill) declared
> that during the course of the last meetings of the Commission
> he had been completely and amply satisfied that there was no
> likelihood that the work of the Commission would result in a
> report based upon the terms of reference provided for it by the
> Articles of Agreement for a Treaty between Great Britain and
> Ireland.[1]

From his Republican headquarters, Éamon de Valera said of the Boundary
Commission:

> Griffith gave as his principal reason for signing the so-called
> Treaty that it meant the end of partition. Lloyd George and
> Churchill had led him to believe that the area of jurisdiction
> of Sir James Craig's parliament would be so reduced by the
> Boundary Commission as to make it an uneconomic holding of
> about two counties.[2]

President W.T. Cosgrave, Kevin O'Higgins and Ernest Blythe went to

London to continue negotiations and on 3 December 1925 reached an agreement between Stanley Baldwin, Prime Minister of England and Sir James Craig, Prime Minister of Northern Ireland.

The Free State lost out badly on constitutional issues. The border between the Free State and Northern Ireland was left as it was. This meant that the entire counties of Tyrone and Fermanagh, along with south Armagh, south Down, the town of Newry and Derry City, where there were nationalist majorities, would remain under the control of the Northern Ireland government. On the other hand Unionists in east Donegal and a portion of north Monaghan had expected, with the adjustment of the border, that they would be under the jurisdiction of the Northern government, so they too were disappointed.

The Free State government benefited financially from the agreement. They agreed to make a one-off payment of around £4 million to the British government for a release from a liability under Article 5 of the Treaty for the service of the public debt of the United Kingdom and they were freed of a financial liability of £5-£10 million annually to the British war debt and to war pensions. W.T. Cosgrave and Kevin O'Higgins issued a statement to the Irish people shortly after signing this agreement: 'Today we have sown the seeds of peace – an instrument which provides a sane and constructive solution born of genuine desire for peace between the two nations has been signed.'

Sir James Craig showed himself satisfied: 'I return to-morrow with nothing but feelings of rejoicing and relief that statesmanship has succeeded in surmounting a grave situation.'[3]

Addressing a large and enthusiastic meeting in Ennis, President de Valera made a passionate speech which he called 'Save Ulster for Ireland'. In this speech he pulled no punches:

> You ask me what is to be done now. Well, I am not a Free Stater and the Treaty policy is not my policy but if it were and the pledge given to Arthur Griffith on the basis of which he accepted the crown and the empire were to be disregarded by the English, then the crown and the empire would be

disregarded by me, and I would trust a united people at home and a united race abroad to back me.[4]

Reaction to the agreement varied widely. Cumann na nGaedheal discussed the agreement and decided to support it in the Dáil but even within the Free State party there were some dissident voices. One such was that of Richard O'Connell, a former leader of the mid-Limerick flying column in the War of Independence, who was elected TD for Cumann na nGaedheal in the Limerick by-election of May 1924.[5]

Pádraig Ó Máille, the former Cumann na nGaedheal TD from Galway, declared on the very day that this Boundary Agreement to amend the Treaty was signed: 'If…any change is being made in the Treaty it ought to be imperative that the change will be made whereby every deputy elected to the Dáil by the Irish people will be permitted to take his seat.'[6]

The Standing Committee of Sinn Féin met and decided to hold a public meeting in Dublin the following Sunday for the purpose of protesting against the partition of Ireland and the 'betrayal' of the North.[7] Austin Stack, an uncompromising Republican, felt so incensed by the Boundary Agreement that he wrote to de Valera condemning the settlement. As if grappling with his own conscience, he argued:

> The boundary business is terrible. The first thing that struck me this morning – when I saw the heading in the press – was that it might be defeated in the so-called Dáil. Then I read in the *Daily Mail* that our forty-seven[8] might go and throw out the proposed piece of legislation. Could we do it? I mean would there be sufficient opposition to enable us to turn the scale? Oath and all, I would be inclined to favour the idea (tho' my mind is not quite made up) if our going in would defeat the proposal…I know you are thinking it over.[9]

The Labour Party declared its opposition to the agreement:

The underlying principle of the Anglo-Irish Treaty and of the Irish Constitution is that Ireland is one and also indivisible, in the sense that its parts could never be completely severed and must eventually be completely reunited.[10]

The Farmers' Party made a non-committal comment: 'We have failed to get the territory which for sentimental reasons we had desired, because the Boundary Commission has proved a fiasco.'[11]

It was believed that the government was prepared to go to the country on the issue if the Boundary Agreement Bill was defeated in the Dáil.[12]

Nationalists and Republicans in most of Northern Ireland were shocked. Cahir Healy, Nationalist MP for Tyrone-Fermanagh, bitterly disappointed with the settlement, declared that the agreement was:

a betrayal of the Nationalists of the North and a denial of every statement put forward by the Free State in the alleged support of our cause since 1921…John Redmond was driven from public life for even suggesting partition for a period of five years. The new leaders agree to partition forever.[13]

At a Republican meeting in O'Connell Street, Dublin, arranged by the Standing Committee of Sinn Féin, Éamon de Valera said that the worst of the bargain was 'that it would be said we had sold our countrymen for money.'[14]

William O'Brien, a former MP from Mallow, County Cork, founder and leader of the All-for-Ireland League, wrote about this new Treaty, as he called it: 'All deputies, sworn or unsworn, should meet together upon a programme of freedom for Ireland.'[15] This was really challenging the abstentionist Republican TDs to do something immediate and bold to oppose this new, permanent partition of Ireland.

Thomas Johnson TD, leader of the Labour Party, Pádraig Ó Máille, former Cumann na nGaedheal TD but by then a member of a new untitled party, and Patrick Baxter, the Cavan Farmers' Party TD, summoned a meeting of all elected deputies to be held in the Shelbourne Hotel, Dublin on 8 December

1925, to give the new agreement the most serious consideration. Gerry Boland TD, an enthusiastic Sinn Féin organiser, was active in the political manoeuvring that led up to this meeting. The Dáil deputies who summoned the Shelbourne Hotel meeting were hoping to persuade the abstentionist Sinn Féin TDs to take their seats, at least on this occasion, to defeat the Boundary Agreement. Labour representatives were convinced for a while that the Republican abstentionist deputies would enter the Dáil but then they detected a changing attitude on de Valera's part and a reluctance to assent to the move.

At a special meeting of Sinn Féin TDs, Austin Stack repeated his call to Republican deputies to enter the Dáil for one day only to vote against the Boundary Agreement. Gerry Boland supported Stack, as did Patrick Ruttledge, but Count Plunkett strenuously objected to Republican deputies even meeting Ó Máille and Johnson under any circumstances and left the meeting. The proposal that Sinn Féin TDs should enter the Dáil for one day only was rejected by a majority of Republican TDs.[16]

Éamon de Valera saw that he would have to uphold the spirit of the November *ard-fheis* motion that 'if, at any time, a change of policy (in regard to abstentionism) is proposed, an *ard-fheis* must be summoned to deal with the proposal.' He suggested at the end of the meeting that the motion should be put to an *ard-fheis* of Sinn Féin as a proposal for the next election.[17] Dev realised that to take any other action at that point would risk splitting the Republican movement from top to bottom without any definite guarantee that, if Republicans entered the Dáil, their numbers would be sufficient to defeat the Boundary Agreement Bill. De Valera was struggling, not too successfully, with the almost impossible task of maintaining unity between three divergent sections of the Republican movement – militant IRA members; the majority section of doctrinaire and principled Republicans unwilling to recognise the Cosgrave-led Free State government under any circumstances; and pragmatic members like Seán Lemass and Seán T. O'Kelly who were seeking effective political action to solve the Oath of Allegiance problem. He issued an appeal to Republican deputies: 'I urge upon all Republican deputies elected at and since the general election of 1923 to be present at the meeting called for the Shelbourne Hotel.'[18]

The Shelbourne Hotel meeting did take place as arranged. Thomas Johnson TD, Pádraig Ó Máille TD and Patrick Baxter TD, the three signatories who summoned the meeting, along with Professor William Magennis TD, Cumann na nGaedheal, were among the earliest arrivals. Nineteen Republican deputies and one Republican MP, Éamon Donnelly (Armagh), attended. Elected deputies from Labour, Cumann na nGaedheal, Independent Labour, the Farmers' Party and the National Group also attended.[19] In all thirty-eight elected representatives attended the meeting. Prominent but unelected members of Sinn Féin were also present – Seán Moylan ex-TD (Cork), Count Patrick O'Byrne ex-TD (Tipperary), Mrs Katherine O'Callaghan ex-TD (Limerick), Dr C. Murphy (Dublin) and Thomas Derrig (Mayo).

The gathering passed a resolution that 'this meeting of elected representatives of the Irish people are opposed to the attempt to partition our country'. A representative committee was then appointed to devise the most effective means to defeat the Boundary Agreement Bill. The joint chairmen were Éamon de Valera, and Thomas Johnson. Joint secretaries were Austin Stack and Professor William Magennis. Others elected to the select committee were Pádraig Ó Máille (new untitled party), Seán Lemass, Patrick Baxter (Farmers' Party) and Dr Patrick McCarvill (Republican).[20]

Many of the opponents of the agreement had been hoping that this meeting would result in the Republicans entering the Dáil to oppose the ratification of the Boundary Agreement but Republicans rejected the requests from the Labour Party to do so.[21] One deputy from outside Sinn Féin, who said he understood the delicate position of the Republican Party on this issue, stated after the meeting that he was not prepared to put any undue pressure on them to enter the Dáil. 'They can make up their own minds now, if they are able to undertake that task, and they can select their own time for entering.'[22] Other non-Republican deputies were not so forbearing. One of these TDs, commenting on the reluctance of the Republican deputies to commit themselves to entering the Dáil, remarked: 'It would be expecting too much of the Republicans to think that they would do the commonsense thing even now.'[23]

The Shelbourne Hotel meeting was not a total fiasco. It was the first occasion that Sinn Féin deputies had met and associated with elected TDs from other political parties. Gerry Boland remarked about de Valera's hesitation to enter the Dáil to defeat the measure: 'Much as I loved Dev – and to know him closely was to love him -there were times when he could not just make up his mind.'[24] But de Valera, always cautious – particularly since the Civil War days – doubted, even if the Republican TDs went into the Dáil at this time, that they would get sufficient support from the other parties to defeat the Boundary Agreement Bill.

This Bill came before the Dáil without delay. During the first stage of the reading of the Bill, Thomas J. O'Connell, Labour TD for Galway, criticised the Free State negotiators for making no attempt to bargain away the article in the Treaty settlement that required Dáil deputies to take the Oath of Allegiance before entering the Dáil:

> There is no attempt to secure unity in the Twenty-Six Counties. Unity in the Twenty-Six Counties does not count. We are going to have unity with Craig on the basis of giving Craig everything he wants but it never seems to have struck our Executive Council that it would be a good thing when the bargaining was in the air that they might have attempted to bargain for Article IV (the Article which required Dáil deputies to take the Oath of Allegiance)...We are asked to accept this Treaty (the Boundary Agreement), which modifies to a very great extent the original Treaty of 1921 without any attempt being made to give a considerable number of elected representatives of this country a chance of expressing their opinions on it...I wonder would the President agree to submit this document to the ratification of (all the) elected representatives of this country?[25]

The President, W.T. Cosgrave, replied: 'Certainly not, sir, not to any person who carries a gun in one hand and a torch in the other. I certainly will not.'[26]

During the second reading of the Bill, John Lyons, Independent Labour TD for Longford-Westmeath, made a long speech in which he also drew attention to the absence of the elected Sinn Féin deputies from the House:

> If the Executive Council can go to London and scrap part of the Treaty at the beck and call of England, then why should not the Saorstát government have the power to scrap another part of the Treaty at the beck and call of Ireland? I say: 'Do away with the Oath.' Why should we deprive a section of the community, that voices the opinion of, at least, thirty-five per cent of the population of the Saorstát, from giving an expression to its views on the matter?[27]

Pádraig Ó Máille TD, Galway, supported John Lyons: 'I, who have no hate in my soul, I believe…that if the Treaty was changed it ought to be made possible for every deputy elected by the people to be free to come in here and take his place in the Dáil.[28]

Other deputies expressed conflicting opinions about who to blame for the absence of so many elected deputies from the House while the rest of the elected TDs were debating and voting on such an all-important issue as the Boundary Agreement. Timothy Murphy, Labour TD, Cork West, strongly condemned the Republican TDs for not entering the Dáil. 'I submit,' he said, 'that if, as a result of our deliberations here today, partition becomes an accomplished fact, the people who are outside the Dáil, and who are supposed to have a monopoly of all the patriotism that is going in this country, cannot acquit themselves of some of the responsibility for that partition.'[29]

Ernest Blythe, Monaghan Cumann na nGaedheal TD and Minister for Finance, could not think of any benefit that would accrue to the country from a policy directed to remove the Oath of Allegiance. 'I think if that clause were removed there would be no gain,' he said, 'and it is not a clause that would be as easy to remove as clauses that have practical importance.'[30]

Wexford deputy Osmond Grattan Esmonde made a vehement speech un reservedly condemning the Republican Party for not entering Dáil Éireann.

He claimed the Republican deputies were 'terrorised by one lady.' It was clear that he was referring to the Sinn Féin TD for Cork Borough, Mary MacSwiney:

> Who is responsible for the fact that we are not a healthy country with alternative governments, so that if one government makes a mistake the other government can step into its place and clear up the mess. Who is responsible for that? There is only one party in this country responsible for that and that is the Republican party. The Republican party has allowed itself to be fooled by the British Oath. It has allowed the whole country to be fooled by the Oath of Allegiance…They (the Republican deputies) are terrorised and paralysed by one lady…Before the terror of her tongue, forty or fifty able-bodied representatives of the Irish people tremble and obey.[31]

Conor Hogan TD, representing the Farmers' Party in Clare, drew the attention of the House to a very serious constitutional matter:

> I believe that with the system we have adopted in the Constitution…there would always be a minority prepared to accept its provisions, to come into the House and work it. That, I contend must create a very serious state of affairs. If, for instance, you had a majority of the elected representatives outside and a minority functioning within, what would be the position. Under the Constitution the minority, having complied with its provisions, automatically becomes the government and all the powers and resources of government automatically fall into their hands. They get control of the exchequer, the army, the police. They are in authority and any persons who acted collectively, even though admittedly they would be representatives of the people, would still be subject to the penal provisions which the Constitution and amending acts provided

for dealing with disturbances of public peace.[32]

Hogan's contribution to the debate could not but cause members of the Free State government to take stock of how the Constitution, as it then stood, could be a source of further conflict in the country in the event of the Sinn Féin Party winning a majority of seats in some future election.

Supporters of the Cumann na nGaedheal government held their breaths as the elected deputies went into the division lobbies to record their votes. When the result was announced government supporters applauded loudly. The Boundary Agreement Bill had passed by seventy-one votes to twenty – an easy government majority of fifty-one votes.[33]

But there were no elected Republican deputies in the chamber to record their votes against the agreement. Instead the abstentionist Republican TDs, in a show of unity, gathered together in the Concert Room in the Rotunda, in the centre of Dublin, to record publicly their total opposition to the Boundary Agreement Bill. Éamon de Valera addressed the gathering. He declared that in another place (the Dáil) other representatives of the people were meeting to decide whether or not they would give their consent to the partition of their country and that they might have, as Republicans, to bow their heads for a time to this enforced partition by a foreign power but that the sanction of their consent partition could never have. 'We deny,' he continued, 'that any section of our people can give away the sovereignty or alienate any part of the territory of this nation. If this generation should be base enough to consent to give them away, the right to win them back remains unimpaired for those to whom the future will bring the opportunity.'[34] De Valera then asked each Republican elected deputy present to sign a declaration that recorded his/her 'unalterable opposition' to the partition of Ireland. Forty-one Republican deputies in turn stood up and recorded their total opposition to partition.[35]

The Republican deputies had chosen the Rotunda Concert Room to record their opposition to the passing of the Boundary Agreement rather than take their places in Dáil Éireann. As it was, the Boundary Agreement passed through the Dáil with the endorsement of a minority of all the elected Dáil deputies returned in the 1923 general election and subsequent by-elections. It was a sad day indeed for the Northern nationalists when they realised that they were now cut off, with little hope of change, from their ancestral homeland of the twenty-six counties.

Many years later de Valera wrote a letter to the *Irish Press* explaining in detail why the Sinn Féin deputies could not attend Dáil Éireann and vote against the Boundary Agreement Bill:

> The Sinn Féin deputies were elected on the understanding that they would not enter Dáil Éireann with or without an Oath. It was obviously impossible for a body so pledged and so elected to act as the Labour deputation suggested…Further it was at the time much more than doubtful whether the addition of the Sinn Féin deputies would be sufficient to defeat the Bill. The probability, indeed, was that the step we were urged to take would, if taken, prove ineffective. Many of the pro-Treaty deputies who might abstain or vote against the Bill, whilst the Sinn Féin deputies were absent could, we feel certain, be drummed up to vote for the Bill and save the government from defeat once the Sinn Féin deputies had appeared upon the scene.[36]

Because of the passing of the Boundary Agreement Bill many members of Sinn Féin began to question their true role in the political life of the country. They were the second strongest political party in the land but they were 'sitting on the fence' while the most serious national issues were being decided in the Dáil without any contribution from them in the assembly that counted. It was also clear at this stage that the vast majority of the women of Cumann na mBan and all the members of the IRA wanted nothing to do with deputies who wanted to enter the Dáil.[37] De Valera's mind was shifting strongly and speedily to the belief that he had to make a definite decision in the near future to enter Dáil Éireann, even at the expense of the unity of Sinn Féin. His whole purpose now was to isolate the question of the Oath of Allegiance and pursue a policy to get rid of it.[38]

Cumann na nGaedheal did not emerge unscathed from the Boundary

Agreement controversy. The party was losing dissidents from its ranks and its numerical strength was being eroded because of its acceptance of policies that looked weak to some of their members from a national point of view.

Notes

1. The *Irish Independent*, 23 November 1925.
2. *An Phoblacht*, 27 November 1925.
3. The *Irish Independent*, 4 December 1925.
4. *Ibid.*, 4 December 1925.
5. John M. Regan, *The Irish Counter Revolution*, p. 256 and UCDA, Mulcahy Papers, P7/C/99, 1 December 1925.
6. Thomas P. O'Neill, 'In Search of a Political Path: Irish Republicanism, 1922 to 1927', *Historical Studies*, 1976, p. 165.
7. NAI, File 2B/82/117/25, Minutes of Standing Committee of Sinn Féin, 2 December 1925.
8. There were forty-eight Sinn Féin elected deputies but Seán McGuinness, Republican TD for Leix-Offaly, had been disqualified from public office following his sentence of eighteen months' imprisonment for assaults on members of the Civic Guards.
9. Franciscan Library Killiney, Austin Stack file, Austin Stack to de Valera, 4 December 1925.
10. The *Irish Independent*, 5 December 1925.
11. The *Irish Independent*, 5 December 1925.
12. *Ibid.*
13. *Ibid.*
14. The *Irish Independent*, 7 December 1925.
15. *Ibid.*
16. *The Irish Times*, 10 October 1968, 'Gerry Boland's Story as told to Michael McInerney'.
17. *Ibid.*
18. The *Irish Independent*, 8 December 1925.
19. The elected deputies (TDs with the exception of Éamon Donnelly MP) who attended the Shelbourne Hotel meeting, according to the *Irish Independent* of 9 December 1925, were as follows:
    Labour Party: Thomas Johnson (Dublin County), Éamonn Doyle (Carlow-Kilkenny), David Hall (Meath), Dan Morrissey (Tipperary), James Everett (Wicklow), Hugh Colohan(Kildare), Patrick Clancy (Limerick), Thomas J. O'Connell (Galway) (8).
    Independent Labour: Seán Lyons (Longford-Westmeath) (1).
    Farmers' Party: P. Baxter (Cavan), Conor Hogan (Clare), Patrick Mulvany (Meath) (3).
    Republican Party: Éamon de Valera (Clare), Caitlín Brugha (Waterford), Mary MacSwiney (Cork Borough), Austin Stack (Kerry), Thomas O'Donoghue (Kerry), Éamon Donnelly MP (Armagh), Seán Lemass (Dublin South), Frank Fahy (Galway),
    Dan Breen (Tipperary), Oscar Traynor (Dublin North), Barney Mellows (Galway),
    Dr James Ryan (Wexford), Patrick McCarvill (Monaghan), Dr John Crowley (Mayo North), Peadar O'Donnell (Donegal), David Kent (Cork East), Patrick Ruttledge (Mayo North), Madame Markievicz (Dublin South), Seán Buckley (Cork West), Brian O'Higgins (Clare). (20).
    National Group: Christopher M. Byrne (Wicklow) and O.G. Esmonde (Wexford). (2).
    Cumann na nGaedheal: Andrew O'Shaughnessy (Cork), Louis J. Dalton (Tipperary), Professor William Magennis (National University of Ireland). (3).
    New Untitled Party: Pádraig Ó Máille (Galway). (1).
20. The *Irish Independent*, 9 December 1925.
21. The Earl of Longford and Thomas P. O'Neill, *Éamon de Valera*, p. 241.
22. The *Irish Independent*, 9 December 1925.
23. *Ibid.*, 9 December 1925.
24. *The Irish Times*, 10 October 1968, 'Gerry Boland's Story as told to Michael McInerney'.
25. *Dáil Éireann Reports*, Volume 13, 7 December 1925, Treaty (Confirmation of Amending Agreement) Bill, pp. 1386, 1387.
26. *Ibid.*, p. 1387.

27. *Dáil Éireann Reports*, Volume 13, 8 December 1925, Treaty (Confirmation of Amending Agreement Bill, p. 1502.
28. *Ibid.*, p. 1605.
29. *Ibid.*, p. 1624.
30. *Ibid.*, p. 1595.
31. *Ibid.*, p. 1710.
32. *Ibid.*, p. 1653.
33. How did this vote of seventy-one votes (for) to twenty votes (against) break down?

For the Boundary Agreement:	For	Against	Abstained	Absent
Cumann na nGaedheal	51	1	2	1
Farmers' Party	10	1	3	1
Labour	–	14	–	–
Independents	9	–	3	–
National Group	–	3	1	–
Independent Labour	1	1	–	–
Total	**71**	**20**	**9**	**2**

Against the Agreement

Cumann na nGaedheal: Professor William Magennis (National University of Ireland)	1
Farmers' Party: Patrick Baxter (Cavan)	1
Labour Party: entire party	14
National Group: O.G. Esmonde (Wexford); Christopher Byrne (Wicklow); Pádraig Ó Máille (Galway)	3
Independent Labour: John Lyons (Longford-Westmeath)	1
Total	**20**

Abstained

Cumann na nGaedheal: Denis McCullough (Donegal): Louis Dalton (Tipperary)	2
Farmers' Party: Patrick J. Mulvany (Meath); Michael Doyle (Wexford): John Dinneen (Cork East)	3
Independents: Alfie Byrne (Dublin N.); William Redmond (Waterford); James Cosgrave (Galway)	3
National Group: Francis Bulfin (Leix-Offaly)	1
Total	**9**

Absent from Dáil (indisposed)

Cumann na nGaedheal; John Prior (Cork West)	1
Farmers' Party: P.J. McKenna (Longford-Westmeath)	1
Total:	**2**
Elected abstentionist Republican deputies, absent from Dáil and did not vote	**48**

34. The *Irish Independent*, 11 December 1925.
35. Dorothy Macardle, Dorothy, *The Irish Republic*, p. 895. The forty-one Sinn Féin TDs who signed were: Mary MacSwiney (Cork Borough); Constance Markievicz (Dublin South); Charles Murphy (Dublin South); Patrick Smith (Cavan); Éamon de Valera (Clare); Brian O'Higgins (Clare); Daniel Corkery (Cork North); Seán Buckley (Cork West); David Kent (Cork East); Peadar O'Donnell (Donegal); Joseph Doherty (Donegal); B. Ó Maoilíosa (Galway); Proinsias Ó Fathaigh (Galway); Lughaigh O'Dea (Galway); Austin Stack (Kerry); Thomas McEllistrim (Kerry); Thomas O'Donoghue (Kerry); Patrick Cahill (Kerry); Seán Farrell (Leitrim-Sligo); Bernard McGowan (Leitrim-Sligo); Laurence Brady (Leix-Offaly); Seán Carroll (Limerick); Conor Byrne (Longford-Westmeath); James Killane (Longford-Westmeath); Frank Aiken (Louth); Patrick Ruttledge (Mayo North); Dr John Crowley (Mayo North); Thomas Maguire (Mayo South); Michael Kilroy (Mayo South); Patrick McCarvill (Monaghan); Thomas George Noble (Count) Plunkett (Roscommon); Gerald Boland (Roscommon); Dan Breen (Tipperary); Patrick Ryan (Tipperary); Caitlín Brugha (Waterford); Robert Lambert (Wexford); James Ryan (Wexford); Seán Lemass (Dublin South); Dr John Madden (Mayo North); Oscar Traynor (Dublin North); Samuel Holt (Leitrim-Sligo);.
    Of the seven deputies who did not sign, Seán T. O'Kelly (Dublin North) and Dr Kathleen Lynn (Dublin County) were in the USA, Ernie O'Malley (Dublin North) was in Catalonia and Seán

McGuinness (Leix-Offaly) was in prison. Michael Shelley (Carlow-Kilkenny), Frank Carty (Leitrim-Sligo) and James Colbert (Limerick) were absent through illness.

36. NAI, File S2768, Letter to the *Irish Press* by Éamon de Valera, 18 March 1957.

37. UCDA, File P80/847 (123), Papers of Desmond Fitzgerald: Intelligence Report from Agent No. 199 to Director of Intelligence about Sinn Féin Policy, 21 November 1925.

38. Draft speech by Éamon de Valera, undated but *c.* 1925, Thomas P. O'Neill, 'In Search of a Political Path: Irish Republicanism, 1922 to 1927', p. 168.

10

OLD FRIENDS PART

Many prominent Republicans attended a Sinn Féin rally, organised by the Ranelagh *cumann*, in a crowded Rathmines Town Hall in Dublin on 6 January 1926. During the course of a lively speech Éamon de Valera referred to the Free State Constitution and said that it acknowledged in every vital article the supremacy of a foreign power and contained a distasteful Oath of Allegiance. Then he made the startling statement that 'he would be quite satisfied to go into any representation of the Irish people and work for them if there were no formulae of that kind.'[1] But, he added, 'the acceptance of partition and the acknowledgement of foreign supremacy by the Oath of Allegiance has been definitely excluded by the Republicans, and rightly so, in my opinion, by the *ard-fheis* of the organisation.'[2] In essence this meant that he was prepared to enter the Free State Dáil if he was not obliged to recognise partition and if there were no Oath of Allegiance required of him to do so.

This was the first time that de Valera had ever expressed such an intention in public. It showed that he, as President of reorganised Sinn Féin, was giving deep consideration to the future of Irish Republicanism.

The *Ard-Chomhairle* of Sinn Féin met on 13 January. When the meeting opened President de Valera brought up the abstentionist policy of Sinn Féin.[3] One wing of the party favoured entry into the Dáil if the Oath of Allegiance were abolished. But the more extreme wing supported the continuation of abstention in both the north and the south. The *Ard-Chomhairle* decided to summon an extraordinary *ard-fheis* for Tuesday, 9 March, to debate the whole matter. The interval was intended to give the organisation in the country reasonable time to discuss the question and appoint and instruct delegates accordingly.[4]

The *Midland Tribune*, a newspaper that had hitherto staunchly supported the Free State government, was having second thoughts about some of the legislation passed in the Dáil, 'which would not have been adopted had a real opposition been present'. In particular the newspaper referred to the Boundary Agreement, 'which had been an eye-opener'. Welcoming the coming extraordinary *ard-fheis* of Sinn Féin, the editor commented: 'Sooner or later an effective opposition will have to be formed in the Dáil and for this reason, the extraordinary *ard-fheis*, if it but clears the air, is a very important factor.'[5]

The Republican political organ, *An Phoblacht*, welcomed the decision to hold this extraordinary *ard-fheis*. But it counselled that it was commonsense 'to think that the *ard-fheis* will have enough foresight and wisdom to find some common platform upon which all shades of Republican opinion within the organisation can agree and, at the same time, go forward more actively.'[6]

In the meantime the political parties began to focus on the two by-elections that were due to be called in a short time, as a result of the death of Darrell Figgis, Dublin County, and the disqualification of Seán McGuinness, Republican TD for Leix-Offaly, after he received a prison sentence for assaulting Civic Guards. To complicate matters further, McGuinness had since escaped from Mountjoy Gaol.[7]

Sinn Féiners believed that their party was making some headway, slowly in some places, rapidly in others. Members of the general public were, in the words of *An Phoblacht*, 'beginning to talk openly of the day when the Republicans will be strong enough to oust Mr Cosgrave'.[8] Could this progress be maintained in these two coming by-elections?

At a meeting of the Standing Committee of Sinn Féin in mid-January some members were surprised when President de Valera brought up the question of whether or not Sinn Féin should contest the by-elections in Leix-Offaly and Dublin County. The Standing Committee had received some letters giving different opinions as to what action they should take. A long discussion took place and opinions varied as to the best course of action. In the end de Valera asked for a preliminary indication of opinion by a show of hands from those present. Twenty members were in favour of contesting

Leix-Offaly and five were against. Fifteen favoured contesting County Dublin and thirteen were against. The secretary was instructed to notify the local sections of the organisation and to ask for their considered proposals in the circumstances.[9]

Seán Lemass continued his series of articles for *An Phoblacht*. He was more straightforward in his language than in 1925, now that the extraordinary Sinn Féin *ard-fheis* was fast-approaching. In the issue of the newspaper published in the third week of January he wrote: 'There are some who would have us sit by the roadside and debate obtuse [sic] points about a *de jure* and a *de facto* this or that, but the reality we want is away in the distance and we cannot get there unless we move.'[10] In a more explicit article a week later, Lemass referred to the 100 per cent perfection aspiration that Republicans had always been prone to demand. 'The people,' he wrote 'will not return to Republicanism because Republicanism asks too much from them – the overthrow of seven hundred years' domination in a single effort.'[11] He believed that the immediate objective of Republicans should be the removal of the Oath of Allegiance but he counselled that it must be an objective 'that the people can attain by their own strength and without war – above all it must be an objective capable of realisation within a reasonable period of time.'[12] In a subsequent article he emphasised that Sinn Féin should think of other important aspects of the nation's welfare besides the constitutional matters that took up so much of its time. He asked:

> Who could walk through the slums of Dublin and see the squalor and the misery which foreign domination has brought in its train and console himself with this grandiloquent philosophy? Who has known the blood of Easter Week, who has seen the horrors of Black and Tan regime and of the Civil War and can placidly contemplate their children enduring it all again? We must win and that soon.[13]

This question of the Oath of Allegiance to a foreign king had to be seriously tackled by Sinn Féin before the issue became entirely intractable. At a meeting of Roscommon County Council in late February 1926 a Councillor Hogg expressed the opinion that all county councillors and national teachers should have the Oath of Allegiance administered to them because, he claimed, some national teachers 'try to instil ideas into the minds of children that might be detrimental to the welfare of the country afterwards.' The editor of *An Phoblacht* commented sardonically: 'In the opinion of some (like Hogg) it is detrimental to have Gael occupying the land instead of Scotch or English planters.'[14]

At the request of the Standing Committee, Sinn Féin in Leix-Offaly held a convention on Sunday, 24 January, to consider the whole question of contesting the forthcoming by-election. This private conference took place in Clonaghdoo and lasted for four hours, chaired by Éamon de Valera, accompanied by Laurence Brady, Republican TD for the constituency, and Éamon Donnelly MP, Armagh. The fact that de Valera presided shows that the local Sinn Féin Party may have had divided opinions on whether they should fight the by-election at all. However the delegates decided to enter the contest and chose Art O'Connor as their candidate. Art had failed to win a seat in Kildare in the 1923 general election. He was at this time Minister for Economics in the Republican Second Dáil cabinet. He was a surprise choice because it was generally believed at that time that he rejected de Valera's new policy of entering Dáil Éireann if the Oath of Allegiance were abolished. The Standing Committee of Sinn Féin endorsed his candidature so that the people of Leix-Offaly 'should be afforded the opportunity of re-affirming their loyalty to the ideal of the Irish Republic free and undivided.'[15]

Two other candidates were nominated to fight the by-election in opposition to Art O'Connor. Cumann na nGaedheal selected thirty-nine-year-old James Dwyer. He was from Borris-in-Ossory and Vice-Chairman of Leix County Council. John F. Gill, Edenderry, organising secretary for the ITGWU, was selected as the Labour candidate.

A slight majority of the Standing Committee of Sinn Féin was still in favour of fighting the County Dublin by-election and the committee requested Liam Gilmore, a representative from that area, to convene a local convention to select a candidate. Count Plunkett TD (Roscommon) was appointed by the Standing Committee to represent them at the convention[16], which was held at the end of January 1926. After long deliberation, the County Dublin Sinn Féin executive decided unanimously not to put forward a candidate. They had two reasons for their decision. In the first instance they pointed out that they had outstanding debts, no funds on hand and no prospect of raising any. Secondly, in the circumstances that prevailed with the possibility of a critical change in Sinn Féin policy in the near future, the selection of a candidate might give rise to a division in their ranks.[17] The Standing Committee accepted the executive's decision but there was a feeling that clouds of dissension were beginning to gather.

At this time, representatives of many shades of political thought both from the twenty-six counties and Northern Ireland came together in the Mansion House and, after a long discussion, formed a new constitutional party that they named 'Clann Éireann' or 'The People's Party'. Professor Magennis, a former NUI Cumann na nGaedheal TD, became leader of the party. Other prominent members of the committee were P. Ó Máille TD, Leas-Cheann Comhairle [Deputy Speaker] of the Dáil, who had previously made a attempt to form a new party; Senator Colonel Maurice Moore; Dr P. McCartan; ex-Colonel Jerry Ryan, Thurles; Seán Gibbons, ex-Cumann na nGaedheal TD and ex -National Group from Carlow-Kilkenny and C.M. Byrne, ex-Cumann na nGaedheal TD, Wicklow. This committee also included several War of Independence veterans.[18] Part of its policy aimed to restore the unity of the territory of Ireland and to do away with the Oath of Allegiance.[19] The proposed new party intended to enter the Free State Dáil and act in opposition to the Cumann na nGaedheal government. Professor William Magennis later explained the general policy of Clann Éireann and how it differed from the principles of Éamon de Valera and his followers:

> While de Valera aimed at unity and sovereign independence,
> he (de Valera) and his followers would not go to Leinster House
> because they regarded the Oath as something contrary to their
> principles. Clann Éireann took no such view but held that they
> should make use of every agency that came to their hand.[20]

No doubt de Valera saw that a new party such as this could be a threat to Sinn Féin, which was still functioning as an abstentionist party.

The Republicans opened their Leix-Offaly election campaign with great gusto on the last Sunday in January. A torchlight procession accompanied the speakers to the Town Hall, Portlaoise. De Valera described the candidate, Art O'Connor, 'as a man who would not run away from his Republican principles.'[21]

The Labour Party leader, Thomas Johnson TD, addressed a party meeting in Edenderry, County Offaly: 'We would be prepared to abolish the Oath of Allegiance or any other Oath, but we are not going to let it stand in the way of our service to the working-class people, no matter to whom the Oath might be.'[22]

At a Cumann na nGaedheal meeting in Abbeyleix, Paddy Hogan, Free State Minister for Agriculture, said the government would not abolish the Oath of Allegiance to get de Valera out of his dilemma. 'Well they can make their minds easy: we are not going to reopen the issue to save de Valera's face.'[23]

The by-elections in County Dublin and in Leix-Offaly were held on 18 February. In County Dublin, William Norton (Labour), general secretary of the Postal Workers' Union, caused a big surprise when he emerged victorious in a three-cornered contest with Thomas F. Healy (Cumann na nGaedheal) and Patrick Belton (Independent). It was the first by-election that the Labour Party had won and increased the strength of the party to fifteen. The *Irish Independent* wrote: 'The result of the election in County Dublin is a severe disappointment to the government.'[24]

The result of the first count in Leix-Offaly was as follows:

James J. Dwyer (Cumann na nGaedheal): 16,618
Art O'Connor (Republican):15,400
John F. Gill (Labour): 9187

When Gill was eliminated his second preferences were distributed: Art O'Connor got 3123 and James Dwyer 2727. There was a large non-transferable vote – 3337 in all. The Republicans were disappointed that more Labour supporters had not given Art O'Connor their second preferences.

The final figures gave Cumann na nGaedheal a majority of 822 votes over Sinn Féin and Dwyer was declared elected. *An Phoblacht* commented: 'The cause of the Republican failure to capture Leix-Offaly was, of course, the failure of Labour electors to give their second preferences to O'Connor. Had the 'plumpers' for Gill carried out the suggestion of their own leaders the seat would not have been carried by the bitterest opponent Labour has.'[25] Cumann na nGaedheal gained a seat previously held by Sinn Féin. But the result showed an increase of 4000 in the Republican vote, continuing a pattern that started in the Dublin South by-election of 1923.[26] Many committed Sinn Féiners like Tom Maguire, a member of the Second Dáil and a serving Republican TD for Mayo South, were happy with this consistent improvement in their voting strength and did not agree with Éamon de Valera that they could not achieve a Dáil majority without ending their abstention policy.[27]

A letter from the Standing Committee of Sinn Féin gave a detailed description of de Valera's motion for the extraordinary *ard-fheis* of the movement to be held on 9 March. Far from being a short statement, it contained six sub-sections, each emphasising a different aspect of the proposal. Section two was crucial, stating: 'At the next general election it shall be the policy of the organisation (Sinn Féin) to put forward candidates, who, if elected, will assert their right to enter any assembly where the other elected representatives of the people meet for public business without having as a preliminary to deny publicly the national faith.' The next section described how the Sinn Féin representatives would act once the Oath of Allegiance no longer existed: they would enter the Dáil and 'use it in the national interest, this line of action being the most peaceful, and under existing conditions, the most effective way of working politically towards the achievement of Republican aims.'[28]

The Sinn Féin Standing Committee also informed all local branches of the organisation that Reverend Michael O'Flanagan, Leas-Uachtarán (Vice-President) Sinn Féin, had given notice that he intended to propose a direct negative to de Valera's proposal. His motion was straightforward: 'That it is incompatible with the fundamental principles of Sinn Féin, as it is injurious to the honour of Ireland, to send representatives into any usurping legislature set up by English law in Ireland.'[29]

Seán Lemass TD, referring to Father Michael O'Flanagan's motion, stated that he (Lemass) had come to the conclusion that Father O'Flanagan was under the impression 'that he was a kind of spiritual chaplain and political pope to the Sinn Féin organisation.'[30]

The Sinn Féin honorary secretaries, Austin Stack and Dáithí Ó Donnchadha, directed that a special meeting of each *cumann* of Sinn Féin should be held to discuss the issues involved in the two conflicting resolutions and to elect delegates to represent them at the extraordinary *ard-fheis*. The Standing Committee suggested to all these bodies 'that they consider the advisability of leaving their delegates free to decide each question when they have weighed the arguments put forward at the *ard-fheis*.' Éamon de Valera concurred with this view[31] but Stack and Ó Donnchadha, secretaries of Sinn Féin, pointed out: 'The bodies (*cumainn*) concerned are free and have the right to act as they themselves think best.'[32]

The various branches of Sinn Féin held meetings very soon after they received the circular and covering letter. Some area branches (*comhairlí ceanntair*) like Bandon, County Cork, decided to send a delegate to the extraordinary *ard-fheis* but directed that 'said delegate must be instructed to voice the considered opinion of his collective *cumann* and to vote accordingly.'[33]

There was a feeling throughout the whole Sinn Féin organisation that these two conflicting resolutions might lead to a serious split in the Republican movement. Frank Gallagher, a well-known Sinn Féin activist for many years, wrote to *An Phoblacht* advising that the discussion on the resolutions should be 'kept free from every hint of that passion and personal abuse to which, God help us, we Gaels are so greatly given.'[34] Many members of Sinn Féin, having discussed the position at their local *cumainn* meetings, expressed through branch resolutions the view that they would prefer if this extraordinary *ard-fheis* had never been called at all. Tralee's Roger Casement *cumann* unanimously moved that the resolutions of both de Valera and Father Michael O'Flanagan be withdrawn from the agenda of the *ard-fheis* without discussion.[35] Waterford *dáil-cheanntar* proposed that: 'as the question of the removal of the Oath from the Free State Constitution is still a hypothetical matter, no decision be taken at the *ard-fheis*.'[36] Wexford *Comhairle Ceanntair* called on the Standing Committee 'to take steps to secure the closer unity of the organisation by setting up a joint committee.'[37] The general feedback from grassroots Sinn Féin members was that they did not support any change of policy that would cause the party to split. However there were many in the party who were convinced that, come what may, a decision could not be put off any longer.

The extraordinary *ard-fheis* of Sinn Féin was held in the Rotunda, Dublin on Tuesday 9 March 1926. There was a very large and representative attendance of five hundred delegates for this *ard-fheis* that was to mark a watershed in the history of Sinn Féin. The morning session was occupied with explaining de Valera's resolution but the actual motion was not moved because some delegates proposed that, in the interests of party unity, it should not be discussed at all. However, this proposal was defeated.

After the lunch break Éamon de Valera proposed: 'That Sinn Féin elected deputies enter the Dáil or Six-County assembly if the Oath of Allegiance were removed.' P.J. Ruttledge TD (Mayo North) seconded the proposal. Father O'Flanagan then proposed his amendment and M. Smith (Cavan) seconded this motion. A full discussion followed which concluded only at 10.30pm, without any decision being reached. This entire sitting had lasted for twelve hours and thirty-five delegates had spoken on the motions.[38] The *ard-fheis* then adjourned until Wednesday morning.

It had become clear during the day that there were three sections involved in the debate. These were: (a) supporters of de Valera's new policy; (b) those in opposition to it; and (c) the in-between group, a large body of delegates who did not wish to see the issue put to a vote lest this cause a split.

The *ard-fheis* reconvened on Wednesday morning and the discussions resumed. Many delegates spoke but each speech was limited to five minutes. In the course of the debate Mary MacSwiney commented that so far as going into Leinster House was concerned: 'Once the first step is taken the descent into hell would be easy.'[39] It was then decided that Father Michael O'Flanagan should speak for fifteen minutes on his amendment and Éamon de Valera for fifteen minutes on his resolution and that the vote should be taken without further discussion.[40] Father O'Flanagan's amendment was put to the conference at 6pm. It was carried by 223 votes to 218 – a majority of five.[41]

Subsequently Father Michael O'Flanagan asked for permission to withdraw the words 'as it is injurious to the honour of Ireland' from his motion as some members considered that it belittled the genuine motives of de Valera and those who supported him. Permission was granted and the altered amendment was put as a substantive motion. To the surprise of many delegates the new version of the motion proposed by Father Michael O'Flanagan was this time rejected by two votes, 179 to 177. But a comparison of the two results showed that seventy-five fewer delegates had voted on this substantive motion. The second vote was taken at 11pm – five hours after the first vote – and the likelihood was that a large number of the country delegates had gone home before the second vote was completed. The fact that the substantive motion was rejected caused confusion.

The *ard-fheis* sat for a third day from 10 am on Thursday. The confusion caused by the defeat of Father Michael O'Flanagan's substantive motion was quickly cleared up when de Valera made a remarkable statement. He said that he was compelled to regard the decisions taken by the *ard-fheis* the previous day as a vote against his policy.[42] Under the circumstances he felt obliged to tender his resignation as President of Sinn Féin.[43] He had held this position since 1917, through many very turbulent years. During his short speech de Valera added:

> I feel that we are not going to win back the people of Ireland by
> the attitude which we are taking up…Things are settling down.
> The Free State junta is solidifying itself as an institution…If
> these people (Cumann na nGaedheal) get firmly fixed and you
> get the economic interests of Ireland fixed, there will be no place
> in Ireland for a national political party.[44]

Had de Valera won the vote it is likely that he would have remained on as president and retained the name 'Sinn Féin' for his party and that the defeated supporters of Father Michael O'Flanagan would have been obliged to establish a new party.[45] But as it turned out, de Valera lost. After his resignation speech, he proposed that Mary MacSwiney take the chair for the moment. He urged the necessity for future cooperation between both sections of Sinn Féin.[46] Mary MacSwiney echoed de Valera's plea for cooperation. She suggested that the *ard-fheis* adjourn for an interval, that each section meet separately to discuss their positions and that the whole *ard-fheis* reassemble later in the day in order to find a basis for cooperation. A motion to this effect was made by Seán Lemass TD, seconded by Gobnait Ní Bhruadair from Ballinacoona, County Kerry, and when put to a vote it was carried.[47] When the *ard-fheis* reassembled once again at 3pm, it was announced that joint committees for cooperation had been established and the following resolution was passed unanimously:

> That the joint committees be given full powers on behalf of the Sinn Féin organisation to deal with all matters arising out of the present situation and to make all necessary arrangements for cooperation. Meantime the *cumainn* and *comhairlí ceanntair* will carry on work as usual. The important message which goes from this *ard-fheis* is that the division within our ranks is a division of Republicans who are unanimous on this fundamental issue: – that in no circumstances can any Republican take an Oath of Allegiance to an alien king or assent to the partition of our country.[48]

Before the final adjournment of the *ard-fheis*, Father Michael O'Flanagan proposed that all the delegates express their feelings of admiration for President de Valera. Mary MacSwiney, seconding, said that the organisation and the country owed a huge debt of gratitude to Éamon de Valera. One delegate described de Valera as the greatest Irishman for a century. As the *ard-fheis* came to a close, the delegates rose and expressed their great respect for Dev by acclamation.[49] However, not all de Valera's former Sinn Féin colleagues were in accord with this. Dr Kathleen Lynn TD (Dublin County), who backed Father Michael O'Flanagan's resolution, wrote in her diary about the three-day debate: 'Antagonism crept in at once and was not all relieved…I can't say Dev showed up very well.'[50]

The news of de Valera's resignation became known in the Dáil through the early edition of the *Evening Herald*. The Ceann Comhairle, Seán Nolan TD, handed a copy of the newspaper to President W.T. Cosgrave. As Cosgrave was reading the report, Kevin O'Higgins, Ernest Blythe and Professor Marcus O'Sullivan bent over to read the headline. They passed the newspaper to Patrick McGilligan and finally to Peter Hughes. Kevin O'Higgins smiled and whispered a few words to President Cosgrave.[51]

The *Gaelic-American* newspaper, speculating on Éamon de Valera's likely successor as President of Sinn Féin, named Mary MacSwiney as a possible contender – 'if the rank and file are satisfied to be ruled by a woman.'[52]

Reaction to the resignation of Éamon de Valera in the provincial newspapers was varied. The *Sligo Champion* said: 'He had been beaten with his own rod.' The *Tipperary Star* reported: 'The extremist section apparently has carried the day.' The Republican *Dundalk Examiner*, which was sympathetic to Dev, predicted: 'A new party, with a new political policy, with such a leader as de Valera could develop into a very strong political force.'[53]

Republican grassroots waited and wondered what was coming next. One thing was apparent: this extraordinary *ard-fheis* had resulted in the termination of the third Sinn Féin Party – Republican Sinn Féin.

Notes

1. The *Irish Independent*, 7 January 1926.
2. *An Phoblacht*, 22 January 1926.
3. *Ibid.*, 15 January 1926.
4. The *Irish Independent*, 14 January 1926.
5. *An Phoblacht*, 22 January 1926.
6. *Ibid.*
7. The *Irish Independent*, 13 January 1926.
8. *An Phoblacht*, 29 January 1926.
9. NAI, File 2B/82/117/25, Minutes of Standing Committee of Sinn Féin, 18 January 1926.
10. *An Phoblacht*, 22 January 1926.
11. *Ibid.*, 29 January 1926.
12. *Ibid.*
13. *Ibid.*, 5 February 1926.
14. *Ibid.*
15. The *Irish Independent*, 26 January 1926.

16. NAI, File 2B.82/117/25, minutes of the Standing Committee Sinn Féin, 25 January 1926.
17. *Ibid.*, 30 January 1926.
18. *Ibid.*, 26 January 1926 and *The Irish Times*, 26 January 1926. The full committee of Clann Éireann was as follows: Chairman: Professor William Magennis TD; Vice-Chairmen: Senator Colonel Maurice Moore; Dr P. McCartan; Mr Éamon Martin; Treasurer: P. Moylett; Honorary Secretaries: P. Ó Máille TD; M. Fitzgerald; Committee: ex-Colonel Jerry Ryan, Thurles; Seán Gibbons, Kilkenny; D. McDevitt, Derry; Liam Langley; Joseph Stanley, Dublin; Mrs O'Shea-Clancy, Dublin; C. M. Byrne TD; F. O'Donohoe (O'Donoghue), Cork and Mr Gantley, Skerries.
19. The *Irish Independent*, 26 January 1926.
20. *Ibid.*, 17 April 1926.
21. *Ibid.*, 1 February 1926.
22. *Ibid.*
23. *Ibid.*, 18 February 1926.
24. *Ibid.*, 20 February 1926.
25. *An Phoblacht*, 26 February 1926.
26. In the eighteen by-elections contested by Sinn Féin in the Irish Free State from October, 1923 to February 1926, Republicans, with one exception – Dublin South in 1925 – increased the vote they had received in the 1923 general election. The following table shows their gains and losses.

Date	Constituency	Gain/Loss (% or votes)
1923	Dublin South	21% to 33%
1923	NUI	+ 24 votes
1924	Dublin South	33% to 42%
1924	Dublin County	14% to 24%
1924	Limerick	+ 10, 384
1924	Cork Borough	+ 6263
1924	Cork East	+ 5268
1924	Donegal	+ 5304
1924	Mayo North	+ 4184
1924	Dublin South	+ 4151
1925	Leitrim-Sligo	+ 2678
1925	Mayo North	+ 3014
1925	Roscommon	+ 2016
1925	Dublin North	+ 5797
1925	Dublin South	-3397
1925	Cavan	+ 3795
1925	Carlow-Kilkenny	+ 6835
1926	Dublin County	not contested by Sinn Féin
1926	Leix-Offaly	+ 4380

27. Uinseann Mac Eoin, *Survivors*, p. 300.
28. *An Phoblacht*, 19 February 1926 and the *Irish Independent*, 12 February 1926.
29. The *Irish Independent*, 12 February 1926.
30. NAI, File 2b/82/116/6. p. 6, Sinn Féin Funds case.
31. Peter Pyne, 'The Third Sinn Féin Party: 1923-1926', p. 46.
32. *An Phoblacht*, 19 February 1926.
33. *Ibid.*
34. *Ibid.*, 5 March 1926.
35. *Ibid.*
36. *Ibid.*
37. *Ibid.*
38. Peter Pyne, *op. cit.*, p. 46.
39. Mary Bromage, *De Valera and the March of a Nation*, p. 219.
40. *An Phoblacht*, 16 April 1926.
41. *Ibid.* and the *Irish Independent*, 10 March 1926.
    To understand how the Sinn Féin organisation divided almost equally on this issue it is interesting to note the prominent Sinn Féin members who spoke at the extraordinary *ard-fheis* in support

of Father Michael O'Flanagan's amendment and those who spoke in the same debate in favour of
Éamon de Valera's new policy motion.

*Among those who spoke in support of Father Michael O'Flanagan's amendment which won the vote
were*:
Rev Michael O'Flanagan (Vice-President); M. Smith (Cavan); J. Kenny (Miltown-Malbay, County
Clare); P. Murney (Newry); L. Slattery (Harold's Cross, Dublin); Seán Ó Ceallaigh; Count Plunkett
TD (Roscommon and Standing Committee); Cluad de Cheabhasa (Standing Committee); Mary
MacSwiney TD (Cork Borough) ; Éamon Donnelly Republican MP (Armagh); Austin Stack TD
(Kerry and honorary secretary); Gobnait Ní Bhruadair (Kerry); Dr John Madden TD (Mayo
North); Liam Paul (Standing Committee); J. Mitchell (Brothers Breslin Cumann, Dublin); Miss
M. Daly (*Comhairle Ceanntair*, Limerick City); P. Mac Aindriú, (Shragh Cumann); W. Ahearn
(Killarney); Reverend Father O'Connell (London); Dr Kathleen Lynn TD (Dublin County);
Countess Plunkett (Ballsbridge, Dublin); Miss L. Coventry (Standing Committee); Seán
O'Mahoney (Standing Committee); Art O'Connor (Standing Committee); Dáithí Ó Donnchadha
(honorary secretary); Brian O'Higgins TD (County Clare); Máire Comerford (Gorey *Comhairle
Ceanntair*); Tom Maguire TD (Mayo South); Seán Buckley TD (Cork West).

Among those who spoke in support President de Valera's motion, which was defeated, were:
Éamon de Valera TD (County Clare); P.J. Ruttledge TD (Mayo North); Michael Comyn (County
Clare and Standing Committee); Seán Lemass TD (Dublin South); Kathleen Clarke (Dublin);
Hanna Sheehy Skeffington (Standing Committee,); R. Brennan (Ranelagh, Dublin); Rev S. Ó
Ceallaigh (Connemara *Comhairle Ceanntair*, Spiddal); Séamus Robinson (formerly Tipperary);
P. Morrissey (Ranelagh, Dublin); R. Ivers (Fitzwilliam, Dublin); M.J. Corry (County Cork and
Standing Committee); Miss Jacob (Mansion House, Dublin); J. Barry (Charleville, Cork); Patrick
Bryan (Kilkenny); M. Bowles (Dromond and Sligo *Comhairle Ceanntair*,); P. O'Donovan (Sligo);
P. Moloney (Roscrea); Dr H. MacPartland (Ennis); P. O' Donnell TD (Donegal); Séamus Fitzgerald
(Cork); Madame Markievicz TD (Dublin South); Gerry Boland TD (Roscommon); Frank Fahy
TD (Galway); Dr Patrick McCarvill TD (Monaghan); Seán MacEntee (Standing Committee); Mrs
Margaret Pearse (Standing Committee); J. O'Dwyer (Kilrush *Comhairle Ceanntair*); Linda Kearns
(Dublin); Frank Carty TD (Leitrim-Sligo); D.L. Robinson; Michael McSweeney (Kilkenny); P.
Corry (Leix); T. Tynan (Offaly); Reverend T. Burbage CC (Geashill, County Offaly).

42.   The *Irish Independent*, 12 March 1926.
43.   *An Phoblacht*, 16 April 1926.
44.   Maurice Moynihan (ed.), *Speeches and Statements by Éamon de Valera 1917-73*, pp. 129, 130.
45.   Peter Pyne, *op. cit.*, p. 46.
46.   *An Phoblacht*, 16 April 1926.
47.   *Ibid.*
48.   The *Irish Independent*, 12 March 1926.
49.   *Ibid.*
50.   J. Anthony Gaughan, *Austin Stack: Portrait of a Separatist*, p. 253.
51.   The *Irish Independent*, 12 March 1926.
52.   The *Gaelic-American*, 3 April 1926.
53.   The *Irish Independent*, 15 March 1926.

11

The Founding of Fianna Fáil

A few days after the *ard-fheis*, de Valera wrote a letter to Joe McGarrity, his old friend in the US:

> For over a year – since the nine bye-elections, I have been convinced that the programme on which we were working would not win the people in the present conditions. It was too high and too sweeping. The Oath, on the other hand, is a definite objective within reasonable striking distance. If I can mass the people to smash it, I shall have them on the march again, and once moving, and having tasted victory, further advances will be possible…You perhaps will wonder why I did not wait longer. It is vital that the Free State be shaken at the next general election…It seems to me a case of now or never – at least in our time.[1]

In the by-elections to which de Valera alluded, Sinn Féin had won only two of the nine vacant seats and although he put as brave a face as he could on the results he now admitted to McGarrity that he was disappointed and discouraged by that outcome.

Éamon de Valera did not bring all Sinn Féin's sincere Republicans with him in his new departure. One of the most dedicated was Dr Kathleen Lynn, the only elected Republican deputy for County Dublin. Around this time Kathleen wrote in her diary, 'He (Dev) left us, diehards, in possession of the Republic. It is best so may there be no bitterness. DG [Deo Gratias] the uncompromised Republic stands.'[2]

The Standing Committee of Sinn Féin came together on 15 March but it was a poignant occasion: many of the most enthusiastic members who had worked conscientiously and efficiently for the organisation since the split over the Treaty were now missing. Mary MacSwiney TD (Cork Borough) chaired the meeting. The secretary recorded the names of the twenty-one members present[3] and at least thirteen familiar faces were absent.[4] (Michael Colivet, Limerick, was absent, although uncommitted to either side at this stage.)

One member of the Standing Committee asked if the two committees set up at the *ard-fheis* to explore possible grounds for cooperation had issued any report. No correspondence had been received from these committees as to whether they had found any basis for agreement. The Standing Committee decided to request them to complete their deliberations without delay and to make an immediate report of their findings.

Éamon de Valera's policy of getting rid of the Oath of Allegiance as a first step received a boost when Reverend Father Sweetman OSB, late of Mount St Benedict, Gorey, County Wexford, referred to the unhappy divisions among the Irish people in a sermon in Swansea on St Patrick's Day. Alluding to the Oath of Allegiance still required by Britain and by the Free State government, he declared:

> I regard such an Oath to a foreign king as a degradation to Ireland and an insult to Almighty God in so far as it gives to a creature the honour which is due to God alone. I have always sympathised with those who refused to take such an Oath, and because of these sympathies I myself and my brother monks were banished from Ireland.[5]

A few days later, Mary MacSwiney, looking into the future, predicted that those who supported the entry of Republicans into his 'Majesty's parliament' [the Free State Dáil] would one day be responsible for the gaoling of Republicans. She added: 'They may walk out when the day comes but how much better never to walk in.'[6]

The Standing Committee of Sinn Féin soon met again. In addition to those present the previous week, Art O'Connor, Charles Murphy TD (Dublin South), Financial Secretary of Sinn Féin, and Éamon Donnelly MP (Armagh), Director of Organisation, attended. Austin Stack TD (Kerry), Secretary of Sinn Féin, was absent due to illness and Dáithí Ceannt TD (Cork East) also sent his apology for non-attendance.

Members of *Comhairle na dTeachtaí* received notice of a meeting to be held on Sunday 28 March 1926, called to make a decision on the following motion to be proposed by Mary MacSwiney:

> The entry of any member of Dáil Éireann (Second Dáil) into the Free State parliament or any other parliament established by English law is incompatible with membership of the *de jure* government of the Republic (the Second Dáil) and inconsistent with the principles and policy advocated by Republican *teachtaí* and candidates since 1922.[7]

More than forty members of *Comhairle na dTeachtaí* attended this meeting. Éamon de Valera was in attendance. Mary MacSwiney, introducing her resolution, claimed that the Second Dáil was still the lawful government. It was the successor of the First Dáil set up on 21 January 1919 and it had never been dissolved. She added that if a Republican went into the Free State parliament he would forfeit his right to membership of the Republican Second Dáil: 'If you go into the Free State parliament as a minority party, you cannot get the Oath removed. If you are a majority party you don't need to go in at all.'[8] Peadar O'Donnell, the Donegal TD, was anxious to avoid a split at all costs. He asked why they could not continue with *Comhairle na dTeachtaí*, have a majority party in power in that assembly and an opposition minority party in that body as well.[9] Dáithí Ceannt, the steadfast Sinn Féin TD for Cork East, said that the Oath was not the only obstacle preventing Republicans from entering the Free State parliament: 'In my case I object to more than the King's name, I object to the Free State, the Constitution, partition, and the Governor-General.'[10] In the course of a heated discussion Seán Buckley, the Sinn Féin TD for Cork West, asked 'What is Dáil Éireann anyway?'[11] J.J.

O'Kelly who was Ceann Comhairle of *Comhairle na dTeachtaí,* answered: 'The faithful members of the Second Dáil constitute Dáil Éireann.'[12] M.P. Colivet (Limerick), a member of the Second Dáil, proposed two amendments to alter the wording of Mary MacSwiney's motion. Both amendments were passed and as a result two sentences of the resolution were excised. The amended proposal that went before the meeting was:

> That the entry of any member of Dáil Éireann into the Free State parliament or any other parliament established by English law is inconsistent with the policy advocated by Republican *teachtaí* and candidates since 1922.

The motion was passed by twenty-six votes to fifteen.[13] Éamon de Valera then said that he did not accept that this vote definitely rejected the new policy he was putting forward of entering the Free State parliament if the Oath of Allegiance were abolished. He suggested that a vote of no confidence in himself and his executive was the proper way of solving the matter. 'Resignation on my part might be misrepresented as desertion of my post. If I am not the proper person, then your duty is to remove me and put someone in my place.'[14] He said he could not see anything wrong with his policy. 'Is there anything wrong about releasing one prisoner if we have the key because we haven't a key for the other.'[15] Here he was referring to the stepping-stone principle of getting rid of the Oath of Allegiance first and then, as a Republican, tackling the other repugnant articles of the Treaty.

The meeting adjourned at 7.30pm and resumed at 9pm. Mary MacSwiney reopened the proceedings by proposing a more definite and clearly-focused resolution: 'That this assembly does not approve of the policy outlined by the President.'[16]

Dr Kathleen Lynn seconded the proposition.

President de Valera, realising the clear-cut nature of this proposal, said: 'I look upon this as an indirect way of asking for my resignation.'[17] When the motion was put to the meeting, Mary MacSwiney's motion was carried by the narrowest of margins, nineteen votes to eighteen, with some *Comhairle na* dTeachtaí members not voting at all. President de Valera said, 'I regard this as a vote of no confidence and there is no course open to me but to resign the executive position.'[18]

The Sinn Féin ard-fheis had already rejected Éamon de Valera's new departure. Now Comhairle na dTeachtaí opposed it. The majority of the members of two fundamental Republican organisations had gone against him.

The members of Comhairle na dTeachtaí again came together on the following day, 29 March. Early in the proceedings President de Valera said, 'I would find it awkward to represent a body whose confidence I have not. I suggest that the majority party appoint its executive and I am willing to give any help I can.'[19]

Mary MacSwiney said she believed that the only way that Comhairle na dTeachtaí could carry on was to keep 'the uncompromising Republic'.[20] J.J. O'Kelly thought that the President 'should set himself free to go out… and that the representative of the majority party should be chairman in the meantime.'[21]

Then Mary MacSwiney proposed 'that Art O'Connor be appointed chief executive officer until the next meeting.'[22] (O'Connor was the defeated candidate in the recent by-election in Leix-Offaly.) The motion was carried. The members of the Comhairle who remained faithful to de Valera did not vote at all.

At these meetings of Comhairle na dTeachtaí on 28 and 29 March 1926, Mary MacSwiney had become a 'king-breaker' and a 'king-maker', all in the course of two days, as she was able to muster enough support to get her proposals through.

At the end of March the joint committees appointed by the extraordinary ard-fheis to explore possible grounds for cooperation between the two divergent sections of Sinn Féin made their report to the Standing Committee. They had held three joint meetings at which they discussed the possibilities of future cooperation. The committees concluded that it was not possible to arrive at any agreement by which the former unity of the Sinn Féin organisation could be preserved. Art O'Connor, chairman of the joint meetings, signed the report. Republicans who remained uncommitted to either party were disappointed with the conclusions reached by these committees. The meeting ended on a sad note when ten prominent members of the Standing Committee tendered their resignations from that body: Seán Lemass TD; Gerry Boland TD; Seán MacEntee; J.J. Cullen; P.J. Brennan; Dr J.P. Brennan; Linda Kearns; Michael Comyn; Donnchadh Ó h-Éaluighthe and P. Caffrey. Their resignations were accepted on the motion of Mary MacSwiney, seconded by P.J. Bowen.[23] The decision of these individuals to leave the Standing Committee began a torrent of resignations from Sinn Féin by less prominent members.

Tod Andrews, a prominent Dublin Sinn Féiner, commented later on why he resigned from Sinn Féin: 'I was very much for going into the Dáil, if the Oath of Allegiance were abolished. But many of the people I knew were very anti-Dáil, particularly the women, including my own future wife, though she changed her mind before we got married.'[24] *An Phoblacht*, continuing its policy of endeavouring to keep the two sections together, reminded Republicans of either persuasion that 'while there are two policies and two groups there is one movement, grounded on the same ideals of an Éire Gaelic and free, with one objective, the full realisation of the Republic.'[25]

It was decided to fill the vacancies on the Standing Committee by co-opting new members in place of those who had resigned. Among those co-opted were Caitlín Brugha, wife of the late Cathal Brugha, and at that time Republican TD for Waterford; Brian O'Higgins, Sinn Féin TD for Clare; Gobnait Ní Bhruadair, Kerry; Laurence Raul and Margaret Buckley, from the Glasnevin *Cumann*, Sinn Féin. Caitlín Brugha was appointed treasurer.[26] Not unexpectedly, as she supported de Valera's new policy, Madame Markievicz TD resigned from the Standing Committee and her resignation was accepted with regret.[27]

Mary MacSwiney wrote to Joe McGarrity in the USA:

It has been a tremendous lesson to the country that de Valera, in spite of his great personality and the love we all have for him, was not able to gain the majority for this compromise either in

the *ard-fheis* or in Dáil Éireann (the Second Republican Dáil).
We know that he himself will never do anything to disgrace the
country, even though he is letting down the government of the
Republic (Second Dáil), but I greatly fear that just as Collins and
Griffith went over his head and carried the compromise further
than he was prepared to go in 1921, so his present and future
followers may, some of them, do the same.[28]

There were further meetings between the rival Republican groups to seek
out some cooperation but, disappointingly, no progress was made. As he left
one of these meetings, Éamon de Valera told Seán Lemass and Gerry Boland,
both of whom agreed with his new departure, that he was thinking strongly of
resigning altogether from politics. 'I have done all I can,' he said. Both Lemass
and Boland told him that he could not leave them at that time. Lemass then
proposed a new organisation to take the place of Sinn Féin.[29] De Valera did
not immediately agree with this proposition. Vivion, de Valera's eldest son,
later told Charles Haughey that Seán Lemass came out soon after that to de
Valera's home in Cross Avenue, Blackrock, and again said to de Valera, 'We
have to form a political party, we have to get into politics.'[30] This time he
convinced de Valera to set out on this course.

A few days later seven men came together in the home of Colonel Maurice
Moore in Sandymount to form a new party, Dublin: Éamon de Valera, Seán T.
O'Kelly, Seán MacEntee, Seán Lemass, Patrick Ruttledge, Dr James Ryan and
Gerry Boland. With great enthusiasm they founded a new organisation and
elected officers for this new party.

After this inaugural coming together, Éamon de Valera opened offices
in Dublin. The news surfaced in the *Irish Independent* and de Valera made a
statement to a representative of the newspaper:

We are ourselves forming a new organisation. An organising
committee with P.J. Ruttledge TD as chairman, Seán Lemass TD
and Gerald Boland TD as secretaries and Dr Jim Ryan TD and
Seán MacEntee as treasurers, are about to set to work at once...[31]

> We are convinced that the ideal of the majority of the Irish
> people is still broadly the Republican ideal – an Ireland united,
> free and Irish – and that the people can be banded together for
> the pursuit of that ideal…[32]

De Valera said to a representative of *An Phoblacht*: 'We believe that
Republicans ought not to stand aside and allow the country to be utterly
ruined and all except the imperialists to be driven out of it. We intend, at any
rate, to make a trial and see.'[33]

The name of this new party was causing much discussion. Éamon
de Valera wanted the name 'Fianna Fáil', which for him preserved all the
links with 1916. 'These should not be forgotten,' he said. Seán Lemass had
misgivings. He thought that fun would be made of the second part of the
name which, when pronounced in the English fashion, would denote 'failure'.
Lemass wanted the new organisation to be known as the 'Republican Party'.
De Valera got his way but Lemass was appeased when it was decided that
the name 'Republican Party' (enclosed in brackets) would follow the words
'Fianna Fáil'.[34] Lemass described Fianna Fáil as 'a slightly constitutional
Party'[35], a clever description aiming at keeping the old Republican supporters
as well as attracting support from moderates and neutrals.

Fianna Fáil appealed for more members for the party: 'There is a place in
the new organisation for all, who, with Pádraig Pearse, believe in one nation
and that free.'[36] But Gerry Boland admitted that in April 1926 the position
was desperate. 'We hadn't a penny or a journal. We were all abstentionist
TDs, mostly without jobs because of victimisation of one kind or another.'[37]
But there was still hope. Boland later added: 'In any event, all of us were
completely absorbed by politics. It was our whole life.'[38]

A tussle soon began to develop between Sinn Féin and the new Fianna Fáil
party. Sinn Féin wanted to hold on to its members while Éamon de Valera's
group wished to recruit new members. On 12 April 1926, the honorary
secretaries of Sinn Féin – Austin Stack and Dáithí Ó Donnchadha – sent out
instructions to every *comhairle ceanntair* and *cumann* of Sinn Féin to exhort
their members to stand firmly on the bedrock of the Republic proclaimed in

Easter Week, 1916. 'We call upon you to remain faithful to the organisation…
that has consistently refused to send representatives to the usurping
legislatures set up by English law in Ireland.' The circular also suggested that
each *comhairle ceanntair* and *cumann* convene a special meeting at which
they would declare without equivocation 'their allegiance to the Republic'.[39]

Éamon de Valera counteracted this move of Sinn Féin when he claimed:
'The men and women who make up my new party, who had previously
proved themselves willing to give their lives for Ireland, can be depended
upon to give at least ten years national service to the upbuilding of Ireland
with the minimum of remuneration.'[40]

The Fianna Fáil central organising committee held a meeting at 33 Lower
O'Connell Street on 26 April 1926. Prominent former Sinn Féin figures
present were Dr P. McCarvill TD, Monaghan (presiding); Seán Lemass TD,
Dublin South; Gerry Boland TD, Roscommon; Éamon de Valera TD, Clare;
and Thomas Derrig. Gerry Boland, who was secretary, stated in his report
that he had attended three conventions in Roscommon the previous weekend
and that a well-attended convention had been held in County Dublin.
Further conventions were arranged for Kildare, Wicklow, Leix, Offaly, Cork,
Tipperary and Sligo. Boland also reported that units of this new organisation
existed in every county in Ireland.[41]

At the beginning of May 1926, pro-abstentionists were prevailing by small
majorities at the higher levels of Sinn Féin. Of the forty-seven Republican
deputies who had been elected in the 1923 general election and in subsequent
by-elections up to February 1926, twenty-one were now on de Valera's side
but twenty-two had declared that they were against his new policy, while
the four remaining TDs remained uncommitted. Only seventeen of the
thirty-seven members of the Sinn Féin Standing Committee had resigned
and followed de Valera. However at grassroots level the number of *cumainn*
affiliated to Sinn Féin had dropped from 275 to 173 within a month of the
split.[42] Thousands of rank and file members left Sinn Féin to follow Dev into
Fianna Fáil, including many experienced secretaries of Sinn Féin *comhairlí
ceanntair* and *cumainn*.[43] Without a doubt, the Third Sinn Féin Party was
badly wounded.

P.J. Little, a competent editor of *An Phoblacht*, had left the Republican newspaper because he had become convinced that Éamon de Valera's new departure was right.[44] Peadar O'Donnell succeeded him as editor.

In a letter to some friends in the US, Mary MacSwiney wrote that she strongly believed that the new move of de Valera was unnecessary and would fail:

> We are feeling sore that de Valera has split our forces on a mere hypothesis, and that he and his followers are taking a course, to our minds, incompatible with practical allegiance to the existing Republic…We believe that this new policy will be a failure; that the Oath will not be removed until the country is ready to scrap the 'Treaty'.[45]

Where dissension did occur between the two parties, it was not a lethal falling-out as happened during the Civil War between pro-Treatyites and the anti-Treatyites: this 1926 split was a bloodless separation. The claims of both sides were argued in debate and much of the argument took place in the pages of *An Phoblacht*. In an article in that periodical, Dorothy Macardle, author of the *Irish Republic*, and at this time a supporter of Éamon de Valera and his new departure, slammed references Mary MacSwiney had previously made to de Valera's new policy:

> The difference (in policies) is largely one of temperament and it is good that the members of each group should be relieved of the kind of work that makes no appeal to them and be free to concentrate on the work to which they can bring enthusiasm and faith…Many Republicans have been feeling guilty for the last year and more, of a sin of omission, very grievous indeed – the sin of standing by almost idle while Ireland was being driven into even deeper bondage and despair…We have suffered a military defeat and it is impossible for a defeated people to live in their own country, outside or even inside the prisons, without

some compromise with the consequences…One towering barrier there is in the whole national situation…the Oath of Allegiance to the Treaty Constitution and faithfulness to the English king…That Oath, taken with a pretence of willingness by Irish representatives is the badge and emblem of the nation's servitude…The issue rests with the people. It is with the people at the general election that the decision will remain. They can abolish the Oath to England by their votes.[46]

William Norton, the new Labour TD for County Dublin, put pressure on Republicans to enter the Dáil and function as an effective opposition. Norton criticised Sinn Féin and the new Republican party, Fianna Fáil, for their lack of 'a bread and butter' policy. He condemned 'the fanatical nationalism which told hungry men and women that all they wanted was political freedom.'[47]

Fianna Fáil was established in County Kildare and the well-known priest, Father Burbage from County Offaly, who had backed the Republican cause all through the War of Independence and the Civil War, chaired the convention that was held in Newbridge. Domhnall Ó Buachalla, from Maynooth, was among those who addressed the County Kildare delegates.[48]

Fianna Fáil supporters showed great determination and enthusiasm in organising the party. Their TDs spent very few evenings at home but were busy in their own constituencies or travelling to various constituencies throughout the country. Gerry Boland remarked that there was not a village or town in Ireland in which he did not have a friend whom he had first met in jail or on the hills during the War of Independence or Civil War. A big factor in the success of organising Fianna Fáil lay in jail contacts that the leaders had made in British and Irish prisons during those years of conflict.[49]

Sinn Féin wished to remain an All-Ireland political party rather than a twenty-six-county organisation and at a meeting of the Standing Committee in early May they decided to co-opt six members to represent the six northern counties. Éamon Donnelly, Sinn Féin MP for Armagh and Director of Organisation, said he had approached Peadar Murney of County Down to become a Sinn Féin Standing Committee member and Peadar had agreed to do so. Murney was immediately co-opted. Donnelly promised to obtain the consent of five other six-county people to become members of the Standing Committee.[50]

De Valera and his band of enthusiastic workers had done enough work in advance to take the big plunge and formally establish Fianna Fáil. The La Scala Theatre, Dublin, was packed to capacity on 16 May 1926 when Éamon de Valera launched his new party. About a thousand people failed to gain admittance.[51] Madame Markievicz presided and Éamon de Valera, who was then in his mid-forties, was given an ecstatic welcome. During his speech he referred to the Oath of Allegiance:

> No man wants to take an Oath of Allegiance to a foreign government. No man wants to take an Oath of Allegiance to a foreign king. That being so, I believe that it is within our power to get the Irish people to say that, no matter who their representatives should be, they must not degrade themselves and the nation by taking the Oath of Allegiance to a foreign king.[52]

He looked to the future but did not forget his former friends still in Sinn Féin: 'With the Oath removed the Republican representatives will meet the other representatives in common assembly…It is unfortunate that there are Republicans who feel such steps cannot be taken but I believe that it is necessary to separate for the moment in order that we can be united in victory.'[53]

Deputies P.J. Ruttledge, Seán Lemass and Gerry Boland also addressed the meeting.

The new Fianna Fáil party had got off to a flying start. 'Politicus', the political correspondent for the *Sunday Independent*, wrote: 'The division in the Sinn Féin ranks is only now taking definite shape. De Valera's party seems to have gathered to itself a number of former members of the Sinn Féin organisation throughout the country that is in striking disproportion to the support the de Valera view obtained at the recent congress.'[54]

An Phoblacht reported on the enthusiastic La Scala meeting: 'The scenes at La Scala Theatre on Sunday with the great building thronged to the doors and the streets outside filled with masses of people unable to get in, have come as an ugly shock to the Free State managers.'[55] John Devoy's *Gaelic American* newspaper for once made a slightly complimentary remark about de Valera: 'The most suitable thing he has done for many a long day, if he can only be depended to act up to his professions.'[56]

Shortly after the foundation of Fianna Fáil, de Valera was asked, in view of the strong support he had previously had in Sinn Féin, whether it would not have been wiser for him to continue to work within that party to secure a majority for his new policy rather than leave to found Fianna Fáil. He answered: 'It was made quite clear to me...that if the *ard-fheis* [of Sinn Féin] had a considerable majority in favour of my policy, nevertheless, the minority would go out and form a separate organisation and would refuse to give my policy any support. Under these circumstances it mattered very little to me whether we had a majority or a minority at the *ard-fheis*.'[57]

As President of Sinn Féin since the ending of the Civil War, de Valera had never been fully able to impose his leadership on that party, as there was a continuous clash between militants and constitutional Republicans. The constitutional Republicans had founded a new party, in which they were more at home. De Valera was now a stronger leader because those who followed him accepted his new policy without question. He had an extensive cohort of supporters, all singing the same tune.

It was remarkable that Éamon de Valera had no words of condemnation for the Free State President, W.T. Cosgrave, or any of his ministers in his inaugural speech as President of Fianna Fáil. It was clear that he did not wish to offend any of his opponents. He was starting out on a fresh course of action designed to win support from followers of all the other parties in the Free State as this was the only possible way to win over a majority of the electorate to his way of thinking.

Notes

1.   Seán Cronin, *The McGarrity Papers*, p. 141.
2.   Medb Ruane, 'Kathleen Lynn, (1874-1955)', in Mary Cullen and Maria Luddy (eds.), *Female Activists: Irish Women and Change 1900-1960*, p. 81.

3.   NAI, File 2B/82/117/25, Minutes of the Standing Committee Sinn Féin 15 March 1926.
      The following members of the Standing Committee were present: Mary MacSwiney, TD (Cork
      Borough); Father Michael O'Flanagan; Dáithí Ó Donnchadha; Count Plunkett TD (Roscommon);
      Pilip Ó Riain; Miss L. Coventry; Seán Ó Ceallaigh; Dr Kathleen Lynn TD (Dublin County); P.
      Caffrey; Donnchadha Ó h-Éaluighthe; Liam Gilmore; B.P. Bowen; Seán O'Mahoney; Brian Ó
      Maoilíosa TD (Galway); L. de Lacey; Greg Murphy; Liam Paul; Micheál Ó Foghlugha; as well
      as three Ard-Chomhairle delegates -P.J. Little, Editor, *An Phoblacht*; Miss Somers; Gobnait Ní
      Bhruadair. Cluad de Cheabhasa sent an apology for non-attendance.

4.   Familiar names and faces missing were: Éamon de Valera TD, (Clare); Seán Lemass TD (Dublin
      South); Seán MacEntee; Hannna Sheehy Skeffington; Gearóid Ó Beoláin TD (Roscommon);
      Madame Markievicz TD (Dublin South); Mrs Margaret Pearse; P.J. Brennan; Michael Comyn; Seán
      Dowling; Linda Kearns; Martin Henry; J.J. Cullen.
      This list gives an indication of the split in the Standing Committee although it is not definitive as
      some members were absent for various routine reasons.

5.   *An Phoblacht*, 2 April 1926.

6.   *Ibid.*, 21 March 1926.

7.   UCDA, File 150/1948, de Valera Papers, Minutes of *Comhairle na dTeachtaí*, 28 March 1926.

8.   *Ibid.*

9.   *Ibid.*

10.   *Ibid.*

11.   *Ibid.*

12.   *Ibid.*

13.   *Ibid.*

14.   *Ibid.*

15.   *Ibid.*

16.   *Ibid.*

17.   *Ibid.*

18.   *Ibid.*

19.   *Ibid.*, 29 March 1926.

20.   *Ibid.*

21.   *Ibid.*

22.   *Ibid.*

23.   NAI, File 2B/82/117/25, Minutes of the Standing Committee of Sinn Féin, 29 March 1926.

24.   RTÉ Radio 1, *Bowman on Saturday*, 'The Foundation of Fianna Fáil and the Taking of the Oath of
      Allegiance', 5 May 2001.

25.   *An Phoblacht*, 16 April 1926.

26.   NAI, File 2B/82/117/25, Minutes of Special Meeting of Sinn Féin, 31 March 1926 and Minutes of the
      Standing Committee of Sinn Féin, 12 April 1926.

27.   *Ibid.*, 12 April 1926.

28.   Seán Cronin, *op. cit.*, pp. 140, 141.

29.   'Gerry Boland's Story (3) as told to Michael McInerney', *The Irish Times*, 10 October 1968.

30.   John Horgan, *Seán Lemass – The Enigmatic Patriot* (Maureen Haughey interview), p. 43.

31.   P.J. Ruttledge TD represented Mayo North, Seán Lemass TD, Dublin South, Gerry Boland TD,
      Roscommon, Dr James Ryan TD, Wexford, and Éamon de Valera, Clare. Seán MacEntee was a
      defeated Dáil candidate in Dublin County.

32.   The *Irish Independent*, 13 April 1926.

33.   *An Phoblacht*, 16 April 1926.

34.   'Gerry Boland's Story (3) as told to Michael McInerney', *The Irish Times*, 10 October 1968.

35.   *Ibid.*

36.   *Ibid.*

37.   *Ibid.*

38.   *Ibid.*

39.   *An Phoblacht*, 23 April 1926.

40.   *Ibid.*

41.   *Ibid.*, 30 April 1926.

42. Peter Pyne, 'The Third Sinn Féin Party: 1923-1926', p. 47.
43. J. Anthony Gaughan, *op. cit.*, p. 253.
44. *An Phoblacht*, 7 May 1926.
45. Seán Cronin, *op. cit.*, p. 143.
46. *An Phoblacht*, 7 May 1926.
47. *Ibid.*
48. *Ibid.*
49. 'Gerry Boland's Story (3) as told to Michael McInerney', *The Irish Times*, 10 October 1968.
50. NAI, File 2B/82/117/25, Minutes of the Standing Committee of Sinn Féin, 12 May 1926.
51. *The Irish Times*, 17 May 1926.
52. UCDA, Archives of the Fianna Fáil Party, File P176/23 (1), Speech by Éamon de Valera delivered at the Inaugural Meeting of Fianna Fáil at La Scala Theatre, Dublin, 16 May 1926.
53. *Ibid.*
54. The *Irish Independent*, 17 May 1926.
55. *An Phoblacht*, 21 May 1926.
56. *The Gaelic American*, 8 May 1926.
57. Thomas P. O'Neill, 'In Search of a Political Path: Irish Republicanism 1922 to 1927', p. 169.

12

Dev No Longer President of the Republic

The day Éamon de Valera founded Fianna Fáil in Dublin, Kevin O'Higgins addressed a Cumann na nGaedheal meeting in Clonmel, County Tipperary. He began by pointing out that there would be a general election before August 1927. Then he warned the Irish people against de Valera and rebuked him sharply for declaring that it was his immediate intention to remove the Oath of Allegiance from the Irish Free State Constitution:

> It is not incumbent upon our people to imperil their country, to risk international complications, in order to save the face of a man who did his damnedest to cut our country's throat. I have no reason to believe that the British government would agree to the waiving of the Oath, either for the Dáil as a whole or particular members of the Dáil, and if that were not agreed, is it to be suggested that in order to oblige a section of the community that made war on their fellow-citizens and on the economic life of the country, we should take up the position of being willing to break a Treaty that was hard won and hard saved.[1]

It was clear that Kevin O'Higgins and the Free State government would not easily agree to change the terms of the Treaty for the benefit of de Valera and his party. O'Higgins advised his audience to preserve the sanctity of the Treaty: 'Do not imperil the Treaty by agitating against the Oath.'[2]

The *Ard-Chomhairle* of Sinn Féin met on 21 and 22 May 1926 and passed this resolution:

That all *teachtaí dála* (TDs) who are prepared to accept the
new policy of entering either of the foreign controlled partition
'parliaments' in Ireland, if the Oath of Allegiance is removed, are
hereby called to resign their seats to the Ceann Comhairle Dáil
Éireann [Second Dáil] and to notify the honorary secretaries
Sinn Féin of their resignation as they no longer represent the
organisation that nominated them and secured their election.[3]

The same body decided two other matters. It was unanimously
determined: 'that the policy of the Sinn Féin organisation in relation to the
contesting of elections remains unchanged'. This meant that candidates from
Sinn Féin would continue to stand as candidates in general and by-elections
but, if elected, they would not enter Dáil Éireann under any circumstances.
The second big change was that Mary MacSwiney, senior vice-president Sinn
Féin, was promoted to be president of the organisation.[4]

Comhairle na dTeachtaí held a further meeting on 23 May 1926. The chief
executive, Art O'Connor, read the Sinn Féin *Ard-Chomhairle* resolution
that all TDs who were prepared to accept the new policy of de Valera should
resign their Dáil seats. The Sinn Féin grouping at the *Comhairle na dTeachtaí*
meeting demanded that Dev's group of TDs give an absolute undertaking
not to enter the Free State parliament. They also asked Fianna Fáil TDs
immediately to call an all-Ireland parliament if they were returned as a
majority party in any coming general election. De Valera, who still attended
meetings of this body with his supporter TDs, briefly stated that he could not
accept the conditions that Mary MacSwiney and her followers demanded.[5]
Éamon de Valera and his followers did not resign from *Comhairle na
dTeachtaí*. They intimated that they would be happy to serve under a chief
executive who would operate through an advisory council that included
Fianna Fáil participants.

There was a heated debate during the second part of the meeting when
Mary MacSwiney proposed Art O'Connor as President of the Republic: 'I
nominate Art Ó Conchubhair [Art O'Connor] as President of the Republic of
Ireland and Príomh-Aire [Prime Minister] of Dáil Éireann [second Dáil] and

Comhairle na dTeachtaí.[6]

Éamon de Valera TD opposed the motion. He did not consider that the assembly had the authority to propose anyone as 'President of the Republic of Ireland' as that was the function of the Second (Republican) Dáil and not the role of *Comhairle na dTeachtaí.* Other Fianna Fáil representatives – including Countess Markievicz, Seán Lemass, and Seán MacEntee – agreed with their leader. De Valera protested against the proceedings and asked that his protest and that of his followers be registered in the records. The group took no part in the election.[7] Mary MacSwiney's proposal that Art Ó Conchubhair be appointed President of the Republic of Ireland was approved by twenty-two votes to nil. Éamon de Valera and his fourteen Fianna Fáil followers did not register a vote and Art O'Connor was declared the new 'President of the Republic of Ireland.' O'Connor accepted his new title and nominated Austin Stack, Mary MacSwiney, Count Plunkett and J.J. O'Kelly as his ministers.[8] De Valera and his companion TDs had been ousted from the ruling council of the Republican *Comhairle na dTeachtaí.*

The first public appearance of this new fourth Sinn Féin Party occurred in mid-June 1926, when the party held a meeting in the Rotunda in Dublin. It could be deduced from the size of the attendance and from the absence of familiar faces that the schism between Sinn Féin and Fianna Fáil had struck deep into the Sinn Féin ranks. Art O'Connor, who had failed to win a seat in the Leix-Offaly by-election earlier in the year, was introduced by the chairman, Count Plunkett TD as 'President of the Irish Republic.'[9] O'Connor said: 'They must do what they believed to be right, even though there were a thousand to one against them.' Count Plunkett said that de Valera was in no-man's land: 'He left the Republican Parliament and did not join the Free State Parliament.' He added: 'They could not understand de Valera's folly of imitating the people he condemned. They were all agreed as to the evil of the Oath but there were fifty other evils in the Treaty.'[10]

Some Sinn Féin activists admired their new president. Brian Halligan, a member of the Standing Committee, said that they had at least in O'Connor 'a man…determined enough to be honest with the Irish nation.'[11] But not everyone shared his opinion. Describing Art Ó Connor in Uinseann Mac

Eoin's book, *The IRA in the Twilight Years*, Moss Twomey, IRA Chief-of-Staff from 1926 to 1936, said that 'Art Ó Conchubhair, although a nice man, made a milk and water president.'[12]

Some supporters of Éamon de Valera, who had crossed the line with him into Fianna Fáil, still had fears for the future of Republicanism if Fianna Fáil ever entered the Free State parliament. Frank Barrett, who had remained faithful to Éamon de Valera through thick and thin, wrote to a Republican friend, whom he addressed as 'T.M.', expressing this concern:

> The economic conditions prevailing, emigration and un-employment, constitute a formidable argument in favour of change of policy, and Dev would be entitled to a fair chance on his new scheme, as long as he can guarantee that there is no danger in it to Republicanism. He feels he can guarantee this, but personally I have fears…We must hope that things will come all right in time – in our time.[13]

At a Cumann na nGaedheal meeting in Navan, County Meath, Kevin O'Higgins declared that: 'de Valera, who was so fastidious about oaths, was now out on his third split. He went to America and split the movement there; then he came back and split the Sinn Féin movement on the Treaty, and now, with his mathematical bent for sub-divisions, he had split even his own supporters.'[14]

De Valera replied to O'Higgins when he addressed a public meeting in Blackrock Town Hall, County Dublin, organised by the new local branch of Fianna Fáil. 'I am supposed to be fastidious about oaths,' he declared, 'and I admit I am and the Oath is abhorrent to me because it is the acceptance of the right of the foreigner to rule in the country.'[15]

Accompanied by the newly elected secretary of Fianna Fáil, Gerry Boland, de Valera spoke in Roscommon, Boland's home constituency. In the course of his speech he asked his audience: 'Is there any man present who wanted his elected representatives to sign an Oath of Allegiance to a foreign king?' The response was a chorus of 'No'. De Valera then made an important point that he shrouded in very figurative language. 'I, for one,' he said, 'have never had any objection to the policy of taking for any £100 that was owed to me £40 or £50 or £60 of the debt, provided I had not to write a clear receipt and say that all the debt was paid.'[16] No doubt, de Valera intended to impress on Sinn Féin his argument that it was practical to try to abolish the Oath of Allegiance as a first step and then to tackle other parts of the Irish Constitution that gave a say to the British monarch in Irish affairs, provided that there was a firm desire to press ahead until complete independence was achieved.

De Valera went down to his own constituency of Clare to launch Fianna Fáil in the county. He had a special interest in Clare as he had topped the poll there since 1917. He also believed that Clare had a splendid history in defending Ireland's honour. Up to this, 'where Clare led Ireland followed.' Furthermore, Brian O'Higgins, his fellow-Republican deputy in the constituency, had remained a member of Sinn Féin after the March split and would, no doubt, oppose de Valera in Clare in the next election. The chances that Brian O'Higgins would be returned as a TD were not high: in the previous general election in 1923 he had depended on a huge transfer of votes from de Valera to be elected. But de Valera was taking no chances. He got a rapturous welcome from a big crowd of his constituents in Ennis. 'If the Oath were smashed, as I believe it will be smashed,' he said, 'everybody in the country would have an opportunity of working without compromise and with commitment, for the complete independence of Ireland.'[17]

On his tour de Valera visited Ballinasloe, County Galway, and addressed a meeting of Fianna Fáil delegates at the town hall. Recruitment for Fianna Fáil was going well but de Valera was worried about some of the new recruits:

> Nine Republicans out of ten believe in the present policy of Fianna Fáil as a reasonable and progressive one. But some of them think we should take the Oath but they were only deceiving themselves. There is a great question of principle involved, because taking the Oath is practically signing and accepting England's right. There is something wrong about that. To accept the Oath now would be as bad as accepting it four or

five years ago.[18]

The Fianna Fáil leader did not leave Ballinasloe until he had appointed an organising committee to set up a new branch of the party there.

When de Valera spoke at a Fianna Fáil meeting in Clonskeagh, Dublin, he outlined a new plan that was intended to win over members of the electorate who had not previously supported him. The great challenge he faced was that, unless he won new voters to his side, he would never gain sufficient political power to bring about any of the constitutional changes that were a basic element of his policy. He explained:

> There were two large classes (besides the anti-Treatyites) who were not satisfied with the Treaty – the neutrals and those who took it as a stepping stone. Many of these people were greatly disappointed at the result of the Boundary Commission.... These people were ready to help and join the national forces in anything that seemed to be an advance from the present position.[19]

During the summer of 1926, Éamon de Valera continued to tour the twenty-six counties of the Free State, organising Fianna Fáil. In a speech he made in Tralee he said that his new party 'should pay attention to the small farmers, labourers and the working people more than to any other class in the community.' He also declared that the party wished 'to combine Republicans...who constituted a third of the whole people, with the neutrals and if they succeeded they would add a sixth more and would have half of the people with them.' He added that 'he saw no difficulty in getting in the neutrals because they could see in this movement that they would have no physical (force) contest of any kind.'[20]

Sinn Féin decided to take up the Fianna Fáil challenge. They made a plan to hold a series of meetings with a view to increasing their membership. Oscar Traynor TD (Dublin North), still an enthusiastic member of Sinn Féin, presided at the first of these meetings, held in Parnell Square. He declared:

'Within one year there would be a general election and it was the intention of Sinn Féin to put their policy before the people.' Éamon Donnelly MP, Armagh, said: 'It was a pity that any new policy affecting the principles of Republicans had been put forward before the country had a general election, which could offer an opportunity to the people in a few months of definitely expressing their opinion of the bargain which lost the Six Counties.' After the meeting a hundred new members volunteered for membership of Sinn Féin.[21] The party was determined to put up a fight to retain its position as the premier Republican party.

At a Fianna Fáil meeting in Sligo where Frank Carty TD and Samuel Holt TD from Leitrim-Sligo, both former Sinn Féin deputies, joined him on the platform, Éamon de Valera said, 'I am sorry to part from dear friends but we, who sincerely hope to see Ireland free before our death, cannot allow even personal friendships to prevent us doing what seems necessary.'[22]

Armagh Republican MP Éamon Donnelly travelled to Kerry in an attempt to strengthen Sinn Féin there. Addressing a poorly-attended meeting in Tralee, he said that he regretted the split that had happened in Sinn Féin: 'Had the present cleavage not taken place in the Republican ranks and basing my argument on the large increase in Republican votes at the last by-elections and analysing these figures under PR, I am of the opinion that Sinn Féin would probably have won out at the next general election.'[23] Austin Stack, the sitting Sinn Féin TD for Kerry and secretary of the party, sent apologies for his absence: on his doctor's advice he was unable to attend. Stack was telling no lie as his health had deteriorated at this time.

Sinn Féin was experiencing a shortage of funds and at one of their meetings the Standing Committee considered vacating its premises at Suffolk Street for cheaper office accommodation. The committee decided instead to sub-let one of the rooms.[24] It was clear that the party organisation was weakening.

Cumann na nGaedheal realised that Fianna Fáil could be strong rivals in the following year's general election. They began to tackle de Valera on his lack of a good economic policy. William Sears, Cumann na nGaedheal TD for Mayo South, said in Castlebar that 'de Valera at last had broken loose from the leading strings of Miss MacSwiney but the Oath had nothing to do with the Shannon Scheme or protection or emigration and the people wanted a fair opportunity in order to win a decent livelihood.'[25]

Professor Magennis's party, Clann Éireann, was also gearing up for the coming general election and held a meeting in Dublin. Senator Colonel Moore and Paddy Belton joined Professor Magennis on the platform and each in turn addressed the meeting. Paddy Belton was a defeated Independent candidate who had polled well in the Dublin County by-election earlier in the year. That night he appealed for the unity of all the nationalist elements in the Free State: 'We were urged in some quarters not to take the Oath,' he said, 'but if we did not do that, O'Higgins would remain in power.'[26]

Éamon de Valera continued his tour of the constituencies in the Free State to set up branches of Fianna Fáil and addressed crowds in many rural areas of County Cork. He spoke on a fair day at a public meeting in Midleton at which Martin J. Corry, a Cork Fianna Fáil councillor, presided. With regard to the Oath of Allegiance, Dev said that 'for one to accept it honestly was to accept England as a master and to accept it dishonestly made one a perjurer.'[27] It was unusual for Dev to place himself in so tight a corner about anything. Would he have to eat these words in the not too distant future?

The 1926 Sinn Féin *ard-fheis* was held in the Rotunda, Dublin, on Saturday and Sunday, 30-31 October. Mary MacSwiney, President, recalled in her address that, whereas at the previous *ard-fheis* there had been nearly a thousand delegates, at this *ard-fheis*, they had only two hundred delegates in the hall: 'Comrades had wearied and dropped away and they who met there that day must shoulder their share of the burden on their own and go forward bravely and steadily, glad in the thought that it was to them to suffer much for the cause they loved.'[28] Dealing with the break-away of de Valera she commented that: 'even if the Oath of Allegiance were removed, the Free State Constitution could not be worked without disloyalty to the existing Republic.' She asked: 'Was there any chance that the Oath would be removed as a result of de Valera's campaign?' and ventured the answer herself: 'Not one chance in ten thousand.'[29]

Only sixteen delegates voted in favour of a motion not to contest the next general election.

A second motion was passed that 'no pact be made with any political organisation for election purposes.'[30] This decision not to associate with Fianna Fáil or any other nationalist party during or after the next general election was the first sign of a malaise that was creeping into Sinn Féin: a tendency to retreat into isolation.

Seán Ó Ceallaigh was elected President of Sinn Féin. The two vice-presidents chosen were Mary MacSwiney TD and Father Michael O'Flanagan. The honorary secretaries elected were Austin Stack TD and Dáithí Ó Donnchadha. Caitlín Brugha was prevailed upon to continue as treasurer although she expressed a wish not to stand for the office again.[31] More women than before were elected to the executive. Of eight Dublin representatives, three were women; Dr Kathleen Lynn, Margaret Buckley and Lily Coventry. Máire Comerford from Gorey, County Wexford, and Dulcibella Barton were among the Leinster representatives, while Mrs Katherine O'Callaghan, Limerick, and Gobnait Ní Bhruadair, Kerry, were two of the Munster representatives.[32] This time only thirteen elected representatives were present from the four provinces. It could almost be felt in the air that the ruling body of Sinn Féin had gone into decline.[33]

At a Fianna Fáil meeting in Loughrea, County Galway, a letter was read from Most Reverend Dr Dignan expressing regret that he could not attend owing to a long-standing appointment. But he sent his best wishes to the meeting:

> Every true Irishman must wish for a speedy end to partition and for the abolition of an Oath of Allegiance to a foreign King. No Irish state can be set up while these remain.[34]

Bishop Dignan had been the first member of the Irish-based hierarchy to give qualified support to Sinn Féin after the Civil War – but only if they pursued constitutional methods. Now he became the first bishop to come out publicly in support of Fianna Fáil. No doubt Éamon de Valera, who craved some support from the Catholic Church, was very happy with this letter.

The Governor-General, Tim Healy, attended the first annual dinner of the Dublin Chamber of Commerce on 6 November 1926. In his speech he referred to the 'coming general election' and 'the number of persons whom we have never heard of before, except in connection with explosions and assassinations and who could possibly be candidates for office'. He offered this advice to these people:

> To those gentlemen who say they will not enter into the legislature of their country because their principle forbids them to take the Oath to his Majesty, I would say, in the words of Gilbert and Sullivan, 'You are curious optimists: you never would be missed.' They are quite welcome to stay out and the further out they stay the better some of us will be pleased.[35]

The cream of Dublin's commercial and professional life, present at the dinner, applauded these words of Tim Healy.[36] But W.T. Cosgrave, President of the Free State government, took the opposite view. In a letter to O'Higgins he wrote: 'It did us no good, did de Valera no harm and would influence no one except against us.'[37]

The incident sparked off a major debate in the Dáil. Thomas Johnson, leader of the Labour Party, raised the matter: 'If a nominated officer of the state (the Governor-General) is free to enter the arena of political party conflict to denounce deputies and parties who have been elected by the citizens then the nature of the office is different from what has been the general belief.'[38] W.T. Cosgrave replied that Healy's speech 'was not made on the advice of the Executive Council' and that that body 'could not approve of such a speech as had been reported.'[39] Cosgrave understood from Tim Healy that what appeared in the newspapers was not a correct report of what he had said but the journalists in question responded by sending the verbatim account to the editor of *The Irish Times*.[40] Professor Magennis, leader of the new party Clann Éireann and a prolific speaker in the Dáil, declared that 'it is incumbent upon whoever fills the office [of Governor-General]...that he should not meddle with the question of partisan politics in the state over which he himself is Governor-General.'[41] This Dáil debate was a consoling experience for the anti-Treaty deputies and supporters and a frustrating one for so sublime a personage as Tim Healy.

Seán Lemass had gone to canvass in County Donegal for new recruits for Fianna Fáil. He had a list of people to call on, among them Neal Blaney, who had been sentenced to death but reprieved for Anti-Treaty activities in County Donegal during the Civil War. When Lemass entered a farmyard into which farmers were drawing hay by horse and haycart, he saw Neal Blaney at the top of a hayrick. Lemass discussed the founding of a Fianna Fáil branch in the district with him while Neal went on forking hay at the top of the rick. After a while he came down and put on his coat, saying to Lemass, 'Come on and we'll see some of the lads in the village.' As they were passing out of the yard there was a young fellow, a son of Blaney, playing and tossing around in the haycocks, oblivious of the reason his father had stopped work to go on business with Lemass. Years later this youngster, Neil Blaney Junior, would be a Fianna Fáil minister.[42]

President Cosgrave did not like being described as an imperialist by Éamon de Valera and at a well-attended meeting in Athlone, County Westmeath, he replied to de Valera's charge:

> My answer to de Valera, and all his new and old disciples, is just that I refer him to the people of Ireland who are his masters as they are mine. He already knows the verdict of his masters…A greater authority than de Valera, a more final arbiter than even Miss Mary MacSwiney has spoken…de Valera wants the removal of the Oath but the people are entitled to know did he mean to smash the Treaty.[43]

Professor William Magennis, Clann Éireann, was asked if an amalgamation between Clann Éireann and Fianna Fáil was feasible. He replied:

> Clann Éireann, as a constitutional party, accepts the Treaty, the Free State and its parliament…We have made as part of our

programme the removal of the Oath…A Republican vote for
the Clann Éireann candidate is a contribution to the ultimate
removal of the Oath…Amalgamation may not be feasible but
cooperation in the elections might very well be feasible.[44]

Fianna Fáil representatives gathered in the Rotunda in Dublin on 24 and
25 November 1926 for the first *ard-fheis* of Fianna Fáil. De Valera and the
other hard workers on the executive had toured the twenty-six counties for
months before this convention and 467 delegates attended, representing the
many new branches established in every one of the twenty-six counties.

Seán T. O'Kelly TD (Dublin North) who presided in the unavoidable
absence of P.J. Ruttledge TD (Mayo North) said that Fianna Fáil stood for
absolute independence for the whole thirty-two counties.

Éamon de Valera TD, leader of the party, stated that the road should be
opened to free constitutional action and added:

If we should succeed no further in achieving the objectives
they were setting before themselves in the organisation than
in opening that road, that achievement alone would justify
us being assembled here. What a future would lie before the
country if all its children, all who sincerely loved it, were enabled
in freedom to work side by side for its advancement.[45]

Seán Lemass, the organising secretary, stated that in the seven months
since the foundation of Fianna Fáil, seventy-nine organising committees had
been established and 435 *cumainn*.

A resolution was passed that an arrangement should be made with Sinn
Féin for a basis of cooperation and alliance at the next general election. This
contrasted with the Sinn Féin *ard-fheis* motion not to associate with any other
political party.

De Valera referred to the reason he left Sinn Féin: 'because he realised that
if the Sinn Féin programme was not modified to meet the circumstances of
the moment that the object to which Sinn Féin existed was not going to be

achieved.' He continued by saying that the rank and file of Sinn Féin wanted cooperation of a certain kind and he felt there was no power on earth that could prevent those people from helping them [Fianna Fáil] to take over control of the country.'[46]

A number of women were elected to the first executive of Fianna Fáil – Countess Markievicz; Margaret Pearse, mother of Pádraig and Willie Pearse; Kathleen Clarke, widow of the executed 1916 leader, Tom Clarke; Dorothy Macardle; Linda Kearns and Hanna Sheehy Skeffington.[47]

At the Imperial Conference which was held in the autumn of 1926, Kevin O'Higgins led the Irish delegation. O'Higgins did very valuable work for Ireland at this conference. He helped to pave the way for the Statute of Westminster that brought full emancipation to the Dominions at a later date.[48] At a meeting of the central branch of Cumann na nGaedheal in Parnell Square, O'Higgins declared that the Imperial Conference had made it clear that no member of the Commonwealth was bound to any association of states except on the basis of free cooperation. He added that 'there was complete freedom for each state in every aspect of domestic and external affairs.'[49]

As 1926 drew to a close Fianna Fáil had become firmly established and was waging a strong constitutional campaign to get rid of the Oath of Allegiance. Sinn Féin had declined in strength. The Free State government was making plans to hold a general election some time early in the New Year.

Notes

1. The *Irish Independent*, 17 May 1926.
2. *An Phoblacht*, 21 May 1926.
3. The *Irish Independent*, 26 May 1926.
4. *Ibid.*
5. UCDA, File 150/1948, de Valera Papers, Meeting of *Comhairle na dTeachtaí*, 23 May 1926.
6. *Ibid.*
7. *Ibid.*
8. *Ibid.*
9. The *Gaelic American*, 26 June 1926.
10. The *Irish Independent*, 12 June 1926.
11. *Ibid.*
12. Uinseann Mac Eoin, 'Conversations with Moss Twomey', *The IRA in the Twilight Years*, p. 838.
13. UCDA, Archives of the Fianna Fáil Party, File P176/23 (19), Copy of letter from Frank Barrett to 'T.M.', dated 7 June 1926.
14. The *Irish Independent*, 14 June 1926.
15. *Ibid.*, 18 June 1926.
16. *Ibid.*, 21 June 1926.
17. *Ibid.*, 28 June 1926.

18. *Ibid.*
19. *Ibid.*, 5 July 1926.
20. *Ibid.*, 16 August 1926.
21. *Ibid.*, 19 August 1926.
22. *Ibid.*, 23 August 1926.
23. *Ibid.*, 24 August 1926.
24. NAI, File 2B/82/117/25, Minutes of the Standing Committee of Sinn Féin, 10, 11 September 1926.
25. The *Irish Independent*, 28 September 1926.
26. *Ibid.*, 11 October 1926.
27. *Ibid.*, 12 October 1926.
28. *Ibid.*, 1 November 1926.
29. *Ibid.*
30. *Ibid.*
31. Margaret Ward, *Unmanageable Revolutionaries – Women and Irish Nationalism*, p. 203.
32. *Ibid.*
33. The *Irish Independent*, 1 November 1926. Teachtaí Dála present were:.
    Dublin: E. O'Malley TD (Dublin North); C. Ó Murchadha TD (Dublin South); Oscar Traynor TD (Dublin North); Dr Kathleen Lynn TD (Dublin County).
    Munster: Seán Buckley TD (Cork West); Brian O'Higgins TD (Clare): Austin Stack TD (Kerry);.
    Caitlín Brugha TD (Waterford): D. Ceannt TD (Cork East).
    Connacht: Dr Madden TD (Mayo North); Count George Noble Plunkett TD (Roscommon); Tom Maguire TD (Mayo South).
    Ulster: Éamon Donnelly MP (Armagh).
34. *Ibid.*
35. The *Irish Independent*, 8 November 1926.
36. Brendan Sexton, *Ireland and the Crown 1922-1936*, p. 104.
37. NAI, (SPO), S5204, Cosgrave to O'Higgins, 12 November 1926.
38. *Dáil Éireann Debates*, Volume 17, 25, 16 November 1926: 'Governor-General and Deputies' Privileges.'
39. *Ibid.*, Volume 17, 28-30, 16 November 1926: 'Governor-General and Deputies' Privileges.'
40. Brendan Sexton, *op. cit.*, p. 104.
41. *Dáil Éireann Debates*, Internet, Volume 17, 32, 16 November 1926, 'Governor-General and Deputies' Privileges.'.
42. 'The Gerry Boland Story (3) as told to Michael McInerney', *The Irish Times*, 10 October 1968, and author's interview with Kevin Blaney (brother of the late Neil Blaney Junior), 2 April 2011.
43. The *Irish Independent*, 15 November 1926.
44. *Ibid.*
45. *Ibid.*, 25 November 1926.
46. *Ibid.*, 26 November 1926.
47. Margaret Ward, *op. cit*, p. 202.
48. Terence de Vere White, *Kevin O'Higgins*, p. 215.
49. The *Irish Independent*, 18 December 1926.

13

FIANNA FÁIL TAKES THE REPUBLICAN VOTE

On the day in January 1927 that the Dáil was to reconvene after the Christmas break, sudden and startling news made political headlines when Dan Breen, Republican abstentionist TD for Tipperary, but who had followed de Valera into Fianna Fáil, announced that the was entering the Dáil that day as an Independent.[1]

Dan Breen had been one of the half-dozen most prominent guerrilla fighters in Ireland's War of Independence. From the very outset Dan had made it known that he could not agree with the compromises in the Treaty. He had fought with Republican forces in the tragic Civil War and had ended up in Free State captivity. On his release he had suffered hardship and want because he could not obtain suitable employment. Although he was elected for County Tipperary in August 1923 he did not enter the Dáil and as an abstentionist TD he received no remuneration. Breen was in bad circumstances in 1925 and 1926. His War of Independence wounds were afflicting him, as they continued to do for the rest of his life. In desperation he wrote to his friend, Joe McGarrity, in Philadelphia:

> My reason for writing you is to know would you advise me to go out to the States, as I am still idle here. I am after putting a very hard winter behind me. My wounds came against me a great deal owing to heavy frost and rain and I could not get proper care when I had no work and no work spells no money. I don't much mind myself only for the wife and little lad.[2]

Breen was aware that his fellow Republican volunteers who had taken the anti-Treaty side in the Civil War were suffering similar hardship. He fully enunciated his reason for going into the Dáil in a statement he gave the *Irish Independent* on the night before:

> The truth is that for some time past I have found myself in a hopeless position as I watched that share of freedom which the Treaty brought being used rather to submerge Ireland's individuality as a nation than to obtain the fuller freedom which Michael Collins claimed could be achieved through its acceptance. I am now entering the parliament of the Free State with the avowed intention of doing all that is in one man's power to remove the barriers that separate the Irish people. I see no hope of unity and consequently no hope of stability or prosperity in this country until the Oath of Allegiance is removed. I hold no brief for any leader but I do believe that Éamon de Valera is an honest man and an honest leader, and therefore, I shall do my utmost to remove any obstacle that debars him from participating in the government of the country.[3]

Before 2.30pm on 25 January 1927, Dan Breen, accompanied by Patrick Moylett, walked up to Leinster House and was met at the outer gate of the Dáil by Pádraig Ó Máille TD (Galway), Leas-Cheann Comhairle and one of the leaders of Clann Éireann. When he entered Leinster House he was welcomed by C.M. Byrne, the Wicklow TD. Dan signed his name in the Dáil roll book that the Clerk of the Dáil produced. Then he sat in the lobby until questions had concluded but he took a keen interest in the crossfire that took place between some members of the Farmers' Party and the Minister for Land and Agriculture on the subject of the testing of cows for tuberculosis. After that he was conducted by deputies C.M. Byrne and Pádraic Ó Máille to the Ceann Comhairle, Professor Michael Hayes, who officially greeted him as a member of the House. As he did so the House applauded and Kevin O'Higgins, Minister for Justice, joined in the applause. Dan then occupied a seat between

Professor William Magennis and Pádraic Ó Máille, both members of Clann Éireann.[4]

Many years later Dan Breen was asked what his constituents thought of the fact that he had entered Dáil Éireann at that particular time and if he had taken the Oath of Allegiance before taking his place in the House. He made this reply:

> I thought it was pure waste of time and energy to sit outside, do nothing and make bellicose speeches and the best of our youth leaving the country. I thought it was time to go in and take part in whatever was there. I could not keep up a war forever and forever. But then there was a lot of people who felt that the Republic should go on. Because I went in, I was then outside all parties. A lot of people did not agree with me. I never saw an Oath. There was an Oath somewhere but no one asked me about it. I just signed a book. I never read any formula.[5]

General Seán Mac Eoin, an opponent of Dan Breen from the Treaty onwards said that 'when Dan Breen reached a decision that he thought was a right one nothing could stop him.'[6] After Dan Breen had been in the Dáil for about a fortnight, Professor Magennis said that Dan had joined Clann Éireann. In a letter to the *Irish Independent* newspaper he claimed that 'the recent accession of Dan Breen to the ranks of Clann Éireann has augmented its forces considerably.'[7]

When asked to comment on the decision of Dan Breen to enter the Dáil, Éamon de Valera said: 'I feel sure that many who voted for Mr Breen at the last election will feel that he broke faith with them. I do not think that Mr Breen's decision will in any way affect the members of Fianna Fáil.'[8]

Down in his own Tipperary constituency, a large and representative meeting of the Seán Treacy Sinn Féin Cumann passed a resolution proposed by Michael Fitzpatrick and seconded by Seán Black: 'that Dan Breen TD, by his action in entering the Free State parliament and taking the Oath of Allegiance to the King of England, has departed from the Republican principles on which he was elected and has lost the confidence of the Republicans of Tipperary.[9] A motion like this had the potential to wreck the political career of Breen.

Captain William Redmond, Independent TD for Waterford and son of the former leader of the Irish Party, John Redmond, had plans to form a party similar to the defunct Irish Party. It was thought likely that Captain Redmond would approach TDs of the Farmers' Party and other Independent TDs to join the new party, which he proposed to call the National League.[10]

Mary MacSwiney continued to throw cold water on Fianna Fáil's new policy of giving recognition to the 'parliament of Southern Ireland'. She posed the question: 'Supposing de Valera did get a majority for Fianna Fáil in the next election, which he was not in the least likely to do, what would happen?' She proffered her own answer to this query. 'He would go up to Merrion Street or Leinster House only to find the junta (the Free State government) still holding their places, with the help of the Free State Army...and they would tell de Valera's party that they could not enter as they had not complied with the Constitution of the Free State.'[11]

In response, de Valera explained Fianna Fáil's future plans and what would happen if he got a majority in a coming election:

> If Fianna Fáil are returned by a majority at the next election...
> our intention will be to take over the government services of
> the country, and to act on the principle that all authority comes
> from the people....I heard it said...that if we got a majority we
> would not be allowed to take over the reins of government but,
> in the case of my party getting a majority, I do not see any danger
> of a conflict although some people tell us we will be faced with a
> civil conflict.[12]

Seán Lemass, another abstentionist Republican TD, now affiliated to Fianna Fáil, announced an extension to the policy already explained by Éamon de Valera: 'Fianna Fáil *teachtaí*, after the general election, will attend the Dáil. They will assert their right to represent their constituents there without being forced to take an Oath repugnant to them and to all decent Irishmen.'[13]

Wexford man Robert Brennan, once a leading member of Sinn Féin but now a devotee of de Valera, asked the Free State leaders to state what their attitude would be if Republicans gained a majority in the next general election. Shortly afterwards, at a Cumann na nGaedheal meeting in Skerries, County Dublin, Desmond Fitzgerald, Minister for External Affairs, answered Robert Brennan's query: 'If the Irish people are mad,' he said, 'and I do not believe they are – as to return seventy-four or more of de Valera's candidates, the present government will have no option but to make way for him.'[14]

At a meeting of the Standing Committee of Sinn Féin, it was agreed 'to carry out the decision of the *ard-fheis* to contest elections but that where little or no prospect exists that the local organisation be free not to contest.' While the committee was discussing possible candidates to stand for Sinn Féin it was mentioned that Ernie O'Malley, the sitting Republican TD for Dublin North and another of the legendary guerrilla fighters of the War of Independence and the Civil War, had been nominated by Sinn Féin but had said he did not wish to stand.[15]

One day Countess Markievicz spent a whole day in Sligo with a younger lady friend, named 'Baby' Bohan. The younger woman remarked that she could not understand 'how anyone could think of going into the Dáil and taking an Oath to the British king.' The Countess replied, 'I will never take that Oath. How could I ever meet Paddy Pearse or Jim Connolly in the hereafter if I took an Oath to a British king.'[16]

Desmond Fitzgerald condemned de Valera's constitutional policy of getting rid of the Oath of Allegiance. 'Do you realise,' he asked de Valera, 'that to destroy the Oath, you have to destroy the Treaty? You will commit the Irish people to depend on England not to wage war against them because, according to international usages, a breach of the Treaty without formal denunciation amounts to a declaration of war.'[17]

Fianna Fáil organisers were holding numerous public meetings and preaching an optimistic message. Eoin P. Ó Caoimh, a prominent member of the party, said at a public meeting in Rearcross, County Tipperary, that 'considering what one man, Dan O'Connell, could do in 1827 in Westminster, surely sixty or eighty elected members could do the same in 1927 in Dublin.'[18]

At a Labour Party meeting in Castlebar, County Mayo, T.J. O'Connell, TD for Galway, declared, 'I do not think the Oath should be elevated into the position of a national question. The Labour Party is not responsible for having it there and if we get into power we will use our influence to have it removed from the Constitution, but that is not because we want to please some who are waiting outside.'[19]

Some Republican activists opposed the Fianna Fáil policy on how to advance the national question. Liam Paul, a member of the Sinn Féin *Ard-Chomhairle*, speaking at meetings of that party in County Leitrim, where Sinn Féin was still strong, said: 'we have a party in the election known as "Fianna Fáilers" who tell the people the nation can be freed by instalments.'[20] Paul was castigating Fianna Fáil for differing from Sinn Féin at this time in history. Sinn Féin wanted to achieve 100 per cent independence in one giant swoop, while Fianna Fáil aimed to gain independence by a series of jumps.

Dan Breen kept the promise he made when he entered the Dáil that he would introduce a Bill to abolish the Oath of Allegiance as soon as circumstances would allow. On 6 April 1927, less than three months after he first entered the Dáil, Breen introduced a Bill to remove Article 17, which dealt with the Oath of Allegiance, from the Free State Constitution.[21]

That day Dan Breen made his maiden speech in the Dáil as he tried to get a first reading for this Bill: 'When I took my seat in this House I explained to my constituents that I would do everything in my power to get this part of the Constitution removed...I ask the deputies for the sake of the country to give it full consideration.'[22]

The other promoters of this Bill were David Hall, Labour TD for Meath, and James Everett, who represented the Labour Party in Wicklow. The Ceann Comhairle of the Dáil allowed explanatory statements from only two of the three deputies promoting the Bill. As Dan Breen was the first speaker, the promoters agreed that David Hall should make the second explanatory statement.

Hall, supporting the Bill, said he was speaking as an individual and did not wish to involve the Labour Party. 'I believe,' he continued, 'it is only right and proper that the Bill should get a first reading in the Dáil so as to give the deputies an opportunity of considering the Bill and of expressing a broad and more intelligible view on it on the next stage.'[23]

The President, W.T. Cosgrave TD, opposed giving the Bill a first reading:

> I oppose the First Reading of this Bill in the name of the government. I oppose it because it seeks to remove a fundamental provision of our *Bunreacht* (Constitution), a provision which arises from and has its roots in the Treaty. It proposes to take out of the Constitution the Oath prescribed in the Treaty. The Treaty bears the signatures of five plenipotentiaries appointed by Dáil Éireann and it was approved by Dáil Éireann. On the first occasion that the people had an opportunity of registering their opinion they returned a majority of representatives in favour of the Treaty. The Constitution was then considered, amended and passed by Dáil Éireann and during the passage of the Constitution Bill this very issue which the present Bill raises was made a matter of confidence by the government.[24]

Cosgrave demonstrated that the Oath of Allegiance Clause in the Free State Constitution had received the continued approval of the Irish people:

> Within fourteen months another general election took place on a new and extended franchise and the result was an overwhelming majority for the Treaty and the Constitution. We have had since then twenty-one by-elections and the result of these may be summarised as seventeen for the Treaty and Constitution and four against.[25]

Cosgrave concluded that the Free State government was opposing Dan Breen's Bill getting a first reading because: 'we believe in honouring our bond – we believe in the sanctity of international agreements.'[26]

If de Valera had been present in the Dáil, there is no doubt that he would have vehemently contradicted much of what Cosgrave had said.

The Ceann Comhairle of the Dáil allowed no further discussion on the matter. The motion was then put to the House. On a division the result was seventeen votes in favour of giving a first reading to Dan Breen's motion to abolish the Oath of Allegiance and forty-seven votes against.[27]

Dan Breen's motion was declared lost but as only forty-seven deputies voted against his motion, it meant that fewer than one third of all the TDs elected to the Dáil had rejected his proposal.[28] President W.T. Cosgrave's motion not to give a first reading to Dan Breen's Bill was passed with a majority of thirty. The fact that forty-five Republican deputies absented themselves from the Dáil that day because of the Oath of Allegiance meant that Dan Breen's motion might have succeeded if they had entered the Dáil and voted for his Bill. This fact received careful consideration in Fianna Fáil, Sinn Féin and Republican circles. Mr Carberry, a supporter of the non-elected Independent Republican, Michael O'Mullane, addressing a political meeting at Westland Row, pointed out that, if the Republican deputies had been in the Dáil when Breen introduced his Bill for the abolition of the Oath, the first reading might have been carried and the Oath might have been removed even before the general election.[29]

Breen felt let down but he could only expect his Bill to be seen as an initial gesture, taking into consideration that forty-five Republican deputies remained outside the Dáil. It was now clear that W.T. Cosgrave's government had no ambitions to dismantle the Treaty bit by bit as Michael Collins had stated he would do when he described the Treaty as 'a stepping stone'.

Dan Breen's failure to get the Dáil to remove the Oath of Allegiance put his own future political career in jeopardy. The *Nation*, a weekly newspaper that had just been set up by Fianna Fáil to propagate its views, was in no way surprised that his Bill was defeated on its first reading:

'The Oath is the only prop upon which the Free Staters have to depend to keep them in office,' wrote the editor. 'Surely Mr Breen did not seriously expect Messrs. Cosgrave, O'Higgins and Co. to relinquish the power they seized by armed force in 1922.'[30]

Second and third from the left, respectively: Katherine O'Callaghan, widow of Michael O'Callaghan, retired Mayor of Limerick, murdered by Black and Tans on 6 March 1921, and Mary MacSwiney, sister of Terence MacSwiney, who died on hunger-strike on 25 October 1920, on their way in to the Treaty debates in December 1921. Both voted against the Treaty. (Courtesy of the National Library of Ireland. Hogw 87.)

Free State Government meeting, 1922. Included in the photograph left to right (from second left): Joseph McGrath, Hugh Kennedy, W.T. Cosgrave, Ernest Blythe and Kevin O'Higgins. (Courtesy of the National Library of Ireland. Hog 97.)

Red Cross personnel tend to an injured Free State soldier in the south-west during the Civil War (1922). (Courtesy of the National Library of Ireland. Hog 216.)

Michael Sheehan's Tipperary Flying Column in Graiguenamanagh, County Kilkenny (16 July 1922), on its return journey after engaging with Republican forces in north Wicklow at the beginning of the Civil War. John Kissane Collection. (Reproduced by kind permission of Joseph Hehir, Thomastown, County Kilkenny, and Jim Coady, Graiguenamanagh.)

Thomas Johnson, leader of the Labour Party, 1922-7.
(Courtesy of the National Library of Ireland. Ke 193.)

*The Boundary Commission 1924-5. Left to right: Dr Eoin MacNeill, Irish Free State;
J.M. Fisher, Northern Ireland; T.E. Reid (Secretary to Armagh County Council);
T.E. Montgomery; Mr Justice Richard Feetham, South Africa, Chairman of the Commission.
(Courtesy of the National Library of Ireland. Hog 181.)*

Fianna Fáil TDs elected in the general election of June 1927.

Front row: fifth, sixth, seventh from left respectively: Countess Markievicz, Éamon de Valera, Kathleen Clarke.
(UCD Archives: Reproduced by kind permission of UCD-OFM Partnership.)

In no particular order: Éamon de Valera (Clare); Thomas Derrig (Carlow-Kilkenny); Patrick Smith (Cavan); Pat Houlihan (Clare); Sean French (Cork City); Martin Corry (Cork East); Thomas Mullins (Cork West); Sean T. Ó Ceallaigh (Dublin City North); Kathleen Clarke (Dublin City North); Sean Lemass (Dublin City South); Madame Markievicz (Dublin City South); Paddy Belton (Dublin County); Sean MacEntee (Dublin County); Mark Killalea (Galway County); Proinsias Ó Fathaigh (Galway County); Dr Sean Tubridy (Galway County); Thomas T.P. Powell (Galway County); Thomas O'Reilly (Kerry); Thomas McEllistrim (Kerry); William O'Leary (Kerry); Dónal Ua Buachalla (Kildare); Frank Carty (Leitrim-Sligo); Sam Holt (Leitrim-Sligo); Patrick Boland (Leix-Offaly); Thomas Tynan (Leix-Offaly); James Colbert (Limerick); Tadhg Crowley (Limerick); James Victory (Longford-Westmeath); Michael J. Kennedy (Longford-Westmeath); Frank Aiken (Louth); Patrick J. Ruttledge (Mayo North); Michael Kilroy (Mayo South); Eugene Mullen (Mayo South); Matthew O'Reilly (Meath); Dr Patrick McCarvill (Monaghan); Gerald Boland (Roscommon); Dr Patrick O'Dowd (Roscommon); Sean Hayes (Tipperary); Andrew Fogarty (Tipperary); Neal Blaney (Donegal); Frank Carney (Donegal); Patrick J. Little (Waterford); Dr James Ryan (Wexford); Seamus Moore (Wicklow).

Éamon de Valera and Dorothy Macardle with a copy of her book, The Irish Republic, *first published in 1937. (Reproduced by kind permission of UCD-OFM Partnership. P150/3664/6.)*

Brian O'Higgins, President of Sinn Fein 1931-3. (Courtesy of the National Library of Ireland. Ke 91.)

William Norton, Labour Party Leader 1932-60, President Éamon de Valera and Sir Thomas Inskip, British Attorney-General, at Euston Station, 15 July 1932. (Reproduced by kind permission of UCD-OFM Partnership. P150/2181/4.)

President Éamon de Valera, John W. Dulanty, Irish High Commissioner in London, and J.H. Thomas, Dominions Secretary (up to 1935), outside the Dominions Office. (Reproduced by kind permission of UCD-OFM Partnership. P150/2181/08(2).)

*Malcolm MacDonald, Secretary of State for Dominion Affairs (from 1935) and President
Éamon de Valera. (Reproduced by kind permission of UCD-OFM Partnership. P150/2509/2.)*

President Cosgrave dissolved the Dáil on 23 May 1927. Polling day was fixed for 9 June.

As the general election campaign got off the ground, fresh efforts were made to get Sinn Féin and Fianna Fáil to cooperate for the sake of the Republican cause. It then became clear that Sinn Féin, the old Republican party, and Fianna Fáil, the new Republican party, were prepared to work together after the general election in the event of the combined anti-Treaty parties winning a majority of seats. Charles Murphy TD, the Sinn Féin candidate for Dublin City South, speaking at a public meeting in New Street, shed some new light on how the two parties could combine. 'If a majority of Republicans were elected, there would be no difference between Fianna Fáil and Sinn Féin because the first thing we would do would be to summon the Republican Parliament for all-Ireland, scrap the Treaty and get going the Republic as it was in 1921.'[31]

Cumann na nGaedheal feared the possibility that a coalition of small parties would put them out of office after the election. President Cosgrave warned the electorate in his last speech in Kilkenny before polling day that the main issue was to provide a government. 'If we go back only fifty strong, I cannot form a government,' he said. 'Who will supply it?'[32]

Fianna Fáil had candidates in all the constituencies except three. In Dublin University constituency (Trinity College) they did not put up a candidate. In Cork North they left the Republican field open to Daniel Corkery, an Independent Republican, and they did the same in the NUI constituency, in which Professor Arthur Clery stood as an Independent Republican.

De Valera's new party believed in the power of the media and spent a good deal of money in advertising in the daily papers. Éamon de Valera had made a visit to the USA and he had collected a large sum of money from Irish-American supporters to help his party to finance the general election. All Fianna Fáil candidates were obliged to sign a solemn pledge before their names went for selection before a party convention. The pledge was very specific in regard to the candidate's attitude to the Oath of Allegiance:

I _____ hereby undertake that if elected to the office of TD, I will support Fianna Fáil (Republican Party) in every action it takes to secure the independence of a United Ireland under a Republican form of government, and, in accordance with the Constitution (of Fianna Fáil), I will not take any position involving an Oath of Allegiance to a foreign power, and I further undertake that if called upon by a two-thirds majority of the national executive of Fianna Fáil to resign that office, I shall immediately do so.[33]

Due to lack of finance Sinn Féin was able to put only fifteen candidates in the field. They nominated a candidate in any constituency where they thought he/she had a good prospect of success. In no constituency did they put up more than one candidate. The members of Cumann na mBan remained steadfast in their support for Sinn Féin. 'We lost very few from Cumann na mBan to Fianna Fáil,' said Síle Bean Uí Dhonnchadha, who remained faithful all her life to Republican movements.[34] The press and media, not kindly disposed to Sinn Féin, gave scant coverage to meetings of that organisation. *Saoirse na h-Éireann, Irish Freedom,* a small newspaper organ of Sinn Féin, declared that 'hardly a day passes without large and enthusiastic meetings held under the auspices of the Republican organisation being either ignored or reported in a manifestly misleading manner.'[35]

There was a big surprise on nomination day when Dan Breen, who had been affiliated to Clann Éireann for a time, decided instead to stand as an Independent candidate in his home constituency of Tipperary.

The new Editor of *An Phoblacht,* Peadar O'Donnell, was hoping for a Republican victory in the general election but he warned that 'the hesitation in people's minds where Republican candidates are concerned is that a Republican majority might be followed by an immediate declaration of war.'[36] He advised the two Republican parties to unite for the election campaign.

In a letter to *The Nation,* the Fianna Fáil-sponsored newspaper, S.P. Ó Cadhla expressed his anger at the lack of unity between Fianna Fáil and Sinn Féin as an important general election approached:

Fianna Fáil and Sinn Féin are each alike imbued with the same motives, they cherish the same ideals, they strive for the same objects…As we read the list of selected candidates appearing day by day, we are grieved to note that one-time loyal comrades are now in different camps. Barney Mellows and Frank Fahy are, perhaps, to take opposite sides in Galway; Éamon de Valera and Brian O'Higgins in Clare; Dr John Madden and P.J. Ruttledge in Mayo and so on. Republicans, pause in your blind infatuation and criminal folly.[37]

To Mary MacSwiney's credit she wrote to Éamon de Valera, President of Fianna Fáil, on 11 May 1927 and appealed to him to unite their two parties together and make a big effort to win a majority of seats in the election – a feat she believed was possible. But she wanted to do this on her own terms. She could work with de Valera if both their parties combined returned a majority of deputies to the Dáil but if the combined Fianna Fáil and Sinn Féin TDs elected were in a minority position after the election, she could not envisage the Sinn Féin TDs cooperating in any way with de Valera's policies. She put it this way:

The difficulty is the minority position for which directly or indirectly I, for one, would not stand. It has been suggested that a majority is almost a certainty: that we could negotiate for that…but that if afterwards the minority resulted and your people did things we could not stand by, we would not be responsible.[38]

Éamon de Valera replied by letter to Mary MacSwiney three days later. He defended the 'minority' position of Fianna Fáil, which meant that he envisaged that Fianna Fáil would be willing at some stage to enter the Free State parliament as a minority political party provided the Oath of Allegiance was abolished.

What you call the 'minority' position of Fianna Fáil is an essential part of the whole programme, and to give it up would be to cripple the policy as a whole. Knowing your attitude on this question and being as convinced that I am right as you are that you are right, I feel we can only agree to differ. I do not know what Sinn Féin will do in the matter of preference votes in the coming elections, but we, at any rate, are determined to see that no Republican votes on our side are lost. It is a pity that Sinn Féin cannot see eye to eye with us on our policy as a whole, for I believe that together on that programme we would be almost certain of success.[39]

By this stage, Fianna Fáil had probably become aware that the Republican vote was going strongly in their favour and that their policy was more attractive to the electorate than Sinn Féin's. From this point on the party opposed any scheme proposed by the Second Dáil and *Comhairle na dTeachtaí* that clashed with their own brand of Republicanism. De Valera drifted away from his former friends among the Second Dáil Republican TDs and his presence at their meetings and at the meetings of *Comhairle na dTeachtaí* ceased. Sinn Féin went to pains to explain why people should not vote for de Valera's party. Their pre-election handouts described 'Fianna Fáilers' as 'Repealers' and Sinn Féiners as 'Republicans'. 'Vote for Sinn Féin candidates because you are neither a 'Treatyite' nor a 'Repealer' – you are a 'Republican', exhorted the election sheets.

One vital question remained to be decided in the forthcoming election and only the Republican family could decide it. There would be a sub-contest between Sinn Féin and Fianna Fáil to establish who would command the Republican vote for the future.

Peadar O'Donnell, the editor of *An Phoblacht*, wrote an editorial just before the election, emphasising that this election would be fought under the proportional representation system:

We urge all Republicans to vote solidly the complete list of

Republican candidates going forward in their constituency. The executives of Sinn Féin and Fianna Fáil have not been fair to the mass of Republicans in the country but the executives have not succeeded in really splitting the country and a solid Republican vote will be secured, thanks to the good sense of the rank and file.[40]

Just a few days before polling day, the Fianna Fáil newspaper, the *Nation*, stressed that the Oath was the predominant issue of the whole general election;

> In making the Oath of Allegiance to the King of England the issue of this election, Fianna Fáil has not misinterpreted the feeling of the nation nor misjudged the national interests. The people desire that the assembly that legislates for three-quarters of Ireland should be open to all whom they elect to it; that no barrier should be raised or maintained against any of their representatives, and above all that no Oath to perpetuate a status of inferiority or subjection should be imposed on deputies... Those who say that England will wage war on us if our representatives refuse to swear allegiance to her king are inciting her to do so.[41]

For polling day, 9 June 1927, the weather was favourable and although there were some showers in the evening in Munster and Connacht, there was sunshine all day in the other areas. The weather contributed to a heavy poll of 67.6 per cent of the electorate, as compared to 60.7 per cent in 1923.

The general public took a great interest in the election results. Big crowds gathered outside newspaper offices to read the results as they were posted outside. The bright nights of midsummer enticed many people to come out and talk and wait to see the final outcome of what was expected to be a tight contest.

Outside the Fianna Fáil Headquarters in Lower Abbey Street, Dublin, large crowds gathered to hear the results as they were announced. As it became apparent that Fianna Fáil was doing well, celebrations began because a new political party had been born.

It took almost a week to count all the votes in the thirty constituencies. There were a hundred and fifty-three Dáil seats up for grabs. Cumann na nGaedheal won forty-seven seats, Fianna Fáil, forty-four, the Labour Party twenty-two, Independents thirteen, Farmers eleven, the National League Party eight, Sinn Féin five, Independent Republicans two, Independent Labour one. Clann Éireann did not win a single seat.

Cumann na nGaedheal had lost eleven seats in the general election. In the 1923 general election the party had secured 39 per cent of the total votes cast. In this election its percentage dropped to 27.4 per cent.[42] The total Cumann na nGaedheal vote came to 315,000, which exceeded the vote of any other party. The pro-Treaty party won the highest number of Dáil seats of any party and as a result, again emerged as the largest party in the state. But the election result was a severe jolt for the government party. President W.T. Cosgrave had warned the electorate in his eve-of-poll speech in Kilkenny: 'If we go back only fifty strong, I cannot form a government.'[43]

The constituency of Galway returned the highest number of Fianna Fáil TDs: there the party obtained four seats out of nine. But Kerry came very close to this performance when that constituency returned three Fianna Fáil deputies out of a possible seven. The party polled almost 300,000 votes in this election – 26.2 per cent of all the votes cast.[44] Fianna Fáil destroyed Sinn Féin at the polls and won the contest for the Republican vote hands down.

Labour had fifteen seats in Leinster House when the Dáil was dissolved. After the general election their representation increased by seven. Labour polled the very respectable total of almost 144,000 votes – 12.6 per cent of the national vote.[45] This was a remarkable achievement against a full line-out of the various political parties. The fact that eleven of Labour's fifteen Dáil representatives had voted to give a first reading to Dan Breen's Bill to abolish the Oath of Allegiance did not harm them in the eyes of the electorate. In fact the big majority of Labour TDs who voted for his Bill did well in the general election. Support for the removal of the Oath of Allegiance was further boosted in the Labour Party by the election in Galway of a new TD, Gilbert Lynch, who said, while addressing a Labour gathering after his election, that 'he would do everything possible to remove the Oath.'[46] Thomas Johnson, leader of the Labour Party, issued a short statement to *The Irish Times* after the election: 'The results of the election are satisfactory to the Labour Party and have fulfilled our expectations.'[47]

There were fourteen Independents in the Dáil on dissolution day, including Dan Breen. Thirteen Independents were returned in the general election but it was believed that eleven of these could be relied on to support the Cumann na nGaedheal government.[48] Dan Breen, standing as an Independent in his home constituency of Tipperary, was badly defeated and received a very low number of first-preference votes. His Republican supporters did not forgive him for breaking ranks with de Valera and entering the Dáil without receiving a mandate from his local constituents to do so. Dan felt dejected and crestfallen that his own people in Tipperary had rejected him. Soon afterwards he left Ireland for the USA.

When the Dáil was dissolved the Farmers' Party held fourteen seats. They did not perform well in the election, lost three seats and finished with eleven seats and 8.9 per cent of the electorate.[49] Patrick Baxter, Farmers' TD for Cavan, who had voted to give a first reading to Dan Breen's Bill to abolish the Oath, was again elected in Cavan. In general terms the Farmers' Party could be relied on to support the Cumann na nGaedheal government.

Captain William Redmond's National League Party had eight deputies elected to the Dáil. It polled 84,000 votes and got 7.3 per cent of the votes cast.[50] The majority of the seats won by the National League were more personal triumphs than evidence of support for the party's policy, which was not very clearly defined. James Cosgrave, Galway, who had voted to give a first reading to Dan Breen's motion to abolish the Oath of Allegiance, lost his seat in the election. The National League TDs were expected to support the government.

Sinn Féin had a disastrous election. Only five of their candidates were elected: David Kent topped the poll in Cork East; Austin Stack was elected in Kerry; Oscar Traynor in Dublin North; Dr John Madden in Mayo North and Caitlín Brugha was returned as one of the deputies for Waterford. The party polled a mere 41,000 votes and gained only 3.6 per cent of the total number of first-preference votes, though it must be taken into consideration that it contested only fifteen constituencies out of thirty.[51] Mary MacSwiney failed to get elected in Cork City Borough. Other household Sinn Féin figures who failed at the polls were Art O'Connor (Kildare) described by Sinn Féin as 'President of the Second Dáil'; Dr Kathleen Lynn (Dublin County); Brian O'Higgins (Clare); Count George Plunkett (Roscommon); Charles Murphy (Dublin City South); Dr Conor Byrne (Longford-Westmeath); Seán Buckley (Cork West); Charlie Mellows (Galway) and Seán Farrell (Leitrim-Sligo). Mary MacSwiney said of the outcome of the election: 'It is a disappointing result for uncompromising Republicans – it is to be regretted that what the Free State was unable to do in Cork City in 1922 and in 1923 [to defeat Mary MacSwiney] has been accomplished by those claiming to be Republicans. The seats lost by uncompromising Republicans have been taken by the Fianna Fáil candidates.'[52]

Of the four Independent Republicans who stood for election two were successful: Daniel Corkery TD (Cork North), who topped the poll, and Professor Arthur Clery TD who won a seat in the NUI constituency. The *Saoirse na h-Éireann, Irish Freedom* newspaper that expressed the Sinn Féin view of events, congratulated Professor Clery on his election as a Republican candidate for the National University of Ireland and declared: 'He is a life-long worker for Republicanism and will not sit in any parliament but that of the Irish Republic.'[53] After his election in Cork North, Daniel Corkery said that it would not be against his principles to enter the Dáil provided he was not obliged to take the Oath of Allegiance. He declared, 'I will present myself for admission to the Dáil when it opens next week.'[54]

Clann Éireann had nominated eight candidates for the election but none was elected. Both Professor William Magennis and Pádraic Ó Máille lost their seats. The absence of the two Clann Éireann deputies would be felt in the Dáil if another attempt was made to abolish the Oath. Their party had suffered complete extinction.

The total anti-Treaty vote, that of Fianna Fáil, Sinn Féin and Independent

Republicans combined, was 350,000: for the first time since independence it was higher than the Cumann na nGaedheal vote of 315,000. The anti-Treaty Republicans had won fifty-one seats in the Dáil – one third of the total number of seats.

The five constituencies that gave the highest number of first-preference votes to the combined anti-Treaty parties were (in order of percentage): Kerry (44.5 per cent); Clare (43.5 per cent); Mayo North (42.8 per cent); Mayo South (39.4 per cent); Galway (38 per cent). The five constituencies that gave the lowest number of first-preference votes to the combined anti-Treaty parties were National University of Ireland (17.5 per cent); Wicklow (21.8 per cent); Cork City Borough (22.8 per cent); Cork West (22.8 per cent); and Carlow-Kilkenny (23.7 per cent). The small farmers, the agricultural labourers and the people who lived in the working-class areas of the cities contributed most to the anti-Treaty vote. The affluent classes in the big cities, including the academic elite of the universities, and the large farmers who tilled the most fertile lands of Ireland voted for the status quo – and the status quo lay with the Treaty parties.

De Valera issued a statement as the results came to a conclusion:

> The only party which accepted the challenge of Fianna Fáil and fought for imposing the Oath of Allegiance to England was the Free State government party. That party has suffered a signal defeat…The Imperialists, of course, want the Gael outlawed and disfranchised. But Fianna Fáil was founded on faith in the Irish people and belief in their desire to be free…In accordance with the mandate given to them, Fianna Fáil deputies will claim their seats.[55]

At a dinner given in the Mansion House by the Dublin Chamber of Commerce, Séamus Bourke, Free State Minister for Local Government and Public Health, said: 'We were forced into a position that we have to rule the country with a mailed fist, and we could not do that and expect to be elected in strong numbers.'[56] A disappointed W.T. Cosgrave issued a statement: 'The election of the President of the Executive Council is a matter for the new Dáil when it meets.'[57]

The five Sinn Féin deputies would not enter the Dáil as then constituted. It was also unlikely that Professor Clery, the Independent Republican TD for the NUI, would enter Leinster House. But it would be interesting to see what would happen if the forty-four Fianna Fáil deputies and the other Independent Republican TD, Daniel Corkery (Cork North), decided to take their seats in the Dáil within the lifetime of the new government.

Notes

1.   The *Irish Independent*, 25 January 1927.
2.   Franciscan Library, Killiney, de Valera Papers, File 1306, Dan Breen.
3.   The *Irish Independent*, 25 January 1927.
4.   *Ibid.*, 26 January 1927.
5.   Interview with Dan Breen by the author, Jim Maher, in St Joseph's Nursing Home, Kilcroney, County Wicklow, in August 1967.
6.   Franciscan Library, Killiney, de Valera Papers, File 1306, cutting from the *Irish Press*, 19 December 1969.
7.   The *Irish Independent*, 9 February 1927.
8.   *Ibid.*, 26 January 1927.
9.   *Saoirse na h-Éireann, Irish Freedom*, February 1927.
10. The *Irish Independent*, 12 January 1927.
11. *Saoirse na h-Éireann, Irish Freedom*, February 1927.
12. The *Irish Independent*, 14 February 1927.
13. *Ibid.*, 16 February 1927.
14. *Ibid.*, 8 March 1927.
15. NAI, File No; 2B/82/117/26/7, Minutes of the Standing Committee of Sinn Féin, 11 March 1927.
16. Anne Mareco, *The Rebel Countess*, p. 298.
17. The *Irish Independent*, 26 March 1927.
18. *Ibid.*, 28 March 1927.
19. *Ibid.*, 1 April 1927.
20. *Ibid.*, 5 April 1927.
21. *Ibid.*, 7 April 1927.
22. *Dáil Éireann Debates*, Volume 19, 991, 6 April 1927.
23. *Ibid.*
24. *Ibid.*, Volume 19, 991-992, 6 April 1927.
25. *Ibid.*, Volume 19, 992, 6 April 1927.
26. *Ibid.*
27. *Ibid.*, Volume 19, 993-994, 6 April 1927.
     The following are the seventeen TDs who voted to give a first reading to Dan Breen's Bill to abolish the Oath of Allegiance:
     Labour (11): David Hall (Meath); Thomas Johnson (Dublin County); Patrick Clancy (Limerick); Thomas Nagle (Cork North); William Norton (Dublin County); Thomas J. O'Connell (Galway); Hugh Colohan (Kildare); Edward (Éamonn) Doyle (Carlow-Kilkenny); Daniel Morrissey (Tipperary); Timothy Murphy (Cork West); Patrick Hogan (Clare).
     Farmers (2): Patrick Baxter (Cavan); Conor Hogan (Clare).
     Clann Éireann (2): Dan Breen (Tipperary); Pádraic Ó Máille (Galway).
     Independent Labour (1): John Daly (Cork East).
     National League (1): James Cosgrave (Galway). The *Irish Independent*, 7 April 1927.

28. Analysis of how the parties voted on Dan Breen's motion to abolish the Oath of Allegiance:

Party	For	Against
Cumann na nGaedheal	0	34
Farmers	2	6
Labour	11	0
Clann Éireann	2	0
National League	1	0
Independents	0	7
Independent Labour	1	0
Total	**17**	**47**

29. The *Irish Independent*, 11 April 1927.
30. The *Nation*, 16 April 1927.
31. The *Irish Independent*, 7 May 1927.
32. *Ibid.*
33. UCDA, File P176/23 (20) Archives of the Fianna Fáil Party, Fianna Fáil Election Pledge.
34. Uinseann Mac Eoin, *Survivors*, p. 348.
35. *Saoirse na h-Éireann, Irish Freedom*, May 1927.
36. *An Phoblacht*, 6 May 1927.
37. The *Nation*, 23 April 1927.
38. UCDA, Mary MacSwiney Papers, File P48a/43/49, 11 May 1927.
39. UCDA, Mary MacSwiney Papers, File P48a/43/50, 14 May 1927.
40. *An Phoblacht*, 3 June 1927.
41. The *Nation*, 4 June 1927.
42. Richard Sinnott, *Irish Voters Decide*, p. 300.
43. The *Irish Independent*, 9 June 1927.
44. Sinnott, *op. cit.*, p. 299.
45. *Ibid.*, p. 301.
46. *The Irish Times*, 14 June 1927.
47. *Ibid.*, 15 June 1927.
48. The *Irish Independent*, 16 June 1927.
49. Sinnott, *op. cit.*, p. 302.
50. *Ibid.*, p. 302.
51. *Ibid.*, p. 302.
52. The *Irish Independent.*, 18 June 1927.
53. *Saoirse na h-Éireann, Irish Freedom*, July 1927.
54. The *Irish Independent*, 16 June 1927.
55. *The Irish Times*, 15 June 1927.
56. The *Irish Independent*, 15 June 1927.
57. *Ibid.*, 17 June 1927.

14

The Oath Reaches Crisis Point

With the general election over, the first task facing each elected deputy was to take the Oath of Allegiance as provided in Article 17 of the Constitution of the Irish Free State. Part of Article 17 specified that this Oath 'shall be taken and subscribed by every member of the Oireachtas, before taking his seat in the Dáil, before the representative of the Crown or some person authorised by him.' The Clerk of the Dáil, Colm Ó Murchadha, was now the authorised person to administer the Oath and the location was a room set aside in Leinster House.[1]

Seán Lemass TD had declared that he and his fellow TDs would claim their seats in the Dáil without taking the Oath of Allegiance. Daniel Corkery, the Independent Republican TD from Cork North, had announced that he would do likewise. Colm Ó Murchadha, Clerk of the Dáil, sent invitations to all the elected TDs to attend at Leinster House on either Tuesday 21 June or Wednesday 22 June for the purpose of taking the Oath.[2] The Dáil was due to meet on Thursday 23 June.

Fianna Fáil headquarters sent circulars signed by Seán Lemass and Gerry Boland to the secretary of each *cumann* of the organisation. One circular said: 'The Free State parliament will open on Thursday, 23 June. We are very anxious that a monster demonstration should be held in Dublin on that day when the Fianna Fáil *teachtaí* present themselves and demand admission as the elected representatives of the people.'[3]

Support for Fianna Fáil came from a large convention of north Cork Republicans in Millstreet, County Cork, who had advised Daniel Corkery to attend at Leinster House on 23 June, demand his seat without taking any Oath and cooperate with the Fianna Fáil party in their fight for its abolition.[4]

The newly elected representatives of the Fianna Fáil parliamentary party held their very first meeting on 22 June 1927 on the eve of the opening session of the new Dáil. Forty-three Fianna Fáil deputies attended. Éamon Donnelly, Republican MP for Armagh, who had previously taken the side of Sinn Féin, was present at this meeting.[5] On the nomination of Michael Kilroy TD (Mayo South), seconded by Neal Blaney TD (Donegal), Éamon de Valera TD (Clare) was unanimously elected chairman. The meeting considered what action the party should take on the following day. Éamon de Valera read an opinion submitted by counsels A. Wood KC, Creed Meredith KC and George Gavan Duffy BL to the effect that no person had legal authority to exclude from the Dáil, before the election of the Ceann Comhairle, any member who had not subscribed to the Oath. After an intense discussion, a motion proposed by Paddy Belton TD (Dublin County) and seconded by Dr Patrick McCarvill TD (Monaghan) dictated 'that in the event of the Fianna Fáil *teachtaí* (TDs) being present in the Free State Dáil when its Ceann Comhairle (Chairman) is being elected, a member of Fianna Fáil should be proposed for that office.' When this motion had been passed, the meeting decided that Seán T. Ó Ceallaigh (O'Kelly) TD (Dublin North) should be proposed as Ceann Comhairle.[6]

Big crowds had gathered in Lower Abbey Street when de Valera, heading his band of forty-four Fianna Fáil TDs, augmented by the Independent Republican TD Daniel Corkery, emerged from Fianna Fáil Headquarters at 2pm on 23 June 1927. Followed by a large throng of people, the Fianna Fáil deputies reached the junction of Kildare Street and Nassau Street, where a cordon of Gardai was on duty. Éamon de Valera, accompanied by Seán T. O'Kelly, Gerry Boland, and Seán Lemass, were allowed through and the other Fianna Fáil TDs followed. As de Valera and his party disappeared up Kildare Street, the crowd sang 'The Soldiers' Song'.

When the Fianna Fáil group arrived at the entrance to the grounds of Leinster House, a uniformed attendant asked each deputy for his credentials. Each elected TD had to produce his invitation from the Clerk of the Dáil before he was admitted. Colonel Brennan, the superintendent of Leinster House, conducted the party to No. 2 Committee Room, which was directly opposite the main hall of Leinster House. Then the hall was cleared except for police and officials. Colm Ó Murchadha, Clerk of the Dáil, and Mr McGann, Assistant Clerk of the Dáil, entered No. 2 Committee Room. Seán T. O'Kelly said to Colm Ó Murchadha that he wished to proceed to the Dáil Chamber. Ó Murchadha responded that before he could do that he had 'a little formality' for him to comply with.

'What is it?' asked O'Kelly.

'It is Article 17 of the Constitution,' replied Ó Murchadha.

'Read it out,' requested de Valera.

Ó Murchadha read it out for all the assembled Fianna Fáil deputies. The article stipulated that no elected deputy could secure his official place in the Dáil until he first took the Oath of Allegiance.

'I will not take any Oath of Allegiance,' replied de Valera.

'Neither will I,' said Seán T. O'Kelly

'I refuse to do so also,' said P.J. Ruttledge.

'I will never take the Oath of Allegiance,' declared Countess Markievicz.

Colm Ó Murchadha then left the committee room and ordered the door on the passage leading to the Dáil chamber to be locked. When Ó Murchadha re-entered No. 2 Committee Room, Seán T. O'Kelly TD addressed him.

'I am going to the Dáil Chamber,' said O'Kelly. 'There is nothing in the Constitution to prevent me going there.'

'Standing orders prevent you,' answered Ó Murchadha.

'Are they valid?' queried O'Kelly.

'Yes,' replied the Clerk of the Dáil.

The Fianna Fáil deputies then left No. 2 Committee Room and proceeded along the hall towards the Dáil Chamber but Colonel Brennan, Captain of the Guard, and Garda Superintendent O'Gorman intercepted them. Colonel Brennan told Seán T. O'Kelly that he could not enter as he had not complied with Article 17 of the Free State Constitution that stipulated that he should first take the Oath of Allegiance. Éamon de Valera and Seán T. O'Kelly made several attempts to proceed in the direction of the Dáil chamber but each time Colonel Brennan and two Garda superintendents prevented them. At this time practically all the Fianna Fáil deputies had come out of No. 2 Committee

Room and were standing in the hall. A strong force of Gardai in uniform and plain clothes appeared and guarded the door leading to the Dáil chamber. Deputies still stood about in groups.

At 4.20pm a number of Dáil deputies that included Éamon de Valera, P.J. Ruttledge, Seán T. O'Kelly, Seán Lemass, Gerry Boland and Seán MacEntee emerged from Leinster House and were greeted with loud cheers.[7] The Fianna Fáil deputies walked back to their headquarters in Lower Abbey Street where they held an enthusiastic meeting on the street outside. 'As long as we are the representatives of the people, we will never take an Oath of Allegiance to a foreign king,' declared Éamon de Valera amidst cheers.[8] But despite all their determination and enthusiasm they had failed in their attempt to claim their seats in the Dáil. Some commentators felt that their failure to enter the Dáil would so disappoint their supporters 'who have disfranchised themselves' by voting for them that 'Republicanism will henceforth be a failing force.'[9]

The Fianna Fáil parliamentary party came together again that evening. This time there were forty-two elected deputies present: Daniel Corkery, who had been elected as an Independent Republican, had joined Fianna Fáil. It was decided that each deputy present at this meeting should sign the following declaration:

> That the following deputies, wrongfully debarred from taking their seats as representatives of the people because of their refusal to subscribe to an Oath of Allegiance to a foreign king, emphatically repeat their election pledge, that under no circumstances whatsoever will they subscribe to any such Oath.[10]

Every deputy present signed the declaration. The meeting then adjourned.

The Sinn Féin newspaper, *Saoirse na h-Éireann, Irish Freedom*, stated: 'The Irish question is not going to be solved on the issue of the Oath. To abolish the Oath of Allegiance to Britain is good. A better Free State is a good thing – for Free Staters. But it is not what we want.'[11] It was clear from that statement that Fianna Fáil could expect little assistance from Sinn Féin in their efforts to remove the Oath of Allegiance from the Irish Constitution.

Meanwhile the elected TDs of the other parties, who had already taken the Oath of Allegiance before Colm Ó Murchadha in Leinster House during the previous two days, had assembled in the Dáil Chamber to elect a new government. W.T. Cosgrave TD, who had topped the poll in Carlow-Kilkenny, was proposed and seconded to fill the office of President of the Executive Council for another term by two members of his own party.[12] Rather reluctantly W.T. Cosgrave accepted the proposition. He wanted to make it quite clear that he did not seek office. 'If I am to accept and continue in office it will be only on the very clearest understanding that I shall receive sufficient support in this House to carry out my programme.'[13] Cosgrave also stated that he had no intention of tampering in any way with the Treaty:

> As long as the Treaty remains, neither this House nor any other assembly can remove the obligation which the Treaty imposes upon elected representatives of subscribing to the Oath... The Irish people cannot alter it except by agreement with Great Britain, ratified by legislation on both sides, but until it is either denounced or altered, the Oath must remain because the international obligations of any country override its internal laws.[14]

Thomas Johnson, leader of the Labour Party, rose and said that his Party would oppose the re-election of President Cosgrave because of the poor record of the previous government's social measures. Patrick Baxter TD (Cavan), leader of the Farmers' Party, announced that, if there was a division in the House, his party's votes would go to elect President Cosgrave for another term but he would not promise that his party would give undivided support to every measure brought forward by a Cumann na nGaedheal government. The leader of the National League Party, Captain William Redmond, said that his party would certainly not support the proposal to elect Cosgrave.

The Labour Party then called for a division and, as a result, W.T. Cosgrave was re-elected President of the Executive Council by sixty-eight votes to twenty-two.[15] All the forty-four Cumann na nGaedheal deputies present voted for Cosgrave and their votes were augmented by thirteen Independents and eleven Farmers' Party deputies. The twenty-two Labour Party TDs voted against the appointment of Cosgrave and the eight National League deputies abstained.

W.T. Cosgrave had a clear majority but it must be remembered that forty-four Fianna Fáil deputies and one Independent Republican TD had been forcibly restrained from entering the Dáil to vote against him. Five elected Sinn Féin TDs had refused even to attempt to enter the Dáil and Professor Arthur Clery, Independent Republican TD, had remained an abstentionist and had not taken his seat. If the combined total of fifty-one elected Republican TDs had been able and willing to record their votes, W.T. Cosgrave would have been defeated in the vote for his re-election as President of the Executive Council of the fifth Dáil because the combined opposition vote would then have totalled seventy-three.

The *Nation* observed: 'Cosgrave has had to take office without the fifty Cumann na nGaedheal men that he stipulated for.'[16]

Soon afterwards President Cosgrave announced the personnel of the new government. He reappointed almost all of his principal colleagues but there was a surprise when General Richard Mulcahy was made Minister for Local Government as he had been absent from the cabinet since he resigned as Minister for Defence following the Army Mutiny in March 1924. Kevin O'Higgins, who had obtained a huge vote in the general election, strengthened his position in the government. He was appointed Vice-President and Minister for Justice. He was also given the portfolio of Minister for Foreign Affairs.

Saoirse na h-Éireann, Irish Freedom newspaper demonstrated the total lack of interest of Sinn Féin in these parliamentary proceedings. 'It does not matter to us whether Tom Johnson or Paddy Baxter, Willie Cosgrave or Éamon de Valera rules the new parliament. Oath-bound or Oath-free, it is still a parliament of the British Empire. We have no use for it.'[17]

In the meantime ordinary citizens of the Free State were beginning to put strong pressure on the elected Fianna Fáil deputies to take their seats in the Dáil. At their meeting on 26 June the County Monaghan, executive of the Cottage Tenants' Association passed a resolution calling on the Fianna Fáil deputy from that constituency, Dr Patrick McCarvill, to take his seat in the Dáil and use his powers there to help the people.[18] Dr McCarvill replied: 'I presented myself at the opening of the Dáil and if I am not now performing my duties as the elected representative of the people it was for the good reason that I was forcibly prevented from doing so.'[19]

Éamon de Valera and his leading Fianna Fáil TDs openly declared that legal action would probably be taken in reference to the exclusion of forty-five elected deputies from the opening of the fifth Dáil before a Ceann Comhairle was elected. Seán Lemass was doubtful about the chance of success of the proposed legal action and said that it would be 'like arraigning the devil in the court of hell.'[20] Éamon de Valera also said that Fianna Fáil would proceed to secure the necessary 75,000 signatures (with not more than 15,000 in any one constituency) to demand that provisions be made to submit to a referendum the question of the imposition of the Oath of Allegiance on Dáil deputies. He was certain that the Oath would then go. 'It is only the imperialists and the Cosgrave Party,' he said, 'who want the Oath and when the people get the opportunity of dealing themselves with this question they will settle it.'[21] The national executive of Fianna Fáil supported Éamon de Valera's plan to force the Cumann na nGaedheal-led government to hold a referendum on the question of the Oath. The campaign to collect signatures was begun in Cork City and in the counties of Dublin and Wexford.[22]

The declaration that legal action would be taken by Fianna Fáil was formally acted upon a week later when the party filed a writ in the High Court of Justice in the names of Seán T. O'Kelly and Seán Lemass. It asked the Court to declare that O'Kelly and Lemass, duly elected deputies, were entitled to enter the place of meeting of the members of the chamber of deputies assembling to elect a Ceann Comhairle without taking or subscribing to the Oath set out in Article 17 of the Constitution.[23]

While all this was happening, Éamon de Valera and Republicans in Fianna Fáil, Sinn Féin and Cumann na mBan received worrying news from

Sir Patrick Dun's Hospital, Dublin. Countess Markievicz, patriot and lover of the poor in Dublin, lay there in a critical condition. Shortly after returning from her exclusion from the Dáil, where she refused to take the Oath of Allegiance, she fell ill and was rushed to hospital. She underwent an operation for appendicitis. She recovered well at first but then suffered complications. Her surgeon operated a second time.[24] As she lay in bed in a public ward, among the poor of Dublin whom she loved and who never let her down in any election, her doctors feared that she was too weak to make a recovery.

The *Nation* described the characteristics of the people of the Irish Free State who continued to be disfranchised on account of the Oath of Allegiance:

> Republicans are one-third of the people of Ireland, the largest, most united and most resolute of political life. That vote is steady, those who vote Republican do not change – they have overcome the allurements of fair promises, the despairing councils of poverty…No event will change them.[25]

On Sunday 10 July 1927 Éamon de Valera addressed a Fianna Fáil public meeting in Ennis, where he received a rapturous welcome. He said that the Free State government had inscribed in people's minds an image of a Dáil which 'Unionists, Orangemen, anarchists may enter but not a Republican.'[26]

That Sunday, while Éamon de Valera was speaking to his constituents in Ennis, the rest of the country came to a virtual standstill as news spread from Dublin that Kevin O'Higgins TD, Vice-President of the Executive Council of the Irish Free State, Minister for Justice and Minister for External Affairs had been gravely wounded by three assassins on his way to Mass in Booterstown, County Dublin. O'Higgins died from his wounds just before 5pm that day. President W.T. Cosgrave issued a statement condemning the assassination:

> The crime which has been committed is grievous beyond words…This crime has not been committed by private indiv-iduals against Kevin O'Higgins. It is a political assassination of a pillar of the State. It is the fruit of the steady, persistent attack

against the State and its fundamental institutions…We will meet this form of terrorism as we met the other forms of terrorism and we shall not falter until every vestige of it is wiped out from the land.[27]

Even before Kevin O'Higgins died from his wounds, the IRA Army Council issued a statement denying any part in the assassination:

Regarding the attempt on Mr O'Higgins' [sic] life today, the Army Council and General Headquarters Staff of Óglaigh na h-Éireann desire to state most emphatically that they have no knowledge whatever of this act, and repudiate any responsibility for it. We feel certain that responsibility, when tracked home, will not involve any of our volunteers. Our organisation does not countenance private acts of vengeance against individuals.[28]

The IRA Army Council did not deliberately lie in this statement. They were certain that no group within their movement was officially involved in the assassination. But many Republicans who had taken part in the Civil War had revenge in their hearts for Kevin O'Higgins, Minister for Home Affairs at that period, for his support for the executions of seventy-seven anti-Treaty prisoners in 1922 and 1923. A small group of freelance IRA members, who held this viewpoint, had assassinated O'Higgins.

Éamon de Valera, still in Ennis, lost no time in condemning the murder in the most emphatic terms:

The assassination of O'Higgins is murder and is most inexcusable from any standpoint. I am confident that no Republican was responsible for it or would give it any countenance…It is a crime that cuts at the root of all representative government.[29]

Reaction to the assassination of Kevin O'Higgins was swift and widespread. Public bodies, district courts and individuals all over the country expressed horror and indignation at the murder.

Four days after the assassination of Kevin O'Higgins, Countess Markievicz died in Sir Patrick Dun's Hospital. Her condition had worsened at nine o'clock the previous night. At midnight she became unconscious and died within two hours. Among those present at her bedside were Éamon de Valera, leader of Fianna Fáil, Dr Kathleen Lynn, former Sinn Féin TD for Dublin County and still a member of the *Ard-Chomhairle* of that party, and veteran Republican activist Mrs Sheehy Skeffington. Their presence together at her deathbed was a tribute to the rebel Countess – the two sides of the Republican family were drawn together for a few days because they so admired and loved her right up to her final moments on earth. The last public utterance of the noble Countess was when the Clerk of the Dáil, Colm Ó Murchadha, asked her if she was prepared to take the Oath of Allegiance in order to take her seat in the Dáil. 'I will never take the Oath of Allegiance,' she replied. She never did as death intervened to save her from further conflicts of conscience.

The Countess had left Sinn Féin and followed Éamon de Valera into Fianna Fáil when de Valera declared that he would enter the Free State Dáil if the Oath of Allegiance were abolished. The Standing Committee of Sinn Féin usually broke off relations with those who defected from their ranks. Not so with Countess Markievicz. The Countess was not regarded as a political figure but as a national heroine. At the Standing Committee meeting of Sinn Féin on 15 July, Austin Stack, Kerry, proposed and Mrs Margaret Buckley, Dublin, seconded the motion 'that we officially attend Requiem Mass and accompany the remains of Countess Markievicz to the Rotunda tomorrow, Saturday, and the attend funeral on Sunday next.' The resolution was passed with one dissenter – the Kerry delegate, Gobnait Ní Bhruadair.[30]

Three days previously the body of Kevin O'Higgins had been taken to the Oak Room of the Mansion House in the centre of Dublin for his lying in-state. A platoon of military and fifty-two Gardai from the Phoenix Park depot made up a constant guard of honour.

In the case of Countess Markievicz, one of the most prominent Republican leaders from 1916 to 1923, the Dublin City Commissioners refused the use of either the Mansion House or the City Hall for her lying in state. Instead her remains were taken to the Rotunda, where she lay in state for a day.

The third meeting of Fianna Fáil was held in the party's headquarters in Lower Abbey Street after the funeral of Madame Markievicz. There were thirty-four deputies present. De Valera referred to moves that were being made by some of their own supporters to try to get Fianna Fáil members to take the Oath of Allegiance to the Free State Constitution and enter Dáil Éireann. De Valera asked the meeting, 'Is there any member of our Party who would be willing to take the Oath of Allegiance to the Free State Constitution under any circumstances whatsoever?' There was silence in the room for some minutes and he got no reply. Then Paddy Belton said he had no moral qualms about taking the Oath but he had given a pledge not to do so and he would keep it. But he warned that if his stance became untenable, he might have to review his position and resign.[31]

Less than a fortnight after the assassination of Kevin O'Higgins, the Free State government introduced the first reading of two Bills especially designed to end the electoral policies of anti-Treaty elements in the country. The first of these two bills, the Constitution Amendment Bill, was conceived to do away with Article 48 of the Constitution that set forth that on the petition of not less than seventy-five thousand voters on the register, of whom not more than fifteen thousand could be voters in any one constituency, a proposal for a new law could be submitted to a referendum of the people of the country. If the Dáil passed this Bill, it would wipe out Fianna Fáil's plan to change by referendum the requirement for elected Dáil deputies to take the Oath of Allegiance before they could enter the Dáil. The second of the two Bills, the Electoral Amendment (No. 2) Bill, 1927, was the more menacing of the two to the existence of the new Republican party, Fianna Fáil, and the older Republican party, Sinn Féin. It proposed to end the situation whereby people offered themselves as candidates for the Dáil and Senate without any intention of taking their seats. This Bill imposed on candidates for election, as a condition of their nomination, that they give a sworn declaration that, if elected, they would take the Oath of Allegiance and enter the Dáil. If they refused to give this undertaking their names would not appear on the ballot paper as they would be deemed to be disqualified.[32]

At a Fianna Fáil meeting in St Mullins, County Carlow, Seán Lemass said: 'The Free State government has introduced legislation designed to make political action by Republicans impossible in future and to drive us back into a position in which the only effective method we may use to achieve our objects is the method of physical force.'[33]

Paddy Belton, Fianna Fáil TD for County Dublin, ignoring the lesson of Dan Breen, decided to enter the Dáil. The day before the Dáil assembled to consider these two proposed new Bills, he wrote a long letter to *The Irish Times,* announcing he would take his seat in the Dáil the following day. He declared, 'I will not take the Oath of Allegiance to a foreign king because the so-called Oath in the Free State Constitution is not an Oath of Allegiance nor is it an Oath of any kind at all.' He explained that he had attended a Fianna Fáil Dublin County constituency convention that 'decided that I should take my seat. I am not going to resign.' Belton emphasised that it was only inside the Dáil that the campaign against the Oath would succeed. 'The opposition to these proposed new Bills in the Dáil will be supported by about thirty or forty deputies and Fianna Fáil has forty-four. Is it not the course of prudence, wisdom and patriotism to go into the Dáil and defeat these Bills?'[34]

After the publication of the intention of Patrick Belton of taking his seat in the Dáil, de Valera replied:

> As a party we have been elected on the distinct understanding that we would not take the Oath. The fact that the Free State now proposes to block up every avenue by which the Oath could be removed by political action will not alter the attitude of Republicans towards the taking of that Oath.[35]

Seán Lemass and Gerry Boland, honorary secretaries of Fianna Fáil, issued a statement that 'at a special meeting of the Fianna Fáil national executive held on Monday 25 July a resolution was passed unanimously that Mr P. Belton TD is hereby excluded from membership of the Fianna Fáil organisation.'[36]

Belton entered the Dáil on 26 July 1927 after signing the Dáil roll book that contained a copy of the Oath of Allegiance. Colonel Patrick Brennan, Superintendent of the Gardaí, introduced him to the Speaker, Micheál Ó h-Aodha TD.

The fourth meeting of the elected Fianna Fáil deputies took place on 26 July 1927 in Fianna Fáil Headquarters in Dublin. Forty elected Fianna Fáil TDs attended. Éamon de Valera read a draft of a guarantee which he had told representatives of the Labour Party he would be prepared to give to them personally provided his colleagues in the Fianna Fáil party concurred. The draft read:

> In the event of a coalition government being formed and succeeding in securing that all the representatives of the people be free to enter the twenty-six-county assembly without subscribing to any political test, the Fianna Fáil Party will not press any issues involving the Treaty to the point of overthrowing such government during the normal lifetime of the present assembly.[37]

On the motion of Seán French, Cork Borough, seconded by Seán Lemass, the party gave full consent to the action taken by de Valera and he was authorised to sign the document on behalf of the party.

President W.T. Cosgrave TD moved the second reading of the Constitutional Amendment Bill, 1927, which was designed to do away with Article 48 – the clause of the Constitution the Fianna Fáil Party planned to use to submit the Oath of Allegiance to a referendum of the people. Cosgrave pointed out that, from a practical point of view, he could not see how this referendum proposal could ever work. He asked: 'How could it be established that the seventy-five thousand signatures are genuine, that the people who have signed their names are, in fact, on the register, and so on. If proof of all this were undertaken, it…might take two or three years to carry it out.'[38]

Captain William Redmond, leader of the National League party, persuasively opposed this Constitutional Amendment Bill. He objected to the time and method of its introduction. 'It was not until a certain party in the state seemed to think that they could get a political advantage out of exercising what seemed to be their constitutional right that the Executive Council announced that this portion of the Constitution was to be deleted.'[39]

Patrick J. McGilligan, the Free State Minister for Industry and Commerce, supported the Bill to refuse a referendum on the grounds that it would cost the state around £87,000.[40]

On a division, the Constitution Amendment Bill passed its second reading by forty-eight votes to eighteen. The twenty-two members of the Labour Party had left the House in protest over another matter and had not returned in time to record their votes against the measure. The group of eighteen deputies who voted against the Bill and lost the division was made up of eight members of the Farmers' Party, seven National League deputies, two Independents and one ex-Fianna Fáil TD.[41]

President W.T. Cosgrave returned to the Dáil the following morning to ask for a second reading for his Electoral Amendment (No. 2) Bill. He said:

> The object of the Bill is to put an end to the present condition of things in which persons avail of the electoral machinery which has been provided by the State for the selection of members of the Oireachtas…without having any intention of taking their seats or undertaking their duties and responsibilities of the office which they seek. This futile performance has now gone on for five years. At every general election and at most bye-elections, candidates have been on what is described as an abstentionist programme. These candidates claim that such votes as they obtain are votes against the Treaty settlement… This Bill will enable this House to be completed [have all seats occupied].[42]

The leader of the Farmers' Party, P. F. Baxter, said he did not think that the Bill would achieve its purpose, because, if it were passed, the seats might be filled, but would the members be representative of the country?

Thomas Johnson, leader of the Labour Party, said that if they in the Dáil, 'debar people from the opportunity of electing people, of giving their votes to candidates with a certain policy, you are inevitably driving them to other methods.'

President Cosgrave concluded his speech by condemning the abstentionist policy of Fianna Fáil and Sinn Féin. 'The present position of the abstentionist parties in this country is unconstitutional: it is anti-constitutional…The abstentionist policy which is now being pursued by those outside the House is not a parallel with, and has no comparison, with the abstentionist policy which was pursued by the Sinn Féin Party from 1916 to 1920 or 1921.'[43]

By the time the electoral Bill was voted on, the Labour members had ended the protest begun the day before and returned to their seats in the Dáil: nineteen of them voted against it. Six members of the Farmers' Party, six National League deputies, four Independents, one Independent Labour TD, together with Paddy Belton (ex-Fianna Fáil TD) joined them in the opposition lobby to record their votes against the Bill. When the result was announced the second reading of the Electoral Amendment (No. 2) 1927 Bill was carried by fifty-one votes to thirty-seven.[44]

Ex-Fianna Fáil TD, Paddy Belton, summarised the position well when he said: 'In the last two days I have done one man's part to prevent these heinous measures from becoming law and if the other forty-three members of my party had done their part they (the government) would be out now.'[45]

Subsequently, in the absence of the Fianna Fáil and Sinn Féin TDs, the Constitutional Amendment Bill and the Electoral Amendment Bill passed through all their stages in the Dáil without any amendments, except a delaying one in the case of the Electoral Amendment Bill.

Outside the Dáil Éamon de Valera claimed: 'The moment we started on that peaceful road, Cosgrave put his hand up by means of this new legislation and said, "No! – the people must not be allowed to do this thing." The government was trying to make it impossible for Republicans to work on peaceful lines.'[46]

Notes

1. The *Irish Independent*, 14 June 1927.
2. *Ibid.*, 18 June 1927.
3. *Ibid.*, 21 June 1927.
4. *Ibid.*
5. UCDA, Archives of the Fianna Fáil Party, File P176/442.
   The forty-three elected Fianna Fáil TDs who attended the first meeting of the Fianna Fáil parliamentary party on 22 June 1927 were: Éamon de Valera, chairman (Clare); Éamon Donnelly (Armagh); Thomas Derrig (Carlow-Kilkenny); Patrick Smith (Cavan); Pat Houlihan (Clare); Seán French (Cork City); Martin Corry (Cork East); Thomas Mullins (Cork West); Seán T. Ó Ceallaigh (Dublin City North); Kathleen Clarke (Dublin City North); Seán Lemass (Dublin City South); Madame Markievicz (Dublin City South); Paddy Belton (Dublin County); Mark Killalea (Galway County); Proinsias Ó Fathaigh (Galway County); Dr Seán Tubridy (Galway County); Thomas T.P. Powell (Galway County); Thomas O'Reilly (Kerry); Thomas McEllistrim (Kerry); William O'Leary (Kerry); Dónal Ua Buachalla (Kildare); Frank Carty (Leitrim-Sligo); Samuel Holt (Leitrim-Sligo); Patrick Boland (Leix-Offaly); Thomas Tynan (Leix-Offaly); James Colbert (Limerick); Tadhg Crowley (Limerick); James Victory (Longford-Westmeath); Michael J. Kennedy (Longford-Westmeath); Frank Aiken (Louth); Patrick J. Ruttledge (Mayo North); Michael Kilroy (Mayo South); Eugene Mullen (Mayo South); Matthew O'Reilly (Meath); Dr Patrick McCarvill (Monaghan); Gerald Boland (Roscommon); Dr Patrick O'Dowd (Roscommon); Seán Hayes (Tipperary); Andrew Fogarty (Tipperary); Neal Blaney (Donegal); Frank Carney (Donegal); Patrick J. Little (Waterford); Dr James Ryan (Wexford); Séamus Moore (Wicklow).
6. UCDA, Archives of the Fianna Fáil Party, File P176/442, first meeting of the elected TDs of the Fianna Fáil Party.
7. The *Irish Independent* and *The Irish Times*, 24 June 1927.
8. The *Irish Independent*, 24 June 1927.
9. *The Irish Times*, 24 June 1927.
10. UCDA, Archives of the Fianna Fáil Party, File P176/442, Second Meeting of the elected deputies of the Fianna Fáil Party.
11. *Saoirse na h-Éireann, Irish Freedom*, July 1927.
12. *Dáil Éireann Debates*, Volume 20, 23 June 1927, pp. 10, 11.
13. *Ibid.*, Volume 20, 23 June 1927, p. 13.
14. *Ibid.*, Volume 20, 23 June 1927, pp. 14, 15.
15. *Ibid.*, Volume 20, 23 June 1927, pp. 36, 37, 38.
16. The *Nation*, 2 July 1927.
17. *Saoirse na h-Éireann, Irish Freedom*, July 1927.
18. The *Irish Independent*, 28 June 1927.
19. *Ibid.*, 29 June 1927.
20. John Horgan, *Seán Lemass: the Enigmatic Patriot*, p. 47.
21. The *Irish Independent*, 30 June 1927.
22. The *Nation*, 9 July 1927.
23. *The Irish Times*, 9 July 1927.
24. *Ibid.*, 8 July 1927.
25. The *Nation*, 9 July 1927.
26. *The Irish Times*, 11 July 1927.
27. *Ibid.*, 13 July 1927.
28. *Ibid.*, 11 July 1927.
29. *Ibid.*, 12 July 1927.
30. NAI, File 2B/82/117/26/17, Minutes of the Standing Committee of Sinn Féin, 15 July 1927.
31. UCDA, Archives of the Fianna Fáil Party, File P 176/442, 18 July 1927.
32. *The Irish Times*, 26 July 1927.
33. *Ibid.*, 25 July 1927.
34. *Ibid.*
35. *Ibid.*, 26 July 1927.
36. *Ibid.*, 29 July 1927.

37. UCDA, Archives of the Fianna Fáil Party, File P176/442, 26 July 1927.
38. *Dáil Éireann Debates*, Volume 20, 27 July 1927, Constitution Amendment Bill, p. 983.
39. *Ibid.*, p. 995.
40. *Ibid.*, p. 1023.
41. *The Irish Times*, 28 July 1927: List of Dáil deputies who voted against the Constitution (Amendment No. 6) Bill:
    Farmers' Party (8): P.J. Baxter (Cavan); Michael Carter (Leitrim-Sligo); M. Doyle (Wexford); H. Garahan (Longford-Westmeath); M.R. Heffernan (Tipperary); Richard Holohan (Carlow-Kilkenny); T. O'Donovan (Cork West); D. O'Gorman (East Cork).
    National League Party (7): J. Coburn (Louth); W. Duffy (Galway); J. Horgan (Cork); J. Jinks (Leitrim-Sligo); D. McMenamin (Donegal); William Redmond (Waterford); V. Rice (Dublin South).
    Independents (2): A. Byrne (Dublin North); G. Hewson (Limerick).
    Ex-Fianna Fáil (1): Paddy Belton (Dublin County).
42. *Dáil Éireann Debates*, Volume 20, 28 July 1927, Electoral Amendment Bill, pp. 1051, 1052.
43. *Ibid.*, pp. 1107-10.
44. *The Irish Times*, 29 July 1927: List of Dáil deputies who voted against the Electoral Amendment (No. 2) 1927 Bill:
    Labour Party (19): Henry Broderick (Longford-Westmeath); Hugh Colohan (Kildare); Richard Corish (Wexford); Richard Anthony (Cork Borough); Denis Cullen (Dublin North); William Davin (Leix-Offaly); Edward Doyle (Carlow-Kilkenny); John F. Gill (Leix-Offaly); David Hall (Meath); Thomas Johnson (Dublin County); Michael Keyes (Limerick); Thomas Lawlor (Dublin South); Gilbert Lynch (Galway); Patrick Clancy (Limerick); Daniel Morrissey (Tipperary); Patrick Hogan (Clare); T.J. Murphy (Cork West); Timothy Quill (Cork North); James Shannon (Wexford).
    Farmers' Party (6): Patrick F. Baxter (Cavan); Michael R. Heffernan (Tipperary); Michael Doyle (Wexford); Michael Carter (Leitrim-Sligo); Hugh Garahan (Longford-Westmeath); Richard Holohan (Carlow-Kilkenny).
    National League Party (6): Daniel McMenamin (Donegal); William Redmond (Waterford); James Coburn (Louth); William Duffy (Galway); John Horgan (Cork); John Jinks (Leitrim-Sligo).
    Independents (4): Alfie Byrne (Dublin North); Gilbert Hewson (Limerick); Michael Brennan (Roscommon); David Gorman (Cork East).
    Independent Labour (1): John Daly (Cork East).
    Ex-Fianna Fáil (1): Paddy Belton (Dublin County).
45. *Dáil Éireann Debates*, Volume 20, 28 July 1927, Electoral Amendment Bill, p. 1099.
46. *The Irish Times*, 27 July 1927.

15

THE 'EMPTY FORMULA'

At the beginning of August 1927, Éamon de Valera was rethinking his firmly-held decision not to take the Oath of Allegiance under any circumstances prior to entering the Dáil. In a letter to his old Irish-American friend, Frank P. Walsh, he wrote:

> The political situation here has been completely changed by the projected Free State legislation...The Fianna Fáil way of removing the Oath from outside is being made definitely impossible and will, I expect, have to be abandoned.[1]

Fianna Fáil became concerned about how it could overcome the problem posed in the Electoral Amendment Bill that all candidates must make a sworn declaration before nomination that they would take the Oath of Allegiance, if elected, and enter the Dáil.

There were forty elected deputies at the fifth meeting of the Fianna Fáil parliamentary party on 5 August 1927. A general discussion took place that ranged over the then position of the party, the future prospects and the question as to whether commitments made already were such that they precluded Fianna Fáil deputies, even in this emergency, from deviating from the former line of action of refusing to take the Oath of Allegiance before they entered the Dáil. All deputies were asked: if constituency conventions were convened and the present situation explained to them, would these conventions be likely to be for or against Fianna Fáil going into the Free State parliament? Twenty-seven of the deputies present thought their constituents, under these changed circumstances, would vote for going into the Dáil to overturn the recent Free State legislation. Six deputies: Thomas Mullins (Cork West); Daniel Corkery (Cork North); Seán MacEntee (Dublin County); Dr Seán Tubridy (Galway); Frank Carney (Donegal) and Patrick J. Little (Waterford), were unsure whether their constituents would vote for or against the change.[2]

Éamon de Valera asked whether all the members present would abide by the majority decision of the party on the question of entering the Free State assembly. All but three answered 'Yes'. The exceptions were: Kathleen Clarke (Dublin North), who said she would give a reply to Éamon de Valera in two days; Daniel Corkery (Cork North) who said he would have to consult his constituency convention; and Dr Seán Tubridy (Galway) who said he would have to see some people whom he had promised to consult regarding this situation if it should ever arise.[3]

The Fianna Fáil leader then asked one final question of his deputies. 'If ye believe that the Oath of Allegiance formula must, in the conditions of the time, be subscribed to by the Fianna Fáil TDs, do ye think we should do it now rather than leave it to others to do so?' To this query all present answered 'Yes' except Frank Carney (Donegal).[4]

A rough draft of a resolution was then proposed and put to the meeting. It was understood that the resolution would be redrafted later to make absolutely clear the circumstances that caused this decision to be made by this meeting:

> Provided the committee to be hereafter appointed recommends that there is a reasonable prospect of the Party being effective in defeating the measures which the minority government have introduced to provoke civil strife, to suppress rightful political activities, and to deprive the people of their common rights and liberties, the party hereby resolves to take the steps which it considers essential to defeat such measures and save the country from their consequences, by taking their seats in the Free State assembly before the adjournment of that body.[5]

All present, with the exception of Kathleen Clarke, declared themselves in general agreement with the contents of the resolution.[6]

The most prominent members of Fianna Fáil – Éamon de Valera, Seán T. Ó Ceallaigh, Seán Lemass, Seán MacEntee, Gerry Boland and Frank Aiken – were appointed to the committee to examine whether there was a reasonable prospect of the party being effective if TDs took their seats in the Free State parliament. They were to report back to the next meeting of the party. The meeting unanimously agreed that it was not possible to summon an extraordinary *ard-fheis* of the party in a short space of time but decided to call a special meeting of the full national executive within a week, to consider what action the Fianna Fáil TDs should take in the tense political situation of the time.[7]

On 8 August 1927 Seán T. O'Kelly, Gerry Boland and Frank Aiken, on behalf of Fianna Fáil, met Thomas Johnson, leader of the Labour Party and his colleague, William O'Brien. They put certain questions to the Labour Party leader who later replied to them in the form of a memo he gave to Gerry Boland.[8]

On 9 August the national executive of Fianna Fáil held a vital meeting. De Valera explained that, because of the Free State's new Bill that required a sworn declaration from all election candidates prior to their nomination that they would take the Oath of Allegiance, he feared that Fianna Fáil would be forced to give up all political action unless the party entered the Free State Dáil. After a long discussion a resolution was passed by forty-four votes to seven that the elected deputies of the party, as a body, be given a free hand in the matter of deciding whether Fianna Fáil should enter the Dáil or not.[9]

All the elected Fianna Fáil deputies, with the exception of James Colbert (Limerick), came together on 10 August to hear Seán T. Ó Ceallaigh report on behalf of the special committee that had been appointed to examine if the party would be effective in getting rid of the Oath of Allegiance if its elected representatives were to enter Dáil Éireann. Ó Ceallaigh read documents that had been signed by Thomas Johnson TD, leader of the Labour Party, and Captain William Redmond, leader of the National League party, in which they declared that their parties were in favour of the abolition of the Oath of

Allegiance and the setting up of machinery for the initiation of constitutional amendments by the people. If this right were restored, Fianna Fáil would be able to reintroduce efforts to put the Oath of Allegiance to a referendum of the people.

A long debate followed, during which the Fianna Fáil TDs listened to arguments about whether they should adopt a policy to enter the Dáil or suffer possible political extinction. Seán Lemass and Éamon de Valera said that the majority of Fianna Fáil members in their own constituencies of Dublin South and Clare favoured entering the Dáil. All the deputies agreed with the bigger argument that if Fianna Fáil suffered extinction, constitutional Republicanism would become a dead letter and there would be the risk of another civil war.

The Fianna Fáil TDs came to a sensational decision at midnight. They decided to present themselves on the following day to the Clerk of the Dáil and sign the roll book containing the Oath of Allegiance. They would make it quite clear to him that, in doing so, they did not intend to give allegiance to the English king. The party agreed unanimously to have the following official announcement published in the next morning's daily newspapers:

> The Fianna Fáil deputies have met and given careful consideration to the position of national emergency which has been created by the legislation now being passed through the Free State parliament. They recognise that the legislation disfranchises and precludes from engaging in any effective peaceful political movement towards independence, all Irish Republicans who will not acknowledge that any allegiance is due to the English crown. It has, however, been repeatedly stated, and is not uncommonly believed, that the required declaration is not an Oath; that the signing of it implies no contractual obligation; and that it has no binding significance in conscience or in law, that, in short, it is merely an empty political formula which deputies could conscientiously sign without becoming involved, or without involving their nation in obligations of

loyalty to the English crown...The Fianna Fáil deputies hereby give public notice in advance to the Irish people and to all whom it may concern, that they propose to regard the declaration as an empty formality and repeat that their only allegiance is to the Irish nation, and that it will be given to no other power or authority.[10]

Forty-two Fianna Fáil TDs signed the statement, all except James Colbert, TD for Limerick, who was unavoidably absent from the meeting. However, he concurred with the decision to take the Oath of Allegiance and look on it as an empty formula.[11]

For de Valera the night that followed this significant decision was like a nightmare. It was one of the rare nights in his political career that he did not sleep, wondering if the tactics he had planned for the next day would succeed.

At eleven o'clock the following morning, 11 August 1927, the two Fianna Fáil party whips – Gerry Boland and Seán Lemass – arrived at the gates of Leinster House. Thomas Johnson and Captain William Redmond, leaders of the Labour and National League parties respectively, received them warmly. The two party leaders accompanied the Fianna Fáil whips into the main building and introduced them to the Clerk of the Dáil, Colm Ó Murchadha. He asked them to sign their names in the Dáil roll book. They provided their signatures, not taking particular note of what else was in the book. In groups of twos and threes the Fianna Fáil TDs arrived at intervals over a period of one-and-a-half hours and repeated the performance of the government whips. One of the Fianna Fáil deputies, Frank Fahy, said: 'I did not go within feet of the Bible the day I entered Leinster House. I pushed the Bible at least two feet away before I signed the book. I speak for the Fianna Fáil deputies when I say this.' At approximately half-past one, Éamon de Valera accompanied by Frank Aiken, Dr James Ryan and Martin J. Corry, entered the outer doors of Leinster House. All four presented themselves to the Clerk of the Dáil. De Valera addressed the clerk, first in Irish and then in English:

I am not prepared to take an Oath. I am prepared to put my

name down in this book in order to get permission to go into the Dáil, but it has no other significance.[12]

Picking up the Bible on the table in front of him he moved it to the other side of the room and told the clerk again, 'You must remember I am taking no Oath.' He then placed some paper over the Oath at the top of the page and signed his name in a specified place on the same page in the clerk's Dáil roll book. He certainly had an idea that the following Oath was underneath the paper he put over the top of the page:

> I _____ do solemnly swear true faith and allegiance to the Constitution of the Irish Free State as by law established, and that I will be faithful to HM King George V, his heirs and successors by law, in virtue of the common citizenship of Ireland with Great Britain and her adherence to and membership of the group of nations forming the British Commonwealth of Nations.

Afterwards de Valera declared: 'It (the Oath) was neither read to me, nor was I asked to read it.'[13] The three TDs who accompanied him – Frank Aiken, Dr James Ryan and Martin Corry – did the same thing as de Valera. P.J. Little, TD for Waterford and former editor of *An Phoblacht*, said later that 'de Valera put the Bible away in the corner before he signed the book.'[14]

When approached by an *Irish Times* representative for his views on the decision of the Fianna Fáil deputies to take the Oath, President W.T. Cosgrave replied in a tone that was neither triumphant nor condescending: 'I am very pleased to see them coming into the Dáil and I think it is the best thing that has happened during the last five years.'[15] Interviewed after a meeting of Labour deputies and senators at Leinster House, Labour leader Thomas Johnson said that the entry of Fianna Fáil deputies into Dáil Éireann 'is a political event of the first importance – opening up an entirely new and more hopeful prospect.'[16]

The Gaelic American newspaper, edited by John Devoy, who had been a bitter opponent and critic of de Valera for more than seven years, took this opportunity to launch a further attack on him. 'If de Valera had entered the Dáil five years ago with his colleagues all the bloodshed and the destruction as well as Civil War and a hundred other regrettable things would have been averted,' he claimed.[17] Many other commentators took the same view. But this was a simplistic view of the situation. It would have been impossible for Éamon de Valera to lead his party into the Dáil during the latter part of 1922 when the Free State government came officially into operation as a bitter civil war was in train. In addition, the British government at that time would not have accepted de Valera's definition of the Oath of Allegiance as 'an empty formula'. Going into the Dáil was an easier task for de Valera and his Fianna Fáil party in 1927, especially after W.T. Cosgrave's government had passed the Electoral Amendment (No. 2) Bill that left the Fianna Fáil elected representatives with no alternative but to treat the Oath as an empty formula and sign the Dáil roll book, thereby saving the party from extinction.

Some Sinn Féin supporters were prepared to tolerate Fianna Fáil as a Republican party up to the time de Valera signed up to the 'Oath' that he called 'an empty formula'. Eithne Coyle, a prominent Cumann na mBan member and a supporter of Sinn Féin who hailed from Falcarragh, County Donegal, said that 'the spirit of Fianna Fáil was not quite dead in 1927, though I had no respect for de Valera when he took the Oath in order to enter Leinster House.'[18]

On the morning of 12 August 1927, the Fianna Fáil deputies formally took their seats in Dáil Éireann. The public gallery was full to overflowing and for the first time in its history the Dáil itself was over 95 per cent complete. There is no doubt that this episode was a turning point in Irish history. It was a strange sight. Éamon de Valera was sitting on the extreme left of the benches formerly occupied by the Labour Party and facing President W.T. Cosgrave. Dressed in black, the Republican leader was an earnest figure, occasionally turning over the pages of his order paper but otherwise motionless, except once when he smiled broadly as a deputy of the Farmers' Party endeavoured to convince the Ceann Comhairle that he was asking a question and not making a speech. President Cosgrave was in excellent mood and was smiling benignly on all and sundry. The Labour leader, Thomas Johnson TD, was truculent. Addressing President Cosgrave he declared: 'I move that the House do meet again on Tuesday next and that there will then be presented to the House, for consideration on that day, a vote of no confidence in the present Executive Council.'

'Certainly,' retorted the President, 'but I am not to be taken as agreeing to that motion.'[19]

Soon after this the Dáil adjourned until the following Tuesday. A whole new chapter had started in constitutional politics in Ireland.

An editorial in *The Nation* newspaper declared:

> To those upon whom the serious responsibility of making the decision rested, we know it occasioned days and nights of the greatest anxiety. Doubts will have arisen in the minds of many as to the wisdom of the choice made…Republicans who are in doubt as to the wisdom of the decision may withhold their verdict for a time.[20]

A Catholic priest, Father Dunlea, asked for his opinion on the entry of the Fianna Fáil deputies into Leinster House and the method they used to take the Oath of Allegiance, said: 'The proceedings at Leinster House on August 12 were gravely sinful for those who took part in them and for those who counselled them.' The Jesuit *America*, one of the most widely circulated Catholic reviews in the US, published an article by Francis Talbot SJ, one of the associate editors of the paper, on the subject of de Valera and the Oath. Father Talbot said that de Valera made a statement to Colm Ó Murchadha, Clerk of the Dáil, that he was putting his name in the Dáil roll book in order to get the necessary permission to enter among the deputies elected by the people and that no other meaning was to be attached to this act. 'This statement is of such a nature as to absolve de Valera completely from all charge of perjury or any irreverence or impiety,' concluded Father Talbot.[21] Archbishop Mannix, a friend of de Valera over the years, said in the *Advocate*, a Catholic newspaper published in Melbourne: 'There is no perjury where there is no falsehood – and the Republicans proclaimed from the housetops the sense in which they signed the test Oath. No one was deceived.'[22]

On Fianna Fáil's first day in Dáil Éireann, Éamon de Valera and Seán T. Ó Ceallaigh met Labour leader, Thomas Johnson. Johnson conveyed the message to them that he thought Labour would not form part of a coalition with de Valera as head but that he thought he could satisfy the National League party to form a Labour-National League coalition.[23]

Despite this setback, the Fianna Fáil deputies came together that same evening and decided to attend the Dáil on Tuesday, 16 August and vote for the motion of no confidence in the government, notice of which had been given that day by Thomas Johnson.[24]

On 14 August 1927, Lord Birkenhead made an important statement on his own behalf and what he took to be the British government's attitude to any suggested modification of the Irish Free State's Oath of Allegiance:

> I repudiate the notion that the British government would consent to modify the form of the Oath. I drafted the Oath and I would never have signed the Treaty if it had not contained this particular clause. I believe that none of my fellow negotiators would have signed it in the absence of agreement on this point. No modification in the substance of the Oath could be accepted without a fundamental disloyalty to the whole Imperial conception under which a number of self-governing communities profess and accept loyalty to the monarch. We shall be as loyal to Cosgrave and his colleagues as they have been loyal to us and to their bond. Greater loyalty there could never be.[25]

There is no doubt that Birkenhead's statement was intended to prop up the Cumann na nGaedheal government and help it to survive the motion of no confidence to be debated in the Dáil in a matter of two days.

On Tuesday 16 August Thomas Johnson moved the following motion of no confidence in President W.T. Cosgrave's government: 'that the Executive

Council has ceased to retain the support of the majority in Dáil Éireann.'[26] The Labour Party was strongly of the opinion that they had enough votes between themselves, the National League party and Fianna Fáil to defeat the Cumann na nGaedheal government. They planned to set up in its place a coalition government made up of Labour and the National League that would have the support of Fianna Fáil. Johnson said: 'If the present ministry retain office, faced by the main opposition of those who had been hitherto in violent conflict with them [Fianna Fáil]…the possibilities of carrying on parliamentary government successfully…are very much less.'[27]

Captain William Redmond addressed the Dáil, referring to Fianna Fáil's U-turn from violent methods to constitutionalism. He said that his party would vote in favour of Johnson's no confidence motion. He further remarked that if Fianna Fáil could be converted now 'as President Cosgrave and his friends were converted a few short years ago and changed from poachers to being gamekeepers, I can see no reason for the life of me why we should not welcome the process and why we should doubt that they would make as good gamekeepers as President Cosgrave.'[28]

The leader of the Farmers' Party, Patrick Baxter, said: 'the Farmers' Party is not going to turn down President Cosgrave and instal Deputy Johnson in his place.'[29]

Seán T. Ó Ceallaigh was the only one to speak – entirely in Irish – from the Republican benches: 'Fianna Fáil deputies thought it better to say nothing that day as there was a danger that they would introduce bitterness into the debate. But he was sure that everyone would clearly understand that they in Fianna Fáil were of the opinion that this Cumann na nGaedheal government should not continue in office.'[30]

There was a feeling of tense excitement as the deputies crowded together on the floor of the House and began to climb the gangway to the division lobbies. The Ceann Comhairle announced the result: seventy-one deputies voted for Thomas Johnson's motion and seventy-one against.

Comprising the seventy-one who voted for the motion were forty-three Fianna Fáil TDs, twenty-one Labour TDs, six National League TDs and one Independent Republican (Paddy Belton). Those who voted against the motion included forty-five Cumann na nGaedheal TDs, eleven Farmers' deputies, fourteen Independents, and one Independent Nationalist (Vincent Rice, a former National League TD who had resigned from that party).

The Ceann Comhairle stated that in the case of an equality of votes, he had the duty to exercise a casting vote. It was his opinion that this vote of the Chair should preserve, if possible, the status quo and enable the House to review its decision at a later date. Therefore he voted against Johnson's no confidence motion so that the final figure was seventy-one for the motion and seventy-two against. Johnson's motion that 'the Executive Council has ceased to retain the support of the majority of the Dáil' was declared lost by one vote – the casting vote of the Ceann Comhairle.[31] W.T. Cosgrave's government had won a reprieve by the skin of its teeth.

The result was received with loud cheering by the occupants of the gallery. The members of the government were all smiles while the occupants of the opposition benches looked crestfallen and visibly bewildered. The Dáil adjourned until 11 October.

The National League party soon noticed that one of its members, Alderman John Jinks, TD for Sligo, had not taken part in the division. According to Captain William Redmond, Jinks had been present at a party meeting the previous day and had voted in favour of opposing the government. Jinks had been in the Dáil for virtually the whole of the debate. Had he suddenly become ill or had he been spirited away by some scheming politicians? If he had voted for Johnson's motion, as expected, Cosgrave's government would have fallen and this would have led to the abolition of the Oath of Allegiance to the British monarch.

It was the next day before John Jinks explained:

> I was never a supporter of Sinn Féin but stood for the policy of the late John Redmond which I believe still to be the right policy. I was astonished, therefore, when I heard of the proposed arrangement to throw out President Cosgrave and replace his ministry by a government which would be dominated by de Valera...I could not conscientiously support any proposal

which would result in de Valera's coming into power. I did not know whether I should vote with the government or abstain from the division. I just thought the best thing to do was to leave the House before the division and to go back to my hotel. There was no mystery to it. The sensational rumours that I was kidnapped and all the rest of it are sheer invention.[32]

A few days later John Jinks resigned from the National League Party.

The Fianna Fáil TDs were astonished and perplexed when Johnson's motion of no confidence was defeated by one vote. They came together that evening at 8pm, wondering which course to pursue from that on. They decided that they would resurrect the idea of a referendum by the people on the matter of the Oath of Allegiance. The officers of Fianna Fáil also instructed their deputies to go back to their constituencies, familiarise themselves with the needs of their local constituents and deal with these problems. This would help them to increase their votes in future elections.[33]

Peadar O'Donnell, editor of *An Phoblacht,* became highly critical of Fianna Fáil after they entered Dáil Éireann, and in an editorial for the newspaper wrote that 'those that [sic] took the Oath have gone away from us.'[34] Mary MacSwiney, writing in *An Phoblacht* about the fact that the Fianna Fáil TDs had entered the Dáil, claimed: 'if their action were right now, it would have been right in 1922 and it would have saved the lives of Cathal Brugha and Erskine Childers and their other gallant comrades.'[35] Hanna Sheehy Skeffington, a former member of the *Ard-Chomhairle* of Sinn Féin who transferred to the executive committee of Fianna Fáil when the split occurred, wrote to de Valera from France:

The recent step taken by your party, indicates so complete a reversal of policy on the part of the executive of Fianna Fáil that it is impossible for me to remain any longer a member of that body or of the organisation. I beg therefore to tender my resignation.'[36]

Éamon de Valera felt a greater shock and sense of loss when, shortly afterwards, he received notification from Dorothy Macardle of her resignation from Fianna Fáil. Macardle was the author of *The Irish Republic*, an outstanding book on the War of Independence and the Civil War. She said in her letter: 'I feel now that a policy is being adopted with regard to the Oath in which I could not cooperate…I can have nothing to do with asking any Irishman or woman to take the Oath.'[37]

What of the five Sinn Féin TDs – David Kent (Cork East), Oscar Traynor (Dublin North), Austin Stack (Kerry), Dr John Madden (Mayo North), Caitlín Brugha (Waterford)? They had the power in their grasp to put the Cumann na nGaedheal government out of office. If they had done the same as the Fianna Fáil deputies, their votes for Johnson's motion of no confidence would have ousted the Cumann na nGaedheal government. They could then have assisted the Labour, National League and Fianna Fáil parties to abolish the Oath of Allegiance. Instead members of Sinn Féin spent the day of the no confidence vote walking around in circles outside Leinster House, carrying placards and protesting because de Valera and his deputies had taken the Oath. One of the placards read: 'Empty Formula – the slaves.'[38] And where was Professor Arthur Clery, the Independent Republican TD elected for the NUI? He had not featured in the public arena since his election but like the five Sinn Féin deputies he had publicly stated that he would not take the Oath of Allegiance if elected.

Because of the assassination of Kevin O'Higgins there was a vacant Dáil seat in Dublin County and there was also a seat to be filled in Dublin South because of the death of Countess Markievicz. The government named 14 August 1927 as the date of the Dublin County by-election and 24 August for the Dublin South by-election.

Cumann na nGaedheal was first in the field. It selected Gearóid O'Sullivan, Judge Advocate General of the army, to contest the vacancy in Dublin County and Dr Thomas Hennessy as the candidate for Dublin City South. Dr Hennessy had been a member of the previous Dáil as he had won a by-election in this same constituency in March 1925 but had not sought re-election in the June 1927 general election.

Fianna Fáil selected Robert Brennan as a candidate for Dublin County. Brennan, a journalist, had been one of those in charge of the armed action in Enniscorthy, County Wexford, during the 1916 Rising. He was Director of Elections for Sinn Féin in the 1918 general election before he was arrested by the British. To fight the Dublin South seat, Fianna Fáil selected Robert Briscoe, a Dublin merchant who had been an active supporter of Sinn Féin and de Valera throughout the War of Independence and Civil War.

Labour decided not to put forward candidates for the by-elections. As the National League and Independents also decided to stand aside, it was presumed that there would be a straight fight between the government and Fianna Fáil candidates.

At the last minute, however, Sinn Féin decided to put forward Dr Kathleen Lynn in the Dublin County by-election and Charles Murphy in Dublin South. Both had been elected TDs in these constituencies in the 1923 general election but had lost their seats to Fianna Fáil candidates in the election of June 1927. The Electoral Amendment (No. 2) Bill, 1927, that made a sworn declaration obligatory for all Dáil candidates before nomination did not apply to these by-elections as the government had accepted an amendment moved by Professor William Thrift, Independent TD, Dublin University, on the committee stage of the Bill that the measure 'would not come into operation until 1 February 1928 or from the date of the next dissolution of Dáil Éireann, whichever is earlier.'[39] Sinn Féin explained that they were contesting the two vacant Dublin seats 'so that the separatist electorate will have a way of expressing its voice.'[40]

The assassination of Kevin O'Higgins figured very prominently in the by-election speeches and in particular in the constituency of Dublin County, where O'Higgins had topped the poll in 1923 and 1927.

Mary MacSwiney came from Cork to support the two Sinn Féin candidates but condemned Fianna Fáil for entering Dáil Éireann:

> I have felt inclined to shed tears of blood over de Valera's action. All I can do, and ask you to do, is to hope and pray that de Valera, having followed Cosgrave and Mulcahy in that step

of treachery in taking the Oath of Allegiance to King George, will not follow the further degradation of jailing Republicans in defence of their country.[41]

The polls in both by-elections were disappointingly low – about 50 per cent of the electorate in Dublin County and 57 per cent in Dublin South. There was a rise of 17,000 in the Cumann na nGaedheal vote in Dublin County from the general election two months previously. Part of this increase could be attributed to the fact that Kevin O'Higgins represented Dublin County and the majority of the electorate there regarded his murder as a heinous crime. Fianna Fáil retained the same level of support as in the general election two months previously. In Dublin South Cumann na nGaedheal increased its vote by 8000 votes and Fianna Fáil by 3500. The Cumann na nGaedheal nominees, Gearóid O'Sullivan in Dublin County and Dr Thomas Hennessy in Dublin South, were elected with huge majorities. In Dublin South Fianna Fáil lost Countess Markievicz's seat to Cumann na nGaedheal. Sinn Féin put up a poor performance in both constituencies and both its candidates lost their deposits.

No sooner had the government declared that it was pleased with the victory of the Cumann na nGaedheal candidates in these two by-elections than President W.T. Cosgrave, acting on behalf of the Executive Council of the Irish Free State, dropped a bombshell when he issued a proclamation dissolving parliament immediately and announcing a fresh general election. He explained that the Council had taken this decision because of the deadlock in the Dáil caused by the Fianna Fáil deputies taking their seats and making it almost impossible to carry on the government of the country.

Speaking to the political correspondent of *The Irish Times,* President Cosgrave said: 'The result of the two by-elections is too remarkable to be brushed lightly aside... They represent a decisive vote of the stable elements in favour of the retention of the present government.'[42]

Notes

1. Éamon de Valera to Frank P. Walsh and others, 3 August 1927 and The Earl of Longford and Thomas P. O'Neill, *Éamon de Valera*, p. 254.
2. UCDA, Archives of the Fianna Fáil Party, File P176/442(14), 5 August 1927.
3. *Ibid.*
4. *Ibid.*
5. *Ibid.*, File P176/442, 5 August 1927, UCDA.
6. *Ibid.*
7. *Ibid.*
8. *Ibid.*, 8 August 1927, UCDA.
9. Minutes of National Executive, Fianna Fáil, 9 August 1927 and The Earl of Longford and Thomas P. O'Neill, *op. cit.*, pp. 254, 255.
10. *The Irish Times*, 11 August 1927.
11. *The Irish Times*, 11 August 1927: the statement by Fianna Fáil that the party had decided to take the Oath of Allegiance and enter the Dáil was signed by the following elected deputies of the party: Éamon de Valera (Clare); Patrick Houlihan (Clare); Tomás Ó Deirg (Carlow-Kilkenny); Patrick Smith (Cavan); Seán French (Cork); Thomas Mullins (Cork West); Martin J. Corry (Cork East); Daniel Corkery (Cork North); Seán T. Ó Ceallaigh (Dublin North); Caitlín Bean Ui Chléirigh (Dublin North); Seán F. Lemass (Dublin South); Seán Mac an tSaoi (Dublin County); Mark Killalea (Galway); Proinsias Ó Fathaigh (Galway); Seán Tubridy (Galway); Thomas P. Powell (Galway); Thomas McEllistrim (Kerry); Tomás S. Ó Raghallaigh (Kerry); William O'Leary (Kerry); Séamus Ó Riain (Wexford); Séamus Moore (Wicklow); Domhnall Ua Buachalla (Kildare); Frank Carty (Leitrim-Sligo); Sam Holt (Leitrim-Sligo); Patrick Boland (Leix-Offaly); Thomas Tynan (Leix-Offaly); Tadhg Ó Cruadhlaoich (Limerick); James Victory (Longford-Westmeath); Michael J. Kennedy (Longford-Westmeath); Frank Aiken (Louth); Patrick J. Ruttledge (Mayo-North); Micheál Mac Giolla Ruaidh (Mayo South); Eugene Mullen (Mayo South); Matthew O'Reilly (Meath); Patrick McCarvill (Monaghan); Gearóid Ó Beoláin (Roscommon); Patrick O'Dowd (Roscommon); Seán Hayes (Tipperary); Andrew Fogarty (Tipperary); Neal Blaney (Donegal); Frank Carney (Donegal); Patrick J. Little (Waterford).
12. T. Ryle Dwyer, *De Valera: The Man and the Myths*, p. 147 and Conor Foley, *Legion of the Rearguard*, p. 68.
13. Dwyer, *op. cit.*, p. 147.
14. *The Irish Times*, 8 September 1927.
15. *Ibid.*, 12 August 1927.
16. *Ibid.*
17. The *Gaelic American*, 20 August 1927.
18. Uinseann Mac Eoin, *Survivors*, p. 157.
19. *Dáil Éireann Debates*, Volume 20, 12 August 1927, p. 1646.
20. The *Nation*, 20 August 1927.
21. *Ibid.*, 3 March 1928.
22. The *Advocate* (Melbourne), 25 August 1927 and The Earl of Longford and Thomas P. O'Neill, *Éamon de Valera*, p. 257.
23. UCDA, Archives of the Fianna Fáil Party, File P176/442/(12), 12 August 1927.
24. *Ibid.*
25. The *Daily Mail*, 15 August 1927 and *The Irish Times*, 16 August 1927.
26. *Dáil Éireann Debates*, Volume 20, 16 August 1927, No Confidence Motion, p. 1670.
27. *Ibid.*, pp. 1673, 1674.
28. *Ibid.*, p. 1686.
29. *Ibid.*, p. 1693.
30. *Ibid.*, pp. 1730, 1731.
31. *Ibid.*, p. 1750.
32. *The Irish Times*, 18 August 1927.
33. UCDA, Archives of the Fianna Fáil Party, File P176/442, 16 August 1927.
34. *An Phoblacht*, 19 August 1927.
35. *Ibid.*, 27 August 1927.

36. UCDA, Archives of the Fianna Fáil Party, File P176/27 (14), 16 August 1927.
37. *Ibid.*, File P 176/27 (15), 29 August 1927.
38. *The Irish Times*, 17 August 1927.
39. *Dáil Éireann Debates*, Volume 20, Electoral (Amendment) (No. 2) Bill 1927, committee stage, 3 August, p. 1517, 1518: *The Irish Times*, 8 August 1927.
40. *Saoirse na h-Éireann, Irish Freedom*, September 1927.
41. *The Irish Times*, 11 August 1927.
42. *The Irish Times*, 26 August 1927.

16

CUMANN NA NGAEDHEAL MAKES A COMEBACK

The old maxim, 'damned if I do and damned if I don't,' seemed to apply in arguments about the Oath of Allegiance during this general election campaign of September 1927. Now that de Valera and Fianna Fáil had entered the Free State Parliament, they were accused of being perjurers – very often by clergymen who strongly supported Cumann na nGaedheal. At a Cumann na nGaedheal meeting at Mount Temple, County Westmeath, Archdeacon Langan PP declared that 'the Oath that they (Fianna Fáil) took could not be regarded as anything but an Oath. The Bible was there. These men were guilty of perjury. Their action was a mockery of religion.'[1] Reverend Father Murray PP, Caltra, who presided at a Cumann na nGaedheal meeting in Mountbellew, County Galway, said that 'it was sad to think that they had in Catholic Ireland a leader [Éamon de Valera] of a political party – a man in whom the country once had great confidence – declaring a solemn Oath to be an empty formula.'[2]

Sinn Féin took no part in the September 1927 general election. The new Free State legislation required all election candidates to sign an affidavit before nomination that they would take the Oath of Allegiance and enter Dáil Éireann if elected. Sinn Féin did not recognise Dáil Éireann and would refuse to take the Oath of Allegiance under any circumstances and their stance now barred them from electoral participation. This was not the only reason Sinn Féin did not contest the 1927 general election. The Standing Committee issued a manifesto stating: 'that they were forced to withdraw from the election because the financial position of the organisation made it impossible for them to effectively contest the election, and the indecent haste with which the election has been forced leaves no time for an appeal to the friends of the

Republic abroad.'[3] The manifesto added: 'Recent adherents to the Free State – the party calling itself Fianna Fáil – have declared that they have entered the "British parliament" [Free State Dáil] in the interests of the people...This is a repetition of the earlier Free Staters.'[4] The Standing Committee's declaration concluded by pointing out 'that no true Republican can consistently vote for any Irishman who will enter a "British parliament" or give allegiance to the British crown.'[5]

An advertisement by Cumann na nGaedheal in *The Irish Times* stated in big bold print: 'They [Fianna Fáil] took the Oath to save their party – they would not take it in 1922 to save the country from Civil War.'[6]

Frank Fahy TD declared at a Fianna Fáil meeting in Gort, County Galway, that if his party were returned to power, 'we will put the question of the Oath to the Irish people by way of referendum. If the Irish people say they want the Oath abolished, we will go to England and say that it takes two parties to make a Treaty and that it is the opinion of the Irish people to abolish the Oath of Allegiance. I do not believe that England's reply will be to declare war on Ireland.'[7]

Oscar Traynor had been elected a Republican TD in a by-election in Dublin North in March 1925. A master printer, he had been an active Republican for many years since he fought in the Sackville Street area of Dublin with the Irish Volunteers in the 1916 Rising. He was elected Sinn Féin deputy for Dublin North for the second time in the June 1927 general election despite having strong opposition from Fianna Fáil contenders for his seat. He was the only Sinn Féin representative in Dublin City and County to retain his seat in that election. In the general election of September 1927 Traynor was denied the chance of defending his seat when Sinn Féin withdrew from the election.

Oscar Traynor disagreed with this latest Sinn Féin directive: 'No true Republican can consistently vote for any Irishman who will enter the "British parliament" [Free State parliament] or give allegiance to the British Crown.[8] Instead of ignoring the general election altogether, Traynor added his name to the nomination papers of a Fianna Fáil candidate. The Sinn Féin Standing Committee asked Traynor to explain his action and he replied that it was solely to show that 'I was not in agreement with that portion of the Sinn Féin manifesto.' The Standing Committee was not satisfied with Traynor's explanation. Austin Stack TD, honorary secretary, was instructed to write to him and to declare that Sinn Féin no longer recognised him as a member of the party.[9]

There were some bitter clashes between Cumann na nGaedheal supporters and Fianna Fáil politicians during the election campaign. Gerry Boland, Fianna Fáil TD for Roscommon, gave a statement to the *Nation* of what happened when he attended Mass in Ballyforan Church, County Roscommon, prior to addressing a Fianna Fáil meeting on the road outside. He said that Father Neary PP made a political speech from the altar, in the course of which the priest said 'that everyone in the church must vote for Cosgrave's Party and give high preference votes to either Martin Conlon, Andrew Lavin or Joseph Burke – the three Cumann na nGaedheal candidates.' Father Neary added that 'a vote for these candidates is a vote for Almighty God.' He called de Valera 'Lucifer' and further said that 'de Valera was out for the destruction of the Catholic religion and that he had destroyed all the young men and half the young women of the country.' Boland asserted that he was prepared to attest to the truth of these words and that every truthful person who attended Mass that morning in Ballyforan would bear him out.[10]

Polling in the general election took place on 15 September 1927. The turnout was estimated to be close to 70 per cent. There were two winners in the election. The Cumann na nGaedheal Party had forty-eight seats at the dissolution of the Dáil but ended up with sixty-two seats – a gain of fourteen seats. Fianna Fáil had a similar gain. The party had forty-three seats at the dissolution but now held fifty-seven. The fact that the Sinn Féin Party took no part in the election helped Fianna Fáil to increase its number of seats.[11]

A big feature of the election was the number of seats lost by the smaller parties. Labour lost the greatest number of seats. They held twenty-two Dáil seats after the June general election but won only thirteen in this September election. The Farmers' Party held eleven Dáil seats at the dissolution but now had six. The National League Party barely escaped extinction, coming out of the election with two seats instead of the eight it had held after the June election. The Independents obtained twelve seats, a loss of one, and Independent Labour gained one seat in the person of James Larkin who was elected for Dublin North. Sinn Féin, with no candidates, lost the five seats they had won in the previous election.

There was a surprising result in Dublin County where Thomas Johnson, a popular politician and leader of the Labour Party, lost his Dáil seat. There was also a shock in Cavan where P. F. Baxter, leader of the Farmers' Party, ended up at the bottom of the poll. Paddy Belton, Independent Republican, who took the Oath of Allegiance and entered the Dáil before Éamon de Valera and Fianna Fáil decided to do so, lost his seat in Dublin County, paying the same price Dan Breen had paid for a similar action. Alderman John Jinks, formerly a National League TD, who had disappeared and abstained on the occasion of the no confidence motion a few weeks earlier, this time stood as an Independent candidate in Leitrim-Sligo but forfeited his deposit as he polled very poorly.

President Cosgrave, having won in both Cork City Borough and Carlow-Kilkenny, elected to sit for Cork City; this left a vacant seat in Carlow-Kilkenny to be filled in a later by-election.

In this election both Cumann na nGaedheal and Fianna Fáil increased their first-preference votes. Cumann na nGaedheal polled a total of 453,064 votes and Fianna Fáil was not far behind with 411,833 votes. Both parties improved their percentage share of the votes cast – Cumann na nGaedheal from 27.4 per cent in June 1927 to 38.6 per cent in this election and Fianna Fáil from 26.2 per cent to 35.2 per cent.[12]

Fianna Fáil gained a majority of seats in Clare (three out of five); Kerry (four out of seven) and Galway (five out of nine). De Valera's party failed to get a seat in only one contested constituency – the NUI.

Out the twenty-nine contested constituencies, Fianna Fáil got a higher number of first preference votes than Cumann na nGaedheal in eleven – Clare, Kerry, Wexford, Waterford, Cavan, Roscommon, Monaghan, Longford-Westmeath, Kildare, Cork North and Mayo South. This was an indication of how Republican support was increasing in all four provinces.

Cumann na nGaedheal members were not over the moon at what looked like a good result. Ernest Blythe, Vice-President and Minister for Finance, commented: 'The results are not as satisfactory as we could hope for but there is an improvement in the position.'[13] De Valera, pleased with the outcome, said, 'At the dissolution we had forty-three deputies, now we have fifty-seven. Our total first preferences have gone up from 299,000 to 412,000.'[14] The ending of the abstention policy adopted by Republicans since the Civil War period reflected itself in the improved results of this election.

Cumann na nGaedheal's sixty-two seats guaranteed that President Cosgrave's government would remain in power and prominent members of Fianna Fáil realised that they still had a long way to go before they could overtake the government party.

The new Dáil was scheduled to meet in early October. This time Fianna Fáil decided to make the taking of the Oath of Allegiance a low-key affair. They did not issue an 'empty formula' statement as they did previously. Instead small groups of them reported to the Dáil at different times in the two days previous to the reassembly of the Dáil and, with only Colm Ó Murchadha, Clerk of the Dáil, present in his office, they signed their names in his Dáil roll book. Subsequently Éamon de Valera gave an interview to the press in which he announced that the Fianna Fáil attitude towards the Oath of Allegiance had undergone no change and they were determined to have it removed as soon as possible.[15] In answer to some other questions from journalists de Valera gave this longer reply:

> Fianna Fáil deputies do not consider it necessary to define further their attitude towards the Oath of Allegiance. On the previous occasion in order that all whom it concerned might be duly informed we made a public statement explaining the position. There has been no change. The statement and action of each individual deputy when signing his name were strictly in accord with the public statement…Our anxiety to have the Oath removed completely and our determination to remove it as soon as possible is in no way diminished.[16]

Some important changes to the political scene occurred before the opening of the new Dáil. Thomas J. O'Connell TD (Mayo South) was chosen as the new leader of the Labour Party to succeed Thomas Johnson, who had lost his Dáil seat in Dublin County. Michael Heffernan TD (Tipperary) was elected leader of the Farmers' Party to replace P. F. Baxter who had lost his seat in Cavan. An important conference was held between Cumann na nGaedheal and the Farmers' Party and it was decided to form an alliance between these two parties whereby the Farmers' Party guaranteed to support the government party on all important issues in the Dáil. Part of this deal was that the Farmer's new leader, Michael Heffernan, would be offered a post as parliamentary secretary in the new government.[17] This alliance marked the end of the autonomy of another small party.

For the first time since independence, all the elected members were expected to take their seats at the assembly of the Sixth Dáil on 11 October 1927. There were no abstentionists because there were no Sinn Féin TDs or Independent Republican deputies on the list of elected TDs. One seat remained vacant as James Larkin, Independent Labour TD, never attended the Dáil to take his seat but not because he was a abstentionist. William O'Brien of the Labour Party had won a libel award against him that he refused to pay and as a result he was declared an undischarged bankrupt and could not take his seat.

This Sixth Dáil elected W.T. Cosgrave as President of the Executive Council by seventy-six votes to seventy. In the division Cumann na nGaedheal had the support of the Farmers' Party and most Independent deputies. Fianna Fáil and Labour composed the minority vote. The two National League deputies and the Roscommon Independent TD, Michael Brennan, abstained. J.X. Murphy, Independent TD, Dublin County, was absent through illness and James Larkin, Independent Labour, Dublin North, was not in the Dáil chamber.[18]

The only reference to the Oath of Allegiance in the whole day's debate was when Michael Heffernan TD, new leader of the Farmers' Party, turned to Éamon de Valera and said: 'The leader of the Fianna Fáil party some years ago stood on the rock of the Republic but he is now standing…on the shifting sands of an empty formula.'[19]

The following day President Cosgrave submitted the names of his cabinet to the Dáil. There was only one new minister – James Fitzgerald-Kenney KC, TD for Mayo South, who replaced the late Kevin O'Higgins as Minister for Justice. Michael Heffernan was appointed a parliamentary secretary as expected and he was made head of Posts and Telegraphs. He replaced J.J. Walsh, the former Minister for Posts and Telegraphs from Cork, who had resigned his membership of Cumann na nGaedheal before the general election.

Because President Cosgrave had won two seats in the September 1927 general election and had chosen to represent Cork Borough, an early by-election was due in Carlow-Kilkenny.

A Cumann na nGaedheal convention in Kilkenny unanimously selected D.J. Gorey as the party's candidate. Gorey, a former leader of the Farmers' Party, had stood for Cumann na nGaedheal in Carlow-Kilkenny in the September general election but had been defeated, yielding his seat to a Cumann na nGaedheal colleague, Peter de Loughry, a former Mayor of Kilkenny. Gorey's selection and the timing of the by-election was ideal for Cumann na nGaedheal because, as a result of the new alliance between that party and the Farmers' Party, the Kilkenny Farmers' Union had decided to throw in their lot with Cumann na nGaedheal and work with the party for the election of Gorey.

At a Fianna Fáil Convention in Kilkenny City, Michael Shelley of Callan, who had been elected as an abstentionist Sinn Féin TD for Carlow-Kilkenny in 1923, was selected to stand for Fianna Fáil against Gorey. He had stood unsuccessfully as a Fianna Fáil candidate in the general election of June 1927.

Labour decided not to nominate any candidate for the by-election, so the contest became a two-horse race between Gorey and Shelley.

At a Cumann na nGaedheal meeting held in Callan, Osmond Grattan Esmonde, the party's TD for Wexford, declared that the government had found the right medicine for Fianna Fáil and had administered a good dose of it. He added that 'as a result Fianna Fáil had been able to swallow not only one Oath but two Oaths and all their own speeches for the past five years.'[20]

In Clogh, Castlecomer, Patrick Hogan, Minister for Agriculture, said in reference to Frank Aiken, the Louth Fianna Fáil TD, said: 'He has taken the Oath; he has taken it twice, and I think the oftener he takes it, the better he likes it.'[21]

Fianna Fáil took the opportunity of the by-election to condemn the unfair distribution of jobs as far as Republicans were concerned and declared that they were interested in social ideas. At a Fianna Fáil meeting in Bagenalstown, County Carlow, Frank Fahy, TD for Galway, said that 'those seeking public positions should get them by competitive examination but they should not be asked their politics before they got them.'[22]

Polling in the Carlow-Kilkenny by-election took place on 3 November. Favourable weather conditions helped to bring the voters out and the poll was heavier than anticipated (82 per cent in County Carlow and 76 per cent in County Kilkenny). Counting the votes began the following day. It was a neck-and-neck race between the two candidates all the way: the result was so close that a recount was called for. There was great tension among the large crowd gathered outside the counting centre in Kilkenny until the returning officer announced the result.

D.J. Gorey, Cumann na nGaedheal, obtained 23,007 votes and Michael Shelley, Fianna Fáil, obtained 22,734. This gave victory to Gorey by 273 votes.

Cumann na nGaedheal had succeeded in keeping President W.T. Cosgrave's seat in Carlow-Kilkenny but Fianna Fáil had obtained almost 10,000 more votes than it did in the September 1927 general election, picking up many votes from Labour and Farmers' Party supporters in a constituency that had voted sparingly for Republicanism since the state was established.

The editorial in the *Irish Independent* on the day of the result declared that the outcome of the Carlow-Kilkenny by-election was important as 'parties in the Dáil are so nearly balanced that the loss or gain of one seat might make a considerable difference.'[23]

Fianna Fáil's second *ard-fheis* was held on 24 and 25 November 1927 in the Round Room of the Rotunda. There was a an enthusiastic attendance of more than a thousand delegates.

The President of the party, Éamon de Valera, said they were in the Dáil now and the purpose was to clear away all political tests. Referring to members of Sinn Féin, he said they still represented a section of the people who were debarred from having their representatives in the Dáil.

It was clear from the attitude of the Fianna Fáil delegates during the two days' *ard-fheis* that they did not want the Republican ethos of Fianna Fáil to be in any way watered down by the presence of their party in the Dáil. One of the first motions on the *clár* (programme) was proposed by J.J. Cunningham, Dublin, and seconded by Alderman Michael McSweeney, Kilkenny, approving of the action of Fianna Fáil in entering the Dáil 'but recognising that the furthermost limit in compromise has been reached.'[24] The *ard-fheis* passed this motion. On behalf of North Dublin City *Comhairle Ceanntair*, B. Egan moved another resolution, seconded by Joseph Groome, that asked for the *ard-fheis* to give a definite assurance to the people of Ireland 'that our aim is to secure the unity and independence of Ireland as a republic'.[25] The delegates also approved this motion. Seán Gleeson, Thurles, County Tipperary, proposed a motion seconded by John Hanafin, Thurles, that 'this Second *ard-fheis* of Fianna Fáil demands the reinstatement of all national teachers and other civil servants, local government employees and other officers of local authorities dismissed through non-compliance with the political test (an Oath of Allegiance to the Free State Constitution) imposed by the Free State government.'[26] This motion was passed unanimously.

In his closing speech to the *ard-fheis*, de Valera assured all the delegates that Fianna Fáil would remain loyal to its Republican roots:

> When circumstances change, methods must change: but the thing that has not changed is the aim or determination to achieve it; and that aim is to secure the complete freedom of our country. Fianna Fáil wants Ireland not merely free but Gaelic as well. Nothing less than that is worth fighting for.[27]

Sinn Féin held its annual *ard-fheis* in the Concert Hall of the Rotunda on 11 December 1927. Only a hundred and twenty delegates attended, indicating a party in decline. An article in the Sinn Féin newspaper, *Saoirse na h-Éireann*,

Irish Freedom said 'that the *ard-fheis* was smaller by far than many that had been held but it was larger than the pessimists forecasted and full of life and energy.'[28] The whole outlook of the Sinn Féin Party towards the political situation in Ireland was reviewed. It was clear that the President, J.J. O'Kelly, Austin Stack, Mary MacSwiney and Father Michael O'Flanagan held different views on many questions but one thing they all agreed on was expressed in this portion of O'Kelly's speech:

> ...the disposition to compromise had been the bane of the long struggle for Irish liberty. They had the proud privilege of association in one of the most inspiring movements of history but, through the indecision of theorists, it had drifted until the very thought of it filled one with shame and humiliation.[29]

It was decided 'that the whole matter of elections be left in the hands of the Standing Committee.' A motion was passed 'that persons who voted at the last general election and who resigned from Sinn Féin as a result, may be readmitted if prepared to accept the Sinn Féin rules as to voting.'[30]

The events of this *ard-fheis* reflected the internal troubles of a divided Sinn Féin. Earlier in the year disagreements had occurred between Mary MacSwiney and Father Michael O'Flanagan.[31] Although the friction between the two seemed to have been settled, it resurfaced during this *ard-fheis*. From the floor of the congress, Father O'Flanagan gave a fiery speech in which he accused Mary MacSwiney 'of spying for Fianna Fáil.'[32] This charge was not well received by the audience, the majority of which did not believe it to be true, but Father O'Flanagan continued his speech and stressed 'that he would not allow his name to go forward for election to any officership of Sinn Féin.' He was called upon not to act rashly but he persisted, stated that 'he was finished with Sinn Féin' and left the hall. For the first time in many years Father Michael O'Flanagan was not on the officer board of Sinn Féin but he later renewed his connection with the movement.

The Sinn Féin *ard-fheis* then went into private session to review the whole situation of the party – how exhaustively can be surmised from the fact that it was precisely half-past four the following morning when the delegates left the Rotunda Concert Hall for their homes. Most of this record-breaking session was devoted to a long discussion on steps that must effectively be taken to unite the Republican forces. But according to Mary MacSwiney, 'These Republican forces are not to be taken to include Fianna Fáil, the members of which have lost all title to the name Republican and any shadow of claim to be reckoned among the known Republican forces of the day.'[33] The known Republican forces in Miss MacSwiney's reckoning were Sinn Féin, 'the army' (IRA) and Cumann na mBan.[34]

On 15 December 1927, Patrick McGilligan, Minister for External Affairs of the Free State government, issued a statement that 'His Majesty the King has been pleased to approve the appointment of James McNeill as Governor-General of the Irish Free State in succession to T.M. Healy KC whose term of office will shortly expire.'[35] McNeill was a former member of the Imperial Legislative Council of India. After his retirement he played a prominent but unobtrusive part in the Sinn Féin movement before the Truce in 1921 and Michael Collins appointed him to the Provisional Government committee to draft the Free State Constitution in 1922. He was a brother of Dr Eoin MacNeill, former Minister of Education.

In audience at Buckingham Palace that morning the king formally ratified MacNeill's appointment. It was announced that he would be sworn in by the Chief Justice in the Law Courts, Dublin, early in the new year.[36] MacNeill would take the Oath of Allegiance to the British monarch during the ceremony.

The Second Dáil held a meeting on 10 December 1927. Opening the meeting, Art O'Connor (Meath), who had been elected 'President of the Irish Republic' and 'President of the Second Dáil' twelve months previously said:

> In December 1926, you ratified my appointment as President but 50 per cent of those present then, have not been summoned today as they have since entered the Free State Parliament and whether you wish the Dáil (Republican Second Dáil) to continue or what particular function you wish associated with

it, is a matter you have to face today. The amount of functioning the Dáil (Republican Second Dáil) has been able to do since the last meeting has been practically nil…Whether you think that the time has arrived to set up some alternative machinery to take the place of the Second Dáil is for yourselves to consider.[37]

Dáithí Ceannt (East Cork) thought they should not give up because sooner or later the people would come back to them. Miss Mary MacSwiney (Cork City) believed the Second Dáil should be preserved.[38] The meeting agreed with both these sentiments.

The matter of the election of 'President of the Republic' then arose. Art O'Connor had informed his colleagues that he intended to take up the practice of law in the Free State courts. Dr Madden (Mayo North) felt that it would 'be very inconsistent if O'Connor was practising in the Free State Courts where he would have to uphold the Free State Constitution and the Free State laws.' Seán MacSwiney (County Cork) remarked that 'an ordinary volunteer could not recognise the court and you would have the Head of the Republic acknowledging it every day.'[39] At this stage President Art O'Connor formally tendered his resignation to the Second Dáil. The Ceann Comhairle Seán Ó Ceallaigh accepted his resignation with regret.[40] Mary MacSwiney proposed that instead of a President the Dáil elect an executive that would be instructed to establish cooperation with Óglaigh na h-Éireann (the IRA). Dáithí Ceannt seconded the motion and the meeting concurred. Among those elected to executive of the Second Dáil were Brian O'Higgins (Clare); Cathal Ó Murchadha (Dublin South); Count Plunkett (Roscommon); Mary MacSwiney (Cork City); Dáithí Ceannt (Cork East); and Seán Ó Ceallaigh, Meath, as an ex-officio member.

Notes

1. *The Irish Times*, 13 September 1927.
2. *Ibid.*, 14 September 1927.
3. NAI, File 2B/82/117/26/20, Minutes of Special Meeting of Sinn Féin, 28 August 1927.
4. *Ibid.*
5. *Ibid.*
6. *The Irish Times*, 27 August 1927.
7. *Ibid.*, 7 September 1927.
8. Sinn Féin Statement, *The Irish Times*, 29 August 1927.

9. *The Irish Times*, 14 September 1927.
10. The *Nation*, 1 October 1927.
11. The final result of the general election held on 15 September 1927 was as follows:.

C. na nG.	Fianna Fáil	Labour	Ind.	Farmers	Nat. League	Ind. Labour
62	57	13	12	6	2	1

12. Richard Sinnott, *Irish Votes Decide*, pp. 299, 300.
13. *The Irish Times*, 21 September 1927.
14. *Ibid.*
15. The *Irish Independent*, 11 October 1927.
16. *Ibid.*
17. *Ibid.*, 12 October 1927.
18. The following was the result of the division on the election of W.T. Cosgrave as President of the Executive Council:

For (76)	Against (70)	Did not vote (3)
C na nG (60)	Fianna Fáil (57)	National League (2)
Independents (10)	Labour (13)	M. Brennan (Ind, Roscommon) (1)
Farmers (6)		

Absent (2): J.X. Murphy (Ind., Dublin County); James Larkin (Ind. Labour, Dublin North)
Not allowed to vote (2): Ceann Comhairle; W.T. Cosgrave
(W.T. Cosgrave represented two constituencies but had only one vote).

19. *Dáil Éireann Debates*, Volume 21, 11 October 1927, pp. 41, 42.
20. The *Irish Independent*, 17 October 1927.
21. *Ibid.*, 31 October 1927.
22. *Ibid.*, 17 October 1927.
23. *Ibid.*, 7 November 1927.
24. The *Irish Independent*, 25 November 1927 and the *Nation*, 3 December 1927.
25. *Ibid.*
26. The *Nation*, 3 December 1927.
27. *Ibid.*, 28 January 1928.
28. *Saoirse na h-Éireann, Irish Freedom*, January 1928.
29. The *Irish Independent*, 12 December 1927.
30. *An Phoblacht*, 31 December 1927.
31. Denis Carroll, *They Have Fooled You Again: Michael O'Flanagan (1876-1942)*, p. 175.
32. *Ibid.* p. 176.
33. *The Irish Times*, 13 December 1927.
34. *Saoirse na h-Éireann, Irish Freedom*, January 1928.
35. The *Irish Independent*, 16 December 1927.
36. *Ibid.*
37. UCDA, de Valera Papers, File P150/1948, 10 December 1927.
38. *Ibid.*
39. *Ibid.*
40. *Ibid.*

17

Fianna Fáil Must Expand

At the beginning of 1928 Ernest Blythe, Minster for Finance, declared that 'the filling up of the parliament has stabilised conditions as nothing else could have done. Henceforward economic problems will, in the public mind, occupy the place that has heretofore been given to purely political questions.'[1] James Fitzgerald-Kenney, the new Minister for Justice and TD for Mayo South, who replaced the assassinated Kevin O'Higgins, declared at a large Cumann na nGaedheal meeting in Castlebar that it was a great day for Ireland when the Free State Executive Council decided that abstention from the Dáil must cease and brought in the necessary legislation forcing de Valera and his followers to make a hard choice. Fianna Fáil deputies, he said, were forced 'to decide whether they would admit the validity of the Treaty and of the Constitution and take their seats in the Dáil or cease to present themselves for election.'[2]

On I February 1928, James McNeill was installed as Governor-General of the Irish Free State in succession to T.M. Healy. The ceremony, which was dignified and impressive, took place at Leinster House in the presence of a distinguished audience. When they entered Leinster House, McNeill and Mrs MacNeill were escorted to the Ceann Comhairle's room by the Vice-President, Ernest Blythe, who was officiating in the absence of the President, W.T. Cosgrave, who, at that time, was making a state visit to the US. The Chief Justice and his usher, both in robes, slowly entered the room where all the Free State ministers, parliamentary secretaries and judges of the supreme and high courts were assembled. All present bowed. James McNeill handed the Chief Justice the commission of appointment that had been given to him by the British king on the advice of the Free State Executive Council. The Chief

Justice then addressed MacNeill:

> Sir, your commission of appointment being in order, you will
> now take the Oath of Allegiance and of office prescribed by the
> statute, here before me and in the presence of the ministers, the
> Chairman of the Dáil and Seanad, the judges and others here
> assembled.

The Chief Justice duly administered the Oath of Allegiance to McNeill.[3]
Not one Fianna Fáil TD attended the ceremony.

James Larkin (Independent Labour), who had been elected a TD for
Dublin North in the September 1927 general election, was disqualified from
office because he was 'an undischarged bankrupt on the date of his election'.[4]
This decision was taken by a majority of the Dáil Committee on Procedure
and Privileges although the Fianna Fáil representatives dissented. Later the
assembled Dáil passed this motion of disqualification by eighty votes to fifty.
A writ was issued to fill the vacancy in Dublin North and the date of the by-
election was fixed for 3 April.

At this stage the Sinn Féin Party went into isolationist mode. Margaret
Buckley reported to the Standing Committee 'that she had arranged for
the holding of a public meeting of the Political Prisoners' Committee to be
addressed by various speakers, including representatives of Fianna Fáil.'
Brian O'Higgins proposed and Count Plunkett seconded that 'we withdraw
our representatives [James Mitchell and Mrs Margaret Buckley] from the
Political Prisoners' Committee' because members of Fianna Fáil had taken
the Oath of Allegiance before they entered the Dáil on 12 August 1927. The
Standing Committee refused to give Mrs Buckley permission to speak from
a 'composite platform' at any political meeting. The 'composite platform' they
had in mind would be a group of Republican speakers who might include
some members of Fianna Fáil. [5]

Many rank-and-file members of Sinn Féin were not satisfied with
the new policies being adopted by the leadership of the organisation. A
communication from the O'Rahilly Cumann, Dublin North, was read at

a meeting of the Standing Committee, expressing the opinion 'that the organisation was in a semi-moribund condition.'[6]

In the Dublin North by-election three candidates were nominated to fill the vacant seat. Vincent Rice KC was nominated by Cumann na nGaedheal and Kathleen Clarke stood for Fianna Fáil. She had taken the anti-Treaty side and was defeated as a Republican candidate in the June 1922 general election. She followed Éamon de Valera into Fianna Fáil after the split in 1926, won a seat for Fianna Fáil in the general election of June 1927 but lost it again in the general election of September 1927. James Larkin, the disqualified Independent Labour TD, caused a big surprise when he again entered the field.

Unlike previous elections, there was little reference to the Oath of Allegiance in this by-election campaign. The economy, unemployment, housing and the efficacy of each party in tackling these problems dominated on the election platforms.

Only 46 per cent of eligible voters went to the polls. Vincent Rice polled 21,731 votes. Kathleen Clarke 13,322 votes and James Larkin 8232. This meant that the government candidate got 177 votes more than the combined total for Kathleen Clarke and James Larkin: he was elected on the first count. This was a great achievement for Cumann na nGaedheal although they polled 2028 votes fewer than they had done in the September 1927 general election. Fianna Fáil dropped 3198 votes on their September 1927 general election figure, which was disappointing for the party, although the drop in votes for Cumann na nGaedheal and Fianna Fáil could be attributed to the low turnout for this by-election. James Larkin increased his September 1927 vote by 742. Hugh Law, Cumann na nGaedheal TD for Donegal commented: 'Fianna Fáil has suffered a signal defeat – that party is declining in prestige and when the next Dáil elections come it will be of very small account in the country.'[7]

Patrick McGilligan, Minister for External Affairs, claimed in Cork with reference to previous Republican abstention from Dáil Éireann, : 'There no longer remain outside people whose main object in political life is to bring institutions of the state into disrepute and break them, if possible.'[8] For the first time since independence every seat in Dáil Éireann was occupied.

However it could not be claimed that Dáil Éireann was entirely representative and free, as the conditions of the 1927 Electoral Bill precluded Sinn Féin candidates from being named on the ballot sheet unless they guaranteed that they would take the Oath of Allegiance and enter Dáil Éireann if they were elected.

Meanwhile *An Phoblacht* stated that all along the Western seaboard economic conditions were desperate. The *Clare Champion* reported:

> Touching scenes were witnessed at Ennis Railway Station last week. Thirty-three boys and girls took the train for Cobh on their way to American cities. Extra carriages had to be attached to the train for their accommodation for the simple reason that when the train arrived, it was found to be packed with exiles from other areas. All flying, all deserting the homeland: all weeping at the snapping of family ties, breaking into sobs as the last hand-clasp, the last kiss, was exchanged. Why? The answer given to this question was unvarying: 'I cannot get work here and I must go look for it.'[9]

The third Fianna Fáil *ard-fheis*, with a large attendance of delegates, took place on 25 and 26 October 1928. Éamon de Valera was unanimously re-elected President of the party. Seán T. O'Kelly and Patrick Ruttledge were elected vice-presidents. Seán Lemass and Gerry Boland were again chosen as secretaries and the treasurers, Seán MacEntee and Dr James Ryan, re-elected.

There were some surprises among those elected to the national executive. It was interesting that Dan Breen was back again in the Fianna Fáil fold and an elected member of the national executive. Pádraig Ó Máille, a former Cumann na nGaedheal TD and later on one of the leaders of Clann Éireann, was now on the governing body of the party. Colonel Maurice Moore, up to this an independent senator but who always supported the cause of Republican prisoners in the Senate, was also on the national executive. These new entrants to Fianna Fáil showed that the party was growing and picking up important new members who did not agree with Republican abstentionism.

When it seemed that the *ard-fheis* was forgetting the question of the abolition of the Oath of Allegiance, de Valera made his presidential address, enunciating a different policy from heretofore to rid the Constitution of this Oath of Allegiance. He stated that the Cumann na nGaedheal government had taken away the path of the referendum by which he and Fianna Fáil had planned to have the Oath of Allegiance abolished. By doing this the government had torn up the Constitution and violated the will of the people. Now Fianna Fáil must try to get control of the government and take over the machinery of government. He referred to the fact that 'people were now questioning whether Fianna Fáil are or are not Republicans'. He thought the reason for this fallacy was that the party had been forced to travel a different road from that which they wished to travel. He commented:

> Is it necessary to say that I come as a Republican? I have not lost faith in Republicanism. In fact it is because I have not lost faith in it that I am here…I am convinced that the Republican movement can be restored to its former robust strength… But what I want to say is that, as far as I am concerned, if I thought that our organisation was going to be narrowed down and barriers put up to prevent those who took different views and a different stand some years ago from joining it, I would never have attempted it; because the one aim and hope of my life since the Treaty was that I would live to see the same sort of movement which we had from 1917 to 1921, when we had within it everything that was good in the nation…We will never be able to work in a political movement until we have the majority of the people behind us, and how are we going to get a majority if, when anybody who was not with us before wants to come to us, we try to put them off. As I have said, the basic political objective of this organisation is to secure the unity and independence of Ireland as a Republic.[10]

Many Republicans who had stayed with Sinn Féin were still very critical of Éamon de Valera for entering Dáil Éireann. Annie MacSwiney, sister of Mary, writing to another Republican member of Cumann na mBan, Sheila Humphreys, who was at this time a prisoner in Mountjoy Gaol, said of Éamon de Valera:

> Sometimes one stands aghast at the spectacle of people that do not mean badly, doing the wrong thing so calmly and expecting you to be pleased with their wrongdoing because they do not call it wrongdoing. Like Dev – who takes the Oath we all condemned Collins for taking, six years after Collins took it, and then said it wasn't an Oath! As if Dev taking it made it different! What happens them! My mind becomes a blank when I try to understand them. Does yours?[11]

The Sinn Féin *ard-fheis* was held in Wynn's Hotel, Dublin on Sunday, 18 November 1928. Eighty delegates representing Sinn Féin *cumainn* in all parts of Ireland as well as in England and Scotland attended.[12]

In his address to the assembled delegates, the President, J.J. O'Kelly, made a blistering attack on Fianna Fáil:

> Treacherously and in disregard of majority decisions in Sinn Féin and the Dáil [the Republican Second Dáil], Fianna Fáil sent its deputies to Merrion Street and, so far as they could, rendered the Republican government impotent. And what has been the national gain from their entry? The salaries and patronage and other petty comforts that have come to apostates can hardly be regarded as adequate national return…What is happening in reality is that a movement [Fianna Fáil] brazenly professing to be Republican is being swamped by time-servers and broken reeds, who were tried before and found wanting and will as surely be found wanting again in the hour of stress.[13]

O'Kelly pointed out that Sinn Féin was then more an organisation with an educational remit than a political machine for general elections.[14]

Among the resolutions passed was one proposed by Pádraig Mac Aindriú and seconded by Máire Comerford that 'in order to arouse the people of Ireland who are now settling down to their shame by the acceptance of Oath-bound partitioned parliaments that public meetings be held in every town and district constituency in Ireland to preach the Sinn Féin policy on these matters.'[15]

In the first few months of 1929 it became necessary to hold a further by-election in Dublin North. A vacancy was created by the resignation of the Independent TD, Alfred Byrne, following his election to the Seanad. Oscar Traynor, ex-Sinn Féin TD, was surprisingly selected as the Fianna Fáil candidate.

At a meeting in Middle Abbey Street, Oscar Traynor said:

> I have been studying events of the past two years and what I have seen convinces me that the hope of uniting the people of Ireland lies with the Fianna Fáil organisation. I believe that Irish independence can be won constitutionally, without any more sacrifices. That is why I am on a Fianna Fáil platform.[16]

Cumann na nGaedheal nominated a strong candidate to oppose Oscar Traynor: Dr Thomas O'Higgins, brother of the assassinated Minister for Justice, Kevin O'Higgins. Thomas O'Higgins claimed at a public meeting to support his candidature that when Cumann na nGaedheal started to build up a decent, disciplined, healthy and prosperous country:

> Mr de Valera went traveling through the country crying 'Traitor' to all who entered the Dáil, pointing out the horrible offence it was for any Irishman to take the Oath. Then quite suddenly he discovered that the Dáil was the place for the very best Irishmen and that there was nothing horrible or treacherous about the Oath that it was only an empty formula and that anyone could take it. All they had to do was to push the little book away and

write to the evening papers.[17]

Just two days before the election James Larkin unexpectedly spoke at a meeting of railwaymen in the Rotunda and asked all present to vote for the return of Oscar Traynor.[18] As Larkin could speak for about 8000 votes, this development increased Traynor's chances of winning Dublin North.

The election took place on 14 March. When the votes were counted Oscar Traynor at first led by as many as 5000 votes but as the counting progressed O'Higgins steadily made ground and ended up with a very small majority.

The final result was: Dr Thomas O'Higgins 28,445 votes and Oscar Traynor 28,294, giving O'Higgins a majority of 151 votes. It was obvious that the supporters of James Larkin had voted en masse for Oscar Traynor.

O'Higgins declared after the result was announced: 'I think that the result is a big vote of confidence in the government.'

This was the third by-election in Dublin North since the establishment of the state in 1922 and it was by far the largest vote ever obtained by a Republican candidate in the constituency. 'I have nothing to say except that I am quite satisfied with the result,' said Traynor.[19] His supporters assured him that his vote was large enough almost to guarantee him a seat for Fianna Fáil in Dublin North in the next general election.

At this time Republicans were shocked by the deaths of two stalwarts. On 18 April Samuel Holt, Fianna Fáil TD for Leitrim-Sligo, died unexpectedly in Cork Street Hospital, Dublin, at the age of forty-two.[20] He had been taken ill while attending the Dáil. His death would mean another by-election: this was not good for Fianna Fáil as they were experiencing difficulty in winning by-elections at this time.

The death of Austin Stack, secretary of Sinn Féin, was no less unexpected. He died in the Mater Hospital Private Nursing Home in Dublin after an operation for appendicitis with associated complications. Stack, the former Sinn Féin TD for Kerry, was only forty-nine. He had been secretary of Sinn Féin since 1917 and had served loyally and diligently in that office His early death was attributed to abdominal trouble that recurred in the latter years of his life. Austin Stack had taken part in three hunger strikes and several prison protests and his illness was a consequence of the ill-effects of these. Stack remained with Sinn Féin, unflinchingly faithful to the Fenian beliefs that he had inherited, although many of his closest friends had followed Dev and helped to establish Fianna Fáil. His death was a big loss to Sinn Féin and its abstentionist policies.

The final page of *An Phoblacht* on 25 May 1929 announced that Republican Press Ltd. had acquired ownership of the newspaper. Peadar O'Donnell had been editor since P.J. Little joined Fianna Fáil. Proinsias Ó Riain (Frank Ryan) and Geoffrey Coulter would in future act as editors. The announcement declared: 'Henceforth, as hitherto, *An Phoblacht* will preach the separatist creed.'[21]

At a convention in Sligo, Lieutenant-General Seán Mac Eoin was unanimously selected as the Cumann na nGaedheal candidate for the Leitrim-Sligo vacancy caused by the death of Samuel Holt. Seán Mac Eoin had led many engagements against British forces in County Longford in 1921, including the famed Ballinalee ambush, and was sure to be a strong candidate for the vacant seat.

Éamon Donnelly, the ex-Republican MP for Armagh who had left Sinn Féin to affiliate with Fianna Fáil, was selected as the Fianna Fáil candidate for the by-election. Donnelly had been elected an MP for Armagh in the Northern Ireland general election in 1925 but he had never taken his seat. Donnelly was a Republican to the core. He said: 'It is my intention in this election to keep alive the principles of Republicanism, for which I entered Irish public life.'[22]

Seán Mac Eoin warned: 'To smash the Treaty would be political madness and would mean another war with England.'[23]

There was a significant group of Sinn Féin adherents in County Leitrim and rumour had it that their votes would go to the Fianna Fáil candidate. But bad news came for Éamon Donnelly when Brian Cassidy, joint secretary of the South Leitrim Sinn Féin executive, scotched this rumour:

> The Sinn Féin organisation now, as in the past, stands
> for the complete freedom and independence of Ireland.

Either candidate in this contest is prepared, if elected, to swear allegiance to an English King and enter His Majesty's partitioned parliament. It is my duty to see that no member of our organisation is fooled by either lies or false promises.[24]

The by-election was held on 7 June 1929 and resulted in a comfortable win for Seán Mac Eoin. The Cumann na nGaedheal candidate polled 28,598 votes to Éamon Donnelly's 24,621 votes, a majority of 3977 votes.

Fianna Fáil, although it had increased its vote considerably, had once again failed to record a victory in a by-election, something that did not augur well for the future of the party.

Seán Mac Eoin's victory meant that the Cumann na nGaedheal government had again strengthened its position. Since the general election in September 1927, there had been four by-elections and the party had won all four, making three gains: two from Independents in Dublin City (James Larkin and Alfie Byrne) and one from Fianna Fáil in this by-election in Leitrim-Sligo.

By mid-1929 it was evident to de Valera and Fianna Fáil that in order to get rid of the Oath of Allegiance they would have to win a general election and become the government of the country. Although the party was growing in strength it still lacked sufficient support to do this. If Fianna Fáil were ever to become the government of the country it would have to entice into its ranks more and more people who had not heretofore supported them.

Notes

1. The *Irish Independent*, 2 January 1928.
2. *Ibid.*, 24 January 1928.
3. *Ibid.*, 2 February 1928.
4. *Ibid.*, 15 March 1928.
5. NAI, File 2B/82/117/26/32, Minutes of the Standing Committee of Sinn Féin, 24 January 1928.
6. *Ibid.*, File 2B/82/117/26/45, 24 April 1928.
7. The *Irish Independent*, 20 April 1928.
8. *Ibid.*, 7 May 1928.
9. *An Phoblacht*, 28 April 1928.
10. UCDA, Archives of the Fianna Fáil Party, File P176/23(1), Speech by Éamon de Valera delivered at the third *ard-fheis* of Fianna Fáil, 25-26 October 1928.
11. NAI, File Taois/ S 8049, Letter from Annie MacSwiney to Sheila Humphreys.
12. *An Phoblacht*, 1 December 1928.
13. The *Irish Independent*, 19 November 1928.
14. *Ibid.*

15. *An Phoblacht*, 1 December 1928.
16. The *Irish Independent*, 20 February 1929.
17. *Ibid.*, 21 February 1929.
18. *Ibid.*, 13 March 1929.
19. *Ibid.*, 16 March 1929.
20. UCDA, Archives of the Fianna Fáil Party, File P176/443.
21. *An Phoblacht*, 25 May 1929.
22. The *Irish Independent*, 20 May 1929.
23. *Ibid.*
24. *Ibid.*, 1 June 1929.

18

Fianna Fáil Wins Its First By-election

The 1929 Fianna Fáil *ard-fheis* was held in the Mansion House on 17-18 October. Addressing the assembled delegates, Seán Lemass, one of the honorary secretaries of the organisation, said: 'If support for Fianna Fáil has increased in other constituencies as it has in Leitrim-Sligo and North Dublin, as shown by the recent by-elections, then the party will secure a majority at the next general election.'[1] He added: 'Our first object is to establish a Republican form of government in this country in our own time.'[2]

It was noteworthy during this *ard-fheis* that the officers and delegates put more emphasis on the campaign for the retention of land annuities than on the older, still unresolved issue of the abolition of the Oath of Allegiance.

Since Frank Ryan had become editor of *An Phoblacht*, that newspaper had grown critical of Fianna Fáil policy and gave more publicity and support to Sinn Féin. Under the heading, 'The Futility of Fianna Fáil', *An Phoblacht* commented on what it perceived as the party's lack of a Republican policy:

> The personalities that dominate the Fianna Fáil organisation
> might (because of their militant past) lend it a glamour
> of Republicanism, but the policy they pursue led them
> from the beginning not towards revolution but towards
> constitutionalism…Many members of the organisation are
> becoming convinced of that fact.[3]

Ernest Blythe, Vice-President of the Free State government and Minister for Finance, commented in Clonmel shortly after the Fianna Fáil *ard-fheis*:

The other day at the Fianna Fáil *ard-fheis* a leading deputy [Seán Lemass] said that the first step of Fianna Fáil would be to establish a Republican form of government here. If that was their policy it was contrary to the economic interests of the country…The present government was not, as he said, out to get a Republic. We believe that if the twenty-six counties could be made a Republic that it should not be done because if it were done it would definitely make partition permanent.[4]

In reply, Seán Lemass, addressing a Fianna Fáil demonstration in Carrickmacross, County Monaghan, Blythe's home constituency, posed a question for the Minister for Finance: 'We want to know whether Blythe accepts the present status of Ireland as the goal of our national ambitions – we want to know from him if he has now drawn the line beyond which our people must not go.'

About a hundred delegates attended the Sinn Féin *ard-fheis* which was held in Wynn's Hotel, Dublin on 8 December 1929. The President, J.J. O'Kelly, referred to a statement by President W.T. Cosgrave that the writ of Dáil Éireann never ran across the border. O'Kelly replied that the First and Second Dáil did not confine their political activities to the twenty-six counties: 'The two men [Collins and Griffith] who led the way in signing the Treaty,' he said, 'and without whose influence the accursed thing would not have even got a proposer, were representatives of Ulster constituencies in the First Dáil.'[5]

The secretary, Liam Mac Giolla Mhuire, expressed regret at the passing of the party's late honorary secretary, Austin Stack. 'He was one great loss to Sinn Féin,' said Mac Giolla Mhuire, 'and his loss could never be retrieved.'[6] The secretary stated that they had a total of seventy-two affiliated branches of Sinn Féin, one more than the previous year.

Most of the previous year's officers retained their positions. The President was once again J.J. O'Kelly and Riobárd Ó Briain replaced Austin Stack as one of the honorary secretaries. Although Mary MacSwiney remained antagonistic to Father Michael O'Flanagan he was again elected to the standing committee with other veteran Sinn Féiners.

The *ard-fheis* in general gave the impression of an inactive political organisation that remained committed to abstaining from the Dáil. The fourth Sinn Féin party had no intention of contesting elections in the Free State.[7]

When he spoke at public meetings Seán Lemass often referred to Fianna Fáil's plans for constitutional reform. He made a point of doing this in order to reassure new recruits to the party that Fianna Fáil did not intend to return to war with England in order to achieve its objectives. At a Fianna Fáil meeting in Donegal he said:

> There are some people who profess to be uncertain as to the Fianna Fáil attitude to the Free State Constitution. There are some articles in the Constitution which Fianna Fáil will amend, when it gets the opportunity. These amendments can be effected by legislation.…Fianna Fáil asks from the people a mandate to achieve its objects by political action alone.[8]

James Killane TD (Longford-Westmeath) who had belatedly transferred to Fianna Fáil from Sinn Féin, died on 26 April 1930 at the age of fifty-six. Killane had been returned for the constituency in the 1923 general election. He had stood for Fianna Fáil in the general election of June 1927 but had lost out to fellow-party-member, James Victory. However, in the general election of September 1927 he had turned the tables on Victory. His death caused a by-election.

Not surprisingly, James Victory expected to be nominated by Fianna Fáil but instead James Geoghegan KC received the Fianna Fáil nomination after two hours' debate by delegates at a well-attended convention in the County Hall, Mullingar. Geoghegan was a native of Athlone, County Westmeath. He had been an active member of Cumann na nGaedheal and had once offered himself as an election candidate to that party but in 1927 he became prominently associated with Fianna Fáil. As a barrister he had given his advice to Fianna Fáil on the question of the retention of the land annuities. His nomination made for a more controversial by-election campaign.

Cumann na nGaedheal selected Dr Vincent Delany as its by-election candidate in the by-election and Senator Michael Duffy was the choice of the Labour Party. He had a keen interest in the welfare of the farming community.

Fianna Fáil had a good deal of support in Longford-Westmeath and party organisers knew they had a chance of winning the by-election so they resolved to fight a strong campaign.

At the start of the campaign, Éamon de Valera returned from the United States where he had collected large sums of money to start a daily newspaper in Ireland that would reflect the views of Fianna Fáil. Accompanied by bands and banners, he arrived in Athlone and addressed a large meeting:

> The Treaty has been described as a stepping-stone, and it is time now, after nearly ten years, that we took a step forward. If Fianna Fáil is returned to power the first thing we will do is to remove the Oath. The Free State ministers and supporters tell us that we are better off in the British Empire. There was none of that talk in 1916 and onwards to 1920. Am I to conclude that we do not want freedom – that we are so foolish as to think that England holds us for our own benefit?[9]

Patrick Hogan, Minister for Agriculture, addressed a gathering of farmers in Longford: 'Assuming that a Republic is got and that England wants to teach the country a lesson they will have no trouble in getting all the supplies they require from other countries.' He asked, 'How long will Great Britain be dealing with those other countries for all her supplies before the enthusiasm for the Republic and the removal of the Oath will have evaporated?' He answered the question himself: 'It will not be six months.'[10]

During the campaign, the Fianna Fáil candidate, James Geoghegan, said that he would still be in favour of keeping the Treaty if changing fundamental parts of it meant a resumption of war with England. This led to insinuations about the genuineness of his Republican viewpoint and caused *An Phoblacht* to express misgivings about his candidature:

The Fianna Fáil candidate who is being foisted on Longford-Westmeath is not a Republican. To do him justice, in his first electoral pronouncement he made his attitude very clear. His attitude on Irish independence differs in no way from that of the supporters of England's 'Free State' – of which he has been an active supporter. Fianna Fáil headquarters, and not Geoghegan, have changed.[11]

President W.T. Cosgrave was ill throughout the election campaign and unable to take any active part in electioneering. Two days before polling day he returned to the Dáil: although looking slightly pale he was fit and well. He did not visit Longford-Westmeath and no doubt his absence was felt.

The by-election took place on 13 June 1930. There was an 80 per cent turn-out, one of the highest polls at any of the many elections since 1922. As the count progressed it became clear that the Fianna Fáil candidate was polling better than expected and that the Labour candidate was not doing well. Interest continued until the last boxes were counted and the result was announced:

James Geoghegan, Fianna Fáil: 21,881
Dr V. Delany, Cumann na nGaedheal: 16,438
Senator Michael Duffy, Labour: 2525

The Fianna Fáil candidate had a majority of 2918 votes over the combined total of Cumann na nGaedheal and Labour and he was declared elected on the first count. It was a spectacular win for Fianna Fáil. The biggest delight for Fianna Fáil supporters was the realisation that their party had won its first ever by-election, after losing the six it had contested since its foundation. The fact that the party had outpolled Cumann na nGaedheal was an indication that it was possible for it to gain a Dáil majority in the near future and confirmed that the policy of seeking to attract new members who had opposed anti-Treaty policies during and after the Civil War would have beneficial results in future elections.

Seán Lemass said: 'The order to march has been given in Longford-Westmeath. I believe this election will prove to be a turning point.'[12]

President Cosgrave put as good a face as he could on the defeat: 'I have not been in the constituency during the election,' he said, 'the only thing that struck me was that Mr Geoghegan, during the contest, indicated that he is a Treatyite. It is to a certain extent satisfactory that a candidate who, at least, is not against the Treaty has been returned.'[13]

This by-election result heralded the emergence of Fianna Fáil as a definite electoral threat to the Cumann na nGaedheal government. Was the Fianna Fáil victory a flash in the pan or could the momentum be maintained?

Notes

1. The *Irish Independent*, 18 October 1929.
2. *Ibid.*
3. *An Phoblacht*, 26 October 1929.
4. The *Irish Independent*, 28 October 1929.
5. *Ibid.*, 9 December 1929.
6. *An Phoblacht*, 28 December 1929.
7. *An Phoblacht*, 11 January 1930.
8. The *Irish Independent*, 27 January 1930.
9. *Ibid.*, 30 May 1930.
10. *Ibid.*, 2 June 1930.
11. *An Phoblacht*, 31 May 1930.
12. The *Irish Independent*. 16 June 1930.
13. *Ibid.*

19

Expectations Rise

Three delegates from the Free State government attended the 1929 Imperial Conference in London. Patrick McGilligan, Minister for External Affairs, led the delegation, accompanied by Desmond Fitzgerald, Minister for Defence and Patrick Hogan, Minister for Agriculture The conference of 1926, at which Kevin O'Higgins had represented the Free State government, had been epoch-making. It unequivocally and finally acknowledged the equality of the dominions with Britain. Thus Great Britain released the strings of control over the dominions, including the Irish Free State.

When the conference closed in London early in 1930, it issued a summary of its report. This contained a number of clauses for insertion in a statute to be known as the Statute of Westminster and which was scheduled to be passed into law by parliament in December 1931. One of the clauses stipulated: 'No law made by a dominion parliament shall be void or inoperative on the grounds that it is repugnant to the existing or future law of England.' Other provisions established the complete legislative independence of each dominion. If this statute was passed it could have a profound influence on future constitutional developments in the Free State.

Addressing a well-attended Fianna Fáil meeting in Ennis, County Clare, Éamon de Valera referred to the attendance of the Free State government delegation at this 1930 Imperial Conference: 'The Fianna Fáil Party has no interest in the British Commonwealth of Nations and we hold that the government should not be trying to involve us in unnecessary and entangling alliances at the Imperial Conference – Ireland would be happier outside the British Empire.'[1]

The 1930 Fianna Fáil *ard-fheis* opened in the Mansion House on 30

October. Seán Lemass, one of the honorary secretaries, presented his annual report, in which he stated that the previous year had been in many respects the most satisfactory since the inception of the party and that the situation was ripe for a Fianna Fáil victory at a general election. He reported that five hundred and fifty fully registered Fianna Fáil *cumainn* were, at that moment in time, affiliated in the twenty-six counties. Galway constituency had the highest number of registered *cumainn* – sixty-three in all. [2]

Referring to the attendance of three Free State ministers at the Imperial Conference in London he said: 'The fight for political freedom will be won entirely by the courage and determination of the Irish people and not by the slavish crawling around the knees of English ministers in London.'[3]

Dáithí Ceannt, former Sinn Féin TD and one of the Munster represent-atives on the Standing Committee of Sinn Féin, died in his native Castlelyons, County Cork, in November 1930. A short time before his death he had written to the Standing Committee of Sinn Féin regretting that, because of illness, he had not been able to attend as many meetings of the ruling body of Sinn Féin as he would have liked during the previous year.[4] Another Sinn Féin stalwart had passed from the political scene.

Major Bryan Cooper, Cumann na nGaedheal TD for County Dublin, died at his home in Dalkey in July 1930 after a few months of illness. This meant that there would be a by-election in County Dublin, where Fianna Fáil was not strong.

The Free State government fixed the by-election date for 9 December 1930. Cumann na nGaedheal chose a well-known barrister, Thomas. A. Finlay KC, to contest the by-election. Conor A. Maguire BL, another prominent member of the legal profession, was nominated as the Fianna Fáil candidate. As the Labour Party decided not to take part in the contest there would be a straight fight between these two candidates

Ernest Blythe declared at a meeting in support of the Cumann na nGaedheal candidate: 'We have very considerable advantages through association with the British Commonwealth of Nations. We are protected from any attack or encroachment on our rights and liberties because if the British people were inclined to encroach on our rights, they could not do so without incurring the hostility of Canada and Australia and other such countries.'[5]

Éamon de Valera was quick to respond to this comment by Blythe when he spoke at a Fianna Fáil meeting in Rathmines:

> Fianna Fáil stood on the policy of Sinn Féin from 1917 to 1921 – for the right of the Irish people to govern themselves in their own way without tolerating any interference from outside. We ought to be able to have a Republic if the majority of the people wanted that Republic. If the people were free to choose, and if threats were not held before them, they would choose as they chose in 1918, a completely independent Republic.[6]

Polling took place in County Dublin on 9 December. Around 20,000 fewer voters turned out than in the September 1927 general election, which could be attributed to the fact that neither Independents nor the Labour Party contested the seat. The returning officer announced the result in the Town Hall, Blackrock:

Thomas A. Finlay KC, Cumann na nGaedheal	35,362
Conor A. Maguire BL, Fianna Fáil	15,024
Cumann na nGaedheal majority	20,338

This result was no surprise to either of the two contesting parties. Fianna Fáil received almost the same number of votes as in the September 1927 general election but Cumann na nGaedheal polled more than 3000 votes fewer. It was apparent that voters who had previously supported Labour and Independent candidates took very little part in this election.

The defeated Fianna Fáil contender, Conor Maguire, said that his party did not at any time expect a favourable result because in Dublin County: 'the greatest portion of what I might describe as the imperialist element in this country is centred.'[7]

Cumann na nGaedheal held its annual convention in the Mansion House, in May 1931.[8] In his address to the delegates, President W.T. Cosgrave referred to the recent Imperial Conference:

> It has come to be realised that the association of states known
> as the British Commonwealth of Nations can only endure if
> their relations with each other are based on the most complete
> co-equality. We have made it clear that the growth of friendly
> relations between us and Great Britain depends on the complete
> elimination in form, as well as in substance, of any appearances
> of inequality. The process of eliminating these appearances has
> been going on steadily since 1922.[9]

Hugh Colohan TD (Labour), who had taken an active part in the old Sinn
Féin movement, was found dead at his home in Newbridge, County Kildare,
on 15 April 1931. Colohan, who was sixty-two, appeared to be in his usual
health when he retired to bed after returning from a session of the Dáil. His
death meant that there would be a by-election in Kildare. Fianna Fáil's vote
was rising in this constituency and the party had polled well there in the
general election of September 1927.

There were three candidates in the field for this by-election. William
Norton was unanimously selected as the Labour candidate. He had won a by-
election for Labour in Dublin County in 1926 but lost the seat in the general
election in June 1927. John Conlon was the Cumann na nGaedheal candidate.
He was a former Farmers' Party TD who had been elected for Kildare in the
1923 general election but had lost his seat in the general election of June 1927
and subsequently joined Cumann na nGaedheal. Thomas Harris, a county
councillor from Caragh, was selected as Fianna Fáil candidate.

At a Fianna Fáil meeting at Milltown, County Kildare, P.J. Little, Fianna
Fáil TD for Waterford, explained that Fianna Fáil wished to remove the Oath
of Allegiance in order: 'to give an opportunity to those people who took
a stronger, and what was called a more extreme view of Irish nationality, to
come into the Dáil Éireann assembly.'[10]

Polling took place in County Kildare on 30 June 1931 and there was a big
turn-out of voters.

There was a surprise when the result of the first count was announced:

Thomas Harris (Fianna Fáil)	10,041
John Conlon (Cumann na nGaedheal)	8374
William Norton (Labour)	6669

An enormous crowd awaited the result outside the count centre as William Norton (Labour) was eliminated and his second preferences were distributed. Of Norton's votes, 2369 were non-transferable. Of the balance Conlon got 2729, which brought his total to 11,103. Harris got 1571, bringing his total to 11,612. Thomas Harris's majority was 509 votes and he was declared elected.

In his victory speech, Harris said that: 'the government had threatened a general election if they lost in Kildare and Fianna Fáil would welcome the election at any time believing that what Kildare had done would be done by the whole country at the first opportunity.'[11]

Fianna Fáil's second by-election victory gave a strong signal that the party would be a strong contender in any election held in the not-too-distant future.

The 1931 Sinn Féin *ard-fheis* was held on 4 October in 16 Parnell Square, Dublin. Delegates attended from all parts of Ireland and from England and Scotland. Brian O'Higgins, one time Sinn Féin TD for Clare, was elected President. He announced that, in future, Sinn Féin would hold weekly Irish classes in Parnell Square, Dublin, for both beginners and more advanced students and that the works of Pearse would be studied. Sinn Féin would maintain its promotion of Irish history and the Irish language.

Thomas Mullins, who had represented Cork West as a Fianna Fáil TD since the general election of June 1927, disagreed with the Fianna Fáil leadership, alleging that Republican policy within the party was weakening. He had been expelled from the party on 28 October 1930 on the proposal of Frank Aiken, seconded by Gerry Boland.[12] Speaking after his expulsion, in his new role as an Independent Republican TD, Mullins said in Dáil Éireann:

They (the Pro-Treaty parties) made us on this side of the House

come in here and take that Oath of Allegiance to the Free
State Constitution against all our desires, against all our heart,
against all that tradition told us. We had to take that Oath and
bend the knee to his Majesty George V before we could attend
an assembly of the elected representatives of the Irish people...
Where is the liberty that prevents a section of the people of this
state [Sinn Féin supporters] from making their voices felt in the
counsels of this assembly?[13]

Seán MacEntee, Fianna Fáil TD for Dublin County, supported Mullins.
'Remove the Oath of Allegiance,' he declared, 'give these men a chance to
come into the House, give them a chance to put their point of view before us
and I say there will be no communism, no unrest, but there will be unity of
effort.'[14]

De Valera referred in particular to the Oath of Allegiance in his
presidential speech at the sixth annual *ard-fheis* of Fianna Fáil which opened
in the Mansion House on 27 October 1931.

To remove the Oath...will be the first act of a Fianna Fáil
majority...To give effect to the policy implied in the removal
of the Oath, a further general election must be held within a
reasonable space of time, within a period of a year, or two years
at most, so as to give to the section who will be excluded at the
coming elections, an opportunity of securing representation.

Trouble was brewing in Sinn Féin. Peadar Mac Aindriú, one of the
secretaries, submitted to the Standing Committee correspondence between
Mary MacSwiney and the secretaries concerning parliamentary election
policy and stated that 'for some time whisperings had been going the rounds,
not only in Dublin, but also in the provinces to the effect that Sinn Féin was
weakening in its attitude to one of the Free State parliamentary parties and
that the organisation at the next general election in the Free State would
advise the people to vote for Fianna Fáil.' The secretary had written to Mary

MacSwiney directing her attention to an *Irish Press* report to the effect: 'that she had advised the people to vote for Fianna Fáil at the next election and put out the murder gang.' Mary MacSwiney had replied to the secretary's letter: 'That in answer to a questioner [at a political meeting] she said that people who would vote, should vote out the murder gang.' She stressed the point that her advice to voters had not been addressed to members of Sinn Féin. After lengthy discussion, the Standing Committee decided to request Mary MacSwiney to attend a special meeting so that she would have an opportunity to be present when the members of the committee discussed the whole matter further.[15]

References to an impending constitutional crisis and the approaching general election in the Free State figured prominently in the debate in the House of Commons during the Second Reading of the Statute of Westminster Bill that set out to give expression to the Imperial Conference resolutions of 1926 and 1930. Winston Churchill, who was one of the signatories of the Anglo-Irish Treaty in 1921, said that if this Bill were passed it would be open to the Free State parliament, by the powers included in this Bill, if they were so minded, 'to repudiate the Oath of Allegiance embodied in the Treaty.' Eyebrows were raised in Ireland when Churchill added: 'I think that it is a very wrong thing to which we ought not to lend ourselves.' He announced that, with his support, Colonel Gretton would introduce an amendment during the committee stage of the Bill to ensure that there should be a saving clause so that the Statute of Westminster might not apply to the Anglo-Irish Treaty of 1921.[16]

Fianna Fáil Senator, Michael Comyn KC, replied to Churchill that he [Churchill] was now proposing to deny the Irish Free State the development of constitutional liberty that was enjoyed by Canada, Australia and the other British dominions. While according free development to these dominions, Churchill wanted to prevent the abolition of the Oath of Allegiance by an Irish Free State government. 'My reply,' said Senator Comyn, 'is that the freedom of Ireland is the inborn right of the Irish people.'[17]

Despite Churchill's speech in the House of Commons, the Cosgrave government believed that any going back by the British government on the findings of the two imperial conferences would be resented and opposed, not only by the Free State but by most of the dominions represented at the conference. The Free State Executive counted on support from the dominions in their opposition to the watering-down of the findings of the conferences.[18]

During the committee stage of the Statute of Westminster Bill in the House of Commons, Colonel Gretton moved Churchill's amendment. The full text of the amendment proposed that there should be a clause inserted in the Bill 'to prevent the Irish Free State government from repealing, amending or altering the Irish Free State Constitution Act, 1922.' Churchill formally supported the proposal. W.T. Cosgrave had written a letter to the Prime Minister, Ramsay MacDonald, in connection with the amendment and J.H. Thomas, Secretary for the Dominions, read out one of the paragraphs of this letter during the debate on the Bill. W.T. Cosgrave wrote that he sincerely hoped that the British government would not take the course of accepting the amendment relating to the Constitution of the Irish Free State. He continued: 'We [the Free State government] have reiterated time and time again that the Treaty is an agreement which can only be altered by consent [between the two governments].'

Churchill replied to Cosgrave's letter that he (Cosgrave), as President of the Irish Free State, had stood by all the obligations entered into by his late colleagues and signatories of the Treaty. But Churchill intimated that there was a danger that de Valera could come to power and he feared what might then happen to the Free State Constitution: 'A general election is approaching in the Free State,' he warned, 'and supposing that a change of government should occur we will be immediately confronted by a grave crisis on the Treaty.'[19] Cosgrave's letter to the British premier was influential in the defeat of Colonel Gretton's amendment by three-hundred-and-fifty votes to fifty. Soon afterwards Ramsay MacDonald moved the third reading of the Bill without any mention of the defeated amendment supported by Churchill and the Statute of Westminster passed through the House of Commons without a division on 11 December 1931.

The *Ard-Chomhairle* of Cumann na nGaedheal met in the Gresham Hotel in early December 1931. In the course of his address to the gathering,

President W.T. Cosgrave said that the Statute of Westminster confirmed for the British courts the principle of co-equality that was written into the report of the Imperial Conference of 1926. The President added: 'It justified the predictions of Griffith and Collins and it was a monument to the work of Kevin O'Higgins through whose endeavours in 1926 the declaration of equality was written.' At the Imperial Conference of 1926, Kevin O'Higgins had played an important role in the passing of the Balfour Declaration, which established the principle that the dominions were all equal in status, not subordinate to the United Kingdom.

A special meeting of the Sinn Féin Standing Committee was held on 4 December 1931, at which Mary MacSwiney was present and asked to account for her alleged exhortation to the public to vote for Fianna Fáil in the impending election. The President, Brian O'Higgins, chaired the meeting and Mary MacSwiney repeated her argument that her words 'had not been addressed to members of Sinn Féin but to members of the general public.' Seán Buckley, former TD Cork West agreed, in the main, with what Mary MacSwiney said. The former TD for Mayo North, Dr John Madden, said it would be bad policy to issue a statement advising people not to vote while J.J. O'Kelly, former Sinn Féin President, said he would not do or say anything that would help 'the murder gang' [the Cosgrave government] to be returned to power. But there was division on the Standing Committee about the words Mary MacSwiney had used in Cork. Brian O'Higgins, Mrs Margaret Buckley, Father Michael O'Flanagan, Séamus Mitchell, Seán O'Mahoney, Cathal Ó Murchadha and the secretaries, Peadar Mac Aindriú and Liam Mac Giolla Mhuire, disagreed with Mary MacSwiney's views, contending 'that there could not be one policy for the members of the organisation and another for people outside the organisation.' Eventually the following resolution was proposed, seconded and passed unanimously: 'that the attitude of Sinn Féin towards the election of persons to British institutions in this country [Dáil Éireann and the parliament of Northern Ireland] remains unchanged.'[20] This resolution was a rap on the knuckles for Mary MacSwiney.

At the meeting of the Standing Committee of Sinn Féin held on 20 December 1931, Brian O'Higgins, President, stated that he had acted on the suggestion made at the previous meeting to issue a New Year statement dealing with the Sinn Féin position in regard to the forthcoming general election. He read a draft statement that he had prepared for publication, subject to the approval of the Standing Committee. After discussion the Standing Committee approved the President's statement. The draft was edited and finalised on 29 December 1931 for publication in the New Year. In the first part of the statement it was confirmed that 'Sinn Féin will not even consider the matter of putting forward candidates at the general election.' The document continued:

> Sinn Féin is opposed, not to any particular party in the partition assemblies in Dublin and Belfast, but to those institutions themselves. They are British-made institutions, they are symbols of imperialism, they are outward signs of the mutilation of our country. Sinn Féin cannot, even by implication, ask or advise citizens of the Republic to help or vote for any candidate, no matter what his profession or promises may be, who before he can even be nominated, must make a public declaration that, if elected, he will swear an Oath of Allegiance to the king of England. It is not by seeking to reform British-made institutions, but by preparing for their abolition that even the first step towards independence can be taken.[21]

De Valera must have been disappointed when he read this Sinn Féin statement: he would get no help from this section of the Republican movement in his efforts to oust Cumann na nGaedheal and abolish the Oath. But he was confident of two things: he was becoming more convinced that he would win more seats than Cumann na nGaedheal in the next general election and recent developments like the coming into law of the Statute of Westminster would make it easier for him to abolish the Oath of Allegiance, which was the chief aim of his party.

Notes

1. The *Irish Independent*, 13 October 1930.
2. *Ibid.*, 30 October 1930.
3. *Ibid.*, 31 October 1930.
4. NAI, File 2B/82/117/27/50, Minutes of the Standing Committee Sinn Féin, 7 November 1930.
5. The *Irish Independent*, 3 December 1930.
6. *Ibid.*, 8 December 1930.
7. *Ibid.*, 11 December 1930.
8. Elected to the Standing Committee of Cumann na nGaedheal at this national convention were: R. Mulcahy TD, Minister for Local Government; John Ryan (Dublin); Reverend P. Brennan (Kerry); Barry Egan (Cork); Very Reverend Canon Masterson, (Leitrim); J.J. O'Connell (Sligo); Fionán Lynch TD, Minister for Lands and Fisheries; Seán Morrissey (Clonmel); J.J. Collins (Castlebar); P.J. Egan (Tullamore); E. O'Toole (Carlow); and J.J. Smyth (Monaghan).
9. The *Irish Independent*, 6 May 1931.
10. *Ibid.*, 8 June 1931.
11. *Ibid.*, 1 July 1931.
12. UCDA, Archives of the Fianna Fáil Party, File P176/443, 28 October 1930.
13. *Dáil Éireann Debates*, Volume 40, 14 October 1931, p. 130.
14. *Ibid.*, p. 170.
15. NAI, Files 2B/82/117/27/76 and 2B/82/117/27/77, 13 November 1931 and 27 November 1931, respectively, Minutes of the Standing Committee of Sinn Féin.
16. The *Irish Press*, 21 November 1931.
17. *Ibid.*, 23 November 1931.
18. *Ibid.*, 24 November 1931.
19. *Ibid.*, 25 November 1931.
20. NAI, File 2B/82/117/27/78, Minutes of the Special Meeting of the Standing Committee of Sinn Féin, 4 December 1931.
21. NAI, File 2B/82/117/27/81, Draft Statement re forthcoming general election, approved by the Standing Committee of Sinn Féin on 29 December 1931.

20

DE VALERA LEADS

The Sixth Dáil was officially dissolved by a proclamation signed by James McNeill, the Governor-General, on Friday, 29 January 1932. The Minister for Local Government, Richard Mulcahy, fixed Tuesday, 16 February as the polling day for all constituencies other than the universities, the poll for which would take place on 20 February. The new Dáil and Senate would meet on Wednesday, 2 March 1932.

There was mounting clamour from Republicans to persuade Sinn Féin supporters to vote for Fianna Fáil candidates as there would be no Sinn Féin nominees in the field. As the general election approached the former Fianna Fáil TD, Thomas Mullins, an Independent Republican deputy for Cork West, formed a new Republican party that he named Cumann na Poblachta and the party proceeded to select candidates in various constituencies to contest the election. But before nominations closed, Mullins recognised that there was a strong desire in Republican circles to close ranks when it became obvious that there was a good chance that Fianna Fáil might dislodge Cumann na nGaedheal at the polls. Mullins presided at a special meeting of the new party at which the prospective candidates were present. After a three hours' debate a resolution was passed unanimously:

> Cumann na Poblachta, after due consideration of all the circumstances, and a keen realisation of the seriousness of its responsibility, believes that its objects can best be served by allowing the people to make a clear and definite choice on this occasion and consequently has decided that its selected candidates stand down.[1]

The National Council of Cumann na Poblachta endorsed this decision to help its Republican friends in Fianna Fáil to maximise their votes.

It also became clear that, although Éamon de Valera and Fianna Fáil did not solicit votes from Sinn Féin or the IRA, Republican votes from these organisations would go to Fianna Fáil candidates in order to bring about a change of government. However the Standing Committee of Sinn Féin refused to endorse this departure and was as intransigent as ever in its statement of 29 December 1931 that it could not advise or ask any citizen of the Republic to vote for any candidate who made a public declaration before his nomination to swear an Oath of Allegiance to the King of England and take his seat in the Dáil if he was elected.

Each political party had a different view of the urgency of the need to abolish of the Oath of Allegiance. William Norton, the unsuccessful Labour candidate in the Kildare by-election of June 1931, said that in the coming election his party would make the economy the main issue. 'Fianna Fáil,' he said, 'would come into the fight with the Oath as the big issue. He added, 'I think the abolition of the Oath did not matter to the man who was out of work – Labour had no use for the Oath – we would abolish it to-morrow but we are not such fools as to say it matters to the worker.'[2] Patrick Hogan, Free State Minister for Agriculture, addressing a Cumann na nGaedheal meeting at Ballymacward, County Galway, said that 'the Oath was not half so important as the price of pigs.'[3]

A former Cumann na nGaedheal TD, Cork's Professor Alfred O'Rahilly, who was a member of the Constitution Committee established by the Provisional Government in 1922, criticised President W.T. Cosgrave's view on the abolition of the Oath of Allegiance:

> President Cosgrave is indignant with anyone who undertakes to show that the officially announced policy of Fianna Fáil at its last *ard-fheis* is quite capable of being carried out peacefully and constitutionally...And I (Alfred O'Rahilly) have publicly maintained that this can be done, merely by removing the mandatory clause in the Constitution...I have proved in

English law the Treaty is a British Act, similar to those applied to Australia and South Africa and therefore relegated to the Dáil by the Statute of Westminster.[4]

Speaking in support of the Cumann na nGaedheal candidates in North Dublin, Richard Mulcahy, Minister for Local Government, declared: 'Cumann na nGaedheal stands for continuance within the British Commonwealth because they want to maintain the market which we have in Britain.'[5]

As the campaign gathered momentum, it became obvious from the enthusiastic reception that de Valera received throughout his tour of many parts of the country that popular opinion was turning in his favour. In Kerry, despite bitter blasts from a north wind and fast-falling snow, cheering crowds headed by squadrons of men on horseback, marching bands and dozens of torch-bearers greeted him in Killarney, Dingle and Tralee. The largest gathering seen in Dingle in living memory welcomed de Valera with round after round of applause.

Bonfires and tar barrels blazed in Blackpool, Cork, and de Valera was accorded the greatest reception he had ever received in the southern city. The crowd that awaited him was estimated at twelve thousand. Dev was surprised by the support he received during his tour:

> I want to tell you that Cork is not unique. I was in Mayo and it is the same. I was in Kilkenny and it is the same. It is the same in Tipperary and I was in Limerick and the meeting there was almost as large as this here. I was in Clare and in that county I have not seen such enthusiasm since 1917.[6]

President W.T. Cosgrave also received an enthusiastic welcome in many cities and towns. In Sligo, he got a wonderful reception from a very large crowd at an open-air meeting. It was one of the largest meetings he had addressed in the course of the campaign, the culmination of a triumphant journey from Ballina along a route lit with blazing tar-barrels in every town and village.[7] Arriving in Cork from Bandon, President Cosgrave was met by bands and torchlights and accompanied to Patrick Street, where more than 30,000 people were assembled. He was received with the greatest enthusiasm and throughout the whole meeting there was hardly a single interruption.[8]

Two days before the election there was a tragic shooting incident in County Leitrim. Patrick Reynolds, the sitting Cumann na nGaedheal TD, and a candidate for re-election, called to the house of an RIC pensioner and well-known Cumann na nGaedheal supporter, Joseph Leddy, to canvass his vote. Detective Garda Patrick McGeehan, who was on protective duty, accompanied the TD but stayed outside the house. Reynolds accused Joseph Leddy of canvassing against him, an argument ensued and Reynolds aimed a blow at Leddy's head. Detective McGeehan entered the house when he heard the commotion. A bitter row ensued and as the two men left the house, Leddy grabbed his shotgun and fired two shots, killing both Reynolds and McGeehan. Because of the death of Patrick Reynolds, the election in Sligo-Leitrim had to be postponed.

De Valera's final rally was held in College Green, Dublin. The crowd was so huge that the surrounding streets were densely packed. A mass of closely-packed people stretched from Trinity College up Dame Street as far as the eye could see. When de Valera appeared, cheering was intensified. Fianna Fáil enthusiasts were confident that this new upsurge of support would be reflected by the election results: there were twenty-six Dáil seats up for grabs within the Dublin area. Many of the most enthusiastic people at these huge political meetings were young men and women and some Fianna Fáil party activists feared that many of them were too young to have votes.

Polling day, 16 February 1932, brought to a conclusion the hardest-fought general election campaign for years. In no area was the poll less than 60 per cent and in the majority of constituencies it was between 70 and 80 per cent.

It was not until the beginning of the second week of March that the final results were announced. When all the votes were counted the state of the parties that would make up the Seventh Dáil was:

F. Fáil	C. na nG.	Ind.	Labour	Farmers	Ind. Lab.	Ind. Farmer
72	57	11	7	3	2	1

John Daly (Cumann na nGaedheal), of Kilworth, County Cork, who was elected for Cork East, died soon after his election and the seat in that constituency became vacant.

Fianna Fáil gained sixteen seats in this general election, including two in Carlow-Kilkenny: they now held three seats out of five in that constituency where in previous general elections they were able to obtain only one. They gained two further seats from Cumann na nGaedheal in Dublin North, where the government party had been strong since the Civil War. In the Leitrim-Sligo election, which had been postponed, Fianna Fáil confounded the critics by winning four seats out of seven – a gain of two seats. One-seat gains in Cavan, Kerry, Limerick, Longford-Westmeath, Mayo South, Meath, Monaghan, Tipperary, Donegal and the NUI followed the three surprising gains of two seats each.

Cumann na nGaedheal lost eight seats from the total of sixty-five that they held in the previous Dáil. The bulk of these seats were captured by Fianna Fáil. Cosgrave's party performed best in Cork City, Cork East, Wicklow and especially in the constituency of County Dublin where the party polled in excess of 36,000 votes, as against Fianna Fáil's total of more than 23,000.

Captain William Redmond topped the poll in Waterford. He had been the leader of the National League but he left that party in late 1931 to join Cumann na nGaedheal: this marked the demise of yet another small party.

The Labour vote decreased in thirteen of the twenty-two constituencies the party contested and it lost three of its ten seats. Two of the party's members, Daniel Morrissey TD (Tipperary) and Richard Anthony TD (Cork), had been expelled before the election because, contrary to Labour policy, they voted in favour of the Public Safety Act 1931.

At a time of renewed IRA activity in the Free State, this act gave the authorities powers of arrest, detention and trial of suspects before military tribunals not bound by normal rules of evidence, despite the fact that many of the crimes in question carried a mandatory death sentence. Morrissey and Anthony stood as Independent Labour candidates and were elected without difficulty; they were listed as Independent Labour in the election results.

Farmers' Party candidates contested nine constituencies, lost more than half the number of votes cast for them in the September 1927 general election and dropped three of their six seats. John O'Hanlon was elected as an Independent Farmer TD in Cavan and listed as such in the election results.

Independents, a more motley group than usual, won eleven seats, one less than the total they had held after the general election of September 1927. Among the Independent TDs elected was James Dillon, son of John Dillon, who had succeeded John Redmond as leader of the Parliamentary (Irish) Party: he won the second seat in Donegal.

Kerry was the constituency that gave most support to Fianna Fáil in this election: there the party captured five of the seven available seats. Ten constituencies gave Fianna Fáil more than 50 per cent of the total votes cast. In order of merit they were: Kerry (59.3 per cent); Clare (58.9 per cent); Mayo North (56.5 per cent); Meath (56 per cent); Galway (55 per cent); Roscommon (54 per cent); Longford-Westmeath (52.3 per cent); Mayo South (52.1 per cent); Monaghan (50.1 per cent); Tipperary (50.1 per cent).

Nationally Fianna Fáil got 45 per cent of all votes cast. Cumann na nGaedheal obtained 35 per cent, Independents 10 per cent, Labour 8 per cent and Farmers 2 per cent. Fianna Fáil polled higher than any other party in each of the four provinces: Leinster (39.7 per cent); the three counties of Ulster (41.7 per cent); Munster (46.8 per cent) and Connacht, where it did best (53.1 per cent).

General elections always bring surprises and this time Thomas J. O'Connell, leader of the Labour Party, lost his seat in Mayo South to a Fianna Fáil candidate, Edward Moane. Although all the Cumann na nGaedheal ministers were returned, Michael Heffernan, former leader of the Farmers' Party and later Parliamentary Secretary to the Minister of Posts and Telegraphs, who had stood as a Cumann na nGaedheal candidate in this election, lost his Tipperary seat to Fianna Fáil.

Almost the entire Republican vote went to Fianna Fáil. Republicans felt that the Free State government had become too pro-Empire during the 1920s and early 1930s and that it too easily used coercive measures. For these reasons, the IRA actively supported Fianna Fáil in this election and helped de Valera's party to win its seventy-two seats but Sinn Féin maintained its policy of ignoring the election and the Standing Committee did absolutely nothing to help to defeat Cumann na nGaedheal.

The 1932 general election was decisive and historic. Ever since August 1923 – the second general election after the signing of the Treaty – there had been a steady improvement in the Republican vote and now Fianna Fáil held exactly double the thirty-six seats the anti-Treatyites had won in the 1922 general election. Not since the Treaty was signed in 1921 had any single party won as many as seventy-two seats. Nor had any political party obtained as many first-preference votes – 560,000 – as Fianna Fáil received in this election.

Archbishop Mannix of Melbourne sent a telegram to Éamon de Valera: 'May God uphold and guide Ireland and you in these difficult days'.

President W.T. Cosgrave, interviewed by an *Irish Independent* correspondent, was resigned to the fact that Fianna Fáil and the Labour Party would be the most likely group to form the next government: 'I am unperturbed by the situation that has arisen.' He added that he proposed: 'to let the Labour Party and those constituting Fianna Fáil work for prosperity and better prices.'[9]

'The defeat of the Cosgrave government,' remarked *The Times* in London, 'is no doubt due largely to attrition. Their stern maintenance of law and order made many bitter enemies.'

A special correspondent of another London newspaper, the *Observer*, quoted de Valera as saying that he did not see how the removal of the Oath of Allegiance from the Constitution would lead to difficulties with England:

> The Oath is not obligatory by the Treaty but only by the Constitution which we can change. It would be absurd to talk of freedom if we were to be denied the right to take steps which are so essential to internal peace here…We can only get willing obedience if the political test is removed and all sections of the people are free to send their representatives to parliament

without having first to foreswear their principles.[10]

The Sunday Times warned:

> Probably if a new Free State government were to abolish the Oath, Britain's wisest course would be to let its effect operate automatically. By so doing, the Irish Free State would cease to be a Dominion, it would forfeit the right to tariff preferences and the existing double taxation relief, and all Southern Irishmen living in England would become aliens. De Valera will surely think many times before embarking on a whole-hogging policy.

The Labour Party held a meeting of its chief officers to consider the party's course of action in the formation of a new government. Six of the Labour group in the new Dáil attended – the seventh, Timothy J. Murphy (Cork West) was absent because of sickness. The Labour senators, who included a former leader of the party, Thomas Johnson, were present, as were members of the council of the party, among whom was Thomas J. O'Connell, who had lost his seat in the election. William Norton, the new TD for Kildare, presided. The meeting decided that Labour would maintain its position of complete independence in the Dáil and would not enter into an alliance with any other party. It would neither seek nor accept office under the new government but would cooperate and give general support to the government in dealing with social questions such as unemployment, housing and widows' and orphans' pensions when the measures introduced did not conflict with Labour policy. In the matter of the Oath of Allegiance Labour had always opposed it and would continue to support its abolition. The party would nominate Patrick Hogan, Labour TD for Clare, for the position of Leas-Cheann Comhairle (Vice-Speaker) of the Dáil.[11]

J.H. Thomas, Dominions Secretary, replied in the House of Commons to a question regarding British relations with the Irish Free State:

I have indicated quite clearly and definitely that the government's position in this matter is based upon the Treaty. There
are many people in Ireland who have risked their lives for the
Treaty. We have acted honourably up to now in regard to it and
we shall continue to do so. This was undoubtedly clear in the
debate on the Statute of Westminster Bill and the position has
not altered since.[12]

As the time approached for the opening of the Seventh Dáil the executive
of the County Cavan Agricultural League decided that John F. O'Hanlon,
Independent Farmer TD, could use his discretion in the event of a division
for the Presidency of the Free State Executive Council. Mr Rehill, a delegate
to the conference, said that the people had declared their will – they wanted a
change of government and Fianna Fáil, the majority party, should be given a
chance. O'Hanlon said he believed in the will of the people and would never
run against it.[13] This decision enhanced the prospects of Fianna Fáil forming
the new government.

President Cosgrave met the members of his party and in a statement released
to the press after the meeting he returned thanks to all those who during the
previous ten years had steadfastly supported the maintenance of the Treaty and
the policy that had been pursued by Cumann na nGaedheal 'of building up the
country and laying sure foundations for the institutions of the state.'[14]

On the day before the Dáil met to choose a new government a formal
conference was held between representatives of Labour and Fianna Fáil,
represented by deputies Éamon de Valera, Seán T. O'Kelly and Gerry
Boland. On the Labour side were deputies William Norton, William Davin
and Senator Thomas Johnson. The question of the election of a new Ceann
Comhairle was causing friction in Labour's own ranks. The problem was
solved when, after discussion, Labour agreed to support Frank Fahy, the
Fianna Fáil nominee for the position, and Fianna Fáil representatives agreed
to support Patrick Hogan, TD for Clare, for the position of Leas-Cheann
Comhairle.[15] On the night before the Dáil met, Labour unanimously selected
William Norton, TD for Kildare, as its new leader.

Sinn Féin issued a statement on the eve of the resumption of the Dáil that threw a spanner in de Valera's hopes of fashioning a Dáil where all the representatives of the Irish people could take their seats without having to sacrifice any of their firmly-held principles. Sinn Féin stated that its Standing Committee wished to correct a misleading assertion that if the Dáil removed the Oath of Allegiance, Republicans would enter 'the bogus national assembly'. The declaration pointed out that the two obstacles to national unity were 'England's two mongrel legislatures [the Dáil and the Stormont Assembly] – symbols of conquest and usurpation' and that 'there can be no unity until they and all they stand for are repudiated as part of the British connection and our public representatives, as well as our military forces, return to the position of 1919-1921'.[16]

Dáil Éireann reassembled on 9 March 1932. The public galleries were crowded. Mrs Margaret Pearse and her daughter, also named Margaret, sat in the front row, perhaps with memories of an Easter sixteen years earlier. Dan Breen (Tipperary), Seán Moylan (Cork North), and Oscar Traynor (Dublin North), fearless guerrilla soldiers in the War of Independence but now Fianna Fáil elected deputies, conversed as they eyed their surroundings rather apprehensively, still with their hands in their pockets! The ministers of the previous Free State Executive filed confidently into their places and sat down; so did Breen, Moylan and Traynor.

Gerry Boland, TD for Roscommon, rose and proposed Proinsias Ó Fathaigh TD (Frank Fahy) for the post of Ceann Comhairle (Speaker) but the Cumann na nGaedheal leader, W.T. Cosgrave TD, argued against any change in the speakership. The division was called for. The Clerk of the Dáil read the result. Proinsias Ó Fathaigh was elected by seventy-eight votes to seventy-one for Michael Hayes, the former Speaker. The new Ceann Comhairle took his place on the dais.

Then came the most important moment of the day. Michael Kilroy, Fianna Fáil TD for Mayo South, proposed Éamon de Valera as President of the Executive Council of the Irish Free State. He used simple words with no studied phrases. Oscar Traynor, who had been Sinn Féin TD for his constituency of Dublin North as late as June 1927, seconded the proposal.

John O'Hanlon, the Independent Farmer TD for Cavan said that, although he did not agree with all de Valera stood for, he realised that the people wanted him and he would vote for him. Then came a surprise. James Dillon, the youthful-looking Independent TD from Donegal, said that he, too, wished to vote for the Fianna Fáil leader, as it seemed to him that he was the people's choice. W.T. Cosgrave TD replied briefly and without fire: 'I propose to challenge a division on this motion.'[17] The packed House awaited the reaction of William Norton TD, the new Labour leader, as he rose to speak. He said that the first Dáil of 1919 had given a pledge to the workers to introduce a new code of social legislation. Year after year the deputies of the Labour Party had asked the Cumann na nGaedheal government to put into effect the democratic programme of that first Dáil. But they had pleaded in vain. The Labour Party was going to vote for de Valera because they hoped Fianna Fáil would endeavour to implement their promises to set about solving the unemployment and housing problems, to provide a scheme for widows' and orphans' pensions, and to improve and develop the outdated transport system.

The division bells rang and the lobbies filled with voting deputies. The Ceann Comhairle read out the figures. De Valera had been elected President of the Executive Council of the Irish Free State by eighty-one votes to sixty-eight. From the gallery there were piercing cheers, cries of delight and loud clapping of hands that lasted for several minutes.[18]

The full complement of Fianna Fáil TDs – seventy-one in total (the Fianna Fáil Ceann Comhairle did not vote) recorded their votes for de Valera. The seven Labour TDs voted for him as well as two Independents, James Dillon, and John O'Hanlon. The Farmers' Party TD from Limerick, John Shaughnessy, also voted for him.

The House then adjourned while the Governor-General was summoned to sort out the legal formalities of the appointment of the new President of the Executive Council and his ministers. When the House resumed the Cumann na nGaedheal deputies were seated on the opposition side of the House and the Fianna Fáil TDs had taken their places on the government benches, making visible the transfer of power.

President Éamon de Valera TD rose to propose his new ministers. He read the names from a printed document in his hand:

President and Minister for External Affairs: Éamon de Valera

Vice-President and Minister for Local Government and Health: Seán T. O'Kelly

Minister for Finance: Seán MacEntee

Minister for Industry and Commerce: Seán Lemass

Minister for Justice: James Geoghegan

Minister for Agriculture: Dr James Ryan

Minister for Defence: Frank Aiken

Minister for Lands and Fisheries: P.J. Ruttledge

Minister for Education: Thomas Derrig

Minister for Posts and Telegraphs: Senator Joseph Connolly

Parliamentary Secretary to the President: Gerry Boland

The Dáil accepted the cabinet without a division.[19]

An Phoblacht gave a brief and qualified welcome to the new Fianna Fáil government. At the end of an article called 'The Army of the Republic', the writer, Moss Twomey, Chief-of-Staff of the IRA, said: 'The Fianna Fáil party takes office in the twenty-six counties in a partitioned Ireland within the British Empire…Members of Fianna Fáil express friendliness with the ideals of the Volunteers…Fianna Fáil declares its intention to chop off some of the imperial tentacles. Every such achievement is of value and will be welcomed.' [20]

Big things happened in Ireland in early 1932. Fianna Fáil, under Éamon de Valera, had secured a Dáil majority to achieve the party's chief political aim – the abolition of the Oath of Allegiance to the British monarch from every walk of Irish life. But there were still many obstacles in de Valera's path.

Notes
1.   The *Irish Press*, 8 February 1932.
2.   *Ibid.*, 18 January 1932.
3.   *Ibid.*, 25 January 1932.
4.   *Ibid.*, 1 February 1932.
5.   *Ibid.*, 8 February 1932.
6.   *Ibid.*, 12 February 1932.
7.   The *Irish Independent*, 8 February 1932.

8.   *Ibid.*, 16 February 1932.
9.   *Ibid.*, 23 February 1932.
10. *Ibid.*, 22 February 1932.
11. The *Irish Press*, 27 February 1932.
12. *Ibid.*, 2 March 1932.
13. *Ibid.*, 7 March 1932.
14. *Ibid.*, 8 March 1932.
15. *Ibid.*, 9 March 1932.
16. *Ibid.*
17. *Dáil Éireann Debates*, Volume 41, 9 March 1932, p. 28.
18. The *Irish Press*, 10 March 1932.
19. *Dáil Éireann Debates*, Volume 41, 9 March 1932, p. 38.
20. *An Phoblacht*, 12 March 1932.

21

DE VALERA INTRODUCES AN OATH BILL

At this time, a National Government was in office in Britain, made up of Conservatives, National Labour and National Liberals. This government felt very uneasy over the election of de Valera as President of the Executive Council of the Free State. They had followed his election campaign and were convinced that he would take speedy action to abolish the Oath of Allegiance. J.H. Thomas, the Dominions Secretary, a National Labour MP, was in charge of Irish affairs. He was hostile towards de Valera, regarding him as an Irishman who would not easily accept a compromise in national affairs.

The Dominions Office was fully committed to maintaining the terms of the Anglo-Irish Treaty of 1921. The Oath of Allegiance to the reigning British monarch was considered essential in linking the various parts of the Commonwealth. There was a danger that if de Valera abolished the Oath unilaterally, the British government would apply sanctions.

When the Seventh Dáil came together for the second day of its term the deputies elected Patrick Hogan, Labour TD for Clare, as Leas-Cheann Comhairle, by seventy-eight votes to fifty-five.[1] Fianna Fáil voted for him as part of the deal made in return for the support of Labour in electing Frank Fahy as Ceann Comhairle.

On 12 March 1932, the new cabinet with Éamon de Valera as President met to discuss the immediate introduction into the Dáil of a Bill to abolish the Oath of Allegiance. The cabinet decided: 'that the Attorney General should submit heads of a Bill having for its object the removal of the obligation on members of the Oireachtas [Dáil and Senate] to take and subscribe to the Oath of Allegiance as specified in the Constitution'. The cabinet also agreed: 'that it was not necessary that any intimation should be made to the British government preliminary to the introduction of the Bill.'[2] On the same day, Joseph P. Walshe, Secretary of the Department of External Affairs, wrote to de Valera advising a delay of one month and warning that the British government 'could engineer a boycott of our goods – the Argentine could replace our meat in six weeks – Denmark could replace our butter and eggs with hardly any interval.'[3] Éamon de Valera took note of this advice but decided to go ahead with his efforts to abolish the Oath of Allegiance.

On the eve of St Patrick's Day, Éamon de Valera gave an interview to a large gathering of British, Canadian and American newsmen. Asked if he intended to take the Oath of Allegiance out of the Treaty as well as out of the Constitution, de Valera replied that the Oath was not mandatory in the Treaty. He further claimed that 'if Lord Birkenhead and the British draftsmen had wished to make the Oath mandatory in the Treaty they would have done so. Now the Irish people had given the new government a mandate to abolish the Oath.'[4]

J.W. Dulanty, the Irish High Commissioner in London, called to the Dominions Office on 22 March 1932 and lodged a communication from de Valera that the Irish government had received a mandate from the Irish people to abolish the Oath and that the people regarded 'the Oath as an intolerable burden, a relic of medievalism, a test imposed from outside under threat of immediate and terrible war.' The statement added that the removal of the Oath was 'a purely domestic matter'.[5]

The British government considered the situation grave. They set up a special group, the Irish Situation Committee, to deal with Irish affairs. Ramsay MacDonald, the Prime Minister, who belonged to the National Labour Party, chaired the committee and J.H. Thomas, Dominions Secretary, was a permanent member. It was now clear that the dispute between de Valera and the British government over the removal of the Oath of Allegiance would not be easily resolved.

Relations between de Valera, his Fianna Fáil government and the rank-and-file of the IRA continued to be cordial. The IRA was overjoyed to see the downfall of the Cumann na nGaedheal government. 'Fianna Fáil came in because the Cosgrave gang had to be put out. There was no other parliamentary alternative,' wrote the editor of *An Phoblacht*.[6]

In the Senate de Valera said: 'With regard to the Oath, we have got a mandate from our people, and that mandate we intend to carry out. There is nothing more precious to us [Fianna Fáil] than peace among our own people. The essential of that peace is the removal of the test [the Oath of Allegiance] that excludes from our parliamentary assemblies a certain section of the people.'[7] Senator Milroy (Cumann na nGaedheal) replied, 'I dissent most emphatically from the view expressed by the President that he got a mandate from the people to deal with the Oath…We know that the Party that now holds the reins of office was returned as a minority Party of the other House (the Dáil).'[8] Senator Joseph Connolly (Fianna Fáil) retorted: 'I would remind the Senate that the present government has the largest party that has yet acted as a government in the country [since the Treaty].'[9]

J.H. Thomas visited Buckingham Palace and had a half-hour discussion with King George V regarding the intention of the new Free State Executive to abolish the Oath of Allegiance from the Irish Constitution. There was obvious tension in the House of Commons until Thomas returned. He addressed the House: 'It is manifest that the Oath is an integral part of the Treaty and a communication is being sent to the Free State government by His Majesty's Government.' Asked if the communication would be published, Thomas replied, 'Undoubtedly.'[10] James Maxton, a Scot and member of the Independent Labour Party, said that the Westminster government was negotiating with practically every country about the revision of treaties and should not the Irish nation be treated as well as foreign countries.[11] Mr Dulanty, the Irish Ambassador to Britain, was present during the proceedings and immediately afterwards was in telephone communication with Dublin.[12]

The discussion about de Valera's government's intention to abolish the Oath of Allegiance continued in the House of Commons the following day. Dr Morris Jones MP suggested that the House should not attach too much importance to the question of de Valera's attitude to the abolition of the Oath. He thought it was a matter that, if left alone, might settle itself as de Valera retained his leadership in the Irish parliament by only a small majority. Jones added that 'there were forces in Ireland which were working to preserve the loyalty of the Irish people to the Oath and the Constitution created ten years ago.'[13] Again James Maxton backed the Fianna Fáil government and said that 'Ireland, in pursuance of its national democratic rights, has elected a certain government in Ireland. De Valera is head of that government and was elected to carry out a certain policy by the free vote of the Irish people.'[14]

In the Bull Ring in Wexford, William Norton TD, the Labour leader, declared at a well-attended meeting that his party would stand by its policy of getting rid of the Oath and would not allow itself to be bullied:

> The Labour Party will be firm in maintaining the position that this nation of ours is a nation which has rights and that nobody must be allowed to trample on the rights of this nation – of this motherland of ours – that we think more of than any other country in the world. You can be assured that the Labour Party will always be on the side of peace and for the avoidance of strife.[15]

William Norton's statement was encouraging to President de Valera, who gave this statement to the North American Newspaper Alliance:

> There is no parallel in our time in Treaty relationships between states for the imposition by one of the parties of a conscience test on the other. Our people do not want the Oath. They regard it as an intolerable burden and in the last election they have given us a clear and unequivocal mandate to have it removed…The removal of the Oath is an essential preliminary to obtaining the willing obedience of the people to state authority.[16]

It was thought throughout Ireland that there could be a conflict of some kind between England and Ireland if the Fianna Fáil-led government went ahead and abolished the Oath. Clare County Council recognised that President de Valera might need some sign of visible support as he forged ahead with this policy. At a meeting of Clare County Council, the Chairman,

Seán O'Grady, (a Fianna Fáil TD), presiding, a resolution was unanimously adopted congratulating de Valera and his government on the stand they were taking for the deletion of the Oath from the Constitution of the Free State. 'We assure President de Valera,' said the resolution, 'that the people of Clare are now, as ever, solidly behind him in the attitude he has adopted to protect the rights of the Irish nation.'[17]

The Independent Labour Party, the party of James Maxton, held its annual conference in Blackpool. Another MP, George Buchanan, replying to a question concerning the Irish Free State, said that he and Maxton had made a decision on the Irish question that, to some extent, bound other members of the Independent Labour Group in the House of Commons. 'We have decided that we are backing the Irish government in the steps it has taken about the Oath,' he stated to loud cheers.' [18] Before the conference ended, Mr Maxton proposed an emergency resolution that called on the British government to negotiate with the Irish Free State 'on a basis of complete equality between the two nations.'[19]

Dingle Foot, Liberal MP for Dundee and a special representative of the *News Chronicle*, asked Éamon de Valera whether he had read the communication from the British government to the Free State Executive that Thomas had cited in the House of Commons. De Valera replied, 'I have only just got the text. It is merely the same opinion he expressed in the House of Commons.'[20]

'And if the result were a tariff war or even a trade boycott what then?' enquired Foot. De Valera replied:

> Surrendering to the 'threat of immediate and terrible war' gave us the last ten years of misery. We have that warning to save us from surrendering now to a threat of Economic War. In any case our economic position is far stronger than you profess to believe. We can feed, clothe, and shelter our people if all goes to all. Besides you choose to forget that we buy more from you than you buy from us.[21]

It was known that President de Valera was engaged in talks with his Attorney-General, Conor Maguire. In London an official of the Dominions Office, speaking on behalf of J.H. Thomas, the Dominions Secretary, said that a special cabinet committee would give the matter a thorough examination.[22]

The full Executive Council of the Irish Free State met for more than four hours on 1 April 1932. There was just one absentee – the Minister for Local government, Seán T. Ó Ceallaigh, who was suffering from flu and confined to his home. At the conclusion of the meeting Seán Moynihan, secretary to the Executive Council, issued the following statement to the Press:

> The dispatch from the British government was considered and the outline of the proposed reply decided upon. Instructions were issued for the preparation of the draft to be presented at a meeting of the cabinet early next week.[23]

Speaking at the AGM of the Galloway Conservative Association at Stranraer, the British Attorney-General, Sir Thomas Inskip KC, said that unless de Valera realised quickly that it was impossible for him to play fast and loose with such solemn obligations as were contained in the Treaty and the Constitution, he could not expect to have the advantages of connection with the United Kingdom. Then the Free State would very soon regret the day that it handed over its destinies, even for a time, to his Fianna Fáil-led government.[24]

Many of the new Fianna Fáil backbenchers were eager to support de Valera in his policy of removing the Oath. Oscar Traynor, TD for Dublin North, addressed a big meeting in Dún Laoghaire, County Dublin:

> There is no crisis whatsoever. There is an Oath of Allegiance imposed upon deputies going into the parliament here. Part of the policy of Fianna Fáil is to remove that objectionable Oath. We made it very clear to the people before the election that we wanted a mandate to clear away that Oath. We have secured that mandate and we are going to clear the Oath out of the way.[25]

At a general meeting of the *Ard-Chomhairle* of Cumann na nGaedheal, in the Gresham Hotel, Dublin, over which W.T. Cosgrave TD presided, part of a resolution passed unanimously after a discussion stated: 'the *Ard-Chomhairle* of Cumann na nGaedheal records its vigorous opposition to any policy which, by depriving the Free State of the advantages it possesses as a member of the British Commonwealth of Nations, would not only injure it economically but would destroy the hope of national reunion.'[26]

The British government received the Irish cabinet's reply to the note from J.H. Thomas on 6 April. In it de Valera condemned the whole Anglo-Irish Treaty settlement, including partition, but he emphasised that they were now dealing 'with the much narrower issue i.e. the Oath.' He said that 'the real issue is that the Oath is an intolerable burden to the people of this state…and that in Ireland it raised brother's hand against brother and gave us ten years of blood and tears.' Éamon de Valera informed Thomas: 'It is the intention of my government, therefore, to introduce immediately on the reassembly of parliament a Bill for the removal of Article 17 [the Oath Clause] of the Constitution.'[27]

Fianna Fáil ministers were already drafting the Bill. A general election would be held if the Bill to abolish the Oath were defeated.[28]

The prime ministers of South Africa, Australia and New Zealand sent messages to President de Valera, who was also Minister of External Affairs, expressing 'concern' at the situation developing between Britain and the Irish Free State. De Valera replied to each letter, declaring that it was the unalterable intention of the Free State government to abolish the Oath: 'We have the fully recognised right to amend our Constitution according to the desire of the people,' he wrote, 'and we intend to remove the Oath from the Constitution through the action of the people's representatives.'[29]

De Valera knew that unless the Irish people stuck with him through this crisis, he would not succeed in his efforts to abolish the Oath. He was heartened by the scenes of intense excitement that he witnessed in Ennis as he was speaking to a huge crowd. 'The people have emphatically declared their will to abolish the Oath of Allegiance to the British crown,' he declared. 'So far as we are concerned there can be no going back. We have nothing to fear if we stand loyally together.'[30] There was thunderous applause in response.

Encouraging expressions of support for the abolition of the Oath of Allegiance came to the de Valera government from the United States. An example of how the Irish-Americans were rallying behind the effort was the fact that the former Supreme Court Justice, Daniel F. Cohalan of New York, since 1919 an avowed enemy of de Valera, now declared that 'under the Statute of Westminster, passed by the English Parliament within the last few months, the right of absolute secession from the British Empire of any of the so-called dominions is unconditionally declared and the right of Ireland to set aside the Oath of Allegiance must of course be included.'[31]

De Valera replied to a statement by Lloyd George that the Oath caused the fiercest controversies during the Treaty negotiations: 'The British government has no more right to impose a conscience test on the Irish deputies than it has to impose a conscience test on French deputies. The Constitution under which we live is our own concern.'[32]

An editorial in *An Phoblacht* referred to the tense situation between de Valera and the British government in relation to the Fianna Fáil policy to abolish the Oath of Allegiance and advised a course of action for the Irish people that was similar to de Valera's policy:

> For our part, let us do our duty. Let us assert our freedom and maintain it – both in its national and economic bases. Let our slogans be: 'No bargaining with England! No connection with the British Empire.'[33]

George Gavan Duffy, a signatory the Treaty, wrote in a letter to the *Manchester Guardian* that 'allegiance is a thing of the past. Except as an out-of-date survival of feudalism in the older kingdoms, it has no place in the modern state where loyal citizenship has supplanted it.'[34]

When the Dáil reassembled on 20 April 1932, there was feeling of tension both inside and outside Leinster House as President de Valera was expected to make an initial step to remove the Oath of Allegiance.

Éamon de Valera was the first speaker to rise; he moved the first Reading of the Constitution (Removal of the Oath) Bill 1932. He explained that the Bill was a measure 'to remove the obligation now imposed by law on members of the Oireachtas [Dáil and Senate] and ministers who are not members of the Executive Council, to take an Oath. The purpose of this Bill would be to amend the Constitution of the Irish Free State accordingly.'[35]

When the Ceann Comhairle, Frank Fahy TD, asked if the motion would be opposed, Ernest Blythe responded that his party, Cumann na nGaedheal, would not oppose this stage of the Bill but would oppose subsequent stages.[36]

Frank McDermot, Independent TD for Roscommon, said that he wished to oppose the introduction of this Bill. He stated that a fundamental question that the government ought to face was if they did or if they did not regard themselves as belonging to the British Commonwealth of Nations. If they did regard themselves as belonging to the British Commonwealth, he submitted that this Bill was a breach of international good manners. He asked: should a Treaty which brought a war to an end not be regarded as binding 'upon the weaker party'? McDermot considered that they did, in fact, regard themselves as members of a partnership, members of the British Commonwealth – a partnership in which the Crown was recognised as a visible symbol of unity. He therefore submitted that the more decent thing to do in approaching this issue would be to get in touch with the other members of the partnership… After reaching a provisional agreement or even in the event of their failing to reach agreement, the government should consult the country by means of a referendum and settle the question once and for all whether the Irish people did or did not wish to form part of the British Commonwealth.[37]

The question was put and the First Reading of the Constitution (Removal of Oath) Bill, 1932, First Stage was declared carried.

The full text of the Bill was published on 22 April 1932:

> An Act to remove the obligation now imposed by law on members of the Oireachtas [Dáil and Senate] and ministers who are not members of the Executive Council, to take an Oath and for that purpose to amend the Constitution and also the Constitution of the Irish Free State Act, 1922.[38]

The Bill would make the Constitution, not the Treaty, the fundamental law in the Free State. Up to that it was the Treaty which was fundamental – a very unusual situation as in no other state was a Treaty made a superior instrument to the Constitution. The Second Reading of the Removal of Oath Bill was fixed for Wednesday, 27 April.

Mrs Margaret Pearse died in St Enda's College, Rathfarnham, Dublin, on 22 April 1932, the very day that the text of this Bill was published. She was seventy-five. As recently as the 9 March she had attended the first sitting of the Seventh Dáil to witness the election of de Valera – whom she supported – as President of the Executive Council. She became ill about a week later but her illness was not considered serious until an hour before she died.

There was more discussion in the House of Commons with regard to the steps that de Valera was taking to abolish the Oath of Allegiance. J.H. Thomas, Dominions Secretary, replying to a question from Dr Morris Jones, said:

> I ought to inform the House that a Bill introduced in the Dáil last week purports to repeal Section 2 of the Irish Free State Constituent Act of 1922 which provided that the Treaty shall have the force of law and that any amendment to the Constitution in any respect repugnant to the Treaty shall be void and inoperative...I have made it clear on behalf of the government that we look upon this matter as the violation of the Treaty. This we have intimated to de Valera in clear and emphatic terms.[39]

On 27 April President de Valera moved the second reading of the Constitution (Removal of Oath) Bill, 1932 in the Dáil before a packed public gallery. He said that before the last election there was widely published throughout the area of the Free State a manifesto to the electors in which Fianna Fáil put forward, in very explicit terms, the items of the programme which, if elected in a majority position, they would endeavour to put into operation. The first item on that programme was 'to remove the Article of the Constitution which makes the signing of the Oath of Allegiance obligatory on members entering the Dáil.'[40] This Bill was intended to give effect to that first item on the programme. He said that when the Treaty was being put before the Second Dáil, one of the arguments put forward in favour of it was that it gave freedom to achieve freedom.[41] He continued: 'Not very long ago, the Statute of Westminster was passed so that now there was no doubt whatever that they could remove Article 17 from the Constitution and do it without violating any contractual obligation whatever that they had with Great Britain.'[42] Alluding to the demand of others that at this point they should leave the British Commonwealth altogether, he said: 'We do not want to exceed the mandate which we asked for without again consulting the people. The moment that the people are ready to stand for an independent republic, we will be quite ready to lead them.'[43]

W.T. Cosgrave moved an amendment to the proposal for the second reading:

> Believing that the rights and liberties and the economic freedom and privileges assured to the people by the Treaty of 1921 are placed in jeopardy by the Bill, the Dáil declines to give it a second reading pending negotiations and agreement between the Executive Council and the British government upon the question at issue.[44]

Cosgrave continued: 'We have regarded relations between this country and Great Britain as being based on the Treaty. The sanction for its observance by both sides rests on a basis solely of mutual respect and confidence in each other's good faith.'[45] He warned that a purely legal action of a unilateral character in respect of an international agreement, as was intended in this Bill, would not commend itself to the representatives of any other nation either in Europe or in the whole world.[46]

Seán MacEntee, Minister for Finance, replied to Cosgrave. He asked if they were to follow the advice of the Cumann na nGaedheal leader and seek agreement in this matter from the British government and if the government in Westminster failed to agree what would the attitude of Deputy Cosgrave and Cumann na nGaedheal be?[47]

A former Minister in the Cosgrave government, Desmond Fitzgerald, said: 'If the British decided that they are going to take punitive action against us, if necessary, are we going to have the sympathy of the world? Certainly not.'[48]

The Roscommon Independent TD, Frank McDermot, who unsuccessfully opposed the first reading of the Bill, proposed an amendment: 'The Dáil declines to give a second reading to this Bill pending a definite declaration of policy by the government on the subject of remaining in the British Commonwealth of Nations.' His amendment was seconded by John F. O'Hanlon, the Independent Farmer TD from Cavan who had supported de Valera when he stood for election as President of the Executive Council.[49]

A lot depended on the outlook of the Labour Party as to whether the second reading of the Oath Bill would succeed or fail. The House waited for William Norton to speak on the Bill: he did so during the second day's debate. His opening sentences gave the impression that Labour was more concerned with economic than with political matters:

> So far as the Labour Party is concerned it has no illusions whatever about the removal of the Oath. We realise, quite clearly, that the removal of the Oath will not provide work for the unemployed man or woman. We realise the removal will not provide houses for people living in slums. We realise clearly that its removal will not provide boots for barefooted children.[50]

President de Valera must have breathed a sigh of relief when, a little further on in his speech, Norton referred to the removal of the Oath of Allegiance in positive terms:

> Although we take that view we realise, at the same time, that there are consequences in retaining it (the Oath of Allegiance) in the Constitution, consequences which may show themselves in the form of political unrest, which may show themselves in

political disorder, may show themselves in political instability…
Other speakers referred to the necessity for negotiations with
the British government…The one and clear fact that emerges is
this. The view of the British Secretary for the Dominions is that
Britain regards the Oath as necessary, as something that must be
retained and, so long as Britain adopts that attitude, what is the
hope of negotiating with Britain?[51]

William Norton summarised his party's view:

The view of the Labour Party in connection with the Oath
is simply we have no use for it as an instrument. I hope that,
even at this belated stage, Britain will take the sensible view,
and realise that the Oath in the form in which it is in our
Constitution is a relic of feudalism, that it has no place in the
modern relations between states…It ought to go and so far as
the Labour Party is concerned we think it ought to go now.[52]

Dan Breen, Fianna Fáil TD for Tipperary, made a brief speech: 'I want to
remind deputies on the opposite benches, especially Deputy Mulcahy and
Deputy Blythe and some other of my old IRB friends, that when they travelled
the country with me in the dark days of 1918 and 1919 they did not then
talk of taking the Oath of Allegiance to a British king.' He added: 'Now I am
surprised that in the course of ten or twelve years they have changed about.
Not alone will they now take an Oath to the British king but they insist upon
the representatives in this country doing likewise.'[53]

General Seán Mac Eoin, the Longford-Westmeath Cumann na nGaedheal
TD who was formerly a leader of an IRA Flying Column in County Longford,
made an interesting and surprising contribution to the Dáil debate. After
advising de Valera to open negotiations with the British government on the
question of the removal of the Oath, he addressed the Fianna Fáil deputies: 'If
you make a good case to the British…you will succeed and you will have my
definite support, and not only that but I shall take off my hat to you and say

you have done a good day's work for this country.'[54]

The debate on the Oath Bill continued for more than three days but William Norton's promise of Labour Party support assured its passing. When the proposal was finally put that the Oath of Allegiance be deleted from the Free State Constitution, at 12.05 am on Saturday, 30 April 1932, it was passed by seventy-seven votes to seventy-one.

When the result of the division was announced there was loud applause from the government benches and from the public gallery. President de Valera's face was wreathed in smiles. Seán MacEntee TD, the Fianna Fáil Minister for Finance, sardonically remarked, 'One vote for every execution.' Dr Thomas Hennessy, Cumann na nGaedheal TD for Dublin South retorted, 'God save poor Ireland.'[55]

Thomas Dowdall, Fianna Fáil TD for Cork Borough, was absent for the vote because of illness: this meant that seventy Fianna Fáil TDs voted for the Bill as well as all seven Labour deputies. [56]

Most Republicans were pleased with de Valera for his determination in getting the Oath Bill through its second reading in the Dáil. The editor of *An Phoblacht* wrote:

> Since coming into office Fianna Fáil has managed to retain public approval. The Irish people are intensely national, and the firm attitude of Fianna Fáil on the questions taken with the British government has evoked praise and general approval among all nationalists.[57]

The committee stage of the Oath Bill was debated in Dáil Éireann on 3 May. During the course of the discussion Éamon de Valera declared: 'When we have got this (Oath) Bill through and settled our own position with regard to our own attitude then let the British talk about it. Let them make their protest against it. We are quite prepared to hear what they have to say.' He emphasised, 'Any dealings with them about this Oath will be as equals.[58]

A question by a Liberal MP, Geoffrey Mander, in the House of Commons as to whether the British government was prepared to submit the matter of the abolition by the Dáil of the Oath of Allegiance to an appropriate judicial tribunal gave J.H. Thomas, Dominions Secretary, the opportunity to make an important statement:

> The matter in dispute is a Treaty agreement between two parties. It is customary when there is a difference of opinion for one or other to ask for a consultation to discuss the difference. In this particular case de Valera, without consultation or intimation of any kind, proposes to break his side of the Treaty. It is not for us as a government, being the other party to the Treaty, to do other than draw attention to the fact that he is breaking the Treaty... The responsibility for the breaking of the ten years of peace that has developed in Ireland as a result of the Treaty must rest with those who are responsible for it.[59]

In answer to Thomas's statement, David Kirkwood, Labour MP for Dumbarton Burghs, remarked: 'When the contract was made the Irish were feeling they were a subject race and they are now feeling that they are a free people.'[60]

Cries of indignation from many members of the House of Commons in protest at Kirkwood's comments signalled that the Dominions Secretary had the support of a huge majority of the members of the British parliament.

The report and final stages of the Constitution (Removal of the Oath) Bill 1932 came before the Dáil on 19 May. After a day of intense oratory, in the course of which the whole Treaty position was again examined, William Norton made a dramatic speech in which he once again promised Labour Party support for the abolition of the Oath of Allegiance in the final vote that was due that evening:

> It (the Oath) is not a matter that Britain ought to interfere in and it is, I think certainly, not a matter to justify Britain using the big stick in the fashion that Thomas has wielded it in the last few months and, in particular, there is no justification for the

threatening manner in which he wielded it in the last week...
The Labour Party's attitude is that we have no use for the Oath.[61]

At 10.30 that night the moment arrived for the final decision of the Dáil. All the amendments to the Bill were defeated in the division lobbies. The third and final stage of the Oath Bill had finally passed through the Dáil. The vote on the final stages of the Bill for the abolition of the Oath of Allegiance was seventy-seven in favour (Fianna Fáil seventy and Labour seven) and sixty-nine against (Cumann na nGaedheal fifty-three, Independents ten, Farmers' Party three, Independent Labour two, Independent Farmer one). The result was received with great enthusiasm by the Fianna Fáil TDs.

There is no doubt that, but for the steadfast support of the seven Labour TDs, de Valera would have been unable to guide the Oath through all its stages in the Dáil without agreeing to negotiate the question with the British government. But the architects of this Bill could not yet relax in the certainty that the Bill would come into operation in the near future. The Bill was shortly due to go before Seanad Éireann and it was unclear what the Upper House of the Oireachtas would decide. The Senate had sixty members and Fianna Fáil and Labour together could only be sure of mustering the support of about twenty of these. The remaining forty members comprised farmers and businessmen, augmented by core supporters of Cumann na nGaedheal and a sprinkling of ex-Unionists. Would the Senate accept the verdict of a majority of the elected TDs of Dáil Éireann or would it use its power to delay for a long period the abolition of the Oath of Allegiance?

Notes

1. *Dáil Éireann Debates*, Volume 41, 15 March 1932, p. 72.
2. Caitríona Crowe *et al.* (eds.), *Documents on Irish Foreign Policy Volume IV 1932-36*; NAI, File DT S2264, Extracts from the minutes of a meeting of the cabinet, (Cab 6/2), 12 March 1932, p. 4.
3. NAI, File DT S2264, 12 March 1932, pp. 4, 5, Letter from Joseph Walshe to Éamon de Valera.
4. The *Irish Press*, 17 March 1932.
5. Crowe et al, *op. cit.*, NAI, DFA Secretary's Files SI, Letter from John W. Dulanty to J.H. Thomas (London), 22 March 1932, p. 26.
6. *An Phoblacht*, 30 April 1932.
7. *Seanad Éireann Debates*, Volume 15, 22 March 1932, p. 610.
8. *Ibid.*, p. 614.
9. *Ibid.*, p. 617.
10. The *Irish Press*, 24 March 1932.
11. *Ibid.*

12. *Ibid.*
13. *Ibid.*, 25-26 March 1932.
14. *Ibid.*
15. *Ibid.*, 24 March 1932.
16. *Ibid.*, 25-26 March 1932.
17. *Ibid.*
18. *Ibid.*, 28 March 1932.
19. *Ibid.*, 30 March 1932.
20. *Ibid.*, 28 March 1932.
21. *Ibid.*
22. *Ibid.*, 31 March 1932.
23. *Ibid.*, 2 April 1932.
24. *Ibid.*
25. *Ibid.*, 4 April 1932.
26. *Ibid.*, 6 April 1932.
27. Crowe et al. *op cit.*, NAI, DT S2264, Despatch from Éamon de Valera to J.H. Thomas (London), 5 April 1932, pp. 31, 32.
28. The *Irish Press*, 7 April 1932.
29. *Ibid.*, 9 April 1932.
30. The *Irish Press*, 11 April 1932.
31. *Ibid.*
32. *Ibid.*, 15 April 1932.
33. *An Phoblacht*, 16 April 1932.
34. The *Irish Press*, 19 April 1932.
35. *Dáil Éireann Debates*, Volume 41, 20 April 1932, p. 171.
36. *Ibid.*
37. *Ibid.*, 21 April 1932, pp. 171, 172, 173, 174, 175.
38. The *Irish Press*, 23 April 1932.
39. *Ibid.*, 27 April 1932.
40. *Dáil Éireann Debates*, Volume 41, 27 April 1932, p. 569.
41. *Ibid.*, p. 573.
42. *Ibid.*
43. *Ibid.*, p. 578.
44. *Ibid.*, p. 577.
45. *Ibid.*, p. 579.
46. *Ibid.*, p. 582.
47. *Ibid.*, pp. 592, 595.
48. *Ibid.*, p. 612.
49. *Ibid.* p. 578.
50. *Ibid.*, p. 739.
51. *Ibid.*, pp. 738 -743.
52. *Ibid.*, pp. 745, 746.
53. *Ibid.* p. 769.
54. *Ibid.*, p. 83.
55. The *Irish Independent*, 30 April 1932.
56. The seven Labour deputies who voted to abolish the Oath of Allegiance were: Richard Corish (Wexford); Patrick Curran (Dublin County); William Davin (Leix-Offaly); James Everett (Wicklow); Patrick Hogan (Clare); Timothy Murphy (Cork West); William Norton (Kildare).
57. *An Phoblacht*, 30 April 1932.
58. *Dáil Éireann Debates*, Volume 41, 3 May 1932, p. 1177.
59. The *Irish Independent*, 6 May 1932.
60. *Ibid.*
61. *Dáil Éireann Debates*, Volume 41, 19 May 1932, pp. 2081, 2085

22

CONFLICT INTERNAL AND EXTERNAL

The British Dominions Secretary, J.H. Thomas, told a meeting in Hove Town Hall that Britain was basing its case on the Oath on the sanctity of treaties and the maintenance of agreements. 'How,' he asked, 'could we negotiate fresh agreements with the Irish Free State if existing ones were not observed?'[1]

President de Valera took the British statesman to task for his insistence on the sanctity of the Treaty at the expense of later agreements, asking: 'Why omit the later agreements – those embodied in the Reports of the Imperial Conferences of 1926 and 1930? Is no sanctity to be attached to these?'[2]

The Prime Minister Ramsay MacDonald castigated de Valera's stance on the Oath question in his Empire Day broadcast:

> The method that regards Treaties as scraps of paper to be altered or ended as it suits either party is the method of disunity. It destroys confidence. It bases all agreements on force, rather than on honour. It strikes at the rule of moral solidarity.[3]

Frank Aiken, Fianna Fáil Minister for Defence, noted that the members of the Senate had the power to prevent the Oath Bill from becoming law for eighteen months by failing to ratify it. 'I am glad that the Bill has gone through the Dáil and I hope it will go through the Senate.' He warned: 'If it doesn't go through the Senate, the people will see to the Senate when they get the opportunity.'[4]

Many representatives of the world Press crowded the public galleries of the Senate to hear President Éamon de Valera move the motion to remove the Oath of Allegiance from the Free State Constitution. He said that it was not his intention or the intention of his government that the Constitution (Removal of Oath) Bill, 1932 should be regarded, as some people had suggested, as a deliberate attempt to sever the Free State from the states of the British Commonwealth.[5] He pointed out that the abolition of the Oath 'is a test, a real test as to whether the declarations of 1926 and 1930 [Imperial Conferences] mean what they say or not. If they mean what they say, there is no offence whatever and there can be no offence in our doing what we propose to do.'[6]

Senator James Douglas led off for the opposition. He claimed: 'Membership of the Commonwealth means a great deal to this country... Outside the Commonwealth we might be theoretically more independent but a hostile Britain could restrict our independence in many ways.'[7] He advised: 'The Senate, however, can see that sufficient time will elapse before the Bill comes into operation to enable the government and the country to find out exactly where we stand. We think that this House has a duty to see that the people of this country know beyond yea or nay where it stands in relation to the Commonwealth if this Bill comes into operation.'[8]

The Fianna Fáil Senator and Minister for Posts and Telegraphs, Joseph Connolly, declared that the plain people of Ireland were backing the government in their attempt to remove the Oath of Allegiance and asked: 'Was one small group – it may be twelve, fifteen or twenty – going to take on setting at nought...all the national aspirations of this country.'[9]

Senator Samuel Brown said that he thought the Senate could best discharge its national duty by passing the second reading of this Bill without a division and then 'inserting on the committee stage an amendment that this Bill shall not come into operation unless and until a valid agreement shall have been entered into with Great Britain.'[10]

After a four and a half hours' debate the Senate passed a motion to adjourn for a week.

Seán Lemass, Minister for Industry and Commerce, made a vigorous speech on the subject to a big gathering in Cork:

It (the Removal of the Oath Bill) is before the Senate now. We have in this country a second legislative chamber not selected by the people and not representative of the people's will... The majority vote in the Dáil has been for the removal of the Oath and consequently the will of the people in that respect is known...It is not for the Senate to stand in the path of progress. They think that they are dealing with fools when they are dealing with the Fianna Fáil government. We want the Bill as the Dáil passed it and it is going to become law in that form whether with the consent of the Senate or against their will.[11]

At a meeting in Cross, County Mayo, James Fitzgerald-Kenney KC, TD, who had been W.T. Cosgrave's Minister for Justice, warned that the Free State government under de Valera could face dire consequences if it continued 'to act like a bully and in this respect no country has treated another in so high-handed a manner as de Valera is now endeavouring to treat England.' He added: 'The British people themselves have already begun to retaliate. Our stuff is already getting so unpopular in England that they will buy nothing from us if they can avoid it.'[12]

In the House of Commons the Liberal MP, Geoffrey Mander, asked the Dominions Secretary if he would state with which of the Dominions trade negotiations preliminary to the Ottawa Conference had been and were taking place and in which cases, if any, there had been no such negotiations. (The Ottawa Conference of 1932 brought together British colonies and self-governing dominions to discuss the Great Depression and to establish a zone of limited tariffs within the British Empire.) J.H. Thomas replied that the preliminary discussions had been taking place with Canada, Australia, New Zealand, the Union of South Africa, Newfoundland and Southern Rhodesia and also with India but no discussions had taken place with the Irish Free State. Mander persisted and asked why the Free State had been excluded. In reply J.H. Thomas said:

Because, as I explained to the House previously, at the present moment the Irish Free State government repudiates an agreement entered into between the representatives of Ireland and ourselves. We feel that no good purpose could be served by entering into further negotiations with people until they show they are ready to observe agreements.[13]

The adjourned second reading of the Oath Bill was resumed in the Senate early in June. Senator James C. Dowdall, for Fianna Fáil, said that he had traded in practically every industrial part of England and 'during those periods political feeling between Ireland and Britain frequently ran high and to the credit of the English trader, I am positively convinced I never lost a bit of business by reason of political ill-will or ill-feeling.'[14]

The Countess of Desart, who had promoted industry, established a theatre and contributed to the opening of a library and the founding of a hospital in County Kilkenny, complained: 'The English people were desperately exasperated with what they considered the want of courtesy displayed by the President of the Executive Council in refusing to discuss the matter of this Oath with the co-equal partners of the Commonwealth.'[15] She added that many who drew incomes from the other side of the channel [sic] gave considerable employment here. She would be forced to withdraw from many activities that involved the paying of salaries and wages if relations with England were to deteriorate.

A well-known War of Independence veteran, Senator Bill Quirke from County Tipperary, a follower of de Valera, said that he felt: 'that if King George and [J.H.] Thomas had been here for the past few debates I am sure they would have been delighted.'[16]

One-time Lord Mayor of Dublin, Independent Senator Laurence O'Neill, supported the removal of the Oath of Allegiance, saying that 'The Bill was a stepping stone, in the words of Collins, to greater freedom which has been so long delayed.'[17]

Senator J. Counihan, Cumann na nGaedheal said: 'The members of the livestock trade are gravely alarmed at the consequences which may ensue if this Bill becomes law.'[18]

Winding up the debate, Éamon de Valera said that it had been suggested that 'we should hold the question up until the people had an opportunity of considering it. The people had considered it for a long time. It has been before the people for ten years.'[19]

The second reading of the Oath Bill was carried in the Senate by twenty-one votes to eight. There were many senators who did not vote at all: they were absent when the division bells rang. The opposition had planned to let the Bill go through its second reading in the Senate without forcing changes but to introduce amendments at the committee stage that was due to follow in a short time.

On President de Valera's instructions, John Dulanty, the Irish High Commissioner in London, got in touch with J.H. Thomas and proposed an early meeting on the subject of trade between de Valera and representatives of the British government so that they could iron out their differences before the forthcoming Ottawa Dominions Conference.[20]

On 6 June 1932, the government issued an official statement that came as a surprise to a great many people in Ireland:

> The President and Minister for External Affairs de Valera has invited the British government to send representatives to Dublin for a preliminary discussion on the present difficulties between the two countries in relation to negotiations concerning the Ottawa Conference. The British government has accepted the invitation and J.H. Thomas, the Dominions Secretary and Lord Hailsham, Secretary of State for War, are crossing to Dublin to-night. They will confer with the President at Government Buildings, Merrion Street, tomorrow morning.[21]

With the Oath Bill certain to be passed, even if the Senate delayed it, de Valera hoped the British government would accept the abolition of the Oath of Allegiance as a confirmed deed. The British government representatives, on the other hand, thought de Valera was proposing a compromise of some kind. J.H. Thomas and Lord Hailsham did indeed come to Dublin on 6 June, accompanied by Sir Edward Harding, Under-Secretary of the Dominions

Office. They conferred for two hours with President de Valera and James Geoghegan, Minister for Justice.[22] De Valera stated he expected the British government to accept the Oath Bill that was at that time before both Houses of the Oireachtas. The British ministers recommended an impartial authority to examine the question but de Valera held that the Oath question was an internal issue.[23]

Afterwards Thomas and Hailsham reported to the British cabinet on this meeting. It was arranged that de Valera should cross to London to meet the Prime Minister Ramsay MacDonald and Stanley Baldwin (Lord President of the Council) on the following Friday. Seán T. O'Kelly, Vice-President and Minister for Local Government, would accompany the President to these talks.

At the beginning of the committee stage of the Oath Bill in the Senate, Senator Sir William Hickie moved the adjournment of the House in view of the negotiations proceeding between the British and Free State governments. But President de Valera saw no reason why the Senate should not continue with the Bill: 'Our attitude as regards the nature of the Bill is unchanged.'[24]

Senator Seán Milroy proposed the insertion into the Bill of a new section that would declare 'that this Act shall not come into force until an agreement has been entered into between the government of the Irish Free State and the British government.'[25] The Senate introduced three further technical amendments during this committee stage. Seán Milroy's amendment was carried in the Senate on a division, by thirty-three votes to twenty-two; the three technical amendments were also carried by majority votes.

An Phoblacht, disappointed that the Oath abolition Bill had been delayed, rebuked the senators:

> The majors and the knights of the expiring ascendancy, reinforced by the leather-lung Milroy and other more recent converts to imperialism, were able to muster enough votes in the so-called Senate, to hold up the Oath abolition Bill. Thirty [sic] senators defied the mandate of the people!...Won't somebody see that the imperial master suitably rewards Milroy's last great

gesture of loyalty with a knighthood?[26]

On 9 June 1932, the day after the Senate debate on the committee stage of the Oath Bill had concluded, a meeting took place in London between President de Valera and Seán T. O'Kelly on behalf of the Free State Executive and Prime Minister Ramsay MacDonald; Stanley Baldwin; the Home Secretary, Sir Herbert Samuel; and the Dominions Secretary, J.H. Thomas, on behalf of Great Britain. Joseph P. Walshe, Secretary of the Department of External Affairs, John Dulanty, the Irish High Commissioner in London and Seán Moynihan, private secretary to de Valera, accompanied the Irish delegation to the London talks. Éamon de Valera was disappointed by the outcome. After the talks an official communiqué announced: 'There was a prolonged discussion on the points at issue but it was not found possible to reach an agreement.' On their way home from London, Éamon de Valera and Seán T. O'Kelly received a rousing send-off from a large crowd of Irish men and women at Euston Station. There were cries of 'Good old Dev' and 'Up the Republic'.[27]

De Valera was finding that abolishing the Oath was 'a hard nut to crack' both at home and in England but he was determined to persist with the task.

The Oath Bill, including the Milroy delaying amendment and the three technical amendments, passed through its final stage in the Senate without a division. The Senate then sent back the amended Bill for the Dáil to approve the amendments. Fianna Fáil and Labour, who had a majority in the Dáil, rejected outright all the Senate amendments. According to protocol this Bill was returned to the Senate and a message read out in that chamber by the Leas-Chathaoirleach (Vice-Chairman): 'Dáil Éireann has disagreed to the Amendments made by Seanad Éireann to the Constitution (Removal of Oath) Bill, 1932.' The Senate again discussed the Bill but persisted with nearly all their amendments. This time the majority of the Senators moved 'that the Seanad do [sic] insist on three amendments out of four' that it had inserted into the Bill. The amendment to delay the Bill until an agreement had been reached between the Irish and British governments was one of the three still included in the Bill. The Oath Bill had now twice failed to be adopted by the

Senate in the form agreed by Dáil Éireann.

The position was that the Act, as passed by Dáil Éireann, would auto-matically become law after eighteen months. Until then the Bill would remain in cold storage but if a new general election took place and a new Dáil passed the Removal of the Oath Bill without amendments, the period of waiting would be shortened to sixty days.

President de Valera made a statement in the Dáil outlining the attitude taken by his government in the talks with the British government in Dublin and London: 'I thought it was my duty to suggest that we might have some friendly discussions – the object being that our respective points of view might be made clear.' He said he had told the British delegation that in regard to the question of the Oath of Allegiance: 'We believed we were doing something that we were entitled to do and which was not, in fact, a violation of the Treaty and that we intended to proceed to put that measure into execution as soon as we are able to do so.'[28]

In the debate in the House of Commons about the discussions between the Free State Executive and the British government, Sir Stafford Cripps of the Labour Party, who had been Solicitor-General in the previous government, said: 'So far as the legal position is concerned, since the passing of the Statute of Westminster, the Irish Free State has an absolute right to abolish the Parliamentary Oath…However undesirable we might think it, the Free State has got a perfect liberty to do what they are doing.'[29]

Sir Harry Batterbee of the Dominions Office, met John J. Hearne, Legal Adviser to the Free State Department of External Affairs, in London on 8 July 1932. Batterbee told Hearne that everybody connected with official life in the Dominions Office had been very much hurt by the treatment the British government had received at the hands of the new Irish Free State government. The attitude of 'declining to discuss' the Oath of Allegiance was quite unprovoked and uncalled for. But the real grievance of the British…was the background of the situation, the fundamental unsettling of things that had been regarded as settled.[30]

It was at this stage that the question of the abolition of the Oath of Allegiance became intertwined with the contention over land annuities that had developed between the Fianna Fáil government and the British government. Éamon de Valera had refused to pay the annuities to the British government but he was putting these payments into a suspense account of his own, pending a settlement.[31] The British Treasury insisted that these annuities should be paid to them forthwith, pending arbitration. J.H. Thomas threatened that the British government would implement special duties on Irish imports into Great Britain in order to force de Valera's government into compliance with the Anglo-Irish Treaty of 1921. De Valera sent a dispatch to Thomas on 3 July pointing out that he would persist in his determination to abolish the Oath and to refuse to pay the land annuities to Britain.

Under pressure from J.H. Thomas, the British cabinet agreed to bring the Special Powers Act into force on 14 July 1932. This act imposed a 20 per cent duty on Irish agricultural exports into Britain: live animals exported to Britain, meats of all kinds, poultry, game, butter, eggs, bacon, pork and cream. The export of cattle and butter to England was of prime importance to Irish farmers and there was no doubt but that these duties would cause an economic crisis in the Irish Free State within a short time.

President De Valera had sent a delegation to the Dominions Conference in Ottawa, led by Seán T. O'Kelly and including Seán Lemass and Dr James Ryan as well as a number of officials. En route to Canada the delegation heard of the duties imposed by the British government in their Special Powers Act. Lemass thought that the Irish government should apply counter-measures. He telegraphed de Valera to advise a duty on coal exports from Great Britain to Ireland.[32] An Emergency Duties Bill was introduced which imposed a duty of five shillings a ton on British coal coming into the Free State and a 20 per cent duty on cement, electrical machinery, sugar products and iron and steel goods.[33] Thus began what is known as the Economic War. British treasury officials believed that, as the economic crisis deepened, the Irish people would reject de Valera and bring an end to his political career.

President de Valera went to London on 15 July and met Ramsay MacDonald. The Prime Minister and de Valera conversed along lines that William Norton, leader of the Irish Labour Party, had suggested to the two men the previous night. The meeting was a failure and de Valera left London without any agreement between the sides to meet again.[34]

An Phoblacht warned the Fianna Fáil government that even if the Oath of Allegiance were abolished, it would not put the IRA out of existence. The IRA would persist in endeavouring to achieve a thirty-two county republic by every means open to it:

> The present Fianna Fáil administration seems to consider that once parliamentary representation is afforded to the IRA that organisation will not longer have a rational ground for existence. Since that supposition is wrong, it is well that the position be made clear once and for all. The mere removal of the Oath in the British-created and British-approved Constitution of Southern Ireland will not radically alter the Republican position. The Irish Republican Army has entered into a solemn compact to guard and defend the Irish Republic against all enemies foreign and domestic.[35]

In a speech at Castlepollard, County Westmeath, Frank Aiken TD, Fianna Fáil Minister for Defence, referred to the disappointment that his government felt because of the fact that the Senate had delayed the abolition of the Oath Bill:

> While the barrier of the Oath remains there are some people who will not enter parliament, and we are asking your [the public's] help to get that barrier swept out of existence. The people have spoken on it, and only a small clique, nominated by Cosgrave, after consultation with the English – the Senate – it is only that small body that is standing in the way of getting rid of the Oath. Before very long we will be asking the people to deal with the Senate so that no longer will they be able to bar the march to national independence and prosperity.[36]

During a speech to seven thousand people in Kilkenny, de Valera said that he believed that when all sections entered the Dáil: 'there can be no possible reason why they should not accept the leadership of the majority of the people's elected representatives.'[37] There had shortly before been a shooting incident in County Clare involving members of the IRA and members of the Civic Guards, and Éamon de Valera was referring to members of the IRA and Sinn Féin when he expressed some doubt that his hopes might not be realised:

> We are told that even if we have the Oath removed that that principle (the principle of majority rule) is not going to be accepted. We are satisfied to wait and see. We believe it will be accepted. We believe if the Oath was gone – and I am speaking to the young people of Ireland – they have commonsense enough to know that that principle (majority rule) should be accepted if there is going to be any ordered progress. I believe we would only have to appeal to the young people and they would rally behind those principles.[38]

On 28 October 1932, Joseph P. Walshe, secretary of the Department of External Affairs, arrived in London with the authority of de Valera to meet members of the British government with the intention of settling the Anglo-Irish dispute. He had two hours' conversation with Sir Edward Harding, Under-Secretary of the Dominions Office and Sir Harry Batterbee. Most members of the British government's Irish Situation Committee favoured a compromise solution by agreeing some modification in the wording of the Oath of Allegiance. The British cabinet approved a statement drafted by the Irish Situation Committee and to be given to Walshe declaring that the British government was anxious for a friendly settlement but that the Irish government should accept the Treaty and give an undertaking not to proceed further with the Oath Bill. Walshe thought that the Irish President would find this quite impossible.[39] He replied that there was the further difficulty, as regards the Oath, that its continuance was regarded in all parts of the Free State as a method of control by the United Kingdom government.[40] This was denied by the British delegation. The talks failed because the British representatives demanded an undertaking that the Irish government should not proceed with the Oath Bill.

Interesting exchanges took place in the Dáil between Seán Lemass, Minister for Industry and Commerce, and James Fitzgerald-Kenney, former Cumann na nGaedheal Minister for Justice. When Fitzgerald-Kenney said that the Cumann na nGaedheal Party stood for the preservation of the Treaty, Lemass quipped, 'And for its restoration?' Fitzgerald-Kenney answered, 'I am pretty confident that there will never be a restoration…because, as a result of the policy of dragging down the country to economic ruin…there will be simply no country left for any government to rule over.'[41]

It was decided at a meeting in Dublin of the Standing Committee of the National Farmers' and Ratepayers' League at which Frank McDermot, Independent TD for Roscommon, presided, that a new party, the Centre Party, should be formed. McDermot believed that the twenty-six counties should remain in the British Commonwealth and this viewpoint was likely to be reflected in the make-up of his new political party.

A prominent Independent member of the Senate, Arthur Vincent, advocated that the party recently formed by Frank McDermot should come together with W.T. Cosgrave's Cumann na nGaedheal and form a new combined party that 'would eventually triumph over President de Valera and his caucus.'[42]

This suggestion was taken up by the Lord Mayor of Dublin, Alfie Byrne, the popular Independent TD for Dublin North and one-time member of the old Redmondite Irish Party. He urged that members of Cumann na nGaedheal; Frank McDermot and representatives of the Farmers' and Ratepayers' League (the new Centre Party); James Dillon, Independent TD, Donegal; John F. O'Hanlon, Independent Farmers' TD, Cavan, and representatives of the Labour Party should together form a national government.[43] W.T. Cosgrave issued a statement welcoming the idea and asking the Standing Committee of Cumann na nGaedheal to meet to consider the proposal.[44] Alfie Byrne later declared in a statement to the press that, among the aims of the new National Party that he hoped to set up, would be: 'to stand by the Treaty which gives us complete powers, legislative and administrative for twenty-six counties. If any changes are found necessary from time to time in the Treaty, these are to be secured by negotiations.'[45]

Fianna Fáil Ministers were seen scurrying around Leinster House during the evening of 2 January 1933. At eight o'clock a hurried cabinet meeting was held at Government Buildings. It was clear from the frenzied activity that a matter of more than usual importance was under discussion. The cabinet met for several hours and, at one o'clock the following morning, ministers emerged tired but excited.

It came like a bolt from the blue. An official government statement declared that President de Valera had called a snap general election. The Seventh Dáil would dissolve immediately. A general election would be held on 24 January 1933 and the Eighth Dáil would meet for the first time on 8 February.

This development took the country completely by surprise. But de Valera's chief reason for going to the country was to get a mandate for the policies he was pursuing with the British government. If he could win a clear victory at the polls, he could negotiate with more strength with the British. If his party returned with an increased number of seats, he would banish from the minds of British ministers, at least for another four or five years, the possibility that Cumann na nGaedheal could oust him from government.

De Valera immediately gave an interview to the press. In reply to questions, he said that the Fianna Fáil association with Labour had been uniformly happy and the dissolution was not due to any differences with Norton's party. The reason for the dissolution, he said, was that 'a hostile Senate is constantly attempting to harass the government by mutilating its measures or wilfully delaying them.'[46]

However the fresh efforts of the opposition parties to unite against Fianna Fáil and get de Valera's government out of office may also have been a contributory factor in the decision of the President, a shrewd political operator, to call an immediate general election in order to outmanoeuvre this strategy before it gained ground.

After fewer than eleven months in office, Éamon de Valera, leader of Fianna Fáil, took a gamble. If he came back as the leader of the next government the Oath of Allegiance to the British monarch would be abolished within sixty days. If he failed to be re-elected President of the Executive Council, there was a distinct possibility that the Constitution (Removal of the Oath) Bill 1932 might be defeated in the new Dáil and the Oath would remain. This and other national questions now depended on the will of the Irish people in the coming general election.

Notes

1. The *Irish Independent*, 21 May 1932.
2. *Ibid.*, 23 May 1932.
3. *Ibid.*, 25 May 1932.
4. *Ibid.*, 23 May 1932.
5. *Seanad Éireann Debates*, Volume 15, 25 May 1932, p. 681.
6. *Ibid.*
7. *Ibid.*, pp. 693, 694.
8. *Ibid.*, p. 696.
9. *Ibid.*, p. 741.
10. *Ibid.*, p. 754.
11. The *Irish Press*, 30 May 1932.
12. *Ibid.*
13. *Ibid.*, 3 June 1932.
14. *Seanad Éireann Debates*, Volume 15, 2 June 1932, p. 844.
15. *Ibid.*, p. 872.
16. *Ibid.*, p. 873.
17. *Ibid.*, p. 904.
18. *Ibid.*, pp. 905, 906.
19. *Ibid.*, pp. 935, 936.
20. Crowe et al. (eds.), *Documents on Irish Foreign Policy 1932-1936*, p. 61, UCDA P150/2179, Handwritten letter from John W. Dulanty to Éamon de Valera, London, 5 June 1932.
21. The *Irish Press*, 7 June 1932.
22. Crowe *et al.*, *op cit.*, p. 61, NAI, CAB 1-4, Extract from the minutes of a meeting of the cabinet, 6 June 1932.
23. Deirdre McMahon, *Republicans and Imperialists, Anglo-Irish Relations in the 1930s*, p. 56.
24. *Seanad Éireann Debates*, Volume 15, 8 June 1932, p. 958.
25. *Ibid.*, p. 985.
26. *An Phoblacht*, 11 June 1932.
27. The *Irish Independent*, 11 June 1932.
28. *Dáil Éireann Debates*, Volume 42, 17 June 1932, pp. 1691, 1692.
29. The *Irish Press*, 18 June 1932.
30. Crowe et al., *op cit.*, NAI, DFA, Unregistered papers, Royal Irish Academy, Dublin, 2004, pp. 78, 79, 80, 81. Memorandum of a conversation between John J. Hearne and Sir Harry Batterbee on the general political situation between Ireland and Britain, London, 8 July 1932.
31. *Ibid.*, NAI, DFA, Secretary's Files S1, Royal Irish Academy, Dublin, 2004, p. 67, Letter from John W. Dulanty to J.H. Thomas (London), Copy, 4 July 1932.
32. *Ibid.*, UCDA P150/2226, Crowe *et al.*, *op cit.*, pp. 86, 87. Letter from Seán Lemass to Éamon de Valera (Dublin), 15 July 1932.
33. Deirdre McMahon, *op cit.*, pp. 68, 69.
34. Crowe *et al.*, *op cit.*, pp. 88, 89, 90, 91; UCDA, P150/2226 Minutes of a meeting between Éamon de Valera and Ramsay MacDonald, London, 15 July 1932.
35. *An Phoblacht*, 13 August 1932.
36. The *Irish Press*, 15 August 1932.

37. *Ibid.*, 12 September 1932.
38. *Ibid.*
39. Crowe *et al.*, *op cit.*, Note by Sir Edward J. Harding of a conversation with Joseph P. Walshe, TNA: PRO DO 35/398/1, 28 October 1932, pp. 189, 190, 191, 192, 193.
40. *Ibid.*, Note by Sir Edward Harding of a conversation with Joseph P. Walshe, TNA: PRO DO 35/398/1, 29 October 1932, p. 194.
41. *Dáil Éireann Debates*, Volume 44, 9 November 1932, p. 1248.
42. The *Irish Independent*, 28 December 1932.
43. *Ibid.*, 30 December 1932.
44. *Ibid.*, 31 December 1932.
45. *Ibid.*, 2 January 1933.
46. *Ibid.*, 3 January 1933.

23

Fianna Fáil Wins Overall Majority

In no time the country and the body politic got into election mode. Gerry Boland was appointed Fianna Fáil Director of Elections. W.T. Cosgrave sent for Frank McDermot TD, founder of the Centre Party, and asked him to join the newly-conceived Cosgrave-Alfie Byrne National Government Party. But McDermot said in a statement, 'I do not think that the sacrifice of our [party] identity and independence would be a good thing for the country.'[1] Two days later James Dillon joined McDermot in his new Centre Party, whose policy at that time was to remain completely independent of Cumann na nGaedheal and Fianna Fáil.[2] One other change was that Daniel Morrissey, Independent Labour TD, Tipperary, joined Cumann na nGaedheal at the invitation of W.T. Cosgrave.[3]

In a speech in Dublin, Cosgrave described the dissolution of the Dáil and the snap election as 'a gambler's throw' and said that Fianna Fáil were 'on the run from the people's wrath'.[4] On the other hand, Labour leader, William Norton, said that his 'party is proud of the stand [to abolish the Oath of Allegiance] which has been taken during the past ten months and in the forthcoming elections we will maintain that stand.'[5]

An editorial in the Republican newspaper, *An Phoblacht*, was interesting in so far as it confirmed the fact that the IRA had given support to Fianna Fáil in the previous, 1932, general election principally because the IRA leaders were most anxious to put Cumann na nGaedheal out of office. But the same editorial posed the question: would the Republican movement repeat this tactic in this upcoming general election?

Under the Fianna Fáil administration...the jailing of Republicans in Dublin, Clare and Kerry has been actually enforced. True, the Fianna Fáil government, with support of Labour deputies, enacted that the Oath, hitherto obligatory on elected deputies, should be abolished. Failure to fulfil that election pledge is due entirely to the anti-Irish Senate holding up the Oath Abolition Bill. The abolition of the humiliating Oath would be welcomed by every Irishman…Should revolutionary Ireland repeat the tactic of February 1932? That is a question now to be answered.[6]

In a statement issued on behalf of the Centre Party, the founder, Frank McDermot, expressed a desire that the Irish Free State should remain within the British Commonwealth. He urged the Fianna Fáil cabinet to consider 'the question of our relation to the Commonwealth' and advised that 'it should be settled for our generation by the vote of the people on that particular issue, since there should be unanimous willingness to accept the decision of the people as to whether they wish to remain in the Commonwealth or to declare a Republic and take the economic consequences of so doing.'[7]

Huge audiences came out to hear Éamon de Valera speak at political meetings around the country. Addressing around 30,000 enthusiastic supporters in Limerick, the Fianna Fáil leader declared that the Bill to remove the Oath of Allegiance 'was held up by the Senate, but in the election you can pass it in spite of the Senate. Once this election is over and we are returned to power the Bill has only to be sent to the Senate and whether they like it or not it becomes law.'[8]

The question posed by the *An Phoblacht* editorial as to whether revolutionary Ireland should again repeat the tactic of supporting Éamon de Valera and the Fianna Fáil Party in this 1933 general election was answered in de Valera's favour when a manifesto issued by a general Convention of the IRA, while criticising Fianna Fáil on many fronts, declared:

The Convention decided to release the Organisation from the restriction that prevented it from taking part in elections, and we are recommending our members, and the mass of national

opinion that looks to us for leadership to work and vote against
the Cosgrave candidates and their so-called Independent allies.
In practice this means that the Fianna Fáil government should
be assisted into office again.[9]

However the attitude of Sinn Féin was different from that of the IRA
The President, Brian O'Higgins, who was an extreme 'diehard' Republican,
submitted a statement to the Standing Committee of Sinn Féin that directed
members of his organisation to take no part in the general election. Margaret
Buckley, Dublin, a prominent member of the Standing Committee, asked if
it would be wise to publish the statement 'in view of the fact that we know
that the order will be disobeyed by some of our members.'[10] The Sinn Féin
President then read the statement twice to the meeting and after that it was
'decided to send it forthwith for publication.'[11]

Tomás Derrig, Fianna Fáil Minister for Education, who had lost an eye
fighting on the Republican side in the Civil War, spoke in Kilkenny after
the local fair: 'When we are returned in this election the Oath will go by the
board. We lay particular stress on that. There will be no justification after the
election for anybody, no matter what their ideals or principles, to resort to
arms or violence.'[12]

When the Fianna Fáil election manifesto was published, it contained one
big surprise – the declaration that the Senate, as at that time constituted, was
to be abolished.

The huge charisma of Éamon de Valera and his great popularity with the
masses continued: everywhere he travelled to address political meetings Irish
men and women gathered in their tens of thousands to listen to him. His
election campaign ended with a massive meeting in College Green on the
eve of the poll. People began to assemble two hours before the meeting was
due to begin. They marched in thousands from the suburbs led by a body of
horsemen, banners flying, torches blazing and bands playing. When de Valera
rose to speak, the frantic welcoming cheer of 60,000 people lasted for several
minutes.[13]

Polling took place all over the country on 24 January 1933. Although the day was dry, it was very cold in places. In parts of County Monaghan sleighs had to be used to bring voters to the polling booths over frozen roads. A noticeable feature of this election was that almost all the men and women coming out to vote wore heavy overcoats and some of the women, old and young, wore warm shawls. Some areas recorded a 90-per-cent vote and in almost every area at least 80 per cent went to the polls.

As the votes were counted the next day, it began to become clear that Fianna Fáil was doing well. The party would be certain to increase its number of Dáil seats. The first completed result was that of the NUI: to the surprise of many, a woman, Helena Concannon, an author who lived in Galway, won a seat for Fianna Fáil, defeating Professor Michael Hayes of Cumann na nGaedheal.

The general public followed the election results with great interest. As the results of the counts poured in, it became apparent that many changes were on their way. Ernest Blythe, former vice-President of the Free State Executive and Minister for Finance, lost his seat in Monaghan. Patrick Belton, this time standing for Cumann na nGaedheal, was elected in Dublin North. He had been a prominent member of Fianna Fáil and had been elected in Dublin County for that party in the general election of June 1927. In Leix-Offaly Laurence Brady, who had been elected as a Sinn Féin TD in 1923 and had sided with Sinn Féin in the immediate aftermath of the split in 1926, but who stood this time for Fianna Fáil, failed to get elected. In Dublin County, Margaret Mary Pearse, sister of Pádraig and Willie Pearse, was elected on a Fianna Fáil ticket. Her mother, Margaret, had failed to win a seat as an anti-Treaty candidate in Dublin County in the 1922 Pact general election.

In Clare, Éamon de Valera polled 18,565 votes out of a total poll of 44,595, which was 42 per cent of the total poll and considered to be the highest personal percentage vote recorded since the state was founded. Fianna Fáil gained more than 50 per cent of all first preferences cast in fifteen out of the twenty-nine constituencies.[14] Fianna Fáil did best in Kerry where it gained 68 per cent of all first preferences, Clare (65 per cent) and Galway (62 per cent). Cumann na nGaedheal performed best in Dublin South (47 per cent of all first preferences), Dublin County (46 per cent) and NUI (45 per cent).

The Fianna Fáil first-preference vote increased by 123,000 to 690,000 and the Cumann na nGaedheal poll fell by 32,000 to a figure of around 420,000. Labour lost 20,000 votes to end up with 80,000 first preferences.[15] In percentage terms Fianna Fáil got 49.7 per cent of the total first preference votes cast, Cumann na nGaedheal 30.4 per cent, the Centre Party 9.2 per cent and Labour 5.7 per cent.[16]

The final state of the parties was as follows:

F. Fáil	C. na nG.	Centre	Ind.	Labour	Ind. Lab
77	48	11	8	8	1

Fianna Fáil gained five seats and Labour one. Cumann na nGaedheal lost nine seats and Independents three. The Centre Party was the big winner, securing eleven seats, but the party had incorporated into its ranks the Farmers' Party that had previously held three seats.

Cumann na nGaedheal was disappointed by the election results, as before the election the party leaders had felt that the controversy over the removal of the Oath and the Economic War would help to bring them back into government. Cumann na nGaedheal Party issued a statement from their Dublin headquarters: 'The election is over and the Fianna Fáil and Labour Party achieved a combined gain of six seats. – so far from suffering any loss of support we have secured an increase of enthusiasm, determination and zeal.'[17]

Frank McDermot had hoped that the farmers of Ireland would rally in great numbers behind his Centre Party but his achievement in obtaining eleven seats was a very creditable performance for a new leader and a new party.

Labour's William Norton said that 'as far as he was concerned he would support by every means in his power any policy that would organise and develop the nation.'[18]

The Fianna Fáil victory was celebrated throughout the country by Republican sympathisers: they had cause for rejoicing because Fianna Fáil had won its first overall majority – of one. The combined number of Labour and Fianna Fáil TDs now exceeded by seventeen the number of Cumann na nGaedheal, Centre Party and Independent TDs combined. Archbishop

Mannix of Melbourne sent a telegram to Éamon de Valera: 'Congratulations. Ireland, with God's blessing marches to final victory.'[19]

The IRA issued an official statement to all its ranks, reminding the Irish people that it had recommended all its volunteers and the masses of national opinion to work and vote against all the Cosgrave candidates and 'their so-called Independent allies'. The statement continued: 'All reports received from unit commanders indicate that the tactic decided on was clearly understood and that the weight of the volunteer organisation thrown behind the Fianna Fáil Party made a big contribution to the defeat of the imperial elements.'[20]

When an *Irish Press* political correspondent asked Éamon de Valera to comment on how he saw the future, he replied: 'The dead who died for Ireland will attend us in our efforts. Our exiled children will sustain us with their thoughts and prayers.'[21] Shortly after the final results of the election were announced de Valera gave an interview to *The New York Times* in which he said that 'following the success of the party at the polls, the Oath of Allegiance to Britain will be removed in a few weeks.'[22]

The administrative council of the Labour Party met the elected deputies and senators of the party to consider the path they intended to take in the coming Eighth Dáil. They issued a report: 'With regard to the Press rumours of the formation of a coalition government, the Labour Party being an independent party does not desire nor will it seek a coalition with any other party. In the next Dáil the Labour Party will give full support to measures which are in accordance with its national and economic policy.'[23] Fianna Fáil was satisfied with this statement as it felt that the declaration pointed to cooperation with them.

The British government had hoped that Fianna Fáil would be defeated in this general election and that W.T. Cosgrave would once again be President of the Executive Council of the Irish Free State. British ministers now realised that Éamon de Valera had established himself as a strong and durable leader of the Irish people and that they had no option but to deal with him in order to solve the Irish dispute.

There was a lot of activity in Dublin on the day before the Eighth Dáil assembled. W.T. Cosgrave was unanimously elected leader and chairman

322 THE OATH IS DEAD AND GONE

of Cumann na nGaedheal. After his election he criticised 'some unworthy methods' employed by Fianna Fáil during the general election. 'Personation, intimidation, slander and misrepresentation were all called into play,' he claimed. 'The fears of the poor and credulous were worked upon, and pains were taken to cast doubts upon the secrecy of the ballot.'[24]

The Centre Party met at its headquarters in St Stephen's Green and chose Frank McDermot as leader of the party for the forthcoming session.

The Clerk of the Dáil, Colm Ó Murchadha, had to be administer the Oath of Allegiance to all the deputies of the Eighth Dáil before they could take their seats. Because the Fianna Fáil deputies were now convinced that this would be the last time they would be obliged to do this, they gave scant regard to what they believed was a make-believe ritual of signing their names in the Dáil roll book.

The Eighth Dáil assembled in Leinster House on Thursday 9 February 1933. David Hogan, author of the very interesting book *The Four Glorious Years*, described the scene in his article for the *Irish Press*.

Above in the public galleries were men and women whose work had made the Dáil, had kept Republicanism alive in the dark days, people little known, priests from many parts, old Sinn Féin workers whose enthusiasm burns still.

Soon there is a whole line of the past sitting together. Kilroy, the Brigadier of the West; Moylan of the South; Breen of the Third Tipperary Brigade; Crowley of Kerry; Harris of Kildare; men of the people who had fought for the people. There were others of the past opposite them, taking their places too; the open-air Seán Mac Eoin, Mulcahy, Dolan, Fionán Lynch, Gearóid O'Sullivan – men who at one time risked life for liberty.

The House is filling quickly. One can pick the new deputies out at once, they are gazing around, they are excited. Miss Pearse sits beside Mrs Concannon, both dressed darkly. Mrs Bridget Redmond, tall and slim, hurries to take her place on the opposition benches. John A. Costello, ex-Attorney-General, is a new face in the Dáil.

Looking down on the House one saw that Fianna Fáil was still the party of the young, of the ordinary man of the fields and man of the towns; while across from them was material comfort and success, middle-aged, secure, placid.[25]

The authoritative voice of the Ceann Comhairle filled the House: 'The next business is the nomination of the President of the Executive Council.' Seán Moylan, Fianna Fáil TD for Cork North, proposed Éamon de Valera – 'the leader of the national advance since 1916.'[26] Micheál Clery, Mayo North TD, seconded in soft Western Irish.

W.T. Cosgrave, leader of Cumann na nGaedheal, stood up. 'We oppose the nomination before the House,' he said.[27] Then he attacked the policy of Fianna Fáil. 'The external policy which has been pursued by the outgoing government has cost this country very dearly.'[28] Cosgrave claimed that Fianna Fáil had divided the nation. 'Their policy is, and their antecedent policy has been to divide the national front.'[29]

The leader of the Centre Party, Frank McDermot, took the floor. 'It is impossible for us to support the re-election of President de Valera,' he said.[30] McDermot claimed: 'President de Valera could have achieved a clear recognition by the British of the moral, no less than the legal right of the Free State to leave the British Commonwealth at any time it desired to do so. Instead he had pursued methods which were bound to create bitterness between the British and Irish governments.'[31] But then came a surprise announcement from McDermot: that his party had given good consideration to what they should do 'and we have come to the conclusion that we cannot vote against him' because 'we must accept the situation and recognise that the result of the election is to make a Fianna Fáil President inevitable.'[32]

William Norton, leader of the Labour Party, followed. Labour, said Norton, would support the nomination of President de Valera for the presidency because: 'We believe that the Fianna Fáil Party can, in the circumstances of this country today, initiate a bold economic and social policy, and in the realms of national endeavour a no less bold policy so far as the national rights of this country are concerned.'[33]

The Independent TD for Louth, James Coburn, declared straight away that he was going to vote against the re-election of Deputy de Valera and one of his reasons for doing so was because 'de Valera still would cherish the hope that he is going to establish an Irish Republic for the whole of Ireland.' Coburn, who was once a follower of John Redmond, believed that 'it is impossible either now or in the near future to set up an Irish republic for the thirty-two counties of Ireland.'[34]

The Ceann Comhairle rang for the division. There was a tense interval until he read from a sheet of paper that was handed to him: 'The result: for de Valera, eighty-two; against, fifty-four.'

Seventy-four Fianna Fáil TDs had voted for the re-election of de Valera, along with eight Labour Party TDs. Forty-five Cumann na nGaedheal TDs, eight Independents and one Independent Labour TD (Richard Anthony, Cork Borough) had voted against the appointment of de Valera. The eleven Centre Party deputies abstained.

De Valera then nominated the Fianna Fáil members he had chosen to become Ministers of the Executive Council. There were several changes in the cabinet. James Geoghegan KC, the Longford-Westmeath TD, outgoing Minister for Justice, had requested President de Valera not to reappoint him to that position as he wished to return to the Bar. Patrick Ruttledge TD, Mayo North, former Minister for Lands and Fisheries, now became Minister for Justice. Senator Joseph Connolly moved from the Department of Posts and Telegraphs to the Department of Lands and Fisheries. President de Valera brought Gerry Boland into the cabinet as Minister of Posts and Telegraphs. The Dáil approved the new cabinet without a division.

The scene was set for President de Valera to remove the Oath of Allegiance to the British monarch from the Irish Constitution. But what would the reaction of the British government be if de Valera unilaterally removed the Oath?

Notes
1.   The *Irish Press*, 4 January 1933.
2.   *Ibid.*, 5 January 1933.
3.   *Ibid.*

4. *Ibid.*, 4 January 1933.
5. *Ibid.*, 5 January 1933.
6. *An Phoblacht*, 7 January 1933.
7. The *Irish Press*, 6 January 1933.
8. *Ibid.*, 9 January 1933.
9. *Ibid.*, 10 January 1933.
10. NAI, File 2B/82/117/27/108, minutes of the quarterly meeting of the standing committee of Sinn Féin, 8 January 1933.
11. *Ibid.*
12. The *Irish Press*, 12 January 1933.
13. *Ibid.*, 24 January 1923.
14. The fifteen constituencies where Fianna Fáil gained more than 50 per cent of all votes cast were Longford-Westmeath ; National University of Ireland; Dublin South; Monaghan; Clare; Meath; Mayo North; Waterford; Limerick; Roscommon; Mayo South; Leitrim-Sligo; Donegal; Galway; Kerry.
15. The *Irish Press*, 28 January 1933.
16. Richard Sinnott, *Irish Voters Decide*, pp. 299, 300, 301, 303.
17. The *Irish Press*, 1 February 1933.
18. *Ibid.*
19. *Ibid.*, 31 January 1933.
20. *An Phoblacht*, 4 February 1933.
21. The *Irish Press*, 28 January 1933.
22. *Ibid.*, 30 January 1933.
23. The *Irish Independent*, 4 February 1933.
24. The *Irish Press*, 8 February 1933.
25. *Ibid.*, 9 February 1933.
26. *Dáil Éireann Debates*, Volume 46, 8 February 1933, p. 19.
27. *Ibid.*
28. *Ibid.*, p. 20.
29. *Ibid.*, p. 21.
30. *Ibid.*
31. *Ibid.*, pp. 21, 22.
32. *Ibid.*, pp. 23, 24.
33. *Ibid.* p. 24.
34. *Ibid.*, p. 26

24

THE OATH BILL BECOMES LAW

Once the Fianna Fáil Party had won an overall majority in the general election of January 1933, the British government realised that the Oath Bill would soon become law in the Irish Free State but were still strongly opposed to de Valera's unilateral course of action.

When the Dáil assembled on 1 March 1933, President de Valera moved that the Constitution (Removal of Oath) Bill, 1932, be again sent to Seanad Éireann in the form it was first sent from Dáil Éireann on 19 May 1932, with one modification – that, owing to the lapse of time, the date 1933 be substituted for 1932. De Valera explained that he was moving this resolution because the Constitution provided that if a Bill was not passed by the Senate or was passed with amendments to which the Dáil did not agree, if a general election was held and the Bill was passed again by the Dáil after the election, it became law within a period of sixty days.[1]

Patrick McGilligan, Cumann na nGaedheal TD for the National University of Ireland and former Minister for Foreign Affairs, opposed de Valera's motion because 'it was a breach of the Treaty'. Cumann na nGaedheal still believed: 'that the only approach to this subject should be by the method of negotiation.' McGilligan added: 'If the President enters into negotiation with the people on the other side of this [the British]…he will have support in these negotiations.[2]

President de Valera's motion to send back the Oath Bill to the Senate, as it was originally passed in the Dáil, was carried in the Dáil by seventy-five votes to forty-nine, a majority of twenty-six. Sixty-seven Fianna Fáil deputies and eight Labour deputies voted for the motion. Thirty-two Cumann na nGaedheal TDs, nine Centre Party deputies and eight Independent TDs opposed the motion. On 1 March 1933, the Bill began its last weary journey back to the Senate but this time, no matter what happened in that assembly, the Oath of Allegiance to a British monarch would be removed from the Irish Constitution in a matter of sixty days.

The senators persisted in using every tactic available to them to delay the Oath Bill from coming into operation. On 8 March the Cathaoirleach read the message sent from the Dáil (dated 1 March 1933): 'that the Bill, to which the agreement of Seanad Éireann is desired, is sent herewith.'[3]

Once again the Senate rejected the Bill by a majority vote. On 15 March the Dáil received a message from the Seanad: 'The Senate declines further to consider the Constitution (Removal of Oath) Bill until it has been made the subject of negotiation...'[4] But the Senate's goose was cooked and although it continued as obstructive as before, it had no power to delay this Bill any longer.

An Phoblacht commented on the composition of the Senate: 'The Twenty-Six County Senate is representative only of the rancher and banker class. The majority of its members, originally nominated by Cosgrave, are avowed imperialists. They assemble in strength only when some measure of reform is to be thwarted by them.'[5]

President Éamon de Valera introduced the Constitution (Removal of Oath) Bill, Motion of Enactment, to Dáil Éireann on 3 May 1933. He explained that a period of sixty days, as stipulated in the Constitution, had elapsed since this Bill had been sent to Seanad Éireann and as the Senate had not passed the Bill within the stated period, this Bill was now deemed to have been passed by both Houses of the Oireachtas in the form in which it was sent to Seanad Éireann on 1 March 1933.[6]

'This is the last step and I hope that we are never going to hear of it again,' said President de Valera. Later on in the course of his speech, he declared, to applause from the public gallery and the government benches: 'We are ending the Civil War and the causes of the Civil War.'

He said that once the Oath was taken away a new day would dawn: 'We must make it clear that no section of the people is debarred from representation in this House.' The President concluded his speech with a warning to any group who wished to subvert the state. 'There is no excuse for anybody to prepare in any way for the use of force. Any attempt to use force or to prepare to use force…is an attempt to establish a dictatorship and there is no justification for it and no government could permit that to go unchecked.'[7]

When the question was put, the motion to have the Oath Bill passed was carried by seventy-six votes to fifty-six – a comfortable majority of twenty votes.

Winning the vote was the cause of big smiles and great rejoicing among the Fianna Fáil and Labour deputies. Immediately after the Dáil had declared the result, the Bill abolishing the Oath was brought by courier to Domhnall Ó Buachalla, An *Seanascal* (the Governor-General), who signed it: it then became law. Dáil Éireann sent a message to Seanad Éireann on 10 May 1933, informing the senators that the Oath Bill was deemed to have been passed into law. The senators of Seanad Éireann had been forced by the express wishes of the people of the Irish Free State, in two general elections, to accept the abolition of the Oath of Allegiance, although the senators protested all the way to the final curtain.

The *Irish Press* lauded the passing of the Oath of Allegiance in its editorial: 'The Constitution by imposing an Oath of Allegiance sought to make the Dáil a sectional assembly. It succeeded for ten years. The abolition of the Oath creates an assembly free of entry to the whole people.'[8]

The editor of *An Phoblacht* was not so convinced that the removal of the Oath of Allegiance would be a cure for all ills:

> We welcome the proposal to abolish the Oath…Yet the Oath is but one item of the Treaty. As it is possible that some unworthy attempt may be made to glorify the removal of the Oath and to argue that Republicans should now recognise the Twenty-Six-County parliament, it is well to reiterate that the war was fought to maintain the Republic – not to remove the Oath or prune the Treaty.[9]

There were still outstanding issues with the British government in the aftermath of the removal of the Oath of Allegiance – issues that would take some time to resolve. Replying to Colonel Grattan in the House of Commons, J.H. Thomas said he had observed the action of the Irish Free State government and parliament in passing a Bill through the Dáil the previous day in relation to the Oath of Allegiance:

> As regards the position which arises on the passing of the legislation, His Majesty's government in the United Kingdom considers that the passing of the Bill will not affect the duty of allegiance to the king or amount to an act of secession…This does not alter the fact that in the view of His Majesty's government in the United Kingdom the removal of the Oath is a breach of the Treaty.[10]

The reaction of Thomas to the removal of the Oath was not as severe as many had expected.

The Standing Committee of Sinn Féin approved unanimously of a draft statement drawn up by its President, Brian O'Higgins, entitled 'Sinn Féin and the Oath' and instructed the honorary secretary to send copies to the daily papers for immediate publication. The statement dashed the hopes of Éamon de Valera that all sections of the Irish people would now recognise the Dáil as the legitimate parliament of the Free State:

> The 'empty formula' has gone out of our partition assembly for twenty-six counties, with its false title of 'Dáil Éireann,' and with all its executive authority vested in the King of England, but that assembly has always been, is today, and will always be a usurpation and even to attach to it a label inscribed: 'This was the parliament of a British dominion yesterday; it is the parliament of a British republic today' would not wipe out the memory of its crimes or make it acceptable to those who are loyal to the living Republic of Ireland.[11]

Mary MacSwiney joined the censure lobby and claimed that the 'stepping-stone' [of Griffith and Collins] was now de Valera's method.[12]

De Valera had to complete another legal procedure to make it possible for all deputies elected to the Dáil or Senate to enter either of these Houses without taking the Oath of Allegiance. He pressed ahead with the removal of the Electoral (Amendment) Bill, 1927. In Dáil Éireann in early June 1933, he proposed a motion to remove the obligation on a person to make an affidavit on oath before a peace commissioner or commissioner of oaths before nomination that, if elected to be a member of Dáil Éireann or Seanad Éireann, he or she would take the Oath of Allegiance and afterwards accept his or her seat in the Dáil or Senate.

During the debate W.T. Cosgrave reminded the Dáil that in 1927 he had introduced the Act this Bill aimed to abolish and that the Act 'might be described as the cause of forcing the Fianna Fáil Party to enter Leinster House.'[13]

The Electoral (Amendment) Bill, 1933 passed through all stages in the Dáil with solid majorities of at least twenty votes. Once again the Labour Party combined with Fianna Fáil to see this Act through the Dáil. Seanad Éireann accepted the Bill without a division. It became law on 13 July 1933.

Before the Oath of Allegiance was abolished, the Clerk of the Dáil, Colm Ó Murchadha, kept a roll book with one page for each Dáil deputy and senator. On the top of each of these pages, the Oath formula was printed and each deputy and senator was obliged to sign under the formula before he or she was allowed to enter the Dáil or the Senate. After the abolition of the Oath, a new roll book without the Oath formula replaced the old book and every TD or Senator duly elected signed his or her name in this open roll book.[14]

President de Valera intended to frame a new Constitution for the Free State and the Oath of Allegiance would be one of the articles that would not appear in this new Constitution. This new Constitution would have to be ratified by a majority vote of the Irish people in a referendum.

To the surprise of many in the British Government, a little-known mediator in international affairs, P.J. Fleming, a native of The Swan, County Laois, arrived in the Dominions Office on 28 July 1933 to negotiate with the British Government, on behalf of President de Valera, on the issues of the Oath and land annuities. Mr. Fleming had been active in the 1916-1921 struggle for independence, during which he became famous as the man the British authorities could not break. He later became a prominent member of Fianna Fáil, whom de Valera and Lemass regarded as an entrepreneur with flair. Fleming mostly met Sir Edward Harding, the permanent Under-Secretary of the Dominions Office. Harding told him that the Oath must remain in any agreement but that the British Government would be prepared to make some modification in its wording. Paddy Fleming retorted that de Valera had taken part in a civil war designed to scrap the Treaty and the Oath and suggested a revision of the whole Treaty. Harding declared that this was not possible. Fleming brought the reply home to de Valera, who considered that no further progress could be made. [15]

On 31 January 1935 came the first move to break the deadlock in the Economic War between the Irish and British governments, when both sides negotiated the Coal-Cattle Pact. The British government agreed to allow the number of cattle imported into Britain from Ireland to increase by a third in exchange for a pledge from the Free State government that it would buy more coal from Britain as well as industrial goods such as telephones. It was not the end of the Economic War but it certainly pointed towards better days ahead.

Speaking in the Dáil on 29 May 1935 with regard to external affairs generally, de Valera said: 'Our position is that we could not be brought into active participation in any war against our will. We have definitely stated that we would not allow our country to be used as a base of attack on Britain by a foreign power and would do our best to defend our own country.'[16]

This statement helped to improve relations between Éamon de Valera and the British government. J.H. Thomas praised President de Valera for the first time ever: 'What I say now is that de Valera made it clear in the Dáil that the Irish Free State government would not permit its territory to be used as a base for attacking Great Britain. I welcome this statement and I am glad that de Valera made it.'[17]

In June 1935 Ramsay MacDonald stood down as prime minister for health reasons and Stanley Baldwin, who replaced him, called a general election in Great Britain and Northern Ireland for 14 November of that year. The national government under Baldwin was returned with a large majority. In a subsequent cabinet reshuffle, J.H. Thomas was shifted from the Dominions Office into the Colonial Office and Malcolm MacDonald became the new Dominions Secretary. The second son of Ramsay MacDonald, he was an energetic young man who wished to conciliate the Irish Free State while maintaining its connection with the British Commonwealth.

A second Coal-Cattle Pact was negotiated in February 1936 between the de Valera and British government. The British agreed to allow the importation from the Free State of 100,000 cattle more than the quota they allowed in 1935. The Westminster government also reduced by 10 per cent the specific duties on live animals and dead meat.

The Irish government agreed to maintain the coal quota and buy at least one-third of the country's cement requirements from Britain. It also promised to reduce emergency duties on these products by 10 per cent. The agricultural community and others who had been adversely affected by the Economic War breathed a sigh of relief as they felt their financial situation ease.

Stanley Baldwin revived the Irish Situation Committee. On 24 June 1936 J.W. Dulanty, Irish High Commissioner in London, called to the new Dominions Secretary 'as a matter of courtesy' and outlined for him some of the constitutional proposals that de Valera had in mind. The Irish president intended to exclude any reference to an Oath to the British monarch in the internal affairs of the Irish Free State but he was prepared to continue to recognise allegiance to the crown for external purposes. Malcolm MacDonald told Dulanty that he wished to meet de Valera, 'as there was unquestionably a strong desire to find some solution.'[18]

The meeting between MacDonald and Éamon de Valera was cordial. De Valera told the Dominions Secretary that the crown would have no function in the internal affairs of the Irish Free State but in matters of common concern between the nations of the Commonwealth, the Free State would recognise the king as the head of the Commonwealth.

On 12 December 1936, President Éamon de Valera introduced the External Relations Bill 1936 in Dáil Éireann. According to the provisions of this Bill, the Executive Council of the Irish Free State appointed all diplomatic and consular representatives but the British monarch was given the authority to sign the credentials that they presented to their assigned governments abroad before taking up office. De Valera introduced the different sections of this Bill:

> It is hereby declared and enacted that, so long as Saorstát Éireann (the Irish Free State) is associated with the following nations, that is to say, Australia, Canada, Great Britain, New Zealand and South Africa, and so long as the king recognised by these nations as the symbol of their cooperation continues to act on behalf of each of these nations (on the advice of the several governments thereof) for the purposes of the appointment of diplomatic and consular representatives and the conclusion of international agreements, the King, so recognised, may and is hereby authorised to act on behalf of Saorstát Éireann for the like purposes as and when advised by the Executive Council to do so.[19]

Éamon de Valera hoped that retaining the symbol of the British crown might eventually entice the Unionist population of the Six Counties into a united Ireland. Declaring a Republic, de Valera felt, would alienate the loyalists of Northern Ireland by removing from the Constitution all references to the British monarch.

Fine Gael joined Fianna Fáil to vote in favour of this Executive Authority (External Relations) Bill 1936 but Labour took the most Republican stance of all the parties and voted against it. William Norton claimed that they would have 'the twenty-six Counties functioning under a status which is certainly not a status of complete independence.'[20] The Bill passed its second stage by ninety-three votes to six, the votes of the Labour TDs. The political parties lined up in the same way at the committee stage of the Bill and it was passed by eighty-one votes to five. The External Relations Act 1936 then became law.

How did the British government react to the External Relations Act

1936? They accepted that it was a big step forward for the government of the Irish Free State voluntarily to recognise the British monarch, although for external purposes only, and to pass legislation to maintain the position of the monarch.

On 1 May 1937, de Valera published the terms of the new Constitution and the second reading of the Constitutional Bill came before the Dáil on 11 May 1937. Frank McDermot, the former leader of the now defunct Centre Party, said that he regretted the omission of the king from the internal affairs of the twenty-six counties: 'Sir, the first great fault of these proposals is the omission of the king, except in so far as he survives, precariously, as an organ or instrument for external use only...I suggest that it would be far more valuable to employ the king as an organ or instrument for securing Irish unity, than as an organ or instrument for appointing ministers to foreign countries.'[21]

The debate on the Constitution continued in Dáil Éireann from 11 May to 14 June 1937. Before the motion: 'That the Draft Constitution, 1937, be and is hereby, approved by Dáil Éireann' was put to the House, Éamon de Valera said in reply to questions:

> If the Northern problem were not there, in all probability there would be a flat downright proclamation of the Republic in this [Constitution][22]...The aim of the Constitution has been to give the greatest amount of concession that the majority here could give [to the Unionists of Northern Ireland] without abandoning what they regarded as their own right and their own principles.[23]

Dáil Éireann approved of the new Constitution on 14 June 1937 by sixty-two votes to forty-eight. The 1937 Constitution contained no reference to an Oath of Allegiance or any political test. The area of the twenty-six counties area was an independent, democratic state but not a Republic because of the External Relations Act. 'Eire' was to be the name of the state.

Neville Chamberlain succeeded Stanley Baldwin as Prime Minister on 28 May 1937. The Irish Situation Committee in Westminster decided to accept the terms of the new Constitution, which meant that the British government would continue to treat the Free State as a member of the British Commonwealth.

Some Republicans, including Tom Barry, the leader of the west Cork flying column, opposed this Constitution on the grounds that 'it did not proclaim the Republic which was destroyed by force of arms in 1922'.[24] A Republican Coordinating Committee that comprised Cumann na mBan, Mná na Poblachta, Cumann na Poblachta and Sinn Féin repudiated de Valera's Constitution because 'he continued to accept the status quo – Ireland partitioned, a British dependency in the North and a British dominion in the South'.[25] Sinn Féin issued a manifesto calling upon the people 'not to participate in the plebiscite which – whatever the result of the voting – is intended by its originators to be used as a semblance of authority for the continued holding of Ireland in subjection to England'.[26] But other Republicans, such as Seán MacBride, former Chief-of-Staff of the IRA, were impressed by the 1937 Constitution.

President de Valera put the new Constitution before the people of the twenty-six counties on 1 July 1937. It was approved by 685,105 votes to 526,945, a majority of nearly 160,000. The percentage in favour was 39, with 30 per cent against. De Valera issued a statement on 7 July 1937: 'The enactment of the Constitution by the people must be a source of joy to everyone who has been working in the cause of Irish independence. It marks an epoch in our national history...Within six months from now the Constitution will be in operation as a fundamental law – the foundation on which the whole political structure of our state will rest'.[27]

The new Constitution became law at the end of December 1937.

The passing of this 1937 Constitution buried for ever the British-imposed Oath of Allegiance that had prevailed in the Free State since the passing of the Anglo-Irish Treaty in January 1922.

Notes

1. *Dáil Éireann Debates*, Volume 46, 1 March 1933, pp. 69, 70.
2. *Ibid.*, pp. 70, 72, 74.
3. Seanad Éireann Parliamentary Debates, Volume 16, 8 March 1933, p. 639.
4. *Dáil Éireann Debates*, Volume 46, 15 March 1933, pp. 972, 973.
5. *An Phoblacht*, 4 March 1933.
6. *Dáil Éireann Debates*, Volume 47, 3 May 1933, p. 423.
7. *Ibid.*, pp. 430, 434, 435, 437.
8. The *Irish Press*, 4 May 1933.
9. *An Phoblacht*, 6 May 1933.
10. The *Irish Independent*, 5 May 1933.
11. The *Irish Press*, 8 May 1933.
12. *An Phoblacht*, 13 May 1933.
13. *Dáil Éireann Debates*, Volume 48, 7 June 1933, p. 85.
14. The *Irish Press*, 26 May 1933.
15. McMahon, Deirdre, *Republicans and Imperialists: Anglo-Irish Relations in the 1930s,* pp. 116, 117, 118.
16. *Dáil Éireann Debates*, Volume 56, 2132, 29 May 1935.
17. *An Phoblacht*, 8 June 1935.
18. Crowe *et al.* (eds.), *Documents on Irish Foreign Policy 1932-1936*, pp. 450, 451, 452, NAI, 2003/17/181, Letter from John W. Dulanty to Joseph P. Walshe (Dublin), 24 June 1936.
19. *Dáil Éireann Debates*, Executive Authority (External Relations) Bill 1936, Second Stage, Volume 64, 12 December 1936, pp. 1386, 1387.
20. *Ibid.*, pp. 1397, 1398, 1402.
21. *Ibid.*, Volume 67, 11 May 1937, *Bunreacht na h-Éireann*, Dara Chéim, pp. 81, 82.
22. *Ibid.*, Volume 68, 14 June 1937, *Bunreacht na h-Éireann* (Dréacht) Tuasgabháil (d'ath-thógaint), p. 430.
23. *Ibid.*, pp. 431, 432.
24. *An Phoblacht*, 22 May 1937.
25. NAI, File 2B/82/117/27/236, Minutes of the Standing Committee Sinn Féin, 4 May 1937; Memo from Republican Coordinating Committee, 2 May 1937, re new Constitution.
26. *Ibid.*, File 2B/82/117/27/243, 22 June 1937.
27. *The Irish Times*, 8 July 1937.

CONCLUSION: THE OATH IS DEAD AND GONE

The Treaty between Great Britain and Ireland signed in London on 6 December 1921 split not only Sinn Féin and the IRA but the people of Ireland. During the Treaty debates it became obvious that many of the Sinn Féin TDs found it impossible to accept the Oath of Allegiance to the reigning British monarch that was part of the Treaty. This group of TDs became committed anti-Treatyites and in the 1922 Pact general election, just before the outbreak of the Civil War, they fared very badly, suffering a significant loss of Dáil seats. Prior to the general election of August 1923, after the Civil War had ended, it was feared that Republicanism might suffer a fatal blow because of lack of public support. But mainly because of enthusiastic Sinn Féin workers in the back rooms and on the canvassing trail, the results surprised all the pundits when the anti-Treaty party emerged with a creditable forty-four seats compared to sixty-three seats for the pro-Treaty Cumann na nGaedheal. This Republican vote continued to increase up to 1926. Sinn Féin, under Éamon de Valera and P.J. Ruttledge, was the party that guided the Republican fraternity through this critical period. But credit for the survival of Republicanism cannot be given solely to these leaders: the rank-and-file members of Sinn Féin did Trojan work to save Republicanism from extinction and to preserve the Republican vote.

At this stage Éamon de Valera, the Sinn Féin president, fully supported the party's policy of refusing to allow its elected representatives to take their seats in Dáil Éireann because the party regarded the twenty-six-county partitioned Dáil as a British institution that demanded an unacceptable Oath of Allegiance. The forty-four Republican deputies represented almost one-third of the elected members of the Dáil. Their abstention from Dáil Éireann did not prevent the new Cumann na nGaedheal-led Dáil from functioning in an efficient manner. Gradually de Valera realised that the only political strategy that might reverse the 1921 Anglo-Irish Treaty was for Sinn Féin to obtain a majority of seats in a general election, a task that seemed impossible unless the party first entered Dáil Éireann.

At Sinn Féin's extraordinary *ard-fheis* on 9 March 1926, de Valera proposed: 'That Sinn Féin elected deputies enter the Dáil or Six-County Assembly if the Oath of Allegiance were removed.' His motion was defeated by a small number of votes. De Valera resigned as President of Sinn Féin and soon afterwards founded a new political party, Fianna Fáil. Sinn Féin had kept Republicanism alive up to that point but following the departure of Éamon de Valera and his followers to Fianna Fáil, the vast majority of Republican voters transferred with them. In their first general election, in June 1927, the Fianna Fáil party secured forty-four seats, in contrast to Sinn Féin, who had only five TDs elected.

After the assassination of Kevin O'Higgins, Minister for External Affairs and Justice in the Free State cabinet, in July 1927, the Cosgrave government introduced legislation that forced Fianna Fáil to enter Dáil Éireann or face extinction as a political party. The elected Fianna Fáil deputies took their seats in Dáil Éireann, claiming that the Oath of Allegiance was just 'an empty formula'. Those who refused to budge from Sinn Féin continued the abstentionist strategy but this course of action meant that the party became an isolated group with no political clout or elected TDs after the general election of September 1927.

The perseverance of Éamon de Valera and his Fianna Fáil colleagues in seeking the abolition of the Oath of Allegiance after 1926 contributed greatly to its demise. But credit for its removal must also be given to the steadfast support the Labour Party gave to Fianna Fáil in the Dáil, a support that enabled bills to abolish the Oath to pass through the Dáil in 1932-3. Successive Labour leaders – Thomas Johnson, Thomas J. O'Connell and William Norton – maintained the party's opposition to the Oath. The people of Ireland also deserve praise for the support they gave to de Valera in 1932 and 1933 when he had to stand firm against the best efforts of British diplomacy.

By a strange twist of destiny Cumann na nGaedheal's Kevin O'Higgins helped to pave the way for the enactment of the Statute of Westminster of 1931 and the full emancipation of the dominions. This piece of legislation facilitated de Valera's abolition of the Oath of Allegiance.

The fact that Dáil Éireann held jurisdiction over twenty-six counties rather than the whole of Ireland prevented other Irishmen and Irishwomen with deep-rooted Republican principles from taking their Dáil seats even after the abolition of the Oath. The vast majority of these men and women remained faithful to Sinn Féin.

Provisional Sinn Féin, under the leadership of Gerry Adams, ended its abstentionist policy in 1986: the abolition of the Oath of Allegiance in the 1930s had cleared the path for members of the party to enter Dáil Éireann. In the 1997 general election, Caoimhín Ó Caoláin, representing Cavan-Monaghan, became the first Sinn Féin TD to take his seat in Dáil Éireann. Gerry Adams himself topped the poll in Louth in the 2011 general election and leads a group of fourteen TDs in the Dáil. However a small group of Republicans who belong to Republican Sinn Féin, continue, because of partition, to refuse to recognise Dáil Éireann or the Northern Ireland Assembly as legitimate parliaments and would not take their seats in either parliament if they were elected.

The Oath of Allegiance to the reigning British monarch that had to be taken by every elected TD and Senator before entering the Dáil or Seanad is dead and gone. No longer is any elected TD or Senator forced to stay outside the Oireachtas because he cannot in conscience swear allegiance to a British monarch.

The chief architect of this liberating piece of legislation – the Constitution (Removal of the Oath) Bill 1933 – was Éamon de Valera. The abolition of the Oath was one of the greatest achievements of this Irish statesman who died on 29 August 1975 in his ninety-third year.

Selected Bibliography
Primary Sources

Archives

UCD Archives
Desmond Fitzgerald Papers
Éamon de Valera Papers
Ernest Blythe Papers
Mary MacSwiney Papers
Moss Twomey Papers
Mulcahy Papers
O'Malley Papers

Franciscan Library, Killiney, County Dublin
Éamon de Valera Papers

National Archives
Aims of Sinn Féin
Department of the Taoiseach (D/T)
Minutes of meetings of the Executive Council of the Irish Free State Parliament
Minutes of Provisional Government
Notes of Colm Ó Murchadha: meeting of the cabinet and plenipotentiaries, 3 Dec. 1921
Sinn Féin Funds Case
Sinn Féin Standing Committee Minutes
Sinn Féin's Organisation Report to Ard-Chomhairle

Fianna Fáil Archives
Fianna Fáil election pledge
Forty-four elected Fianna Fáil TDs, June 1927
Frank Barrett correspondence
Minutes of the National Executive of Fianna Fáil
Speech by Éamon de Valera at the inaugural meeting of Fianna Fáil
Speech by Éamon de Valera at the third *ard-fheis* of Fianna Fáil

National Library of Ireland
Thomas Johnson Papers

Manuscripts
Papers of Father Pat Gaynor (member of Sinn Féin Executive, 1922)
Ua hUalla cháin, Gearóid, *A Scéal Féin*

Parliamentary Sources
Irish Stationery Office and Tithe an Oireachtais: Parliamentary Debates
Dáil Éireann Debates 1919-21, Private Sessions, Stationery Office, Dublin, 1921
Dáil Éireann Debate on the Treaty between Great Britain and Ireland, Official Report
Dáil Éireann Debates 1922-37
Seanad Éireann Debates 1925-33

Interviews
Aengus Ó Snodaigh TD (Sinn Féin)
Dan Breen (Fianna Fáil TD)
Jack Gardiner, Callan, County Kilkenny
Kevin Boland (Fianna Fáil minister, 1957-70, founder of Aontacht Éireann, 1971)
Ruairí Brugha, (Clann na Poblachta, Fianna Fáil TD, Senator and MEP)

Newspapers and Journals
The *Advocate* (Melbourne, Australia)
Carloviana
The *Daily Mail*
Éire
Éire-Ireland
The *Free Press* (Wexford)
The *Freeman's Journal*
The *Gaelic-American*
The *Irish Independent*
The *Irish Press*
The *Irish Times*
The *Kilkenny People*
The *Leader*
The *Nation*
The *Nationalist* (Clonmel)
An Phoblacht
Saoirse na h-Éireann/Irish Freedom
Sinn Féin
The *Sunday Independent*
The *United Irishman* (1905)

Periodicals and Reviews
Historical Statistics of the USA
MacBride, Seán. Review of *The Vatican, The Bishops and Irish Politics, 1919-39. Irish Press*, 1986.
O'Neill, Thomas P. 'In Search of a Political Path: Irish Republicanism, 1922 to 1927'. *Historical Studies*, 1976.
Pyne, Peter. 'The Third Sinn Féin Party, 1923-1926'. *Economic and Social Review*, Vol. I, 1969-70.

Radio Documentary
John Bowman. 'The Foundation of Fianna Fáil and the taking of the Oath of Allegiance.' *Saturday 8.30*, RTÉ, 5 May 2001.

BOOKS

Bell, J. Bowyer. *The Secret Army : The IRA*. Dublin: Poolbeg, 1998.

Breathnach, Máirtín. *Republican Days: 75 Years of Fianna Fáil*. Dublin: Ashville Media Group. 2002.

Bromage, Mary. *De Valera and the March of a Nation*. New York: Noonday Press, 1956.

Carroll, Denis. *They Have Fooled You Again: Michael O'Flanagan (1876-1942)*. Dublin: Columba Press 1993.

Coogan, Tim Pat. *De Valera: Long Fellow. Long Shadow*. London: Hutchinson. 1993.

Coogan, Tim Pat. *Michael Collins: A Biography*. London: Hutchinson. 1990.

Cronin, Seán. *The McGarrity Papers*. Tralee, County Kerry: Anvil Books, 1972.

Crowe, Caitríona, Ronan Fanning, Michael Kennedy, Dermot Keogh and Eunan O'Halpin (eds.). *Documents on Irish Foreign Policy Volume IV, 1932-36*. Dublin: Royal Irish Academy, 2004.

Cumann na n-Uaigheann Náisiúnta. *The Last Post*. Dublin, 1985.

Daly. Paul. *Creating Ireland*. Dublin: Lir Hachette Books, 2008.

De Valera, Terry. *A Memoir*. Dublin: Currach Press, 2004

Dwyer, T. Ryle. *De Valera: The Man and the Myths*. Dublin: Poolbeg Press, 1991.

Earl of Longford, The and Thomas P. O'Neill. *Éamon de Valera*. Dublin: Gill and Macmillan, 1970.

Farrell, Brian. *Seán Lemass*. Dublin: Gill and Macmillan, 1983.

Feeney, Brian. *Sinn Féin: A Hundred Turbulent Years*. Dublin: O'Brien Press, 2002.

Ferriter, Diarmaid. *Judging Dev*. Dublin: Royal Irish Academy. 2007.

Foley. Conor. *Legion of the Rearguard*. London: Pluto Press, 1992.

Garvin, Tom. *Judging Lemass*. Dublin: Royal Irish Academy, 2009.

Gaughan, J. Anthony. *Austin Stack: Portrait of a Separatist*. Blackrock, County Dublin: Kingdom Books, 1977.

Gaynor, Éamonn. *Memoirs of a Tipperary Family: The Gaynors of Tyone, 1887-2000*. Dublin: Geography Publications. 2000.

Hanley, Brian. *The IRA, 1926-36*. Dublin: Four Courts Press, 2002.

Hopkinson, Michael. *Green against Green*. Dublin: Gill and Macmillan, 1988.

Horgan, John. *Seán Lemass: The Enigmatic Patriot*. Dublin: Gill and Macmillan, 1997.

Jones, Thomas. *Whitehall Diary. Volume III. Ireland 1918-25*. (Keith Middlemas ed.) Oxford: Oxford University Press, 1971.

Keogh, Dermot. *The Vatican. The Bishops and Irish Politics, 1919-39*. Cambridge: Cambridge University Press, 1986.

Laffan, Michael. *The Resurrection of Ireland: The Sinn Féin Party 1916-23*. Cambridge: Cambridge University Press, 1999.

Lawlor, Caitriona (ed.). *Seán MacBride. That Day's Struggle*. Dublin: Currach Press, 2005.

Macardle, Dorothy. *The Irish Republic* (4th ed.). Dublin: Irish Press Ltd, 1951.

MacDonagh, Michael. *The Life of Daniel O'Connell*. London: Cassell and Company, 1903.

Mac Donncha, Micheál. *Sinn Féin: A Century of Struggle*. Dublin: Sinn Féin Publications, 2005.

Mac Eoin, Uinseann. *Survivors*. Dublin: Argenta Publications, 1987.

Mac Eoin, Uinseann. *The IRA in the Twilight Years, 1923-1948*. Dublin: Argenta Publications, 1997.

MacManus, M.J. *Éamon de Valera*. Dublin: Talbot Press. 1962.

MacSwiney Brugha, Máire. *History's Daughter*. Dublin: O'Brien Press, 2005.

Maher, Jim. *Harry Boland*. Cork and Dublin: Mercier Press, 1998.

Mansergh, Martin. *The Legacy of History*. Cork and Dublin: Mercier Press, 2003.

Mareco, Anne. *The Rebel Countess*. London: Phoenix Press, 2002.

Martin, Micheál. *Freedom to Choose*. Cork: Collins Press, 2009.

McMahon, Deirdre. *Republicans and Imperialists. Anglo-Irish Relations in the 1930s*. New Haven and London: Yale University Press, 1984.

Moynihan, Maurice. *Speeches and Statements by Éamon de Valera, 1917-73*. Dublin: Gill and Macmillan, 1980.

Murphy, Brian P. *Patrick Pearse and the Lost Republican Ideal*. Dublin: James Duffy, 1991.

Murray, Patrick. *Oracles of God*. Dublin: UCD Press, 2000.

Neeson, Eoin. *Birth of a Republic*. Dublin: Prestige Books, 1998.

Neeson, Eoin. *The Civil War, 1922-23*. Dublin and Cork: Mercier Press, 1966.

Nolan, Aengus. *Joseph Walshe: Irish Foreign Policy, 1922-46*. Dublin and Cork: Mercier Press, 2008.

Ó Cruadhlaoich, Diarmuid. *The Oath of Allegiance*. Dublin and London: Maunsel and Roberts, 1925.

Ó Brádaigh, Ruairí. *Dílseacht: The Story of Tom Maguire and the Second Dáil*. Dublin: Irish Freedom Press, 1997.

O'Hegarty, P. S. *The Victory of Sinn Féin*. Dublin: Talbot Press, 1924.

O'Shea, Dónal. *80 Years of Fianna Fáil*. Castelbar, County Mayo: Manlo Publications, 2006.

Pakenham, Frank. *Peace by Ordeal*. London: Mentor, 1962.

Rafter, Kevin. *Sinn Féin, 1905-2005*. Dublin: Gill and Macmillan, 2005.

Regan, John M. *The Irish Counter-Revolution*. Dublin: Gill and Macmillan, 1999.

Ruane, Medb. 'Kathleen Lynn (1874-1955)', in Mary Cullen and Maria Luddy (eds.). *Female Activists: Irish Women and Change, 1900-1960*. Dublin: Woodfield Press, 2001.

Sexton, Brendan. *Ireland and the Crown, 1922-1936*. Dublin: Irish Academic Press, 1989.

Sinnott, Richard. *Irish Votes Decide*. Manchester: Manchester University Press, 1995.

Taylor, Rex. *Michael Collins*. London: Hutchinson, 1963.

Walker, Brian M. *Parliamentary Election Results in Ireland 1918-92*. Dublin: Royal Irish Academy, 1992.

Ward, Margaret. *Unmanageable Revolutionaries – Women and Irish Nationalism*. London: Pluto Press, 1989.

White, Terence de Vere. *Kevin O'Higgins*. Dublin: Anvil Books, 1986.

Index

Note that individuals whose names appear in the text in both English and Irish forms are indexed in English with a cross-reference to the Irish form.